ORDER AND PARTIALITIES

SUNY Series, INTERRUPTIONS: Border Testimony(ies) and Critical Discourse/s
Henry A. Giroux, editor

ORDER AND PARTIALITIES

Theory, Pedagogy, and the "Postcolonial"

edited by

Kostas Myrsiades
and
Jerry McGuire

STATE UNIVERSITY OF NEW YORK PRESS

Published by
State University of New York Press

Printed in the United States of America

For information, address the State University of New York Press, State University Plaza, Albany, NY 12246

Production by Christine Lynch
Marketing by Bernadette LaManna

Library of Congress Cataloging-in-Publication Data

Order and partialities : theory, pedagogy, and the "postcolonial" / edited by Kostas Myrsiades and Jerry McGuire.
p. cm. — (SUNY series, Interruptions — Border testimony(ies) and Critical Discourse/s)
Includes bibliographical references and index.
ISBN 0-7914-2639-4 (alk. paper). — ISBN 0-7914-2640-8 (pbk. : alk. paper)
1. Colonies in literature. 2. Decolonization in literature. 3. Literature, Modern—Study and teaching. 4. Developing countries—Literatures—History and criticism. 5. Imperialism in literature. 6. Literature and history. I. Myrsiades, Kostas. II. McGuire, Jerry. III. Series.
PN56.C63064 1995
809'.93358—dc20 94-41282
CIP

10 9 8 7 6 5 4 3 2 1

CONTENTS

Part II
Pedagogy: Terminologies, Problematics, Readings

LALITA PANDIT AND JERRY MCGUIRE

Introduction

> If people don't all experience emotional satisfaction and deprivation in the same way, what claim can there be for equality of need? There was fear and danger in considering this emotional absolute as open in any way; the brain-weighers, the claimants of divine authority to distinguish powers of moral discernment from the degree of frizz in hair and conceptual ability from the relative thickness of lips—they were vigilant to pounce upon anything that could be twisted to give them credence. Yet how was that absolute nature of intimate relationships arrived at? Who decided?
>
> —Nadine Gordimer, *July's People*, 64–65

> And now, come home. Bakary told me once that you had no heart, and sometimes I think he is right. I suppose there must be men like you at a time like this—it is very difficult to fight without being able to hate the person you are fighting. I have some time to read now, so try to bring me some books—novels, not too obvious, but not too difficult either—and especially some books about the lives of men in other countries.
>
> —Ousmane Sembene, *God's Bits of Wood*, 226

It is always worth taking note of where one has crossed a border into the territory of the other, and of what one carries over and what one has left behind. It is worth paying attention to what one has crossed when one has crossed a border. A great many Western scholars who have developed a professional interest in the literatures of postcolonial societies fairly recently would do well to keep this advice in mind, for border crossings are threshold phenomena, both desired and dreaded. They mark a gap in experience that is crossed and recrossed by machines of power under whose influence fantasy, prejudice, ambivalence, and dispositions of panic and violence thrive. Indeed, the question is not whether such mythic energies will emerge, but which ones are preferable—which ones will lead not deeper into defensive hostilities towards the unknown into which one enters, but into practical knowledges that render those borders negotiable, even as zones to be dwelt in rather than lines to be crossed.

Of course, such a zone is itself a fantasy, specifiable perhaps as a synthetic or co-assimilative ideal, and it is no less questionable than any other construction of wishes concerning the social, cultural, economic, and political lives of people whose experience would seem to be immeasurably removed from the apparatus of the Western academy.[1] Furthermore, there is no justification for the assumption that all boundaries as such must conform to the same abstract rules: a physiological boundary is not the same as a cultural boundary, and neither is the same as the boundary of an athletic field. In many ways, postcolonial theory in the academy takes from this fact a related set of concerns: what is the nature of the postcolonial threshold? What are its rules? Or is the diversity even here, among various postcolonialities, so great that no comprehensive set of rules can be articulated?

The collection of essays that follows is a theoretical inquiry into the complex and problematic relations among postcolonial literatures and theories, the people who teach them at the university level, and the institutions in which they are taught.[2] Each of the eighteen essays traces its own path through these relations; yet each also comments on the fundamental paradox and contradiction within which these relations operate: that professors of postcolonial literature and theory must engage with the powerful, labyrinthine apparatus of Western cultural hegemony—a set of systematic articulative/interpretative procedures corresponding to, and in the service of, a regime of ideological expectations and its institutional representatives—in order to disengage themselves from its operations. There is no way to teach these relations without entering, oneself, into the entanglements of postcolonial power.

Certainly nowhere in literary scholarship is the program of study so deeply determined by intensely felt political and cultural contestation, which inevitably leads both to wide-ranging particular investigations and to global hypotheses.[3] Sometimes critical positions seem determined by whether we are more distrustful of relativism or of hierarchy. Out of all the noise emanating from the contesting positions of postcolonial theory there repeatedly emerges an insistence on the ways in which some narrations obscure, subvert, misrepresent, or silence others—a politics of silence and alterity, the problematic of the phantom of the subaltern's voice.[4]

One of the problems faced by teachers of postcolonization literatures and theories is that there are a great many ways for this voice to be lost, subverted, obscured, or trivialized. Consider an article that appeared in the 31st May North American edition of *India Today*, a newsmagazine that expatriate Indians read in order to "stay in touch with the homeland" and to supply a cosmetic Indianness to their homes for the benefit of their children growing up in America. In Hiriyadaka (coastal Karanataka, India), women from various parts of the country come together every spring to take part in a festival, an annual ritual inspired by the life story of a semi-mythic, heroic woman named Siri. The purpose of the ritual, which originates in matrilineal systems that were common among communities living on the coast (p. 75), is to empower women by providing them an opportunity for an indigenous form of group therapy. The women take purifying baths, dress in colorful sarees, enter rooms filled with the fragrance of areca flowers. As intricate shadows fall on the walls, amid pensive flames of oil lamps, they sing the story of Siri and dance to music, "bodies...swaying furiously, the hair awry" (74). The pathos of Siri's story is reflected in the lives of these women. They identify with her sorrow, her defiance of patriarchal codes, her wanderings, her quest for freedom, autonomy, and personal happiness. The decline and fall of Siri's lineage when her two granddaughters' lives end in murder and suicide become emblematic of the politico-historical decline of matrilineal traditions.

It seems that this ancient festival received coverage in *India Today* partly because an anthropology professor from California State University is at present engaged in extensive research on what the article characterizes as "the phenomenon" (74). Peter J. Claus's research and the funding that went into it make the festival a valid "human interest story" for *India Today*. In postcolonial India, many precolonial practices and customs have no doubt remained untouched by colonial history. Nevertheless, within the framework of the linguistic and perceptual coloniality of "modernized" India, the Siri festival becomes an exoticized artifact, a cultural commodity packaged to suit the tastes of the elite bourgeois readership of *India Today*, for whom such "customs" have primarily an antiquarian interest. The result is an Indian version of "internal colonialism" related to the metropolitan images of Scottish crofting communities that Martin Padget examines below in "An Iconography of Difference."

India Today's writer gives the article a title, "Driving away the Demons," which immediately sets up these coastal revelers as a community defined by its superstitions. One of the captions describes the ritual as a "bizarre form of mass therapy," a phrase that any European or American tourist/journalist, American-born Indian, or cosmopolitan, modernized Indian might use. But the actual details of the festival make it clear that the therapeutic process works through an imaginary identification with a figure of mythological dimensions. The women "scream, laugh, or cry, and pour out their problems" (74). In a trancelike state, they give communal voice to the silent pain that has accumulated over the course of the year. It is a therapy grounded in the psycho-ecology of their culture: myth, legend, history. If most of the women who take part in this ritual cannot read or write, they are culturally literate in oral practices of communication that their societies have maintained intact. Oral practices and literatures as intricately codified as written texts prepare these women to respond to the aesthetic form of the ritual. The melodic verses of Siri's story invoke epiphanies capable of releasing personal, domestic pain into a symbolic practice that transcends time, making time-honored traditions part of the present. If at some level the women believe in Siri's power to understand them and protect them, such an attribution of authority to an absent, abstract, all-knowing personhood is not generically different from idealizing the therapist-analyst and investing him or her with such authority. Yet this connection remains unvoiced, and the voices of the women themselves are lost, misrepresented, trivialized.

There is nothing of the occult in what *India Today* describes as a "cult." Nor is there a stereotypically "Eastern" mind at work in this ritualized form of psycho-ecology providing release from social pressures that oppress individual women. An expatriate Indian living in the United States might wish to have access to shared experiences of this kind, grounded in the ancient traditions of the home-culture. And while the conflictual wishes and aspirations of such readers perpetrate their distinctive subversion of any "originality" or "authenticity" that might be sought, the very act of writing about it within the received conventions of academic discourse exposes this social practice to distortion by the essentializing categories that shape contemporary discussions on cultural difference.

But if the postcolonial voice can be distorted in a process of objectivization, it can as easily be lost through absorption as it is subordinated to the status of symbolic operator in texts ordinarily regarded as strictly, if not canonically, "Western." Here one might consider William Burroughs—a writer mentioned by *none* of the contributors to this volume—whose reputation as cultural "outsider" is marked both by experimentation with subversions of the conventional expectations of Western readers and by a fascination with ethnic, racial, and national otherness. Again and again his challenges to "normalcy"—his fantasies of violent and illicit sexual behaviors, his documentation of drug hallucination, his violations of narrative expectations—involve representations of an imagined postcolonial environment marked by a total disregard for the legitimacy of differences. One senses that for Burroughs the boundaries between sexes, species, nations, planets, syntagmas, and planes of consciousness are all the same, all governed by the same set of abstract rules of permutation. Within the texts, multiple alter egos play both sides, all sides, repudiating order everywhere. In the words of his narcotics agent from *Naked Lunch*, Bradley the Buyer, who is addicted to "contact" with the junkies he pursues: "Fuck 'em all, squares on both sides. I am the only complete man in the industry."

Yet the wish to be "complete" by denying difference and hierarchy, however provocative as ideological divergence from writerly and institutional conventionality, clearly fails to engage with the otherness of the other, the postcolonial insistence on particularities that the forces of assimilative process can only violate. Not only repudiation of hegemony cuts both ways and plays both sides: so does alterity itself. To participate in a contestatory debate about the subversion of boundaries and the infiltrations of alterity is inescapably both an admission of partiality and an act of faith. No one is "complete"; no one is completely different.

Nor is this partiality identical with the principled ambivalence of deconstructive methodologies; postcolonial authors and theorists repeatedly find themselves not merely immobilized among the paradoxes, but obliged to make choices from among conflicting cultural options. Buchi Emecheta's *Bride Price*, for instance, is not simply a depiction of a culture in conflict with itself; it is a conflictual picture of such a culture. It would be easy simply to celebrate the claims it makes for communal attention to children—that the community consists, for example, of many mothers. Yet it also insists upon the Ibo proverb that says, "On the day of blood relatives, friends go." In this another distinction is drawn, another set of criteria is established, another framework of kinship is suggested. The proverb suggests that the claim of communal parenting is too broad, that (as in other cultures) circumstances dictate adults' responsibilities for care of children. Are we to say, then, that the distinction between Ibo and, say, Belfast Catholic cultures becomes one of degree, not (hierarchical) type? How is this question to be handled in our classrooms?

Early efforts to frame a postcolonial theory, like the enormously valuable *Empire Writes Back*, understandably relied too heavily on a strategy of inversion of values in which a variety of dichotomous structures observed in the relations between (post)-colonized cultures and the metropolitan center—margin/center, order/disorder, reality/unreality, power/impotence, authentic/inauthentic, being/nothingness, and so forth—were reversed in such a way that those values conventionally assigned to the colonized community were now privileged, held to organize and legitimate postcolonized cultural production.

But however radical the gesture of inversion appears, it nevertheless depends upon overdetermined, highly inflexible, and at least partly discredited categories that fail to address the complex, pluralistic energies of postcolonial experience. Indeed, the rigorous mapping of the theories and practices of postcolonial authors undertaken by postcolonial scholars itself seems to reflect the workings of an exclusionary rhetoric that confines, demarcates, constrains. Such classificatory processes are systematically related to those that segregate localities and populations via colonization, and many contributors to this volume see in the production, circulation, and consumption of postcoloniality a reincarnated, recycled colonialism, imperialism, and capitalism. Of course, Western logic will defend itself—will insist that it articulates the terms for distinctions and comparison, not sliding equivalencies, approximations, and metaphoric excess; and that the characteristic intellectual gesture of ideological polemic is the fallacy called slippery slope. Nevertheless, it seems necessary to find ways to speak of the degrees of discomfort that Western interpretative methods can give rise to, especially when they hurl themselves over borders into a world where their authority is admittedly partial.

In many ways, the essays collected here constitute a discourse on, and of, partiality—of the failure of global models, global aspirations, global assumptions, of the necessity to recognize distinctions and the subversion of distinctions, of a new regime of inquiry marked both by passionate intensities and the peculiar demands of multicultural selectivity. What emerges is a postmodern multidiscipline whose analysis of postcolonial pedagogy repeatedly reflects back on its own enmeshed participation in the global exercise of postcolonial power. The diverse approaches reflect the varied intellectual foci and institutional situations that such pedagogy faces: historical analyses of complex traditions of cultural production; reexamination of pedagogy as a set of productive-receptive operations whose terms depend upon—and change their form in relation to—cultural and political specificities that Western pedagogical theory has largely ignored or misrepresented; reconsideration of the forces involved in the construction of processes of reading; inquiries into the ways in which colonial/postcolonial experience intersects with the experience of gender, class, and/or race; challenges to canons; efforts to preserve and/or establish canons; efforts to define the possibilities for constructing a cross-cultural poetics; skeptical challenges to any pluralistic opportunism whatsoever; and repeatedly, from the most varied perspectives, readings of texts by "postcolonial" authors and readings of Western canonical texts in "postcolonial" ways.

These issues circulate, cross, and recross in these essays in as many ways—in more ways—than there are authors. The temptation towards hands-off relativism (simply to present them in random order and without comment) itself crosses, in a gesture that is itself implicated in the entanglements in question, with the desire to provide an order or orders that will at least map out our own interested participation in the interrogation of postcoloniality. We have opted to divide these essays into two broad groups, "theoretical" and "pedagogical," both of which clearly demonstrate the kinds of partialities, multiplicities, ambivalences, and contestations that inevitably confront scholars attempting to theorize postcoloniality in postmodernity.

Some issues come up here so frequently that another set of hands might well have used them to establish a more minutely articulated structure for the book: the commodification of alterities, for instance, or the construction of postcolonial subjectivities, or cultural hybridity. The interest of such issues lies, however, not in their distinction but in their interrelationships, and to treat them as clearly distinguishable would be to lose our intended focus on the relations of postcolonial theory with pedagogical praxis. No doubt the same objection could be raised against our decision to distinguish "Theory" from "Pedagogy." Our rationale is simple, however: the organization of the literary profession in Western academic institutions is such that most scholars interested in the intersections explored herein will *begin* from one of these positions. Their involvement, that is, will likely be motivated and defined in the first instance by the professional segregation of "literary" and "cultural" theory from pedagogical concerns. Our purpose is thus not to lead anyone toward this bipartite division of the "postcolonial," but, by presenting materials with one foot in hegemonic structuration and the other—indeed, many others—afloat in "postcolonial" multiplicity, to lead them away from it towards a more progressive imagination of professional possibility.[5]

The first part, "Theory: New Histories and (Multi)cultural Poetics," attempts to address some of the ways in which historical and formal tendencies overlap in efforts to theorize "postcolonial" discourse. The "new" histories in question are new in quite different ways. Abiola Irele coordinates historical observation and ideological analysis to arrive at a new contextualization of contemporary African discourse. Martin Padget examines a set of British lantern-slide travelogues of the nineteenth century to give a sense of the relations between material conditions in the internal colonies and the ideological fantasy-constructions that underlay their representation and falsification. In so doing he confers historical meaning on communities who had previously served the inscriptive needs of hegemonic self-justification. Poonam Arora examines the mythic/symbolic dynamics of the Indian *tawaif* or courtesan film to historicize a "chasm between history and memory" whose sources extend to the transfer of Muslim and non-Muslim populations between Pakistan and India in 1947 and whose effects continue to resonate in patterns of repression and proscription of desire in contemporary, multicultural India.

Efforts to address the formal parameters of "postcolonial" discourse—to enunciate a poetics of such discourse—exhibit all the crossings, entanglements, and ambivalences noted above. Indeed, whatever their differences of scope, focus, and intent, they share a preoccupation with the central ambivalence of the literature and theory in question, namely, the wish to formulate a model that permits occupation of the border territories defined by postcolonial thought—a model sufficient to, responsive to, respectful of the complexity of those borders. At issue is the ethical and logical problem of theorizing border crossings whose spatial and conceptual dynamics can hardly be assumed to be commensurable. Hence there appear here a variety of skirmishes and clashes, negotiations and assimilations. And while all of them turn in some way around the focal conflictuality of colonizer and colonized, they are variously informed by the phenomena of other borders—colonial/indigenous (Hogan), cultural center/margin (Lionnet), nationalism/pluralism (Taylor). In addition, Joline Blais investigates a revision of Freudian and Fanonian patriarchal treatments of colonial subjectivity by a gender-sensitive "hystery" as practiced by Marguerite Duras, and Laura Donaldson demonstrates a synthesis of Gayatri Chakravorty Spivak's "affirmative deconstruction" and Gloria Anzaldúa's "new *mestiza*."

The last two voices of the Theory section, those of Teresa Ebert and Amitava Kumar, are distinguished by their (quite different) challenges to many critical assumptions currently vying for prominence in the field. Ebert confronts the postmodern discursive turn particularly as it shapes efforts by Western feminists to identify with and empower the speech of the subaltern, and proposes in its place a practice of materialist critique in the service of the struggle against the global division of labor imposed by late capitalism. Kumar, like Ebert, objects to the trivialization of oppositional thought—its burial under obfuscatory and mystificatory idioms and its straitening under institutional regimes concerned only with maintaining in-house order and hierarchies of professional privilege. Unlike Ebert, however, Kumar leans away from any one overarching model and toward energetic localizations of change. Together they surely indicate that "postcolonial" theory remains an open project, constantly in need of revision and development. And they clearly signal, as well, the theoretical complexities with which teachers of postcolonial texts and issues must contend.

The second part, "Pedagogy: Terminologies, Problematics, Readings," combines essays concerned with supplying analysis and definition for a number of terms and notions that are frequently contested both in general scholarship and within these covers and essays focused more directly on ways of introducing and elucidating "postcolonial" texts. No doubt all teachers ought to be attentive to the relationship between their larger project of teaching and the texts they use to realize it. But for postcolonial scholars, this relationship is a matter of intense concern. As Rajeswari Mohan explains, "Whether texts serve an agenda of commodity fetishism or radical critique...would depend on the discourses that mediate them into the classroom." The nature of such mediation is the principal topic of her essay, which reflects upon and contextualizes a number of "Questions for Postcolonial Pedagogy" that undergo a variety of transformations and exemplifications in the essays that follow. Some of these questions might be explicitly stated as follows: What definitions are critical for scholarly clarification of postcolonial complexity? What relations inhere between postmodernism and postcolonialism? How are postcolonial challenges to conventional canonicity affected by institutional structures in the academy? How should we handle comparisons between American or European modernist writers and postcolonial or Third-World writers? How do questions of race, gender, and economics figure in the pursuit of a postcolonial pedagogy? How might an emergent and oppositional postcolonial pedagogy relate to an assimilationist multicultural project in Western academic institutions? Above all, where and how can we prepare a space in the ideological configuration of academic institutions for antihegemonic resistance to find a foothold?

This last question, especially, is vigorously scrutinized by Stephen Slemon and Allen Cary-Webb. Slemon theorizes a postcolonial pedagogy that turns historical and institutional conflictuality to its best advantage to create a pedagogical space conducive to social change. And Carey-Webb, despite his warning against a "superficial multiculturalism that actually legitimates a monocultural perspective" and "simplistic and goodwill incorporation of difference," focuses in the last half of his essay on an integrative pedagogy that challenges both conventional canonicity and conventional teaching. He distrusts pluralism because "it offers acceptance of the presumedly 'Other' on the terms of the 'Self' and in a way legitimates the 'Self' as contained and independent," but in his conclusion, he argues on behalf of postcolonial pedagogical structures that allow two or more systems to encounter each other and reconstitute frames of cultural reference to question established institutional structures and habits of perception.

The "Readings" that close out this part might be expected to be both more concrete in their pedagogical concerns and more "Western," more colonizing or assimilative in their interpretative approach. For as professors of literature, we might too easily agree with Nadine Gordimer's Maureen about the fundamental reality and necessity of "the humane creed":

> [it] depended on validities staked on a belief in the absolute nature of intimate relationships between human beings. If people don't all experience emotional satisfaction and deprivation in the same way, what claim can there be for equality of need? (*July's People*, 64–65)

Yet these readings differ from conventional professional interpretative responses to canonical texts. On one hand (and despite being self-consciously informed by theory of several sorts), they are often more like meditations on processes of production and response than like instructions for processing or maps of analysis. Aware of the distinctively contestatory spaces of pedagogical reading (one of the few venues available for self-reflexive exploration of what it means to enter into shared contexts of imaginal experience), and of their various ambivalences of orientation with regard to students, institutions (of learning, publication, political authority), and language(s), the authors who concentrate on reading particular texts (and all the authors, to the extent that they involve themselves with such readings) are clearly caught up in a predicament of complex partialities defined in such a way that no one avenue of escape or transcendence avails itself without at the same time subverting its own assumptions.

On the other hand, these are readers with a purpose, and that purpose must be understood to comprehend a repudiation of oppression, and of all violations of subjectivity, community, property, tradition, and spirit, particularly those global miseries deriving from the systemic injustices of Western hegemony. These are all readings projected out of an awareness of the threatened vitality of cultures under duress. Yet if *Order and Partialities* resonates with a shared determination to disable the inequities of the order that has prevailed, it indicates not a distinct unity setting itself up in opposition to the old unity of Western cultural dominance, but a decisive energy of differences exploring new possibilities of selection and combination of the intellectual, political, and cultural materials of the postmodern world, a kind of bricolage without a bricoleur. Against the old world order is not a new world order, but a new understanding of partiality leading to radical options of self-conscious self-reconstruction. And if our partialities are cast up against a countervailing order that seemingly knows no limit and does not care, so that for every instance in which another hegemonic "absolute" rears its head we must demand, like Gordimer, "Who decided?," we still are partial in that other way that accepts the risk of partial knowledge because it knows the risk of complete ignorance, and that trusts, even as it doubts, the desire it shares with the great Sembene: for books, however difficult, that will help make the men and women of the world real to one another.

NOTES

1. Edward Said has shown, however, that the penetration of Western power into the lives of postcolonial people has employed academic/scientific collaborators as vanguard agents (see "Representing the Colonized").

2. Perhaps the context of these essays—the institutions that generate them and to which their claims might be applicable—should be further specified as Western; but such a generalization ought to be argued, not assumed.

3. That it also leads, or ought to lead, to specific kinds of *actions* beyond the scope of traditional Western scholarship is a point taken up by a number of writers in this collection. See especially the essays by Gardner and Kumar in this volume.

4. In his introduction to *Culture and Imperialism*, Said writes, "The power to narrate and to block other narratives from forming and emerging is very important to culture and imperialism, and constitutes one of the main connections among them" (xiii). Concern for control over the voice is evident among many of the authors most frequently cited in these essays, such as Ashcroft, Griffiths, and Tiffin, Homi Bhaba, and Gayatri Spivak.

5. No doubt many would wish to see here a third category designating those whose interest derives from an immersion in political praxis rather than theory or teaching. See note 3 above, and the essays by Ebert, Gardner, and Kumar.

WORKS CITED

Burroughs, William. *Naked Lunch*. New York: Grove Press, 1959.

Emecheta, Buchi. *Bride Price*. New York: Braziller, 1976.

Gordimer, Nadine. *July's People*. New York: Viking, 1981.

Said, Edward. *Culture and Imperialism*. New York: Knopf, 1993.

———. "Representing the Colonized: Anthropology's Interlocutors." *Critical Inquiry* 15.2 (Winter 1989): 205–25.

Sembene, Ousmane. *God's Bits of Wood*. London: Heinemann, 1986.

Part I

THEORY

New Histories and (Multi)cultural Poetics

1

ABIOLA IRELE

Dimensions of African Discourse

It is now more than 200 years since, as Africans, we have been using the European languages for self-expression.[1] The circumstances in which these languages (English, French, and Portuguese, in particular) became available to us are too well known to require elaboration. What needs to be recalled for my theme is the fact that they bear the stamp of a tragic irony which, with a remarkable prescience, Shakespeare has dramatized in the antagonistic relation between Prospero and Caliban in *The Tempest.* An important component of this relation, as the play stresses, is constituted by the question of language, that is, of the modes of perception and of representation which govern the master/slave dialectic.[2]

These circumstances, in their real historical manifestations, have determined the very contours of modern African expression in the European languages. The themes and preoccupations that are central to the development of this expression, and the uses to which the acquired literacy upon which it is grounded has been consciously put, point to an imperative of consciousness: the intensive exploration by the African writer, both at the imaginative and conceptual levels, of a peculiar and singular historicity. Whether in the form of imaginative literature or in directly ideological terms, writing has served us as a means of appropriating the European languages in an endeavor to transcend the vicissitudes of a problematic experience, in an effort towards an expressive grasp of the world in which that experience unfolds.

The close correspondence between the two channels of African discourse I have indicated becomes evident when it is observed that the themes and textual modes of the imaginative literature regularly present themselves as imagistic transpositions of explicit preoccupations at the level of the ideological; they give the indirection of form and of metaphor (in the large sense of the term) to sentiments, attitudes and ideas—to activities of consciousness—that stem from an immediate engagement with experience. Both can thus be regarded as alternative and even alternating modes of the same textualized response to a collective experience, exemplifying in a particularly striking way what Edward Said has called "the situation of writing in history" (*Literature and Society*, Introduction).

The imaginative and ideological forms of African expression in the European languages thus constitute a specific configuration of discourse, which, though not by any means uniform, univocal, or homogeneous, is nonetheless coherent, centered as it is upon a dominant issue: that of our historic encounter with and continuing relationship to the West and the varied implications of our modern experience as it has been determined by this historic encounter.

My intention in this presentation is not to propose one more exposition of the themes of African writing (to go over ground that has already been well surveyed) but to highlight those aspects of African response to the incursion of Europe and the West that may help to clarify the processes and issues involved in the development of African discourse, in the broad sense in which I'm taking the term here. I'd like to proceed by situating African writing within the three contexts that seem to me to bring out its proper dimensions: first, as racial reference, its central place within black expression and hence its specific affiliation to the movement of black affirmation in the Americas; second, its relation to the emerging discourses of the Third World, as part of a general contestation of the hegemony of the West; and finally, its relevance to certain currents of thought in the West itself, with which it can be placed in a certain relation of congruence. In this last respect, we witness a transformation of African discourse in the postcolonial period into an internal debate that inaugurates a distinctive form of public discourse in Africa, focussed on the question of modernity. My overall aim is to present African discourse as an affective and cognitive process whose textual expression continuously interacts with the concrete reality of history, and significantly bears upon the urgent preoccupations of the contemporary world.

The most striking aspect of African discourse is of course its character as a movement of contestation. Starting with the work of the eighteenth-century black writers, this discourse has determinedly confronted European representations of Africa and of the black race, dedicating special attention to the objective historical conditions of the race, first during slavery and later, colonialism. A conditioning factor of African response has thus been, quite simply, an acute racial consciousness directly reacting to the negativizing premises of Western racist ideology.

Thus African discourse has been historically projected in an essentially adversarial posture and has thus assumed a polemical significance. In whatever accents African response has been given expression, whether in an openly combative form or a discreetly pathetic one—with gradations in between—the discursive project has taken the form of an ongoing, principled dispute with the West over the terms of African/black existence, and ultimately, of being. The example of Aimé Césaire, whose poetry embraces in its scope the African experience in its full ramifications—historical, moral, and even metaphysical—becomes especially instructive in this regard. All his expression is predicated upon what he calls "the true operative power of negation," upon the subversive impulse of a poetic language resolutely pitted against Western prescriptive terms ("Barbare," in *Cadastre*, 56; also in *Collected Poems*, 212). His work sets in train, as it were, a poetics of aggression which elaborates a system of "counter-interpellations" (to use Althusser's term) opposed to the co-optive force of Western imperialism and cultural impositions.

Writing has also served us as the means of a pointed indictment of the white man in the relentless documentation our literature provides of the stark realities of the black experience as a historical consequence of conquest and domination. The resort to the autobiographical form by the early black slave writers (Equiano and others) attests to the function of witnessing that the African writer has been constrained to assume from the very beginning. There is perhaps no better instance of this immediate documentary and testamental significance of African writing than that offered by the ironic fictions of Ferdinand Oyono, whose depiction of colonial violence is built upon the image of the prison as the fundamental institution from which it is generated and by which it is maintained. And it is the concrete grasp of the actualities of the colonial experience laid bare in works such as these that Frantz Fanon has enlarged upon in his analyses of the colonial situation to present a graphic description of what, with Foucault, we now recognize as the "carceral society."

The point that emerges from this aspect of African discourse is its strongly articulated sense of historical grievance. The fact itself has further implications, beyond its immediate reference to the West: it has determined in African (and black) thinking and attitudes a conflation of the categories of race and culture which still exerts an axiomatic force even in the postcolonial period. The positing in this discourse of a sharp dichotomy between an aggressive Western civilization and a humane African sensibility has implications for the African debate on modernity which we shall have occasion to consider. For the moment, we might note that the moral perceptions that inform the African sense of racial and historical grievance issue into a comprehensive critique of the West, a questioning of its assumptions about itself and of its vision of the world. Under the pressure of experience, our writers have had to undertake a critical reassessment of the colonizer, of the philosophy of life which is assumed to underlie his civilization and his very disposition towards the world, anticipating in the course of this reassessment some of the key strategies of contemporary Western analyses.

The complementary aspect of this stance of negation is the mobilization of the collective will and consciousness which African writing has sought to enact at the discursive level. Our expression in the European languages has not only functioned as a mode of contestation of the colonial ideology but also served an emancipatory project. It is, of course, in this respect that the various theories of Africanism that have sprung up in the black world have had their strategic importance. Of some of the relevant figures, let me simply refer here in passing to Blyden and his concept of the "African personality," Delaney and Garvey, with their various exemplifications of the "Back to Africa" movement, Du Bois with his militant Pan-Africanism, and of course, Senghor and his theory of Negritude.

The ideology of race promoted by the theories of Africanism associated with these figures, going hand in hand with movements of racial solidarity, sustains in the literature a form of romanticism which seeks to legitimize and underwrite a myth of universal black identity. In the African context, this has had the largely salutary effect (though not without its problems and contradictions) of a revaluation and celebration of indigenous cultures, a process exemplified in the gravitas that writers as different as Senghor and Achebe ascribe to the universe of life that they posit as their true antecedent (what Senghor calls *le royaume de l'enfance*—"the realm of childhood") and on which they stake their sense of origins. That the process of revaluation embraces the modes of expression associated with the traditional African world gives rise to what I've called elsewhere an "aesthetic traditionalism," a poetics of indigenism that shapes the formal structure of much of the imaginative literature ("African Letters"). For, in the discursive context of the colonial situation, language, as an essential medium of human articulations and cultural processes, becomes a strategic site of African revendication, a significant modality of cultural nationalism. The tremendous effort of historical scholarship that went with this cultural nationalism gives further density to African affirmation by seeking to project African being-in-time along an autonomous axis of historicity.[3]

The immediate import of these imaginative and intellectual efforts is perfectly clear: as "counter discourses," they represent not only a repudiation of the negative representations of the "native" in the imperialist ideology, they also articulate the claim to an alternative cultural history to the Western. It is especially in this connection that theories of Africanism assume an incisive relevance for black intellectuals in the New World, in what has come to be known, by analogy with the Jewish condition, as the "Black Diaspora": they imply a reinvestiture of the black self, a reincorporation, in the strong sense of the word, which establishes a new compact of the racial and historical community through a coincidence with origins. For the black intellectual in Africa and the New World, severed from a sense of immediate connection with the original community, an appeal to the background of African traditional life and history represents a form of spiritual homecoming, in the sense of *nostos*.

The preoccupation with the racial question thus provides a primary dimension of African discourse. This dimension, which incorporates all the significant aspects of cultural nationalism that the discourse promotes, gives it an immediate link with black consciousness movements in the New World. It ought to be noted in this respect that the historical and thematic links between modern African expression in the European languages and African-American and Caribbean literatures proceed in formal terms from their common origin in the work of the early black slave writers of the eighteenth century. These links have determined a cycle of reciprocities that finds a pointed illustration in the derivation of the Negritude movement itself from the Harlem Renaissance, as a direct outgrowth of the thematic and ideological expression of Afro-Americans (see Kesteloot). And the idea of black identity to which the Harlem poets and artists strove to give expressive form finds with the French-speaking black intellectuals its ultimate formulation in a concept of black racial essence.

The essentialism implied by this concept, which informs the various theories of Africanism of which Negritude is a summation, still holds sway in some crucial respects: for instance, what I've called the cycle of reciprocities between black discourse in the New World and in Africa is being sustained at the present time in the work of a prominent segment of the black intelligentsia in North America. Such recent developments as the Black Aesthetic movement initiated by Addison Gayle, Stephen Henderson, and others, and the Afrocentrism of Molefi Asante, constitute restatements in African-American terms of the essential tenets of Negritude: they proceed from the same vision of a common backcloth of origin, of culture, of expression and of sensibility. And in the critical work of scholars such as Houston Baker Jr. and Henry Louis Gates Jr., who are promoting a theory of "vernacular" literary and cultural expression of the black community in the United States with direct reference to African-derived paradigms, we observe an effort to conceptualize the black self as a continuous process of self-realization with organic roots in the ancestral soil. Whatever value one is inclined to attach to the propositions which these various scholars offer of the black estate in the Americas, they attest to the fact that there remains a wide area of overlapping between African discourse and African-American imaginative self-awareness and intellectual self-reflection.

The manifestations of black racial consciousness that I've reviewed here denote a form of collective self-projection through a strategy of differentiation. We need not enquire here into the validity or truth claims in strict anthropological or philosophical terms of the formulations proposed by African discourse and its extensions in the New World. Because they present themselves essentially as a refutation of the category of the radical "other" imposed on the black colonized, they function, ipso facto, as a repositioning of the collective self in what may be considered a willed act of renewed self-apprehension.

In its polemical stance then, African discourse presents itself as a thorough-going deconstruction of the Western image of the native, the black, the African. Because we were represented as the absolute "other," we were well placed to develop a minoritarian discourse which marks out the extreme position of dissent from the systematizing, totalizing thrust of the Western imperialist system. This dissent has force not only in its bearing upon the application of the Western conceptual system, in its concrete effects, to our historical situation, but upon the very structure and the universalist ambitions of this system itself.[4] In this sense, the discourse of Africanism as elaborated by black intellectuals on both sides of the Atlantic must be seen as a reinscription of an antecedent Western monologue on Africa and the non-Western world, its displacement and transformation by a new, assertive self-expression on the part of a subjugated and voiceless humanity.

The general pattern of this challenge to Western discourse has been indicated for the colonized writers of English expression by Ashcroft, Griffiths, and Tiffin in their comprehensive survey, *The Empire Writes Back*, and the mechanisms they have described as typifying this expression can be identified in anti-colonial and postcolonial literatures in other languages. The pattern involves notably the refusal of privilege to the language, literature, and thought systems of the colonizer, and to the framework of references stipulated for the colonized writer by the metropolitan paradigm. This refusal is complemented by an assiduous cultivation of a sense of place, which finds expression in a localized idiom made coterminous with a radical sense of identity. What is implied here is a determined inversion of the order of precedence decreed by the colonizer from an entrenched center of power. The conceptual formulation of this new disposition discernible in Third World discourses is carried through an intellectual effort that runs parallel to the imaginative expression. Edward Said's *Orientalism* represents perhaps the most powerful instance of this effort in the elaboration of a "postcolonial discourse" whose theoretical implications are being explored today in the work of other Third World intellectuals such as Abdelkebir Khatibi, Gayatri Spivak, and Homi Bhabha (for a broad discussion, see also JanMohamed and Lloyd).

The historical reference for this dimension of African discourse in its transactions with Third World literary and intellectual responses to Western imperialism may be taken to be the Bandung conference of 1955, considered as the primal event of decolonization in our time.[5] The specific impulses at work in the postcolonial literatures that may be related to this event thus operate as potent factors to decenter and relativize the conceptual and moral order of the Western world and to promote a pluralism of voices with a legitimate claim to universal hearing. The pressures they exert move towards what one might call a global "deregulation" of the Western paradigm, as much in feeling and expression as in thought.

The allusion to Bandung and to decolonization underscores the constitutive role of African and Third World discourses in the formation and consolidation of anti-colonial nationalism in contemporary times. These discourses assume a political significance as an integral component of ideologies of national independence that gave orientation to anti-Western sentiments in the non-Western world, culminating in the emergence of new nation states in Africa and Asia after the Second World War. The rhetoric of cultural and racial affirmation involved in these ideologies thus served as the mental levers in the struggle against the objective structures of imperial domination and colonial dependency.[6]

The implication of African discourse in these developments extends its affiliation to the literature of race and black identity, giving it a relevance with more than a circumscribed significance. But despite this extension of its primary affiliation, it is probably correct to affirm that the African/black response to the West remains very particularized, as much in the specific terms of its expression as in its general thrust.[7] The nationalist project in the imaginative literature and ideological writings in the African context was centered primarily on considerations of the historical fortunes of the black race, of which the African continent was taken to represent the ancestral core and spiritual homeland. African nationalism thus developed as a continuous progression from Pan-Africanism, the continent assuming the attributes of a "nation" in the comprehensive vision of black peoples that Pan-Africanism fostered. Nationalism in Africa only assumed distinctive territorial expressions in its final phase, in relation to the spheres of domination determined by the partition of the continent among the imperial powers (see Irele, "Pan-Africanism and African Nationalism," in *African Experience*, 117–24).

It is thus in a large and diffuse sense that imaginative literature and other forms of discourse came to serve nationalism in Africa. And as in all forms of literary expression dedicated to the promotion of nationalist consciousness, the dominant symbols tend toward a celebration of community projected through imaginative form. The master text in the case of Africa remains Chinua Achebe's *Things Fall Apart*, by reason both of its innovative role in the emergence of modern African literature and its ideological significance as a vindication of a unique mode of life and apprehension, despite the inevitable ambivalence that runs as an undercurrent to its portrayal of an indigenous African society and culture. Here, as elsewhere, literature provides an aesthetic and moral sanction for an idealized vision of the community, defined, on the one hand, in terms of inclusion—of the indigenous group's singularity, its commonality of history, culture, and sentiment (in Africa and Third World nationalisms this commonality does not generally extend to language, however); and on the other hand, in terms of an exclusion of the colonial master himself from the human category to which the group feels and indeed knows itself to belong. The claim to self-determination thus becomes grounded in a cult of difference all the more plausible in that it seems ratified by the visible imprint of racial and ethnic characteristics.

This insistence on difference involves an apparent irony of the nationalist posture as it emerges from African and Third World discourses, for it seems to imply an assent to the terms of the colonial ideology, predicated as this is on the very idea of the incommensurability of the human essence of the colonizer and that of the native. It thus appears as if what I've called "the strategies of differentiation" that animate much of African discourse produce the paradoxical result of an entrenchment of the categories of the colonizer.[8] The essential point, however, is that this affirmation of difference not only authorizes the claims implied in the nationalist project to an autonomy that is political, it also in its fullest sense enacts a movement towards an absolute form of self-recovery, toward repossession in cultural and existential terms.

This observation points to what is perhaps the most salient aspect of the idealism (in all the senses of the word) inherent in myths of the nation constructed by African and Third World discourses—the utopianism and even millenarianism with which they are pervaded. These myths articulate the aspirations of colonized, non-Western peoples to a new mode of insertion into the flow of history, as well as to a modernity in which their sense of initiative can receive unhindered play. This second aspect of African and Third World utopianism has implications for the further development of the intellectual adventure of the non-Western world, for it happens to be the case that, in the particular circumstances of decolonization in the twentieth century, the accession to modernity can only take place under the rubric of the nation-state, both as a notion inherited from the West and as a functional unit for modes of social organization and economic production compatible with the exigencies of the modern world—a point to which we shall soon return.

Thus, if nationalism in Africa and the Third World aspires in each domain of its expression towards a reintegration of the communal past within the collective awareness, it has perforce to acknowledge an epochal break with that past provoked by the colonial, Western incursion. The historical consciousness implicit in nationalism thus involves in this case an acute sense of discontinuities in the history which the colonized themselves have undertaken to refashion. In the African context, the career and work of Kwame Nkrumah strikingly exemplify the nexus introduced by this logic of decolonization between a celebratory traditionalism mandated by his nationalist convictions and a utopian vision of African reconstruction in the contemporary world.[9]

As an idea, then, colonial emancipation is predicated on the hopes of a new beginning for historical communities striving for a new mode of existence; it is thus enmeshed in an unusually complex relation between past, present, and future. In African discourse, especially, this relation is inscribed within the tense dialectic of tradition and modernity. The high valuation of racial and cultural antecedents, of what is imagined and projected as their coherence, has had to be balanced against the recognition of the new imperatives of modernization dictated by the impact of a triumphant West. What this implies is nothing less than a drama of conflicting normativities,[10] and it is this drama that defines for Africans today the specific form of what has come to be termed "the dilemma of modernity" (Cahoone).

It is especially in this respect that the contemporary climate of thought in the West interests us—an interest that is the most recent indication of the deep and long-standing imbrication of African thought in the movement of ideas in the West. In very significant ways, African discourse, along with other "minority discourses," has urgently anticipated some of the current preoccupations in Western thought. These anticipations were not necessarily theorized, or if they were, as in the case of Fanon mentioned earlier, they were not formulated in exactly the same terms as in the currents of thought now commonly grouped under poststructuralism and postmodernism. But the ideas that are coming out of the Western world today strike us with a certain familiarity, for they address issues of authority, pluralism, and especially the relation between discourse and power. These ideas are concerned crucially with the question of discursivity and its crucial function in the claims to legitimacy and normativity in the social sphere, a question that goes to the very heart of our modern experience stemming from our encounter with Europe.[11]

This parallel simply confirms the fact that there have been significant points of intersection between the unfolding of African discourse along its polemical trajectory and intellectual and social developments in Europe, at least since the eighteenth century: African discourse, by the very force of circumstance, has had to integrate important elements of the Western structure of mind to which African intellectuals have had perforce to relate. This is obvious enough in the case of what we may term the "liberal" tradition of Western thought, within which very powerful voices have been raised on our behalf since the beginning of our encounter with Europe, voices with which we have found good cause to identify.[12] The critical interrogation going on today within Western thought of its own systems of knowledge and values corresponds in certain important respects to the exigencies of this liberal tradition. Moreover—and this is the point I wish to stress—it accords with the perceptions of African intellectuals of the contradiction between the humanist claims of Western civilization and its practical effects on subject races, in other words, of its profound dissimulations.

But the real significance of the "convergence" that can be claimed between African discourse and the critical activity now taking place in the West emerges from the wider perspective of a global debate on the question of modernity. It is at this level that one discerns a third dimension of African discourse. The "dynamics" inherent in contemporary discourse in Africa, as indeed in the Third World as a whole, takes us well beyond the immediate ideological and nationalist project the discourse patently subserves. It involves not only a reappraisal of the terms of the relationship between the West and indigenous cultures and societies, but also an interrogation, often anxiety-ridden, of these very societies themselves. This interrogation is inherent in the very nature of the nationalist project itself, in the peculiar conjunction between the archaisms that modulate its deeply affective function and the prospective significance of the utopianism by which it seeks to mobilize the collective will.

It is important to place this process of self-interrogation as it has manifested itself in Africa in the wider historical and philosophical framework of modern experience worldwide, in order to grasp this dimension of African discourse I'm trying to elucidate. Modern nationalism, in Europe and elsewhere, has derived much of its impulse from the pressures brought about by the vast social transformations set in train by the industrial revolution,[13] which profoundly modified the modes of transactions between individuals and between communities and redefined their relation to the world. Much of modern thought and scholarship has been conditioned by the need to confront the existential implications of these changes. Thus the Enlightenment has come to represent the point of cleavage between what Karl Mannheim has called "Conservative Thought" on one hand, and on the other, the various ideologies of progress that have derived from the unprecedented development of science and its technological applications since the eighteenth century.[14] The massive reorganization of life in political, economic, social, and cultural terms brought about by the industrial revolution has provoked varying responses on the part of writers and thinkers in the West, some of which might be said to offer parallels to "nativistic" movements in the non-Western world, providing a common ground for the debates on culture and the whole question of modernity both in the West and in the Third World, most especially in Africa.

In the more significant of these responses, the quest is for a mode of experience that retains the immediacy of the "simple life" of traditional societies, conjoined with an inwardness of experience, as opposed to the complex organization of industrial society and the spiritual disarray and alienation which it is taken to entail. This quest is obvious in literary Romanticism in Europe, and a "Romantic" strain can be said in this sense to pervade the conservative ideology of Burke, the nationalism of Herder, and can even be discerned behind Hegel's idea of the "organic society."[15] The tension which all these responses address is summed up in the distinction made by Tonnies between *Gemeinschaft* (Community), with its connotation of close bonding between the members of a determinate and specified group, and *Gesellschaft*, implying an impersonal order of social organization. This distinction reflects a concern for a warmly human rather than the purely rational scale of values that Max Weber has singled out as the organizing principle of modern society.[16] And it is in the general light of a profound dissatisfaction with this principle that a reappraisal is taking place in contemporary Western thought of "instrumental reason" as a factor of modernity.

The interplay between thought and change—evoked in these very terms in the title of Ernest Gellner's book—which underlies the responses I've evoked above, becomes directly relevant to a consideration of African discourse, for it sketches out the background to the felt pressures of modernization in all societies and cultures that have experienced the impact of industrialization, either directly, as in Europe and in North America, or indirectly, through foreign influence or imperialism, as in non-Western societies.[17] The point then is that a general preoccupation with the dilemmas of modernity runs as a *leitmotif* in Western thought, at least since the Enlightenment; it is hardly surprising therefore that it should also constitute the unifying theme of the reflexive activity embodied in African discourse, which has developed both in the context of Western cultural impositions and of the far-reaching dislocations which these have engendered in African cultures and societies.

The combined effects of the humiliated feeling of colonial dependency and of cultural malaise flowing from these dislocations have determined something of a standard trope of the African imagination in which Africa, associated with the security of origins, is represented as being violated by an aggressive and unfeeling Europe. This is, of course, the basis of the Romanticism that informs what I've alluded to as the myth of identity in African discourse, and that conditions the disaffection towards Western rationality, associated both with colonial domination and an unsettling modernity that is its immediate consequence. African literature in its genesis and development has revolved so much around the theme of culture conflict carried by this "master trope" that it has become a commonplace of its reception and analysis.

Yet, it is important to note that what appears to be a fixation on the dialectic of tradition and modernity also reflects a quest for a new direction of collective initiative, for the intellectual foundations of African renewal. The theories of "African socialism" propounded by figures such as Senghor and Nyerere in the immediate aftermath of African independence have no other significance; indeed, they issue largely out of the utopianism that, as we've seen, underlies the nationalist consciousness in Africa. And as is evident in the case of Nkrumah's "consciencism," they represent a focused endeavor to negotiate a mode of accommodation between Africa and the West (see Senghor; Nyerere; Nkrumah, *Consciencism*).

This aspect of contemporary African thought has been thrown into special relief by the current debate on the question of African philosophy. An extension of the Negritude debate, the present discussion centers upon an argument about the philosophical status of traditional African systems of thought and their capacity both for providing a satisfactory explanation of the world comparable to Western systems of knowledge and for enabling effective action in the modern world. The epistemological issues involved in the debate have thus been subordinated to a consideration of the options open for the process of renovation in Africa, options that condition strategies for ensuring the destiny of her peoples in a world governed by the institutional imperatives of the nation-state and dominated by a universal technicity, in short, for the instauration of an acceptable order of life in Africa in contemporary times.

What the intellectuals associated with this debate—such as Marcien Towa, Paulin Hountondji, and Achille Mbembe (see also Bjornson)—have achieved is to initiate what one might call a "contradictory discourse" that breaches the consensus around a uniform vision of Africa, and is more in tune with the dynamics of the social and cultural processes at work in cultural and intellectual production in contemporary Africa. By fostering a new orientation towards a critical appraisal and revision of the earlier formulations of African discourse, they have given a new focus to intellectual activity in Africa in the postcolonial period.

The Zairean philosopher Valentin Mudimbe has argued that the development of African discourse has been essentially a function of what he calls, in Foucauldian terms, the depositions of the Western archive. From a consideration of what I've called its dimensions, it is indeed perfectly legitimate to postulate a close connection between African intellectual efforts and Western discourse, and specifically today, critical activity in the West. The immediate conclusion one can draw from this connection is that African discourse is not marginal but, on the contrary, central to contemporary concerns.

But while there exists a congruence between the temper of contemporary thought in the West and African concerns, it does not seem to me that this quite indicates a coincidence of interests. Western thought at the moment, in its distinctive anti-foundationalist current, is engaged in the process of unraveling its tradition, precisely that tradition which came into sharp focus in the eighteenth century; it is marked in other words by a comprehensive skepticism with regard to its defining legacy of rationalism, by a disengagement from its predicates arising from a profound distrust of what has come to be seen as its reifications. On the other hand, the direction of African discourse has been towards the privileging of thought as an active modality of existence. It seems to me, therefore, that the terms of late twentieth-century Western thought do not correspond to the imperatives of intellectual enterprise in the present African context.

We cannot then, as Africans, have much use for what can be described as the uncharted nihilism of this aspect of contemporary thought in the West—for the morose anti-humanism of Foucault, or the corrosive intelligence of Derrida.[18] An active intellectual vigilance can therefore be said to be in order on our part. The plain fact is that history has not been for us a phantom play of mirrors, but rather a harrowing experience, vividly rendered in our imaginative expression and reflected in the general tenor of our discourse. This fact imposes on the African intellectual a certain moral responsibility, for at this stage of our historical and intellectual adventure, we cannot do with anything less than a forward movement of thought and, above all, of will.

NOTES

1. This essay is a revised and expanded version of a paper delivered at the annual convention of the Modern Language Association held at Chicago in December 1990.

2. Shakespeare's play has understandably served as a reference for reflection on this theme by writers in the Caribbean, notably the Cuban Roberto Fernández Retamar (see "Caliban: Notes towards a Discussion of Culture in our America," in *Caliban and Other Essays*) and Lamming. Aimé Césaire's play, *Une Tempête*, is a polemical reworking of Shakespeare's play in such a way as to emphasize its continuing relevance to the black situation. For a fuller discussion, see Nixon.

3. For a review of African historical scholarship in this light, see Gordon.

4. The most extensive and radical effort to call into question the Western conceptual system by an African is contained in Pathé Diagne's little known work, *L'Europhilosophie*. See also Outlaw.

5. The historic significance of the Bandung Conference has been summed up in the following terms: "the national movements of Asia and Africa gradually developed into a universal revolt against the west, a

rejection of western domination which found expression in the Afro-Asian conference at Bandung in 1955. The Bandung conference symbolized the new-found solidarity of Asia and Africa against Europe" (Barraclough, 159).

6. The ideological significance of Third World literature in the context of the anti-colonial struggle is comprehensively examined by Barbara Harlow.

7. The historical, sociological and cultural factors which give a specific character to Third World anti-colonial nationalism are examined by Anderson, esp. chapter 7, "The Last Wave" (104–28). See also Brennan and the three essays by Edward Said, Terry Eagleton, and Fredric Jameson in Deane's *Nationalism, Colonialism and Literature*.

8. Stanislas Adotevi's acerbic critique of Negritude in *Négritude et Négrologues* is essentially a denunciation of what he takes to be the complicity between Senghor's ideas and the propositions of European racist ideology with regard to the black race.

9. The utopianism of Nkrumah is in full evidence in *Africa Must Unite* (1964), published while he was still President of Ghana. For an excellent presentation of Nkrumah's career and political ideas in this perspective, see Rooney.

10. This dilemma as it relates to Africa and the Third World has been well summed up by Paul Ricoeur in these words: "On the one hand, the developing world has to root itself in the soil of its past, forge a national spirit, and unfurl this spiritual and cultural revendication before the colonialists' personality. But in order to take part in modern civilization, it is necessary at the same time to take part in scientific, technical and political rationality, something that very often requires the pure and simple abandonment of a whole cultural past" (quoted in Brennan, 46).

11. These issues form the very core of Foucault's work (see *L'Ordre*). Bakhtin's concept of the "logosphere" in its designation of the social sphere as a site for contending discourses is equally fundamental to these issues.

12. Consider, in France, the tradition of pro-black literature that runs from Abbé Grégoire in the eighteenth century down to Sartre in the twentieth.

13. Ernest Gellner's interpretation of the rise and development of nationalism in Europe is based largely on this premise; see *Nations and Nationalism*.

14. The prime example of what I call here ideologies of progress is Comte's positivism, to whose spirit much of nineteenth-century Western

thought, including Marxism in its elaboration by Marx and Engels, can also be related. See Pollard.

15. That this system of valuations underlies Romantic literature is made clear by its theoretical formulations, notably in the writings of Coleridge on the imagination; for an extensive discussion, see Abrams. Eagleton offers a more recent consideration, situated within a resolutely Marxist perspective, of the relation between historical and social factors and theories of art.

16. See Kumar. Both Leo Marx and Edward Shi have traced the same development and concern in American literature and thought. This "romantic" strain is resurfacing today more generally in the ecology movement, of which Ernest Callenbach's *Ecotopia* is perhaps the best-known literary expression.

17. The case of Russia, which remained more or less on the fringe of Western civilization for much of its history up to the Bolshevik Revolution, is particularly illuminating in this regard. Movements such as that of the Russian Slavophiles, with their affinities to the mysticism of the Tolstoyans and even to the philosophical anarchism of Kropotkin, offer perhaps the most revealing instance of the way in which the advance of modern civilization has produced malcontents even in Europe. The Russian case offers close parallels to the African situation which bear reflecting upon (see Avrich).

18. Consider the very forceful critique of Ferry and Renaut of the trend represented by these philosophers and others associated with them. An especially lucid and also critical appraisal of the same trend is provided by Sim. My remarks here are prompted by what I see as an uncritical and possibly disabling fascination with these French philosophers on the part of a new generation of French-speaking African intellectuals, particularly Valentin Mudimbe, on whom the pertinence of Foucault's analyses and the power of his intellect seem to have made a profound impression. By comparison, Edward Said's more circumspect endorsement of Foucault in *The World, The Text and The Critic*, while allowing for these qualities in his work, proceeds from the kind of intellectual vigilance I'm recommending here.

WORKS CITED

Abrams, M. H. *The Mirror and the Lamp: Romantic Theory and the Critical Tradition*. New York: Oxford University Press, 1953.

Achebe, Chinua. *Things Fall Apart*. London: Heinemann, 1959.

Adotevi, Stanislas. *Négritude et Négrologues*. Paris: Union Générale d'Editions, 1972.

Anderson, Benedict. *Imagined Communities*. London: Verso, 1983.

Asante, Molefi. *The Afrocentric Idea*. Philadelphia: Temple University Press, 1987.

Ashcroft, Bill, Gareth Griffiths, and Helen Tiffin. *The Empire Writes Back: Theory and Practice in Postcolonial Literatures*. London: Routledge, 1989.

Avrich, Paul. *The Russian Anarchists*. New York: Norton, 1978.

Baker, Houston A., Jr. *Blues, Ideology and Afro-American Literature: A Vernacular Theory*. Chicago: University of Chicago Press, 1984.

Bakhtin, M. *The Dialogic Imagination*. Trans. Caryl Emerson and Michael Holquist. Austin: University of Texas Press, 1981.

Barraclough, Geoffrey. *An Introduction to Contemporary History*. Hammondsworth: Penguin, 1967.

Bhabha, Homi. "DissemiNation." In Bhabha, ed., *Nation and Narration*. London: Routledge, 1990, 291–322.

———. "Signs Taken for Wonders: Questions of Ambivalence and Authority under a Tree outside Delhi." In Gates, ed., "*Race*," 163–84.

Bjornson, Richard. *The African Quest for Freedom and Identity*. Bloomington: Indiana University Press, 1991.

Brennan, Timothy. "The National Longing for Form." Bhabha, ed., *Nation and Narration*, 44–70.

Cahoone, Lawrence E. *The Dilemma of Modernity*. New York: SUNY Press, 1988.

Callenbach, Ernest. *Ecotopia*. New York: Bantam Books, 1976.

Césaire, Aimé. *Cadastre*. Paris: Seuil, 1961.

———. *Collected Poems*. Trans. Clayton Eshleman and Annette Smith. Berkeley and Los Angeles: University of California Press, 1983.

———. *Une Tempête*. Paris: Seuil, 1969.

Deane, Seamus, ed. *Nationalism, Colonialism and Literature*. Minneapolis: University of Minnesota Press, 1990.

Diagne, Pathé. *L'Europhilosophie*. Dakar: Editions Sankoré, 1982.

Eagleton, Terry. *The Ideology of the Aesthetic*. Oxford: Basil Blackwell, 1990.

Fanon, Frantz. *The Wretched of the Earth*. New York: Grove, 1967.

Ferry, Luc, and Alain Renaut. *French Philosophy in the Sixties*. Trans. Mary S. Cattani. Amherst: University of Massachusetts Press, 1989.

Foucault, Michel. *L'Ordre du discours*. Paris: Gallimard, 1971.

Gates, Henry Louis. *"Race," Writing and Difference*. Chicago: University of Chicago Press, 1986.

———. *The Signifying Monkey*. New York: Oxford University Press, 1989.

Gayle, Addison, ed. *The Black Aesthetic*. New York: Doubleday, 1987.

Gellner, Ernest. *Nations and Nationalism*. Ithaca: Cornell University Press, 1963.

———. *Thought and Change*. London: Weidenfeld and Nicholson, 1965.

Gordon, D. *Self-Determination and History in the Third World*. Princeton: Princeton University Press, 1971.

Harlow, Barbara. *Resistance Literature*. London: Methuen, 1987.

Hountondji, Paulin. *Sur la "philosophie africaine."* Paris: Maspéro, 1983.

Irele, Abiola. *The African Experience in Literature and Ideology*. Bloomington: Indiana University Press, 1990.

———. "African Letters: The Making of a Tradition." *The Yale Journal of Criticism* 5.1 (Fall 1991): 69–100.

JanMohamed, Abdul, and David Lloyd, eds. *The Nature and Context of Minority Discourse*. New York: Oxford University Press, 1990.

Kesteloot, Lilyan. *Black Writers in French*. Trans. Ellen Conroy Kennedy. Washington, DC: Howard University Press, 1991.

Khatibi, Abdelkebir. *Maghreb Pluriel*. Paris: Denoël, 1983.

Kumar, Krishan. *Prophecy and Progress: The Sociology of Post-Industrial Society*. Hammondsworth: Penguin, 1978.

Lamming, George. *The Pleasures of Exile*. London: Michael Joseph, 1960.

Mannheim, Karl. *Essays on Sociology and Social Psychology*. Ed. Paul Kecskemeti. London: Routledge and Kegan Paul, 1953.

Marx, Leo. *The Machine in the Garden*. New York: Oxford University Press, 1970.

Mbembe, Achille. *Les Afriques indociles*. Paris: Editions Karthala, 1988.

Mudimbe, Valentin. *The Invention of Africa*. Bloomington: Indiana University Press, 1988.

———. *Parables and Fables: Exegesis, Textuality and Politics in Central Africa.* Madison: University of Wisconsin Press, 1991.

Nixon, Rob. "Caribbean and African Appropriations of *The Tempest.*" *Critical Inquiry* 13.3 (Spring 1987): 557–77.

Nkrumah, Kwame. *Africa Must Unite.* London: Heinemann Educational Books, 1964.

———. *Consciencism.* London: Panaf Books, 1970.

Nyerere, Julius. *Ujamaa: Essays on Socialism.* London: Oxford University Press, 1973.

Outlaw, Lucius. "African Philosophy: Deconstructive and Reconstructive Challenges." *Contemporary Philosophy: A New Survey.* Ed. G. Fløstad. Vol. 5: African Philosophy. Dordrecht: Martinus Nijhoff, 1987.

Oyono, Ferdinand. *Houseboy.* Trans. John Reed. London: Heinemann Educational Books, 1966.

———. *The Old Man and the Medal.* Trans. John Reed. London: Heinemann Educational Books, 1967.

Pollard, Sidney. *The Idea of Progress.* Hammondsworth: Penguin, 1971.

Retamar, Roberto Fernández. *Caliban and Other Essays.* Trans. Edward Baker. Minneapolis: University of Minnesota Press, 1989.

Rooney, David. *Kwame Nkrumah: The Political Kingdom in the Third World.* New York: St. Martin's, 1988.

Said, Edward. *Literature and Society.* Baltimore: Johns Hopkins University Press, 1980.

———. *Orientalism.* New York: Random House, 1978.

———. *The World, the Text and the Critic.* London: Faber, 1984.

Senghor, Léopold Sédar. *On African Socialism.* New York: Praeger, 1964.

Shi, Edward. *The Simple Life.* New York: Oxford University Press, 1985.

Sim, Stuart. "Lyotard and the Politics of Antifoundationalism." *Radical Philosophy* 44 (Autumn 1986): 8–13.

Spivak, Gayatri Chakravorty. *In Other Worlds: Essays in Cultural Politics.* New York: Routledge, 1988.

Towa, Marcien. *Essai sur la problématique philosophique dans l'Afrique actuelle.* Yaoundé: Editions CLE, 1971.

2

Martin Padget

An Iconography of Difference: Internal Colonialism, Photography, and the Crofters of the Highlands and Islands of Scotland

IMPROVEMENT, ROMANCE, AND CROFTING

Michael Hechter argues that the nineteenth century saw the consolidation of a long process of internal colonialism in Britain and Ireland, whereby Celtic populations were transformed into ethnic peripheries set against an anglicized core culture. Distinct cultural practices in peripheral areas were more or less subsumed by new forms of labor, law, religion, kinship, skills, and language associated with the dominant national culture. In the case of the Highlands and islands of Scotland, it was only after 1745, in the wake of the Battle of Culloden and the suppression of the clan hierarchies, that the region was incorporated into the newly cohering British state.

Over the following century far-reaching changes were wrought on the land and the types of agriculture and population it sustained, as former clan chiefs were either dispossessed or anglicized. Quickly the land shifted from a population base for the old clan ranks to a capitalized resource. Improvement transformed communal landholdings into the privatized estates of landowners, rationalizing agriculture through clearance, enclosure, and the allocation of former clan lands to sheep farms and, later, deer forests. Economic principles of self-interest were to supercede the "barbaric" commonality of the clan. The land itself was set the task of yielding a profit. The former clan members were reformed into a crofting community—a population of only partly subsistence farmers who would pay a cash rent for land allotted to them by

Fig. 2.1 Oban (No. 2). Oban will be found a most convenient point to start from on board one of Mr. McBrayne's well-appointed steamers, so with the last bell and the steam whistle sounding in your ears, the steamer glides gaily through Oban bay, passing Dunolly Castle on the right and Kerrera on the left, then enters the South of Mull. Still steaming on, you pass Duart Castle with its gloomy memories of the treacherous Maclean, while away on the Morven shore stands the remains of Ardtornish Castle, where at one time the Lords of the Isles held their rude parliaments and discussed ways and means for the subjugation of Scotland, which for them ended disastrously at the battle of Harlaw. The first place of importance we touch at is Tobermory.

their landowner.[1] And the region as a whole was increasingly drawn into international networks of trade and communication.

Ironically, at the very point when improving discourses were at their most powerful and hegemonic in the Highlands and islands, a disapproving romanticism began to resist what was seen as the breakdown of "natural" relations between people and the land that sustained them. Peter Womack argues that the period from the suppression of the Jacobite Rebellion in 1746 to the publication of Sir Walter Scott's *The Lady of the Lake* in 1810 saw the mythologization of the Highlands and islands as capitalism's other—as a repository of stable meaning in a world continually rent by social and economic change. For much of the 140-odd years after Culloden, crofters of the West Highlands and islands, among whom the Gaelic language and old clan loyalties tended to be the strongest, were represented by travelers as a naturalistic people endowed with Edenic intuition and a prelapsarian social unity. Crofters populated a geographically marginal and politically peripheral area of the country that was perceived by most leisured visitors as an "exotic" location within the British Isles. As such, the Highlands and islands were regarded as a region remote from "practical" life, where adventure and a contemplative relationship with nature could be pursued.[2] By the 1880s, however, when Scottish photographer George Washington Wilson traveled to the Highlands and islands, crofters throughout the region were in the midst of resisting the continued enclosure of former common lands and the conversion of no longer profitable sheep farms into sporting estates. In creating his lantern slide narrative, *The Road to the Isles*, Wilson had to negotiate the contemporary unruliness of crofters, acknowledge their often desperate poverty, and realize that distress and discontent were an unavoidable facet of the Highlands and islands landscape.

According to Steve Humphries, *The Road to the Isles* was one of the most popular magic lantern slide packages of late Victorian Britain.[3] Typically pointed toward a largely urban and middle-class audience, lantern slide travelogues matched reportage with advertisement, and were a highly popular form of both public and domestic entertainment in the last two decades of the nineteenth century. Composed at the juncture of tourism, advertising, ethnology, and news commentary, Wilson's images depicted the Highlands and islands as a region in which a pre-industrial order seemed, at least outwardly, to have survived the ravages of industrialization and the concomitant despoiling of many areas of "natural" beauty in Britain. At the same time, improved communications and cheapened costs of travel in the late nineteenth century allowed increasing numbers of tourists from throughout Britain to have direct access to the region itself. Accordingly, Wilson marketed his images toward an audience of both armchair and potential travelers, who possessed the financial means to tour Scotland.

The Road to the Isles takes viewers from Oban, the main commercial center of the west Highlands of Scotland, to the geographical periphery of the British Isles. The travelogue follows the passage of a steam ship calling at the Inner Hebridean islands of Mull and Skye before moving on to the Western Isles, and beyond to St. Kilda, the country's most remote inhabited island until its evacuation in 1930. Land travel complements the passage by sea, and the tour "takes in" all manner of sights that are commented on in the text. These sights include: the "pleasant picture" of the little town of Tobermory, which "takes heart and eye at once"; Eigg's "remarkable cave, which was the scene of one of the most hideous atrocities narrated in Scottish annals"; the "Old Man" of Storr, a pinnacle 160 feet high in which "the mimicry of a ruined city is reproduced, and wonderfully realized by the presence of clouds on the hill"; the "fantastic forms" of the Cuillin range of mountains on the Isle of Skye; Dunvegan Castle, which "is supposed to be the oldest inhabited house in Scotland"; the "megalithic, cruciform, Druidical circle, called the Circle of Callanish" on the Isle of Lewis; the site of Bonnie Prince Charlie's landing on South Uist; the birthplace of the Prince's fabled helper, Flora Macdonald; Kiessimull Castle at Castlebay, "which was at one time the stronghold of the Macneill of Barra"; and the "Parliament" at St. Kilda, "the most remote and probably the most inaccessible of the British Isles."

By examining the slide sequence in relation to contemporary crofter agitation we come closer to understanding how Wilson, as an agent of representation, romanticism, and tourism in the late nineteenth century, both alluded to and elided regional unrest. Wilson's photography moved from representing rural tranquillity to making social commentary on the condition of impoverished crofters' housing in Skye, from advocating certain improvements in local agricultural practice to celebrating the virtues and terrors of picturesque and sublime landscapes, and from ruminating on the myths of Highland history to considering the qualities of a "primitive" existence in far-flung St. Kilda. Beginning at the bustling town of Oban, the slide sequence threads disparate land groups through its passage out into space and back into time. The voyage ends at the geographical periphery of Britain at what was construed as its precapitalistic past.

Through his images of the region Wilson created an iconography of cultural difference—difference as registered through a selective rendering of locale, landscape, and history. In order to account for the popularity of the slides, we need to ask how Wilson's narrative produced the Highlands and islands for domestic audiences at the high point of British imperialism, to consider what sort of cultural capital was invested in the photographic enterprise, to speculate on how the images were implicated in the dynamic relationship between core and periphery, and to insist that through these photographs the crofting population was not merely subjected to the unreturnable gaze of tourists and metropolitan authority.[4]

At the same time we should not forget Wilson's commercial intentions. While as modern viewers we may never know exactly how Wilson related to his subjects—how were they posed? were they paid? how did Wilson explain his intentions? were subjects informed of how images were to be used?—we do know that image-making involved ethnographic interaction between photographer and photographic subjects. In the images themselves, this interaction is effaced. Indeed, Wilson's photography gives the appearance of direct access to the "reality" of life in the Highlands and islands. This emphasis on ethnographic exactitude had an ironic effect, however, for in the process of photographing crofters, their homes, and their livelihood, Wilson made it obvious that crofters were neither the fabled folk of Celtic lore nor a population that could be simply ignored while tourists "enjoyed" the area. The presence of a series of crofting images in the slide sequence casts a conflicting light on romanticism, for the crofters' residual beliefs and practices straddled the divide between what was perceived as belonging to the past and to the present.

Wilson's thematic equivocation is complemented in the structure of the narrative, which is organized so as to shuttle back and forth between images that at various points complement, contradict, and disregard one another. Thus the sequential placement of slides neutralizes the impact of images and words that might appear overly favorable to the crofters' cause in ongoing unrest in the Highlands and islands. Finally, before taking a closer look at the images, we should note that implicitly, if not explicitly, Wilson's narrative raised two important questions for late Victorian audiences: first, what happens when the "exotic" other appears impoverished within the geographical boundary of the British Isles; and second, on what philosophical basis should crofters' residual practices be seen in a positive light and worthy of public aid?

AN ICONOGRAPHY OF DIFFERENCE: CROFTING THROUGH THE CAMERA

The Road to the Isles is interspersed with periodic references to "the present crofter agitation." Eight images round out the "picture" of ordinary life in Skye: "Crofters Dwellings," "Washing Day," "The Spinning Wheel," "Octogenarians," "Corn Grinding," "The 'Cas Chrom,'" "Crofter and Daughter," and "Girl with Creel." The condition of housing, domestic cleanliness, the prevalence of old people in the area "notwithstanding the neglect of sanitary laws," anachronistic work procedures, outmoded craft skills, and an

Fig. 2.2. Crofters' Dwellings (No. 9). Such a home savours a good deal of Robinson Crusoe life, but a taste of the Skye climate, with all its accompanying discomforts, would very speedily dissolve any enthusiasm for living in such a dwelling. The average dwelling of the West Highlands is not a model edifice, and is open to wind and always pervious to rain. An old bottomless herring firkin, stuck in the roof, usually serves for a chimney, but the blue peat reek disdains the aperture, and streams wilfully through the door and the "crannies" in the wall and roof. The interior is seldom well lighted. What light there is proceeds rather from the orange glow of the peat fire, on which a large pot is simmering, than from the narrow pane, with its great bottle-green bull's-eye. The rafters, which support the roof, are black and glossy with soot. The sleeping accommodation is limited. The floor is the beaten earth; the furniture is scanty, there is hardly even a chair, stools and stones worn smooth by the usage of many generations have to do instead. The door usually opens into the byre, which is separated from the living room by a low partition, sufficient to keep "crummy" out, while fowls cluck about and assert their co-tenancy with the crofter and his family; the darkness of the outer apartment is impenetrable, excepting directly opposite the entrance, while outside there is usually a pool of stagnant odiferous liquid, in which one or two dirty duck guddle.

ironic reflection on the difficulty of women's labor compared to that of men are all commented on in the images and words.

The ninth image in the sequence, "Crofters' Dwellings," reveals Wilson's ambivalent glance on life in Skye. Here, through the reference to Robinson Crusoe, the commentary begins by criticizing a romanticized way of seeing "primitive" life. The ensuing description of "the average dwelling in the Western Highlands" emphasizes the discomfiture it affords its inhabitants (or, more accurately, the discomfiture of viewers in their imagined habitation of the homes), speaking of "the blue peat reek" of smoke, the interior's lack of light, and its general want of cleanliness and hygiene. The allusion to a "Robinson Crusoe life" also points to the implicit correlation between life in the Highlands and islands and the condition of indigenous peoples in the British colonies. By invoking the motif of an impenetrable darkness that is exactly the other side of romanticized primitivism, Wilson transfers local life to another spatial sphere and temporality—as though such housing cannot truly exist in contemporary Britain. The image of opacity is inspired by Wilson's repugnance at the absence of a firm division between byre and human living space in the cottage. This lack of an adequate differentiation between the domestic sphere of humans and the habitats of beasts marks the limit of a visual and written discourse through which Wilson tries to look impartially at the livelihood of crofters. Here an ostensibly objectified viewing of crofting practices quickly gives way to a morally improving perspective that, in turn, resonates with late Victorian standards of property and propriety.

Curiously enough, the image itself is picturesque in composition, fitting the rudiments of that way of seeing with its combination of stacked dry-stone walls and irregular thatch. As Wolfgang Kemp notes, the picturesque involves the separating out of utility and perception. It is not so much the object itself that claims the attention of the viewer, but the act of looking itself, where the individual's re-creative vision is foregrounded. The picturesque involves the smoothing out of rough edges through the balancing perception of an aestheticized consciousness. If we take the picturesque as "that which is multifarious, irregular, unevenly lit, worn and strange" (Kemp, 104), then the image of the crofters' cottages surely qualifies as worthy of the category. However, this claim contradicts the import of the accompanying words, which hardly separate utility and perception. When taken together, then, the image and text embrace the dual and often contradictory function of the slide narrative. While the image is of a conventionally picturesque sort, the text takes its cue from the language of social reform and sanitary improvement that had already led to the enacting of slum clearance initiatives throughout the industrial centers of Britain in the latter half of the nineteenth century.[5]

The difficulty of reconciling curiosity with the need to intervene in the lives of others is demonstrated in a later image in the sequence. "A Poorhouse" (No. 44) depicts an old woman sitting outside the entrance to a decrepit cottage. Here there is no picturesque quality to the image and the landscape resembles a blasted wasteland. Since nature appears to be without aura, no romance can be conjured out of the scene. Instead, sheer poverty registers the end of Wilson's discourse, while also implying the beginning of another discourse—the acknowledgment of the need to manage rural poverty. Wilson literally cannot imagine how people live in such conditions, and in his implicit recommendation for some form of change to make provision for the rural poor a certain humanitarianism comes to the surface of the narrative. However, this nascent welfarism remains couched in a groundless sympathy rather than a substantial call for action to be taken. Wilson avoids further comment on the issue by continuing the voyage outward with an image of the island of Eriskay, while the accompanying text delves back in time to consider "the forlorn days of 'Bonnie Prince Charlie.'" Thus the sequence as a whole slips across the surface of contemporary Highland and island life, taking care to balance out its newsworthy items with numerous images that depict the romantic past of the region and the "timeless" physical attributes of its landscape.

"The 'Cas Chrom'" (figure 2.3) provides an opportunity for Wilson to advocate agricultural improvements. The "laziness" of crofters stands in direct contrast to the unarticulated but presumed industry of photographer and audience. The commentary announces: "The haste and hurry of the nineteenth century has not taken hold of the Islesmen yet." In practical terms, this means that clock-time and the regulatory regime of work shifts had not yet entered into the lives of crofters. Wilson's rationale of greater efficiency and maximum yield in labor has the quality of self-assured and naturalized logic about it, although Wilson does moderate his criticism of "inefficient" farm practices by referring to adverse natural conditions. Since crofting land is so often located on "steep and rocky" ground there is difficulty in asserting that more self-discipline and greater application will actually yield substantial "profit" from the earth. This concession granted, Wilson then elides the very question of access to more fertile land and the historical process of peripheralization whereby crofters were pushed to the geographical margins of their landowners' holdings. While the commentary stakes out grounds for improve-

Fig. 2.3 The "Cas Chrom" (No. 14). The method of cultivating the ground in the Hebrides, and in some parts of the Highland mainland, is no less primitive than grinding the corn; and a Highlander will tell you that the crooked spade is a certain indication of poverty. The ordinary croft of the Islesman is small, and often so steep and rocky that the use of a plough is out of the question, even if a crofter could possess and man one.

Yet a little more energetic cultivation would in many cases bring its own reward, as the crooked spade, or "cas chrom," only turns the surface of the soil; and the crofter's plot being so small the same ground is turned over year after year, the result being a very poor return of oats or potatoes. The former is often never matured, or it may be devoured by the proprietor's game, while the latter is not infrequently frosted. The haste and hurry of the nineteenth century has not taken hold of the Islesmen yet, for they take everything very easily, and even in the spring of the year, when they may be said to be very busy getting the "croft" ready for seed, it is unusual for them to commence working until three or three-and-a-half hours after sunrise; but to give them credit, they will work as long as they can see.

ment with a small series of conditional phrases—"yet a little more energetic cultivation would in many cases bring its own reward," "they are not careful to look after the cow droppings, which a practical husbandman considers very valuable"—the facts of ongoing resistance to what crofters saw as landowners' abuses of their tenants' rights to the use of enclosed grazing lands are left out of the account.

In briefly considering crofter agitation, Wilson suggested that precisely because crofters had not broken the old ties of dependency, they lacked freedom to pursue their self-interest. Or, put more succinctly, they lacked knowledge of what their true self-interest should be. Following the argument of early improvers, Wilson advocated the instigation of the principle of private property into the lives of ordinary people as a remedy for the Highland and island "problem." This, according to popular wisdom outside the crofting community, would offset crofters' social and moral dependency on what remained of the old clan system. First articulated in late eighteenth-century social critiques of the region, the charge that rank-and-file clanspeople had been imprisoned to hierarchy and slave labor, and conditioned into a dependency relationship with clan chiefs remained a familiar justification for improvement until the mid-nineteenth century.[6] James Hunter argues that against the concept of private ownership as it pertained not only to the land but to all that thrived upon it (both animal and vegetable life), crofters clung to the deep-seated belief that those who worked the land had the right to occupy it. Crofter agitation, profuse by the early 1880s, focused on the occupation of lands that had been enclosed by landowners earlier in the century for sheep farms. In some cases sheep farms were later converted into shooting estates—here the land shifted from agricultural production to a leisure resource for an elite few. For land-hungry crofters and cottars these estates became potent symbols of land deliberately left underdeveloped and kept out of circulation.

In his slides Wilson clearly did not set out to explain crofters' grievances, although unrest had excited widespread public interest in the region; instead, he capitalized upon that interest in framing the slide sequence. Consequently, Wilson's narrative was constructed so as not to be overtly partisan in terms of politics and ideology. The continued movement of the sequence away from the mainland and the Western Isles toward remote St. Kilda, whose population of 77 showed few signs of rebellion, allowed Wilson to avoid a more overt confrontation with the issues at hand in conflicts over land ownership and land use in the Highlands and islands.

ST. KILDA: "PRIMITIVISM" THROUGH THE LENS

Forty-five miles west of the Uists, and 110 miles from the mainland, Wilson's sequence ends its voyage to the geographical and cultural margins of the British Isles. St. Kilda, a tiny archipelago

Fig. 2.4 Parliament (No. 56). Being beyond the reach of the laws that govern this realm they make their own laws. The solitary minister on the Island may advise in certain matters, and certainly has a limited influence, but it is their Parliament that fixes matters beyond appeal, and no stranger dare take part in its deliberations.

This Parliament meets daily, discusses the weather and state of the sea, &c. &c., in a few Gaelic phrases; and by a majority the order of the day is fixed, and no single individual takes it upon himself to arrange his business until after they unitedly decide what is best.

in the midst of the often tempestuous Atlantic, appealed to the touristic imagination precisely because of its remote location and the adventure that was an inherent part of getting there—for example, it was not uncommon for visiting ships to fail in off-loading summer tourists at Hirta, the group's main island, because of unfavorable sea and weather conditions. Wilson's slide sequence deliberately plays up the remoteness of St. Kilda in order to bolster its appeal to viewers. Such a gesture necessarily implies the increased capacity of a core culture to claim its periphery through improved communication systems and such technological apparatuses as the camera. The major sign of Wilson's incorporative claim on the St. Kildans is not to be found in the simple fact of photographing islanders for commercial profit, but more precisely in how he manufactured a sense of danger to audiences in the final image of the sequence, "Group with Queen." Here depicted are five women and two girls whose bold gazes back at the camera appear not to allow for a sentimentalized view of their remote island culture. Can the steadfast quality of the women's look back at the camera be viewed today as the sign of more generalized resistance to the outside codification of island life? Or does the image flirt with a notion of sexual danger in order to boost the touristic appeal of St. Kilda as an "exotic" and semi-"barbaric" location? I will come back to these questions at the end of this section.

Tourist visits to St. Kilda began in the 1830s, but until the 1870s were mostly reserved for the well-to-do. The popular tourist trade began in earnest in June 1877 with the introduction of a steamship, the Dunara Castle, which made regular passages from Glasgow to St. Kilda. The Victorian response to life in St. Kilda mixed touristic fascination for an exotic other with an impulse to inquire into and codify the domestic economy, customs, and "superstitions" of the islanders. Travelers desired to see St. Kilda as the repository of "real" cultural difference, as a uniquely distinctive culture that should not be quickly compared with "primitive" communities elsewhere in the world.[7] Wilson wrote in the commentary for the image "Boreray":

> Being so isolated it is not to be wondered at if in many things they are behind the age, and the occasional tourist who would treat them as they would South Sea Islanders gets a poor reception, but one who lives amongst them for a time will find them hospitable and trustworthy, and, like all Western Highlanders, they are very superstitious. They also wear an extraordinary load of flannel clothing, and declare that the arrival of a stranger gives them the cold. (No. 55)

The first sentence consists of a curious piling up of conjunctives: instead of the last clause qualifying the assertion that the St. Kildans are "hospitable and trustworthy" with an observation of such behavior, we are told of their superstitiousness. Here we see how "fact," observation, truism, and cultural comparison follow one another in such a way that the structure of an individual sentence complements that of the image narrative as a whole in its sequential piling up of clauses and visual statements.

Of particular interest to viewers was the annual harvest of fulmars, a sea-bird found in thousands around the archipelago, which islanders gathered for food, oil, and feathers. In the absence of diversified husbandry and because of the meager return the soil gave on the few crops planted on Hirta, the St. Kildans were reliant on the fulmar as an essential foodstuff. In the words of the commentary: "Instead of using the crooked spade, and in return receiving a miserable crop of potatoes and oats, you will find through the aid of the hair rope combined with their unparalleled agility in scaling the precipitous cliffs, thousands of Fulmar are secured and salted down for the season's use" (No. 54). By the end of the nineteenth century these "natural" gymnastic abilities had become staged in simulated harvests by the island men for tourist audiences.[8] This theatricalization of island life, and the revenue such displays afforded, did much to undermine the finely balanced culture of the St. Kildans. In time, with greater exposure to mainland goods and cultural values, the islanders grew self-conscious about the limitations of their own isolated lives and became aware of their home culture as marginalized and different from that of the tourist incomers.

Tom Steel claims that by the end of the nineteenth century islanders had grown wise to extracting a maximum of profit from the tourist trade. Prices charged for blown egg shells, homespun gloves and stockings, and permission to take photographs steep-ened according to the market tolerance for the purchasing of "authenticity" and cultural novelty. Photography, which marked the visualized trace of the tourist's visit to places far from home, became pervasive on St. Kilda. In time, caught between the insatiable desire of the tourist to possess a product of living anachronism and a growing sense of their geographical and cultural remoteness, the islanders became more dependent on the petty cash that the tourist trade provided to buy off-island goods and move out of their localized economy.

In the mid-1880s, however, tourist visits by steamers were limited to four or five each summer. Since between October and May islanders generally received fixed communications from neither their proprietor nor tourists, it is fair to say that at the moment of Wilson's slide narrative islanders remained isolated. This claim is corroborated by the fact that in the testimonies of two local men to a government commission in 1883, neither Donald MacDonald nor Angus Gillies made anything but a passing reference to island visitors.[9] It seems that in 1883 the 77 islanders were far more interested in maintaining their own way of life than comparing their lot to that of outsiders. This is not to say that they lived completely secluded lives, however, for St. Kildans relied on their proprietor, MacLeod of MacLeod, for the delivery of essential foodstuffs and to pick up the feathers, oil, cloth, and cattle with which their rent was paid. But it does mean that when Wilson photographed St. Kilda in the mid-1880s, he was at the beginning, rather than the middle, of what became an established practice of image-making by visitors to the island.

In his images of St. Kilda, Wilson was at pains not to compare the islanders' livelihood with "primitive" populations elsewhere. Far from being made into a synecdoche for a more general primitivism, their lives were inquired into at the micrological level. Commenting on the text for the "Parliament" image, Ian Spring notes that although Wilson probably described the operation of the island's governing body of men accurately, he did so only with reference to concepts originating outside of St. Kilda. Wilson at once appealed to a long tradition of "Golden Age" representations of St. Kildans, starting with the traveler Martin Martin in 1697, that stressed the Utopian aspect of "simple," isolated island life, while he also alleged that the actual governance of the island naturalistically followed the form of Britain's democratic Parliament. Consequently, in making his image of the St. Kilda men, Wilson yoked together a series of what would normally be thought of as oppositions. Thus, while insisting on its geographical isolation, Wilson arrived at St. Kilda by way of a modern steamer, then proceeded to register the cultural antiquity of the Gaelic St. Kildans through the mechanized lens of the camera, and finally explained "their Parliament that fixes matters beyond appeal" by referring to contemporary anglicized democracy.

It is exactly this act of bridging the constructed domains of dominant and marginal cultures that late nineteenth- and early twentieth-century tourists thrived upon in later visits to St. Kilda. In the text for an image of gannets' nests, Wilson comments on the disruptive role of tourists: "They [the islanders] also use largely as an article of food, wild fowls' eggs; many of these egg shells they preserve and sell to the insatiable tourist, who occasionally visits this remote Island" (No. 58). The insatiable tourist who visits only occasionally: although the statement may at first seem contradictory, it does express a simple recognition of the fragility of life on St. Kilda. Arguably Wilson foresaw the disruptive impact of continued visits by tourists and fellow photographers to the island, yet this did not prevent him from capitalizing upon the trade that his own photography encouraged.

The sequence ends with an image of five women and two girls that is entitled "Group with Queen." What are we to make of it?

Did these women come to Victorian viewers as enigma personified? Were contemporary audiences meant to take seriously the threat of castration that resounds in the prospect of the "queen's" revenge on a certain "faithless" male should he return to St. Kilda? If we claim that the women's resolute gaze back at the camera caused the discomfiture of (male) viewers, is it too much to speculate that the sexual anxiety provoked by the one image evokes the larger fear of potential rebellion among "native" populations throughout the empire? For viewers were informed that "the natives have a significant way of enforcing their disapproval of any body's misconduct" (figure 2.5). These questions aside, however, we can assert with confidence that with the final comment the narrative ends on a nervously facetious note.

Fig. 2.5 Group with Queen (No. 62). St. Kilda is not without its queen, who is said to be the best-looking woman on the Island, and was first styled thus by a gentleman who visited the Island a good many years ago, and spent some months among its natives with the view of reforming his habits. He is known to have won her affections, and she always on the arrival of a steamer makes inquiries regarding the faithless one. He, however, along with several others, would do well to give St. Kilda a wide berth, as the natives have a significant way of enforcing their disapproval of any body's misconduct.

Exactly how audiences in lantern slide lectures across late Victorian Britain reacted to the image of the St. Kilda women, it is hard to say. Through one scenario, we might characterize lantern slide lectures as shows in which St. Kildans' clothing, mannerisms, customs, and "arcane" practices were scrutinized and remarked upon, shows through which the islanders were drawn into discourse and incorporated into bourgeois society via the image made commodity. It is probable that Wilson paid the women to pose for the image and that they were willing to cooperate with his instructions, sitting patiently until he had taken the photograph. Yet what the women thought of Wilson, of the camera, whether they had any comprehension of how their images would be displayed in photographic albums and projected on to large screens in lantern slide shows, it is impossible for us, now looking at the "same" women, to know.

The final image culminates a slide sequence that simultaneously expresses and elides "native" unrest throughout the Highlands and islands. Having found crofter agitation amid the spectacle of picturesque and sublime natural scenery in Skye, the sequence moves on to the Western Isles only to find poverty spoiling the general view, and beyond to St. Kilda, where in the process of representing the island's population Wilson creates a symbolic danger out of the stern appearance of the women before the camera lens.

CONCLUSION: "A NURSERY OF GOOD WORKERS AND GOOD CITIZENS FOR THE EMPIRE"

In 1883 popular rebellion among crofters did much to push William Gladstone's Liberal government into appointing the Napier Commission to report on the livelihood of the crofting community. Its commissioners "convoked, by public invitation, 71 meetings at sixty-one stations, and received the testimony of 775 persons" (*Report*, 1). The following year, official findings were published in the *Report and Evidence of the Commissioners of Inquiry into the Conditions of the Crofters and Cottars in the Highlands and Islands of Scotland*. In framing the subsequent Crofters Act of 1886, Gladstone's government had to wrestle with the central ideological problem of how to reconcile crofters' collective belief in their right of access to land enclosed in the aftermath of Culloden with Liberal support for the rights of property owners. During the infamous Clearances, most of which took place between the late eighteenth and mid-nineteenth centuries, crofters had lost communal land-holdings through the application to the region of laissez-faire capitalism, with its strict principles of maximized agricultural and industrial production. But toward the end of the century, when crofters collectively asserted their "right" to land they judged had been stolen from them, it was the morality rather than the legalistic substantiality of their claim which the *Report* and act responded to.

For crofters, the Report with its several thousand pages of appendices, statistical evidence, and painstakingly recorded oral testimonies put their voices, both as individuals and as a collectivity, into public written discourse for the first time. The respect with which crofters' grievances were heard and the co-equal status of their testimonies with statements made by landowners, their factors (landowners' agents), and clergymen is itself telling, and a vital sign of a democratizing of procedure in the collecting of state information. However, it would be naive to suggest that crofters simply gained complete cultural enfranchisement through the Crofters Act.[10] Instead, government aid was contingent upon crofters' greater participation in the British economy.[11] In the final part of this essay I will briefly examine the language of the *Report* so as to understand why the commissioners appeared to go against the Liberal government's prevailing belief in free market economics in order to make the "anachronistic" gesture of supporting the crofters' political struggle.

I opened the essay by referring to Michael Hechter and his suggestion that nineteenth-century Britain witnessed the consolidation of a process of internal colonialism that had begun in sixteenth-century England. As Hechter notes, "differences in language, kinship structures, inheritance systems, modes of agricultural production, patterns of settlement, legal systems or the lack thereof, religious beliefs, and most generally styles of life" (5) marked the distinction between the practices of the anglicized core culture and its peripheral cultures. Hechter continues by providing a general model for national development: "The core and peripheral cultures must ultimately merge into one all-encompassing cultural system to which all members of the society have primary identification and loyalty" (5). If this is true, then why, among other recommendations favorable to the support of crofters' cultural identity, did the *Report* actively encourage the use of Gaelic in church and schools? Surely the prevalence of a separate language in a geographically marginal area of Britain would hinder the more complete incorporation of crofters into a single national culture?

In answering this question we should remember that the *Report* was constructed so as to propose a pragmatic solution to prevailing unrest in the Highlands and islands. Anxious to avoid violent rebellion on the scale of the Irish troubles, where the exemplary struggles of the Irish Land League had resulted in peasant farmers' security of tenure and the right to fair rent in 1881, the commissioners recognized the value of crofters' residual beliefs, but only by framing the crofting community as a national cultural resource. Thus, the commissioners argued, crofters' sedimented values and "natural" relations with the land needed to be supported so as to avoid "lasting traces of resentment and alienation" (*Report*, 110) against landowners and authority. Specifically, if "restored to tranquillity, confidence, and the exercise of their natural good sense" (111) crofters would return to a condition of calm morality. In other words, the commissioners demonstrated a greater governmental capacity both to acknowledge and administer cultural difference for the greater "good" of the nation as a whole.

By the time the Napier Commission visited the Highlands and islands, crofters had been emigrating to British colonies for almost a century and a half. In the conclusion to their report the commissioners directed their attention to the channeling of emigration to a productive and ameliorative end:

> The crofting and cottar population of the Highlands and Islands, small though it be, is a nursery of good workers and good citizens for the whole empire. In this respect the stock is exceptionally valuable. By sound physical constitution, native intelligence, and good moral training, it is particularly fitted to recruit the people of our industrial centres, who without such help from wholesome sources in rural districts would degenerate under the influences of bad lodging, unhealthy occupations, and enervating habits. It cannot be indifferent to the whole nation, constituted as the nation now is, to possess within its borders a people hardy, skilful, intelligent, and prolific, as an ever-flowing fountain of renovating life. (110)

Thus the report ends by invoking the language of not only economic production but also of environmental influence in order to justify a positive government initiative, or "artificial remedy" (108), to keep crofters on the land. The reference to "exceptionally valuable" "stock" makes it clear that one of the fundamental considerations behind the commissioners' acknowledgement of crofter grievances was the extension of capitalistic principles to the reproductive capacity of the crofting population as a whole. Taken in their totality of "40,000 families or 200,000 souls" (108), crofters could produce a significant surplus population with which to service the empire both at home and abroad. Government recognition of crofters' right to their continued livelihood, then, was contingent upon them maintaining stability, morality, and productivity in agriculture, fishing, and human reproduction.

In conclusion, I suggest that while the language of productivity is pervasive in the final pages of the *Report*, the incorporative strategy of the Napier Commission did not have a wholly detrimental effect for crofters. Although the commissioners' official recognition of crofters' livelihood was too late for the thousands of people who had been expelled from former common lands and forced to emigrate during the Clearances, it was the first time that crofters' right to the land gained legitimacy in the eyes of the British government. Grass-roots political organization and agitation continued in the aftermath of the Crofters Act, and helped forge political and cultural unity among Highlanders and islanders that, while hardly without tensions, remains particularly strong in the late twentieth century.[12]

Returning to Wilson's photography, we should realize that precisely because the production of his images was rooted in a particular historical moment, the images are liable to counter-hegemonic viewings. As Raymond Williams reminds us, "The residual by definition, has been effectively formed in the past, but it is still active in the cultural process, not only and often not at all as an element of the past, but as an effective element of the present" (122). This statement should serve as a reminder that while the crofting population was represented by Wilson as a residual rural population, in the 1880s crofters could not be simply sentimentalized as other-worldly. At the same time, we see that through his images of St. Kilda, Wilson strived to end the slide sequence by taking viewers beyond the fringe of crofting unrest and stranding them in Britain's geographically and, arguably, culturally most peripheral place. Viewing *The Road to the Isles* today enables us to see how Wilson struggled to rein in the cultural contradictions of the Highlands and islands at the very point when crofters began to collectively assert their dynamic and politically emergent cultural identity.

NOTES

1. In the *Report* the Napier Commission defined the word "crofter":

> By the word crofter is usually understood a small tenant of land with or without a lease, who finds in the cultivation and produce of his holding a material portion of his occupation, earnings, and sustenance, and who pays rent directly to the proprietor. The term cottar commonly imports the occupier of a dwelling with or without some small portion of land, whose main subsistence is by the wages of labour, and whose rent, if any, is paid to a tenant and not to the landlord. (3)

Hunter explains further: "[T]he crofter is not a subsistence agriculturalist but a man who, while retaining his stake in the land, has always had to have an occupation ancillary to that of farming his holding" (3). For detailed discussion of the emergence of the crofting community in the context of Scotland's fuller incorporation into the British empire in the eighteenth and nineteenth centuries, see Hechter; Hunter; Richards; and Smout.

2. For critical analysis of how the Highlands and islands and Gaelic people became mythologized in the eighteenth and nineteenth centuries, see Chapman; McArthur; and Womack.

3. The images reproduced in this essay were made from the original glass-plate slides in the possession of L. M. H. Smith, and appear by his kind permission. They and the accompanying text are to be found in Smith's *The Road to the Isles: The Hebrides in Lantern Slides.* All references are to the image numbers in the slide sequence rather than their pagination in Smith's book. The slides were found by chance in the early 1980s, after Taylor's critical biography of Wilson was published. I thank Smith for permission to reprint images and for information on the slides. In a personal letter, he has informed me that slides, in the form of $3^1/_4$-inch glass plates, were printed from Wilson's vast repository of glass negatives and handcolored by his staff before being distributed through Riley Brothers of Bradford, England.

4. The idea of "production" is borrowed from Pratt's study of European travel writing, *Imperial Eyes.* For a somewhat similar use of the idea of internal colonialism to explain the use of the folkloric past in nineteenth-century novels, see Armstrong.

5. It is worth noting that Wilson's photographs share their historical moment with fellow Scots Thomas Annan, who photographed Glasgow's slum areas, and John Thomson, famous for his journalistic photo/text series *Street Life in London* (1877)—produced in collaboration with writer Adolphe Smith—and a number of images of China taken in the aftermath of the Opium Wars. Arguably, the urban poor of major cities constituted another internal colony. For discussion of the uses of photography in late nineteenth-century slum clearance initiatives, see Tagg.

6. For a discussion of this motif of ideological imprisonment within the hierarchy of the clan, see Womack. The liberation of the individual from clan sentiment—or, according to Thomas Newte in 1791, "voluntary slavery"—in real terms meant the unconditional suppression of Gaelic cultural difference. As Womack puts it: "The freedom which is caught in this paradox is of an ideologically peculiar kind; and the case of the poor Highlander, for whom it meant new labour discipline, new state power, and new rights of private property, was calculated to strain its limits" (14).

7. For an invaluable, although somewhat romanticized history of St. Kilda, see Steel.

8. Spring notes that in the nineteenth century, "a tradition of representation developed whereby the particular practice of cragsmanship is transferred in meaning from a simple acquired skill to an inbred propensity" (160).

9. When the Napier Commission visited St. Kilda in June 1883 to hear the testimonies of Free Church minister Reverend John McKay and two crofters, Donald MacDonald and Angus Gillies, its members were at pains to assess not only the economic condition of the islanders but also their morality. Thus McKay was asked if any "spirituous liquors" (*Report*, 865) were sold to islanders by steamer passengers. He answered in the negative, but added: "Some of these passengers are very loose in their character, and some of them are drunk when they come ashore, but the people avoid them as far as they can" (865). When asked what some of the troublesome visitors did, Mckay replied: "They go about the hills, and go seeing through the windows and striking the dogs and one thing and another" (865).

10. The act gave crofters security of tenure and the right for compensation from landowners for improvements made on their crofts, but did not address crofters' and cottars' major grievance, the lack of available land. Cottars, in particular, continued to agitate well into the twentieth century. For details, see Hunter; and Richards.

11. For thorough historical analysis of the operations and reportage of the Napier Commission, see Hunter; Richards; and Smout.

12. While conceding the popularity of crofter agitation, the Napier Commission was at pains to emphasize the role of outside agents (especially those of the Highland Land League) in helping crofters articulate their complaints to the commissioners: "Intervention from without of this character was to be expected in a free country, and it may not have been without justification, and even utility, among a population in a dependent and precarious condition, unused to combination for a public purpose" (*Report*, 2).

WORKS CITED

Armstrong, Nancy. "Imperialist Nostalgia and *Wuthering Heights*." *Emily Bronte: Wuthering Heights*. Ed. Linda Peterson. Case Studies in Contemporary Criticism Series. Boston: St. Martin's, 1992, 428–49.

Chapman, Malcolm. *The Gaelic Vision in Scottish Culture*. London: Croom Helm. Montreal: McGill-Queens University Press, 1978.

Hechter, Michael. *Internal Colonialism: The Celtic Fringe in British National Development, 1536–1966*. Berkeley: University of California Press, 1975.

Humphries, Steve. *Victorian Britain through the Magic Lantern*. London: Sidgwick and Jackson, 1989.

Hunter, James. *The Making of the Crofting Community*. Edinburgh: John Donald, 1976.

Kemp, Wolfgang. "Images of Decay: Photography in the Picturesque Tradition." 1978. Trans. Joyce Rheuban. *October* 54 (1990): 102–33.

McArthur, Colin. "The Dialectic of National Identity: The Glasgow Empire Exhibition of 1938." *Popular Culture and Social Relations*. Ed. Tony Bennett, Colin Mercer, and Janet Woollacott. Milton Keynes: Open University Press, 1986, 117–34.

Pratt, Mary Louise. *Imperial Eyes: Travel Writing and Transculturation*. New York: Routledge, 1992.

Report of Her Majesty's Commissioners of Inquiry into the Condition of the Crofters and Cottars in the Highlands and Islands of Scotland With Appendices. 1884. British Parliamentary Papers (Agriculture) 21–25. Shannon: Irish University Press, 1969.

Richards, Eric. *A History of the Highland Clearances*. Vol. 2: *Emigration, Protest, Reasons*. London: Croom Helm, 1985.

Smith, L. M. H. *The Road to the Isles: The Hebrides in Lantern Slides*. Loanhead, Scotland: Macdonald, 1983.

Smout, T. C. *A Century of the Scottish People, 1830–1950*. London: Collins, 1986.

Spring, Ian. "Lost Land of Dreams—Representing St. Kilda." *Cultural Studies* 4.2 (1990): 156–75.

Steel, Tom. *The Life and Death of St. Kilda*. London: Fontana, 1975.

Tagg, John. *The Burden of Representation: Essays on Photographies and Histories*. Amherst: University of Massachusetts Press, 1988.

Taylor, Roger. *George Washington Wilson: Artist and Photographer, 1823–93*. Aberdeen: Aberdeen University Press, 1981.

Williams, Raymond. *Marxism and Literature*. Oxford: Oxford University Press, 1977.

Womack, Peter. *Improvement and Romance: Constructing the Myth of the Highlands*. London: Macmillan, 1989.

3

Poonam Arora

Sanctioned and Proscribed Narratives in Indian Cinema: A Bicultural Reading of the Courtesan Film

> Much that has been suppressed in the historical creation of post-colonial nation-states, much that has been erased or glossed over when nationalist discourse has set down its own life history, bears the marks of the people-nation struggling in an inchoate, undirected and wholly unequal battle against forces that have sought to dominate it.[1]
>
> —Partha Chatterjee

On 15 August 1947, when the Indian subcontinent became independent from British rule, my father saluted the Pakistani flag in a proud gesture of allegiance.[2] My grandparents, who were Hindus, had opted for Pakistani citizenship and my father, a sixteen-year-old student at a junior college in Lahore, shared his parents' faith in the secular ideals of the Pakistani state. Two weeks later, when my father's family found itself increasingly isolated and therefore vulnerable in a Muslim majority state, it decided to risk the journey to India through regions that were seething in bloody ethnic riots. The move, they believed, was to be a temporary one. Once on the other side of the national divide, my father's family was made to swear allegiance to the Indian flag. Thus, in less than a month, my father went from being a subject of a British colony, to opting for Pakistani citizenship, to unwittingly becoming an Indian citizen. Nor was this an exceptional history. Fourteen million people were involved in a two-way demographic shuffle.

In the absence of any formal policy on the transfer of populations between the two nations, only very ad hoc and inadequate arrangements were made to feed, house, and transport these people. Muslims and non-Muslims traveling in opposite directions clashed with each other and terrible atrocities were committed on both sides. Rape and physical torture were deployed as weapons of warfare in what has now, in a different context, come to be called, "ethnic cleansing." Over half a million people are believed to have died. In the almost half century since the formal partition of the subcontinent into India and Pakistan, historians and sociologists have neither been able to explain the violence that accompanied Partition nor establish its role in the move toward modernity that the nation states were supposed to accomplish. This crucial omission from the history of the postcolony has opened a huge chasm between official histories of the two, now three nation-states, and the popular memory of these events.[3] Whereas virtually all non-Muslims living in what became Pakistan either left for India or were killed, a sizeable number of Muslims remained in sections of India which were not contiguous with Pakistan. The continuing presence of the Muslims in India has been the source of an intermittent and escalating cycle of violence between Hindus and Muslims in contemporary India. In this essay I will show how popular film texts have, in some small measure, bridged the chasm between history and memory by generating narratives that are encoded with those desires of Hindus and Muslims who participated in the chaotic formation of nations and which have since been repressed/proscribed by the nation-state.

From its very inception, Indian nationalism has drawn on the mythology of Hindu religion for its discursive elaboration. Indian Muslims who do not share in this mythology were at first heartened by the Nehruvian moment,[4] which promised to imbue the project of nation-building with a multicultural complexity. These Muslims believed that the state's heavy reliance on Hindu symbols and rhetoric would be redressed, thereby opening up for the Muslims of India a legitimate space in Indian national life. This hope has been tragically belied. Hindu nationalists, in their attempts at self-definition, have not only closed off access to cultural forums in which Muslims may define themselves as loyal Indian subjects, but they have persisted in constructing the Muslim community as their cultural other. The construction of the Muslim as masculine, fundamentalist, and separatist has become indispensable to

Hindu nationalists' formulation of their own identity as adaptive, "Gandhian" (encoded as nonviolent), and inclusive.

Despite its lip service to secular ideals, Indian cinema in general has contributed significantly to the celebratory construction of Hindu nationalist discourse. It has done so by reviving precisely those tenets of social organization and gender politics which have been invoked by the nationalist discourse and which are derived from Hindu mythology. It is notable, however, that a specific genre within Indian cinema—the Muslim film[5]—reverses the binarism of Hindu and Muslim identities. This genre represents the Muslim not as masculine, fundamentalist, and separatist, but rather as feminine, exotic, and seductive. This apparent anomaly has been explained by Faisal Devji in his recent essay, "Hindu/Muslim/Indian." Devji argues that the latter "benign" construction of the Muslim in popular texts fulfills a dual function for Hindus. First, it counters the putative threat of the Muslim, who is commonly viewed as the "enemy within" (9). Second, the representation of the Muslim woman as a figure of romance in literature and film "elicit[s]...pleasure in the shape of a rape fantasy" (9). Devji reads this fantasy as a mock punishment meted out to the Muslim whose presence not only reactivates the painful memory of the partition, but who is also believed capable of reenacting that violent history. This rape-fantasy functions for the Hindu nationalist imaginary as a displacement of the "original sin" of partition. Thus the collective Hindu imaginary abdicates responsibility for the carnage that took place at the time of the partition by displacing this community's guilt onto the Muslim.

Devji's argument convincingly explains the popularity of the Muslim film for Hindu audiences. I shall extend Devji's argument by illustrating that, in a specific subgenre of the Muslim film—the tawaif or courtesan film—not only does the representation of the Muslim woman as a tawaif seduce her Hindu audiences (by, in effect, "asking for" her rape), but the focal point at which this occurs is during certain key scenes in which the tawaif unveils herself to the pro-filmic and, by extension, to the film audience. What Devji's argument does not address is the popularity of the tawaif film with its equally devoted Muslim audience. Nor can the argument that the film extracts a public confession from the Muslim imaginary for the internalized "guilt" of being different within an aggressively homogenizing national culture, explain that appeal. I will argue via *Pakeezah* (Kamal Amrohi, 1971) and *Umrao Jaan* (Muzaffar Ali, 1981) that the tawaif film interpellates

"Hindus" and "Muslims" into different subject-positions by deploying divergent textual strategies.[6] I have chosen these particular films because, unlike those films which feature the tawaif as one character among many, *Pakeezah* and *Umrao Jaan* are centrally about their eponymous protagonists.

Hegemonic readings, of Muslim films in general, and the tawaif film in particular, conducted by film critic Iqbal Masud, for instance, laud the bicultural appeal of these films by highlighting "the mutual respect and regard of the Hindu and the Muslim" (Masud, 7). Masud claims that these films are popular with audiences because their plots, at the most overt level, elide issues of Hindu-Muslim strife in the contemporary context, in favor of the representation of "stately, beautiful women, majestic, brave and dignified men and elaborate social rituals" (Masud, 7). Films like *Pukar* (1939), *Anarkali* (1953), *Mughal e Azam* (1960), *Chaudavin ka Chand* (1960), among others, appeal to the Hindu by countering the construction of the Muslim as a dangerous subversive who may be conspiring with the national enemy (Pakistan), through a representation which depicts him as nothing more than an ardent devotee of a luxurious obsolescence.[7] On the other hand, the films' fascination for Muslim audiences, according to the above hegemonic readings, is explained by their ability to return the latter to a mythic and romanticized precolonial past in which Mughal kings and nawabs (aristocrats of Mughal India) ruled justly and graciously over a predominantly Hindu populace and even partook of the cultural life of the Hindus.

These hegemonic readings thus rely on the films' removal of the tawaif from the ghettoized space of Muslim cultural life and positioning of her as public spectacle in the "secularized" space of filmic discourse. The tawaif films can make the case for the "healthy" coexistence of Hindus and Muslims in contemporary India chiefly through their strategic deployment of the syncretism of Hindu and Muslim artistic traditions. Tawaifs have traditionally danced in the kathak style; and whereas the films acknowledge that the dance is an amalgam of two very different traditions—the Muslim court and the Hindu temple—the dancer herself is unequivocally constructed as a Muslim woman. What is more, despite the overtly Muslim context of the actual performance, the kathak dance form itself is adapted from the original artistic tradition of the devdasis[8] (traditional, Hindu temple dancers) and Lord Krishna (a Hindu god who is the tutelary deity of kathak).

Even though the *kotha* (performance house of the tawaif) has now come to be associated with the artistic accomplishments of the Mughal aristocracies of the nineteenth century, key aspects of the tawaif's performance have been derived from Hindu artistic traditions. The tawaif film highlights this multiculturalism of the courtesan's performance and such syncretism plays a crucial role in suturing both Hindu and Muslim spectators into the film's narrative.[9] In a sequence in *Umrao Jaan*, for example, the dance of two women is intercut with close-ups of paintings which depict the romance of Lord Krishna and the gopis (cowherd women). Even though the paintings are done in the miniature style of Mughal India, the subject is a familiar religio-erotic theme from Hindu mythology. In addition, the music accompanying this dance sequence is characteristically Indian.

Devji has argued that the tawaif seduces her Hindu audiences ("asks for" her rape) and thus carries the burden of Muslim guilt. I want to suggest further that the Muslim woman's transgression of culturally imposed injunctions to silence, in the case of the tawaif indirectly qualifies her to articulate an otherwise repressed desire on behalf of the disenfranchised Muslims of India. This deliberately and, as I shall show, necessarily coded articulation, concerns the Muslim community's desire to escape to an illusory, originary homeland which holds the promise of "respectability" and equality. I want to clarify that what I am calling the desire for an idyllic homeland is an escapism from a social context wherein the vast majority of Indian Muslims feel marginalized and silenced rather than, as political groups like the BJP (Bharatiya Janata Party) have charged, a concrete aspiration for the state of Pakistan. Whereas other audiences, such as workers who have recently emigrated to cities in search of work, or women who have left behind their parents' homes to live with their husbands' families, may freely identify with the tawaif's yearning for an originary home, Muslims must encode this yearning for fear of its being read as a renegade move.

It is not surprising that it is the figure of a woman that condenses and articulates the coded desires of the Muslims of India. Rosie Thomas, discussing the representation of woman in that quintessential Indian melodrama *Mother India* (1957), shows how in Indian cinema the "discourses around female sexuality and modern nationalism...intersect and feed on each other, with significant political effect" (13). The chaste, sexually controlled and selflessly devoted Hindu woman of *Mother India* and countless other films underscores the narrative of the "triumphant emergence of the new India from both feudal and colonial oppression" (18). But there is an underside of the state-sponsored and triumphant nationalist narrative, and it is embodied in a particular version of Muslim womanhood.[10] If the construction of woman as "Mother India" in Hindi melodrama writes the sanctioned narrative of a unified and teleologically formed nation, the erotic, seductive, and independent tawaif writes the proscribed narrative of a fissiparous and still contingent nation. Nor are the symmetries between the two versions of the nation fortuitous: the chaste Hindu wife/mother may be in sharp contrast to the seductive and independent Muslim courtesan, but, in the ultimate analysis, each is symptomatic of the competing ideological forces operative within the Indian political context.

Despite the centrality of Hindu-Muslim strife in Indian cultural politics for well over three-quarters of a century, this strife has been conspicuously absent in the corresponding period of Indian films. The official explanation for this omission is that the representation of "communal" themes in Indian cinema may offend either religious community. This argument has a colonial ring to it, inasmuch as "[t]he term (communalism) is a colonial one, both historically and ideologically, because it presumes the existence of primordial and irrational hatreds which call for government by a modern, rational and third party" (Devji 4). The Indian nation-state professes, rather like the British colonial state, to rise above the religious fray of Hindus and Muslims. In reality, the Indian state has come increasingly to appropriate the rhetoric of Hindu nationalism from which it had at first tried to distance itself. Thus, even though the concept of the "communal" has been emptied of the original connotations of irrepressible religio-political conflict which called for "management" by the colonial power, today it implies the initial articulation of a Muslim point of view and a subsequent Hindu reaction to it. Thus the contemporary state has tried to manage the eruption of sectarian violence through systematic precautionary measures directed at the Muslim community. These include police brutality, espionage and, most pertinently here, precensorship of cinema and other mass media.

Take, for instance, the state's response to *Garam Hava* (1975), a docu-drama about a working-class Muslim extended family in the early 1950s. The film, which is based on a short story by Bhishem Sahni and directed by M. S. Sathyu (both non-Muslims), reflects the suspicion and injustice which a typical Muslim family suffered under during Partition, and depicts how this family copes with its hardships. Initially, "anticipating communal riots," the film's producers and distributors withheld the film's release for over a year until after national elections had been held. When the film "did not unleash violence or resentment (against the Muslims)" the state co-opted the film and, following its favorable reception at the 1974 Cannes Film Festival, bestowed on it India's top award "for serving the cause of 'National Integration'" (Sachdev, 149). This eventual favorable reception afforded to this pro-Muslim film, however, cannot be interpreted as the state's shift in attitude toward Muslims or Muslim sympathizers, for both continue not only to be regarded with suspicion but to be characterized as anti-national.[11] Despite the fact that the film has escaped censorship, *Garam Hava*'s delayed release bears witness to the state's control over those issues which it deems as having a bearing on "(i) the sovereignty and integrity of India, [and] (ii) the security of the State" (*Film Policy Report*, 77).[12] To those familiar with the rhetoric of the Indian nation-state, the "threat" to the "sovereignty and integrity" of the state is commonly understood as a reference to the challenge that the minority communities (the Muslims being foremost among them) pose to the thinly veiled Hindu nationalist agenda of the state. It is largely due to the propaganda of Hindu political parties that minority communities are believed to embody the potential for creating "another Pakistan," and therefore to merit a close surveillance of their activities.

It is against the backdrop of these censorship practices that the Muslim film is compelled to code its message. This is not, I might add, a message of political strife, far less of political divisiveness. On the contrary, the films embolden those who suffered the trauma of Partition but were forced to repress it thereafter, to reckon with the psychological and political realities of post-partition India.[13]

The narratives of *Pakeezah* and *Umrao Jaan* both play out the internalized guilt of the Muslim diaspora quite explicitly. *Pakeezah* initially introduces a woman who, because she is a tawaif, is rejected as an unfit bride by her lover's family. She subsequently dies after giving birth to a daughter who later also becomes a tawaif and falls in love with a man who is her father's brother's son. This patriliny is unknown to the lovers. The daughter, in turn, is spurned by her lover's family. This man, however, rejects his family in favor of the tawaif whom he wishes to marry. In an effort at rehabilitating the tawaif and giving her a new identity, he gives her a new name—Pakeezah—meaning "pure woman." The name resonates with the associations of another name—Pakistan—which literally means the homeland of the pure. Despite her love for the man, Pakeezah refuses to consent to the marriage, because she is ashamed of being a tawaif and is unwilling to ruin the man's good name. Pakeezah consents to the marriage only when, in a highly melodramatic final sequence, she is revealed to be the daughter of the very family that had rejected both her and her mother as unfit brides. Thus it is only when Pakeezah is reunited with, and accepted by, her father that she can honorably marry her lover/cousin. Since in Muslim kinship groups, marriage between paternal first cousins is considered the ideal match, this marriage reconciles Pakeezah to both her natal family and her family through marriage. What is more, order is restored through a rehabilitation not just of Pakeezah but, belatedly, of her wronged mother as well. The fact that the roles of both mother and daughter are played by the same actress—Meena Kumari—is significant because this dual role establishes a continuity between the suffering of mother and daughter.[14] In the film's last scene, Pakeezah is bid farewell by her father and received into her husband's family. This movement—daughter to bride—is exceptional for a tawaif, who is, by definition, outside the institution of marriage and the arena of respectability.[15] The unusual nature of her trajectory is underscored by the following voice-over, which occurs in the final scene:

> Hazȧrō sȧl nargis apnē bānürē pā rōtē ha,
> Barē müshkil sā hōtȧ ha chaman maī dēdȧvar paida.
>
> [For thousands of years the lonesome Nargis flower
> Bemoans her desolate and uncharmed existence,
> For it is after many misfortunes
> That this flower meets an admirer.][16]

Despite the happy ending, *Pakeezah* remains a profoundly pessimistic film. It is not the happy ending that the film is remembered for, rather it is its gloomy portrayal of unsheltered women which is memorable.

Umrao Jaan is based on the life of a tawaif, Umrao Jaan Ada, who lived in Lucknow in the second half of the nineteenth century. The plot of this film is strikingly similar to that of *Pakeezah*.

Like Pakeezah, who grows up an orphan, Umrao Jaan is kidnapped from her natal home and is raised away from her parents. While still a child, she is inducted into the institution of the *kotha*.[17] As a tawaif, Umrao Jaan falls in love with a nawab from her native town, who she expects will marry her and thereby return her to respectability. However, the latter is prevented by his mother from marrying Umrao and is instead married to a maid-servant of the mother. Like Umrao, this maidservant too had been kidnapped from her parents' home and subsequently spent a few days of captivity with Umrao. This shared childhood experience figuratively makes the two women into close siblings, one of whom marries the man. A despondent Umrao, meanwhile, continues to devise ways of escaping from the *kotha* and returning to her natal home.[18] When she does eventually return, Umrao is rejected by her family because she has lived as an unsheltered woman and sullied the honor of the family.

The protagonists of both films seek their natal families and attempt to gain acceptance in respectable society through marriage with the men that they love. Whereas Pakeezah finds such acceptance, Umrao continues to be a social outcast. The final shot of *Pakeezah* shows the veil lowered on the bride; this signals the reclamation of the hitherto unsheltered woman into respectable society. Conversely, since no man is prepared to protect Umrao's honor, she remains an outsider and the final shot of the film shows her facing her solitary image in a mirror.

The different endings to the careers of the two tawaifs reflect the Muslim community's changing perceptions of their prospects of a reconciliation with their separated (now Pakistani) kin as well as of their acceptance into mainstream Indian society. The production of *Pakeezah* began in 1955, but it was not until 1971 that the film was finally released. During this period the optimism of those Indian Muslims who believed that they would one day find a legitimate space within Indian nationalist culture was dampened considerably by three successive wars between India and Pakistan and spates of Hindu-Muslim communal tension and violence. While majority populations in India have refused to recognize Muslims as equal partners in the nationalist project, Muslims, for fear of jeopardizing their claim to Indianness, have been unable to build political, religious, economic, or cultural alliances with Muslims elsewhere. This double crisis came to a head in 1971 (the year of *Pakeezah*'s release) when India and Pakistan fought a major war over the secession of Bangladesh from Pakistan. Thereafter, any normalization of relations between India and Pakistan became an even more remote possibility.

By the time *Umrao Jaan* was released in 1981, the ongoing hostilities between India and Pakistan no longer permitted the Muslims of the subcontinent to entertain even the fantasy of a reconciliation with their brethren. Umrao's abortive quest for reunification with her family is symptomatic of this futility and *Umrao Jaan* is the last film made by a Muslim director to address the nostalgia for a "pure" and innocent homeland either in its narrative or in the lyrics of the film's songs.

The lyrics of the songs in *Pakeezah* and *Umrao Jaan* extend and underscore the political resonances of their ostensibly conventional romantic plots. Songs play a crucial role in Indian popular cinema. Audiences remember the psychological import of a film's narrative through its songs, which are in mass circulation well beyond the film's exhibition. The most prominent songs of *Pakeezah* and *Umrao Jaan* are sung in the films by the respective tawaifs. Audiences understand that the lyrics of the songs are composed by the tawaifs themselves, since the most famous tawaifs, Umrao Jaan among them, were eminent poets. Their songs generally express the singer's disillusionment with the world she lives in, and they articulate a wish to escape to an idyllic, innocent, and originary/natal homeland, where the tawaif may be able to transcend her "sullied" reputation. Even though the tawaif's tainted reputation derives from her open sexuality, her desire to escape from her present ignominious existence, either by returning to a childhood past or to a future in another idyllic world, resonates meaningfully with her Muslim audiences. Hence, for example, when the protagonist despairs of her status as an unsheltered and therefore tainted woman she confesses as follows:

> Jō kahē gayē nȧ mujhsā vo zamȧnȧ keh rahȧ ha,
> Kā fasȧnȧ ban gayē ha mārē bȧt taltā taltā.
>
> [The secret which I had virtually repressed, the whole world speaks of it now,
> My story has become a household scandal.]

The tawaif goes on to sublimate this guilt/dishonor with her lover. Together they sing:

> Chalo dildar chalo, chand ke paar chalo.
>
> [O beloved, let us escape to the other side of the moon.][19]

It may be suggested that the tawaif's lyrics both elicit, and are symptomatic of, the Muslim community's sense of separation from those who are now on the other side of the national divide. Further, in the absence of acceptance by the majority Hindu population, the tawaif's lyrics may be seen to express the Muslim community's desire for recognition in the Indian state.

Let me illustrate this via a scene from *Umrao Jaan* in which the tawaif finally returns to her parents' home and attempts to exonerate herself. Umrao Jaan sings:

> Yā kyȧ jagā ha dōstō, yā kaunsȧ dyȧr ha,
> Hadā nigȧh tak jahȧn ghůbar hē ghůbȧr ha....
>
> Tamȧm ůmr kȧ hisȧb mȧngti ha zindagē,
> Yā mārȧ dil kahā tō kyȧ, yā khůd sā sharmsȧr ha....
>
> Bůlȧ rahȧ ha kaůn mujhkō chilmanō kā ůs taraf,
> Mārā liyā bhi kyȧ kōē ůdȧs bākarȧr ha....
>
> [Oh, what a place is this, what a home is this,
> Where till the limits of one's gaze one sees only destruction....
> Now an account of my entire existence is demanded, as the precondition of my life,
> What can I say to explain my actions, when I am so full of shame and guilt....
> Who beckons me from the other side of the divide?
> Is it possible that in my absence, others have been as sad and restless for me as I have been for them?]

During this scene in her parental home the camera pans from the public/masculine space of the home where Umrao is performing before an audience of men to the private/feminine space. The two spaces are divided by a bamboo screen which conceals Umrao's mother from her. In a gesture uncharacteristic both of the tawaif who may not leave her audience, and the mother who is not permitted to come out of the *zenana* (female quarters), both women traverse the distance that divides the public and the private domain. They meet in a half-way space where they have the following conversation:

> Kyȧ tům hē Lucknow sā ayē hō?
> Jē hȧn.
> Tůmhȧrȧ nȧm kyȧ ha?
> Nȧm jȧn kar kyȧ kariyāgȧ?

Kyȧ tu̇m zȧt kē patu̇riyā ho?
Jē nahim, hȧlȧt nā banȧ diyȧ ha.
Kucch tō batȧō bātē apnā bȧrā māī. Kaun hō tu̇m?
Kyȧ batȧoō kā man kau̇n hoō.
Tu̇mhȧrȧ aslu̇ vatan kahȧn ha?
Aslē vatan tō yahēn ha jahȧn mai kharē hoō.

Mother: Are you the one who has come from Lucknow?
Daughter: Yes.
Mother: What is your name?
Daughter: What is the point of knowing my name? [She has been renamed since her abduction.]
Mother: Are you a prostitute by birth?
Daughter: No, circumstances have made me one.
Mother: Please tell me something about yourself. Who are you?
Daughter: How shall I say who I am?
Mother: Where is your actual home?
Daughter: My actual home is right where I am standing.

It is significant that Umrao uses the word "*vatan*" to refer to her natal home. Even though *vatan* in Urdu originally meant homeland, the word has now taken on connotations of the word "nation." Umrao's choice of the word *vatan* casts her yearning for acceptance by her natal family in distinctly diasporic terms. The brief meeting between the mother and the daughter is the climactic and cathartic moment in the film. If Umrao suffers from the shame of being an impure woman, her parent suffers from the shame of failing to protect her from that ignominy. Neither, however, can erase the past.

The scene between the daughter and the mother is intercut with flashbacks from the opening sequence of the film where the young Umrao was being ceremoniously adorned for her engagement ceremony. By emphasizing that Umrao is engaged but never married, the film reinforces the fractured nature of an otherwise archetypal narrative. The mother-daughter reunion is cut short by Umrao's brother, who disowns her and asks Umrao to leave the family home. Umrao returns to her house where, in the last shot of the film, she wipes a dusty mirror to gaze more clearly at her image. Given the traumatic separation from the mother in the previous scene, the final shot in which Umrao's unveiled gaze is directed at herself in the mirror portends the formation of a new and mature identity. It is significant that the film does not recount the entire life-history of *Umrao Jan Ada*, as the biography on which this film is based had done.[20] Instead it terminates at the point where the woman decides to reconcile herself to her life as an outcast and eschew continued attempts at reconciliation with her natal family.

Despite her ultimate rejection, Umrao's ability to return, albeit briefly, to her natal home is a fitting climax for this narrative of yearning, separation, and arrested growth. To audiences who have identified with the tawaif's sense of displacement and subsequent desire to return to her originary home wherein she seeks the acceptance of traditional kinship groups, the film sends a clear message: it is no longer possible to return to formerly unified social orders and old identities. To want to do so is regressive. Nevertheless, Umrao's career is laudable, especially from the point of view of the Indian Muslim diaspora, because by attempting to return to her natal home she figuratively erases those cultural and political boundaries which continue to be highly restrictive.

Pakeezah, too, emerges as a narrative about loss, and it too in some ways encodes the Muslim subject's search for respectability in post-Partition India. In the last decade of the independence movement, the Muslims who lived in what has now become India were uncertain of their fate. Unlike the Muslim League, which made it clear that Hindus living in the predominantly Muslim parts of the subcontinent would have to leave, the Indian National Congress, because of its professed secular ideals, did not actively repatriate the Muslims. Consequently, Muslims living in what was certain to become India had to make conscious and very difficult choices as to whether they should stay behind in the concentrated Muslim pockets of a putatively secular India where they had lived for generations, or make a very dangerous journey through bloody riots to get to a new country with whose population they shared a religion but not a language or local customs. The eventual division of the Muslim population of the subcontinent into Indians and Pakistanis (and later Bangladeshis) tore asunder thousands of close-knit communities and extended families, who lost contact with each other for long periods of time. The governments of these separate nations forbade their respective citizens from having any contact with the "enemy," during this period. The tawaif film transforms the forced separation of the Muslim community into a romantic narrative; it dissimulates that secret yearning which has all too often been read as a dangerous political statement of defection into a melodramatic narrative.

Key here is the film's use of the motif of "dead" letters, and letters written on trains. Both are charged signifiers in the historiography of the South Asian Muslim diaspora, for train and postal services between India and Pakistan were suspended for extended periods between 1947 and 1977 and, when postal services were resumed, letters were regularly intercepted and censored.

The narrative of *Pakeezah* hinges on two nearly "dead" letters. The first is written by Pakeezah's mother to her lover informing him of the birth of their daughter and asking him to come and take charge of her. The letter does not get to the addresser until seventeen years later. By then, the daughter, of whose existence the father is unaware, has become a tawaif. The second letter is written by Pakeezah's lover-to-be, and left for her to discover when she wakes up in a train carriage. Pakeezah, who is touched by the sentiment of the letter, falls in love with its writer, a man she has no way of tracing. It is only by accident that she meets him again. Thus, in the film, those who send the letters and those who receive them frequently lose each other. These letters mark not only the tenuous connection between separated lovers, but are treasured, even fetishized, by the protagonists as the only hope of their eventual reunion.

A crucial scene in *Pakeezah* depicts a man accidentally entering a train carriage where Pakeezah is fast asleep. He believes her to be in purdah[21] and so, even though the man has seen Pakeezah's unveiled face, social decorum demands that he not acknowledge that fact. The man writes to apologize for his intrusion and extols the beauty of Pakeezah's feet: "Apkā pȧo dākhā, bahu̇t hasēn haī. Inhāī zamēn par mat u̇tȧriyāgȧ, mailā hō jȧyāngā." [I happened to have seen your feet, they are beautiful, please do not place them on the ground for they will be sullied]. There are several ironies implicit in this encounter: the man, in giving Pakeezah the benefit of the doubt, believes her to be in purdah; hence the displacement of his compliment to her feet. The fact of the matter is that Pakeezah, because she is a tawaif, is not in compulsory purdah. What is more, as a dancing girl she makes her living precisely by "sullying her feet." It is the letter-writer's acknowledgment of Pakeezah as a "respectable" woman that makes her fall in love with him. Even though Pakeezah's friend tries to disabuse her of her hope of being rehabilitated into "respectable" society, Pakeezah, nevertheless, treasures the letter as proof of the existence of a savior who will one day rescue her from her ignominious existence and return her to "respectability." The actual letter and the sound of trains keep the hope of her rehabilitation alive.

I have argued that the tawaif film contains a repressed narrative which speaks to the sense of displacement and loss felt by the Muslim minority within India. I have also indicated that these films are extremely popular with Hindu audiences. In this section, I want to analyze what is, undoubtedly, the climactic moment of each tawaif performance and, to a lesser extent, of the tawaif film: the moment in which the tawaif unveils herself. It is this unveiling which is definitive in the tawaif film's ability to interpellate its discrete audiences, and its ability to perform this differential interpellation hinges largely on the differing epistemologies of the veil in Muslim and Hindu cultures.

According to the traditional etiquette of the *kotha*, the tawaif's performance begins with her obeisance to the most senior nobleman present and is followed by her unveiling herself either literally or symbolically through hand gestures (see figures 3.1 & 3.2). This ritual is scrupulously followed in the tawaif's filmic performance, with one crucial modification. Instead of the tawaif's gaze being directed at her aristocratic audience, in the film's mise-en-scene her gaze is directed at her filmic audience in frequent and extreme close-up of her eyes. Such cinematography creates for the audience an illusion of proximity and physical intimacy that was historically the privilege of the Muslim nawab in a *kotha*.[22] The tawaif's dance, adapted from the dance of the *devdasis*, transforms what was meant to be the homage paid to the Hindu deity into the homage paid to the Muslim aristocrat. Within the cinematic apparatus, this transformation is taken a step further: the tawaif addresses viewers who may be interpellated as the deity[23] or the nobleman depending largely, though not exclusively, upon their religious conditioning and orientation.

Anthropologist Sylvia Vatuk notes that

> whereas Muslims use (veiling) practices *to safeguard their women from men outside the family* and to keep (the women) in their own separate world, Hindus use the same devices to enforce women's subordination to their in-laws, to maintain an asymmetrical relationship between bride-givers and bride-takers, and generally *to order the domain of family and kinship.* (55–56, emphasis mine)

Fig. 3.1. Rekha in a pose of unveiling in *Umrao Jaan*. Courtesy of National Film Archives of India.

Fig. 3.2. Rekha facing the film audience and with her back to the aristocratic patron in *Umrao Jaan*. Courtesy of National Film Archives of India.

Given that the cultural codes underlying the veiling practices of Hindus and Muslims are so dissimilar, it is possible to argue that each community of spectators interprets the unveiling of a woman, in the filmic context, according to its cultural conventions. Among Hindus once a woman is veiled she has the status of the bride of the social group to which her husband belongs (as opposed to being the daughter of her natal social group).[24] Despite the proximity of men and women in an extended family, men in an orthodox Hindu context are forbidden from directly addressing, or looking at, the brides (or veiled women) of the extended family. This practice, which is intended, of course, to discourage any sexual alliance between a married woman and any other man in her husband's family, makes the veil a far more sexually charged sign within a Hindu context than it is within a Muslim one. Among the latter, women are veiled primarily to protect them from those men who are outside the faith, that is, Hindu men. Hence, in Muslim social life veiled women are more likely to be strangers rather than women within the family. Thus, even though the filmic scene of a hitherto veiled tawaif unveiling herself signals her deliberate seduction of the Hindu and the Muslim spectator alike, the gesture is more sexually charged for the Hindu as compared to the Muslim man, precisely because of the former's taboo against looking at any veiled woman. Moreover, since in principle the Muslim woman is veiled precisely to prevent Hindu men from looking at her, the Hindu viewer's scopophilic pleasure in being able to look at a Muslim woman is heightened by this knowledge.

Thus, even though diegetically the tawaif seduces a Muslim nobleman, the sexual pleasure that the Hindu subject derives from this deliberate seduction has to do with strong social taboos against any contact with a veiled woman who is another man's wife. Consider now that the protagonist of *Pakeezah* is introduced to the viewer through a song and dance sequence in which she enacts the various scenes of her somewhat coerced unveiling. She complains about this coercion in her song: "Inhē lōgō nā lā lēnȧ dủpattā mārȧ" [These very people have snatched my veil from me]. The pleasure that such a scene elicits for the Hindu subject should be understood in a sociocultural context. Even though in the nineteenth century, tawaifs entertained upper-class Hindu and Muslim men alike, the institution of the *kotha* and the figure of the tawaif have in the popular consciousness come to be associated almost exclusively with the Mughal aristocracy.[25] Because brahmins and Hindu reformers in the nineteenth century had colluded with the British in the censure of the "decadent" cultural practices of the Muslim aristocracy, Indians today mistakenly believe that Hindus, like the British, did not frequent *kothas*.

Whereas in the nineteenth century Muslim aristocratic men prided themselves in having acquired their social graces by frequenting *kothas*, Hindus began to construct themselves in opposition to this cultural practice. As a result the *kotha* culture became taboo for staunch Hindus. The tawaif film has relaxed the boundaries of an otherwise segregated cultural field by permitting the Hindu subject a vicarious participation in the tawaif's performance. In India's contemporary cultural context, where the public domain is still largely segregated along religious lines, the Muslim film's creation of a discursive space wherein a Hindu subject may gaze at a Muslim woman with impunity has far-reaching sociopolitical implications. Following Devji's claim that the Muslim's threat is minimized for the Hindu through the construction of the Muslim woman as the figure of a rape fantasy, I want to show that it is the tawaif's gesture of unveiling herself that is crucial to the elaboration of this fantasy for the Hindu spectator.

It is also, however, crucial in the interpellation of the Muslim audience, and I will now turn to the pleasure that the tawaif and her unveiling afford to her Muslim audiences specifically. Even though tawaifs have lived in a ghettoized cultural space where they are visited by men alone, they have historically enjoyed considerable freedom of mobility. Apart from performing at the *kotha*, which is a semi-public space (often in the commercial part of town), it was, at least in the nineteenth century, not uncommon for tawaifs to be invited to the homes of aristocratic Muslim families to perform at family festivities before an exclusively female audience. At such occasions the tawaif would have been treated, even by the women of the household, as an accomplished artist and an honored guest. If we understand the veil to be metonymic of the curtain or door that divides private and feminine spaces from public and masculine cultural spaces,[26] the tawaif, as the figure who can cross over from one to the other, embodies the challenge to other comparable and similarly drawn traditional boundaries—those between the Hindu and Muslim parts of a town or village.

Thus, according to the "negotiated" readings of the tawaif film as performed by its Muslim audiences, when the tawaif draws attention to her veil which, in her lyrics as well as in her dance, is a reference to her gaze, she bespeaks, not merely the "immodesty" of her gaze, that is, her sexual/moral transgression, but, more importantly, her ability to cross traditionally drawn cultural boundaries. Since it is the political boundary dividing the national spaces of Hindustan (the Urdu name for India) and Pakistan (its religious, political, and cultural other) that most concerns the Muslims of post-partition India, it is this boundary, rather than of gendered or topographic spaces, that the tawaif invokes.

The tawaif's ability to freely lift her veil and thereby erase the boundary between traditionally separate and gendered spaces, along with her capacity to trespass into the domain of the domestic, makes her a fitting agent of transgression of that other absolute boundary—one that divides national spaces in the Indian subcontinent. In *Pakeezah* the tawaif threatens to bleed to death by dancing on shards of glass until she is recognized as the daughter of the family. Through this suicidal gesture, Pakeezah transforms the performance space into a familial space and ultimately blurs the distinction between these two mutually exclusive spaces. Likewise, when Umrao breaks the bounds of the public space of her performance to enter the domestic space of the *zenana*, she violates the sanctity of those spaces and calls that unified, reconfigured space her *aslē vatan*—real nation. There are Hindus and Muslims among the audiences of the tawaif film for whom the emotional scars of the partition of the *vatan*—the undivided subcontinent—are still raw. Though Hindus may decry the politics of Partition, the Muslims, however, must avoid denouncing it for fear of arousing the suspicion that they are something less than Indian. Under these circumstances, the tawaif's veil becomes a sign not only of the curtain between a woman and a man, or the separation between the gendered spaces of the home and the world, but of the emotionally charged boundary between one nation and another. Since it is not possible to erase that political boundary, the text entrusts the tawaif with the responsibility of making it permeable, at least temporarily.

The fact that in the tawaif film the Muslim woman has access to language and is an independent agent, permits Muslim audiences to decode what for Hindu audiences is the sexual appeal of the tawaif in distinctly political terms. Even though in India women in general lack a voice in the public sphere, among Muslims these injunctions to silence are more codified.[27] Under these circumstances, the tawaif's singing, her unsheltered status, and her relative independence violate virtually every ideal of femininity in the Muslim cultural order.[28] Those who are familiar with the conventions of Urdu poetry, fully understand that the tawaif as poet and as someone who, against the strict dictates of Muslim personal law, encouraged men to drink, has been inextricably linked with the Bohemian lifestyles of religious and political dissenters.[29]

Even though the last two decades have witnessed a revival of ghazal poetry, this revival has concentrated on the themes of romance and unrequited love rather than the political themes for which this genre has historically been renowned. As a result, audiences have taken the tawaif's ghazal themes of romance and decadence at face value and invariably missed the political import of her poetry. Since the tawaif has historically defied the feminine ideal of silence within the Muslim social order, that social order, in turn, has sanctioned her to defy the political silence imposed upon it from without. For Muslim subjects who have systematically been silenced in post-Partition India, the coercion of the woman into silence becomes a synecdoche for the coercion of the Muslim into silence. The tawaif's ghazals and her singing break both silences simultaneously.

Since the veil conventionally circumscribes the world of "sheltered" women, the tawaif's license to unveil herself may be read as the prelude to her poetic license.[30] Further, the metaphor of light becomes associated with this rhetorical freedom since, in Urdu poetry, a candle is traditionally a metaphor for poetic license. It was customary at a mushaira (assembly of poets) to place the candle before the person who was reciting his/her poetry. Thus when Umrao sings the following ghazal, in which she alludes first to her unveiled gaze and then to the candle burning in front of her, she conflates two dominant metaphors:

> In ȧnkhō kē mastē kā mastȧnā hazȧrō haī,
> In ȧnkhō sā vȧbastȧ afsȧnā hazȧrō haī.
>
> [There are a thousand devotees of these inebriated eyes,
> There are a thousand legends pertaining to these eyes.]
>
> Is shammā farōzȧn kō ȧndhē sā darȧtā ho,
> Is shammā farōzȧn kā parvȧnā hazȧrō haī.
>
> [Those who threaten to extinguish this burning candle
> Must remember that there are a thousand protectors of this light.][31]

The devotees of the tawaif's eyes, and those who zealously protect her poetic license, are none other than those disenfranchised

Muslims of India for whom she has become a spokesperson. The tawaif film resorts to a kind of ventriloquism through which silenced minorities may acquire a voice.

Muslim intellectuals who chose to stay in India after 1947 have, by and large, professed secular ideals and have openly condemned the "fundamentalism" of Muslim politicians and religious leaders. Any expression of an emotional need to unite with their separated kin in Pakistan, or to seek the recognition of the latter, runs a very high risk of being read as a renegade act. By projecting the articulation of the emotional need of the Muslims to return to an originary home where they would be treated as equals or, alternatively, the desire for equality in post-Partition India, onto the figure of a woman, the tawaif film disguises the political import of such a statement. It is interesting in this respect to consider that Kamal Amrohi and Muzaffar Ali—the directors of *Pakeezah* and *Umrao Jaan*—and Kaif Bhopali, Majrooh Sultanpuri, Kaifi Azmi, and Shahryar—poets who have composed the lyrics for the two films—are all Muslim intellectuals who are also some of the leading writers and poets of Urdu literature in contemporary India. What is more, the film *Umrao Jaan*, though based on the well-known biography of the historical figure, does not use the poetry for which the woman herself was most renowned. Instead, the film creates a space for the poetry of contemporary Muslim male poets who, by adopting the persona of an articulate, unsheltered, and independent woman, find a forum for that which the state is likely to proscribe.

Muslim film directors who stayed on in Bombay after Partition have maintained silence on the religious situation of the subcontinent. The only mature treatment of the Muslim culture and its emotional response to the partition has come from a non-Muslim filmmaker—M. S. Sathyu—in *Garam Hava*. There is a very good reason for this silence on the part of the Muslim artistic community. Mehboob Khan, a Muslim and an important filmmaker of postindependence India had in 1947, the year of India's independence, made *Elan*, which conveyed what can best be termed a weak expression of Islamic socialism. The Censor Board of India banned the film presumably because of the already volatile nature of Hindu-Muslim relations at that time. Mehboob Khan was to go on to restore his reputation with film audiences and the Censor Board a decade later when he made *Mother India*, a supreme tribute to India's progressive and egalitarian ideology. The fate of *Elan*, however, must have served as a lesson for Muslim filmmakers who, for fear of either being dubbed fundamentalist or alienating their majority audiences, have ignored the unequal status of the Muslims within a Hindu majority culture and concentrated on cementing over the ever-widening cracks between the Hindus and the Muslims of India by staying with historical and romanticized narratives and eschewing overtly political ones. I have argued that some of these historical and romantic narratives are coded to respond to the psychological needs of the Indian Muslims.

The history of antagonism between Hindus and Muslims in India has taken the shape of a contest over the appropriation of specific and overdetermined signs, namely, the cow, the sanctity of a mosque and the space surrounding it and, most recently, the Babri Masjid/Ram Janmbhoomi. While Hindus and Muslims contest power through attempts to appropriate these signs, the figure of the tawaif works to temporarily resolve cultural conflict by permitting two radically different types of investment therein.

NOTES

1. Partha Chatterjee, *Nationalist Thought and the Colonial World—A Derivative Discourse?* London: Zed Books Ltd., 1986, 170.

2. This essay owes much to the insightful comments of Katrina Irving and Gail Minault and to my parents' memories of Partition.

3. I am indebted for this idea to Gyanendra Pandey's talk, "Writing the History of the Partition," at the University of Michigan, in fall 1993.

4. Jawaharlal Nehru, the first prime minister of independent India (1947–64), believed that the national state, as opposed to the colonial state, would be able to deal with the ubiquitous problem of "communalism" by concentrating on rapid industrialization and the guarantee of civil rights to all citizens, regardless of their caste or religion. According to Nehru's political philosophy, economic development was certain to weaken the stranglehold of sectarian ideologies.

5. A genre of films devoted centrally to the courtly tradition of the Mughal empire and its legacy of cultural sophistication which the films depict as being continued by the Muslims of such cities as Lucknow, Hyderabad, and Delhi.

6. I do not mean to imply that viewers of a tawaif film are Hindus or Muslims in any essentialist way, for these categories are overdetermined sites of nationalist, class, and gender conflict. Rather, I want to emphasize how popular texts perform an ideological function by constructing Hindu or Muslim subject positions, thereby stabilizing what may

otherwise be somewhat unstable subject positions at any given historical moment. My father's history, with which I began this essay, is exemplary of such an instability.

7. I use the pronoun "him" to gesture self-consciously to the masculinist construction of the Muslim in these films.

8. See Faubion Bowers, *The Dance in India* (New York: AMS Press, 1967) 97–104.

9. Noted tawaifs in Mughal and subsequently colonial India were accomplished dancers in the kathak style of classical Hindu India; they sang ghazals and thumris which while borrowing a vocabulary from Arabic and Persian languages, were based on ragas, or the musical moods of classical Hindustani music. What is more, tawaifs often composed poetry in Persian and Sufi styles which was rendered in Urdu, a language which is a hybrid of Hindi and Persian. Until a few decades ago, the educated class of North India, regardless of its religious affiliation, was fluent in Urdu.

10. See Gyanendra Pandey's "In Defense," in which he writes the counter-history of those "fragments" of Indian society who "might be said to represent 'minority' cultures and practices—[and who] have been expected to fall in line with the 'mainstream' (Brahminical, Hindu, consumerist) national culture." Foremost among these fragments, Pandey identifies the Muslims of India. Pandey's defense of the "fragment" is eloquent; however, his charge that Indian cinema colludes in the writing of the nationalist historiography by generating a "collective amnesia" about Partition, cannot be fully sustained in relation to the tawaif film.

11. For an elaboration of this idea see Pandey's essay "In Defense."

12. The wording of this section of the *Report* is taken directly from the Constitution of India.

13. When I first presented a version of this paper at a conference, all three Indians present in the audience "cautioned" me against the possibility that my argument may be co-opted by the Hindu nationalists to their own ideological ends. The implication is that if one gives credence to the religious as a political force, one has already descended to the level of the religious fundamentalist. As one well-intentioned respondent put it: "Your essentialist categories of 'Hindu' and 'Muslim' make me uncomfortable. Who are these 'Hindus' and 'Muslims'?" I interpret my fellow Indian expatriate's discomfiture with my categories of analysis as symptomatic of the very condition of postcolonial modernity, wherein post-Enlightenment, rational, and pseudo-Western intellectuals, we have been taught to discredit religion as one of the coordinates of postcolonial identity. I would argue that "to give into" religion as a category of analysis

is not necessarily to betray one's secular ideals, quite the contrary. It is time the Indian intellectual got her hands dirty, for religious violence (along with its various forms of repression) must be analyzed before the postcolony can arrive at its own specific version of modernity.

14. Meena Kumari, who died soon after *Pakeezah* was released, was one of the stars of the studio system in India. Despite her immense popularity, the film industry could not take the risk of revealing to her audiences that she was a Muslim. Like many other Muslim stars of her generation, Meena Kumari always went under a Hindu screen-name, this even when she played the role of a Muslim woman, as in *Pakeezah*.

15. See Oldenburg's essay, "Lifestyle as Resistance: The Case of the Courtesans of Lucknow," in which the author has established that "courtesans with their private ideology stand out as a group that has historically existed in a patriarchal society without suffering from its worst constraints and repressions by avoiding the inevitability and challenging the 'respectability' of the central patriarchal institution—marriage" (25–26). It is interesting that even though actual tawaifs have lived as extremely wealth and independent women who invariably shun marriage and prefer lesbian relationships (as Oldenburg has shown), the narratives about them persistently represent them as wanting to escape from their lives into "respectable" heterosexual marriages.

16. Pakeezah's mother, who died in the sorrow of rejection, was called Nargis. Nargis is also the Indian name for the Narcissus flower. This and all subsequent translations are mine.

17. A *kotha* was an important institution of Mughal India. Here women entertained aristocratic men with poetry, song, and dance. Kothas were run by former tawaifs, extremely wealthy women who gave their young initiates a rigorous training in the fine arts. In a context where few women received formal education, the *kothas* were responsible for some women's extremely high achievements in literature and music.

18. It is the politically turbulent time of the 1857 insurgency against the British which allows Umrao to escape to her hometown. For those who were affected by the trauma and upheaval of the partition of 1947 and others who witnessed the dual exodus of millions of people, the scene of hapless refugees, fleeing with their meager belongings, in the film, is strongly reminscent of the 1947 partition of the Indian subcontinent.

19. The moon is a symbol of romantic love in Indian culture. Moreover, a crescent moon and star is an Islamic symbol and appears on the flag of Pakistan.

20. See Mirza Mohamad Hadi Ruswa's *The Courtesan of Lucknow: Umrao Jan Ada*, trans. Khushwant Singh (Delhi: Hind Pocket Books, 1970).

21. Purdah implies not merely the veil that respectable women must wear, it is the condition of living in segregated quarters. In India, women traveling without a male escort travel in train carriages which are designated as *zenana khana* or ladies section.

22. Prior to the patronage that Mughal kings extended to kathak—the dance form which the tawaifs performed—all forms of Indian dance go back to the prototype of the *devadasi* who danced for the entertainment of the deity in a Hindu temple. The *devadasi*, much like the tawaif, did not marry, although she did have children and the daughters typically carried on the tradition.

23. In Hindu culture a woman is believed to be married to a deity first and to a man next. The husband—*patidev*, lord husband—is believed to be a form of the deity.

24. Among traditional Hindus, only married women wear the veil, whereas, among traditional Muslims even adolescent, unmarried girls may be veiled. Hindu women when they visit their natal homes do not veil themselves since there they have the status of the daughters of the family and are believed to be safe from the advances of men.

25. It was the British that coined the disparaging term "nautch girl" (c.a. 1800–10) for the tawaif. The term was part of the larger discourse of censure that the British deployed against, what they termed the "effete" and "ineffectual" practices of the Mughal aristocracy and which discourse was effectively mobilized to justify the takeover of the richest Mughal state of the nineteenth century—Oudh.

26. The word *purdah* literally means "curtain" or "screen."

27. Even though in the Indian context women in general are denied a public voice, there is one significant exception in the Hindu context; a woman singer is a sanctioned cultural stereotype; a devotee often speaks from the subject position of a woman singing devotional/romantic songs to her beloved—the deity. Among Muslims purdah practices include not just the veiling of the eyes but the veiling of the voice as well. See Sylvia Vatuk's discussion of "nazar ka parda aur avaz ka parda" (the veiling of the eyes and the veiling of the voice) in "Purdah Revisited: A Comparison of Hindu and Muslim Interpretations of the Cultural Meaning of Purdah in South Asia," *Separate Worlds: Studies of Purdah in South Asia*, ed. Hanna Papanek and Gail Minault (Delhi: Chanakya Publications, 1982).

28. See Aijaz Ahmad's *In Theory: Classes, Nations, Literatures* (London: Verso, 1992), where he discusses the "incipient feminism" of Mirza Hadi Hassan Rusva's biography *Umrao Jan Ada*, on which the film is based. According to Ahmad, Rusva's early-twentieth-century account of the historical Umrao Jaan was the first to establish that tawaifs were perhaps "the only relatively free women in our society" (117).

29. Peter Manuel in *Cassette Culture: Popular Music and Technology in North India* has argued that "[ghazals] extolling wine and inebriation traditionally suggested an antinomian, nonconformist hostility to social orthodoxy, which was personified in the figure of the Muslim priest" (100). The figure of the tawaif who encouraged wine drinking, which is strictly forbidden according to the Koran, has been regarded as the Manichean opposite of the priest.

30. Historically some tawaifs have been known for the explicitly political nature of their poetry, which consequently was banned by the monarchy and the priesthood.

31. The protector of the candle's flame is the moth which is both an ardent devotee as well as its protector. In a song sung in the climactic scene of *Pakeezah*, when the secret of the tawaif's parentage can no longer be concealed, the unveiled gaze and the candle are similarly conflated:

> Ȧj ham apnē du̇aō kȧ asar dākhān gā,
> Tērā nazar dākhān gā, zakhmā jigar dākhān gā....
> Jȧn lāvȧ ha mu̇haobat kȧ samȧ ȧj kē rȧt,
> Shammȧ hō jȧyāgē jal jal kā dhu̇an ȧj kē rȧt.
>
> [Tonight we will test the power of our will,
> The power of this gaze to pierce the heart of the beloved.
> Tonight the atmosphere of love is deadly,
> This candle will be reduced to mere smoke, this night.]

WORKS CITED

Chatterjee, Partha. *Nationalist Thought and the Colonial World: A Derivative Discourse?* London: Zed Books Ltd., 1986.

Devji, Faisal Fatehali. "Hindu/Muslim Indian." *Public Culture* 5 (Fall 1992): 1–18.

Government of India. Ministry of Information and Broadcasting. *Report of the Working Group on National Film Policy*. New Delhi: Government of India Press, 1980.

Kishwar, Madhu and Ruth Vanita. "Women Allowed Strength Only If Men Fail Them: Yeh Nazdeekiyan, Jeevan Dhara, Shradhanjali, *Umrao Jaan*." *Manushi* 11 (1982): 47–50.

Manuel, Peter. *Cassette Culture: Popular Music and Technology in North India*. Chicago: University of Chicago Press, 1993.

Masud, Iqbal. "From Shahenshah to Mianbhai." *Indian Express*, Sunday edition, 16 November 1986: 7.

Oldenburg, Veena Talwar. "Lifestyle as Resistance: The Case of the Courtesans of Lucknow." *Contesting Power: Resistance and Everyday Social Relations in South Asia.* Berkeley: University of California Press, 1991, 23–61.

Pandey, Gyanendra. "In Defense of the Fragment: Writing About Hindu Muslim Riots in India Today." *Representations* 37 (1992): 27–55.

Ruswa, Mirza Hadi Hasan. *The Courtesan of Lucknow: Umrao Jan Ada.* Trans. Khushwant Singh. Delhi: Hind Pocket Books, 1970.

Sabbah, Fatna. *Woman and the Muslim Unconscious.* Trans. Mary Jo Lakeland. New York: Pergamon Press, 1984.

Sachdev, Arun. *Film India: The New Generation, 1960–1980.* New Delhi: Directorate of Film Festivals, 1981.

Thomas, Rosie. "Sanctity and Scandal: The Mythologization of Mother India." *Quarterly Review of Film and Video* 11 (1989): 11–30.

Vatuk, Sylvia. "Purdah Revisited: A Comparison of Hindu and Muslim Interpretations of the Cultural Meaning of Purdah in South Asia." *Separate Worlds: Studies of Purdah in South Asia.* Eds. Hanna Papanek and Gail Minault. Delhi: Chanakya Publications, 1982.

4

Patrick Colm Hogan

The Gender of Tradition: Ideologies of Character in Post-Colonization Anglophone Literature

TRADITION UNDER COLONIALISM

Perhaps the most insistent theme in post-colonization writing, especially that from the "occupation colonies," is the conflict between indigenous traditions and the colonial culture.[1] Whether one conceives of this conflict as the immediate result of inherently antagonistic cultural relations, or as the more distant product of antagonistic political structures (see, for example, Bhabha, "Signs," 156), the final result is the same: the political, economic, social, and ideological infiltration of colonial culture—here, English culture[2]—into the cultures of Africa, South Asia, and Ireland, and the concurrent denigration of indigenous traditions, forced the indigenous populations to reconsider their relation to these traditions, as well as to locate themselves with respect to the new culture.

We may divide a subject's possible relations to indigenous and colonial cultures into six broad categories: (1) The maintenance or resumption of genuine tradition, uncorrupted by colonial influences. Tradition in this sense is neither rigid nor static; it is not "fossilized," but living and developing. A genuine or "orthodox" traditionalist wishes to return to an autonomous development which was cut short by the violence of colonialism. (2) The fashioning of what I will call "reactionary traditionalism," a traditionalism which is a reaction against foreign cultural incursions or similarly threatening elements. Such a traditionalism is usually absolutist and xenophobic and it is almost invariably untrue to actual indigenous traditions; indeed, it is necessarily unorthodox as it seeks to purge tradition of those elements which appear to make it weak in the face of the foreign (or related) threat. This reactionary traditionalism is frequently, though misleadingly, termed "fundamentalism."[3] Both reactionary and orthodox traditionalism are likely to be suffused with a nostalgia for an idealized indigenous past, a prelapsarian time when indigenous society lived up to its own ideals; in other words, both are likely to be forms of romantic traditionalism as well, or at least to involve romantic elements. (3) Genuine assimilation achieving genuine or "orthodox" Englishness—actually an option only for the English; Africans, Indians, and to a lesser extent the Irish, were historically barred from orthodox Englishness due to English racism. As Homi Bhabha put it, "to be Anglicized, is *emphatically* not to be English" ("Of Mimicry," 128). (4) Reactionary assimilation or "mimeticism," which is to say, the almost phobic denial of the distinctive elements of indigenous culture, and the imitation of English culture, especially its most alien elements. This is, in effect, the re-creation of English culture such that the elements it shares with indigenous culture are purged or diminished; reactionary assimilationism is thus the mirror image of reactionary traditionalism. (5) Cultural disintegration involving a sense of alienation from all cultures, being "no longer at ease" (in Chinua Achebe's phrase) in any culture, finding a home neither in indigenous tradition nor in Europeanization. Clearly, alienation is not in itself an experience one chooses to have; it is, rather, an inability to enact any choice—an inability, as we shall see, frequently associated with emotional and mental disintegration. (6) Synthesis or universalism, which is to say, the combination of elements from both indigenous and colonial traditions in order to forge a new culture which one hopes will be superior to both.[4]

As Ashis Nandy has pointed out, the colonial denigration of indigenous culture consistently involved an assimilation of cultural hierarchies to sex hierarchies. Specifically, the indigenous cultures were seen as feminine or effeminate and the colonial culture as masculine. Colonialists who promulgated this view stressed or fabricated elements of indigenous culture putatively indicative of effeminacy (passivity, weakness, irrationality, wiliness, etc.) and elements of colonial culture putatively indicative of masculinity (aggressiveness, strength, rationality, honesty, etc.). Correspondingly, they downplayed or denied the aspects of both cultures which did not fit this schema.

As Nandy emphasizes, colonial ideologists tended to focus particular attention on indigenous men, in effect denying their manhood. On the other hand, the ideological position of women was enormously important as well. First of all, indigenous women were viewed as the most passive creatures possible. Subservient, even to the point of lacking separate will, they were the shadowy tittering figures on the margins of *A Passage to India*: "all the [Indian] ladies were uncertain, cowering, recovering, giggling, making tiny gestures of atonement or despair" (36). Or "those Indian women...silly, pretty, flimsy nincompoops" of Virginia Woolf's *Mrs. Dalloway* (10). At best, they were fitting objects of pity for Western liberals, including Western feminists.[5] In this way, colonial ideology tended to "feminize" indigenous men and "hyperfeminize" indigenous women.

But this feminization did not merely involve seeing indigenous people as passive. As, for example, Homi Bhabha has stressed, the colonizer always views the colonized as dual, both subservient and uncontrollable. Bhabha assimilates these two aspects to the fetish and phobic object analyzed by psychoanalysis. But, in fact, this dualism seems to be nothing other than the dualism of misogynist stereotypes, more like virgin and whore than fetish and phobic object. Indeed, the dissembling or duplicity which allows for this duality is itself a misogynist stereotype. Thus indigenous peoples came to be viewed in colonial ideology as seemingly passive and subservient, but harboring hidden violence and lust. Out of sight, they were drugged and lecherous, immoral and dissolute. These are the "Eastern excesses," bacchic "opposites" to European "values" (57), the putative "lechery" and "debauchery" (62) explored by Edward Said in *Orientalism*.

This racist and sexist view was applied cross-culturally by colonial ideologues, but there were some important variations in degree. In particular, the more vicious the cultural denigration, the more sexualized was the image of colonized people. This denigration reached its nadir with respect to sub-Saharan Africa. Thus it helped give rise to the racist image of the sexually indefatigable African man, with huge reproductive organs and inexhaustible drives—a psychologically deep, historically persistent, and ideologically functional image, as Frantz Fanon demonstrated in *Black Skin, White Masks*. In this way, the ideological feminization of colonized people paradoxically contributed to the narrowly genital hypertrophy of male sexuality in the ideological representation of the African man.[6] This is not to say that women did not suffer from this ideological sexualization. Quite the contrary. Here, too, indigenous women were hyper-feminized, which in this case means assimilated as a group to prostitutes, or rather to a fantasy of the prostitute, an imago of an insatiable, scheming, threatening (perhaps castrating) temptress.

In part as a result of this colonial imposition of gender models on cultural relations—and in part as a result of a cross-cultural tendency to assimilate important social divisions to the division between men and women—many indigenous anglophone writers too came to see the opposition between tradition and colonial culture as bound up with gender issues. Indeed, a great deal of characterization in post-colonization anglophone literature may be viewed as a direct, if partially unconscious, response to this ideological feminization of indigenous people.

STRUCTURES OF LITERARY CHARACTERIZATION

More exactly, we may conceptually organize the possibilities for gender identity in parallel with those for cultural identity: (1a) orthodox masculinity and (1b) orthodox femininity. These are, of course, cultural categories—not because gender identity is "constructed" (that is, formed through acculturation), but rather because it is ideological. In all cultures, conceptions of masculinity and femininity are determined not by what men and women are like—whether this results from nurture or nature—but by the function of these concepts in structuring social hierarchies. Thus "orthodox masculinity" here is masculinity as understood in the culture in question (e.g., traditional Ibo society, traditional Hindu society); the same holds for "orthodox femininity." This category is obviously parallel to that of orthodox tradition, and it is normative within that tradition (that is, a definition of "masculinity" or "femininity" indicates a standard, not an empirical belief about real people).[7] (2a) Reactionary masculinity, that is to say, a refashioned masculinity from which all elements of putative femininity have been purged in order to avoid the threat of feminization. This is sometimes referred to as "machismo." (2b) Reactionary femininity, a scrupulous adherence to an ideological ideal of femininity, purged of any hint of the degeneracy projected by colonial ideologues onto colonized women. These are clearly parallel to reactionary traditionalism, and are also normative within that tradition. Both varieties of gender category (orthodox and reactionary) are subject to the same sort of romanticization on which we remarked in connection with traditionalism. Specifically, in their romanticized versions, both varieties posit a precolonial, prelapsarian time when men were "real" men and women were "real" women, unlike the present. (3) Transsexualism, or one's complete assimilation into the other sex, specifically the complete masculinization of a woman. This is parallel to the genuine assimilation of a colonized person into orthodox English tradition or culture. And, in this case too, the assimilation is most often blocked by members of the dominant group. (4) Degenerate effeminacy, the loss—usually by men, but also by women—of all ideologically masculine characteristics, and the exaggeration of putatively feminine vices (e.g., lasciviousness and duplicity). (As with the preceding category, hierarchization of male over female tends to exclude from this category the opposite sort of assimilation; in other words, it in effect disallows the category of "degenerate masculinity.") This is linked with mimeticism. (5) Complete loss of gender identity, usually as part of a broader loss of personal identity; this, of course, corresponds to cultural disintegration. (6) A synthesis of masculine and feminine properties, sometimes referred to as "androgyny," in other words, a forging of gender identity which combines the putative virtues of both sexes into a new, superior identity—a process parallel to cultural universalism or synthesis.

These six gender categories, along with the corresponding categories of cultural relations, map out a structure of possible character formations with respect to gender and culture. In the rest of this essay, I hope to show that, in a wide range of post-colonization anglophone works, patterns of characterization are organized by this structure. In other words, although they do not formulate it explicitly in these terms, post-colonization writers have implicitly recognized these patterns, and used them to explore the complex ideologies of colonialism and gender with which they have been so often, and necessarily, concerned. Before going on to discuss specific examples, however, it is worth specifying some of the literary properties which are associated with these categories, and noting some of the variants in their treatment.

Beginning with the first and second categories, we may remark that orthodox masculinity and orthodox femininity necessarily involve competence, as well as strength and a degree of fortitude, in traditional spheres of activity. This is necessarily part of any literary representation of characters of this sort. On the other hand, there are, not surprisingly, differences between the representations of traditional roles by men and those by women. Indeed, in literature by men, traditional women are frequently replaced by a romanticized, patriarchal ideal of feminine behavior. Correlatively, in literature by women, the strength and competence of traditional men is less in evidence, and their abuse of social, economic, and physical power is more likely to be exposed.[8]

Both men and women recognize a sort of reactionary femininity and a reactionary masculinity. In connection with these, it is important to recall that colonial ideologies deny the masculinity of indigenous men and the "purity" of indigenous women. Thus a reactionary masculinity and a reactionary femininity will operate differently. They are opposed not to one another, but to colonial stereotypes. In other words, the reactionary traditionalist man defines himself not against the traditional woman, but against the degenerate effeminate stereotype of colonial culture; the reactionary traditionalist woman defines herself not against the traditional man, but against her derogatory hyperfeminization in colonial ideology. Indeed, as reactionary femininity is opposed to a colonial hyperfeminization, it may involve stereotypically masculine traits, such as strength and anger, even violence and cruelty, especially insofar as these are aimed at the colonizer or at other threats to tradition. Indeed, as varieties of reactionary traditionalism, both reactionary masculinity and reactionary femininity are intolerant and sectarian not only with respect to European culture, but with respect to alternative indigenous cultures as well; this is a necessary part of their rigidity.

As we have seen, degenerate effeminacy has defined the standard European view of colonized men and women (and, it is worth adding, it has defined one standard view of Europeans who have assimilated or "gone native"). This view has no doubt been held by reactionary assimilationists as well. However, canonical post-colonization writers rarely if ever advocate assimilation. Thus they repudiate this colonial view, and many tend rather to reverse it.[9] In other words, a number of post-colonization authors see European culture as lascivious and degraded. Thus, they view Europeanized Africans or Indians as degenerate, both dissolute and duplicitous—most often duplicitous about political corruption. Specifically, they see such characters as concealing their assimilationism behind a mask of traditionalism, usually reactionary traditionalism. In this category, too, there are some differences between male and female authors, especially with regard to women characters. A number of male authors associate their Westernized female characters with objectionably loose sexuality; women authors are more likely to avoid this stereotype or to criticize it.

Having repudiated the preceding alternatives, canonical post-colonization authors tend to advocate either cultural synthesis or orthodox tradition. Of course, they may unconsciously adopt reactionary traditionalist or assimilationist attitudes; however, their self-conscious views almost invariably fall into the other two categories. Advocates of cultural synthesis, both male and female, tend to identify this with androgyny. Advocacy of true tradition is more narrowly male, and thus is linked with orthodox masculinity and a romanticized femininity, as already noted. Thus we frequently find either an orthodox masculine, orthodox traditionalist, or a partially androgynous advocate of cultural synthesis as the hero of a post-colonization anglophone work. And we frequently find this character opposed to a degenerate and effeminate mimic or a hypermasculine, reactionary traditionalist.

This framework is, of course, not fixed in stone. Many characters fit only partially or blur categories. We are isolating paradigm cases, after all, not delimiting necessary and sufficient conditions. Characterizations vary with author's sex, as we have noted, as well as with factors ranging from individual personality to regional history. Thus, as we shall see, African male writers seem somewhat more likely than Indian writers to value what they take to be genuine tradition and genuine masculinity; indeed, Indian writers rarely even develop central characters of this type. This is, in part, the result of the precolonial valorization of androgyny in Hinduism, as well as the far more vicious European denigration of African tradition and African people. Nonetheless, the paradigmatic structure we have outlined allows us to systematize characterization across a wide range of works in what I believe to be a politically clarifying manner, especially when these cultural, historical, and other differences are kept in mind.

LITERARY INSTANCES

I shall be drawing primarily on Indian and African works, for in these colonies, the cultural opposition, and concomitant racial division, were more thorough-going and ideologically brutal. However, I should like to begin with an Irish example, drawn from *Ulysses*. Though not usually interpreted in the context of post-colonization literature, Joyce's novel contains many of the themes and structures which recur in African and Indian writings. It, too, is concerned with the issue of cultural identity, and with the relation between this and sexual identity. Stephen and Buck are in part defined by degenerate effeminacy and reactionary assimilationism. They are drunken and lecherous, and there are many hints that they have strong homosexual impulses as well—most famously in the passage in which Stephen thinks of "[Mulligan's] arm: Cranly's arm" in conjunction with "Wilde's love that dare not speak its name" (41).[10] Buck is in part an anglified Oxfordian, now chumming with Haines, a paternalistic liberal who has crossed the Irish Sea to study the natives. Stephen is assimilated not in British but in French culture. He has turned his mimeticism from one colonial metropolis to another—but it is still mimeticism. The opposite of Stephen is a reactionary masculinist and reactionary traditionalist, the Citizen. Athletic, aggressive, violent, and intensely xenophobic, the Citizen seeks to resurrect the most hypermasculine elements of traditional Irish culture, particularly its competitive sports. In contrast with all three is Leopold Bloom. Half Hungarian Jew, half Irish Christian, baptised as a Protestant and a Catholic, Bloom combines an array of cultures, colonized and colonial, in personal history and in temperament. He is, in addition, explicitly androgynous: "the new womanly man," Joyce calls him (403).[11]

Turning to Indian literature, we find this same structure repeated in a variety of works. Take, for example, Tagore's *The Home and the World*. There are two main male characters. Nikhil, the hero, is explicitly synthetic in his views. He opposes imperialism, and adheres to many aspects of indigenous culture. However, at the same time, he advocates the adoption of more Western freedoms for women, and he strongly opposes the sectarian impulse of reactionary traditionalism. Furthermore, he combines traditionally masculine and traditionally feminine virtues. Sandip, in contrast, is a reactionary traditionalist and reactionary masculinist—hypermasculine in his use of violence and in his deceptive sexual conquests, sectarian in his attacks on Muslims. In addition, Sandip is corrupt—his reactionary traditionalism barely concealing a reactionary assimilationism. This novel also contains the rather diminished figure of the teacher, who has characteristics of orthodox tradition and orthodox masculinity; but, as is typical of Indian literature, his role is downplayed.

We find a similar opposition between the hypermasculine and hypertraditional Gora and the synthetic and androgynous Binoy in Tagore's *Gora* (Gora himself being eventually converted to a synthetic view). The militantly Islamic Saleem and his cousin the Gandhian Asad form a similar pair in Attia Hosain's *Sunlight on a Broken Column*. And Salman Rushdie takes up this structure in *Midnight's Children*, with the androgynous and synthetic Saleem opposed to the hypermasculine and reactionary nationalist Shiva, as well as to the mimetic Mr. Sinai, who sinks into drunkenness and dissolution after being assimilated into British customs on the Methwold estate, where his skin begins allegorically to whiten (212). Moorthy, of Raja Rao's *Kanthapura*, is a synthetic and androgynous hero as well, contrasted with the collaborationist Swami, who provides another good example of a duplicitous character, both a reactionary traditionalist and a greedy glutton, corrupted by European culture; he is, as Rao puts it, one of "these fattened Brahmins who want to frighten us with their excommunications, once the Government has paid them well" (91).

Khushwant Singh's *Delhi: A Novel* provides what is in effect a history of India in these terms. Indeed, Singh's book is particularly interesting for the present study, for it focuses not only on English colonialism, but on earlier Mughal, Persian, and other colonialisms—which presented Indians with precisely the same cultural dilemmas. In virtually every age he portrays, Singh isolates one or more violent, hypermasculine, and corrupt reactionary traditionalists—ranging from the drunken rapist and murderer, Mirza Mughal during the Sepoy Mutiny to the Hindu fundamentalists who assassinated Gandhi. He most often contrasts these with an androgynous and syncretistic figure. Gandhi is one clear example of this in the novel. Other examples would include Musaddi Lal, a thirteenth-century clerk who follows both Hinduism and Islam, and says that this makes him a sort of *hijda* (55), that is, a hermaphrodite. There are also occasional instances of orthodoxy—for example, Nihal Singh, a brave, strong, and merciful Sikh soldier fighting, unexpectedly, with the British against the Mughal emperor (because this emperor's ancestor had murdered one of the great gurus of Sikhism).

In Nihal Singh, there is a very slight valorization of orthodoxy, though syncretism is clearly the author's strong preference. This pattern is typical of post-colonization anglophone Indian literature, as we have already noted. However, there are exceptions. R. K. Narayan's *The English Teacher* concerns a young man, Krishna, whose wife dies, leaving him "both father and mother" to their daughter (97); he teaches English literature, but seems less assimilationist than synthetic. Contrary to the more common plot development, Krishna becomes both less androgynous and less synthetic over the course of the novel. By the end, he gives up the child into the care of her grandparents, stops teaching English (repudiating the "Western mind" which is "classifying, labelling, departmentalizing" [179]) and becomes part of a non-British school. In other words, he becomes more of a traditional man. He does not, however, become hardened, violent, or sectarian—quite the contrary, in fact; this is a hopeful movement back to an orthodox, open, developing tradition, not a reactionary traditionalism.

Bapsi Sidhwa's *The Bride* is interesting in this context as well. This novel contrasts the "strangely effeminate" (21) urban and partially Westernized Pakistanis with the masculine, traditional tribesmen from the hills. Qasim—one "hero" of the book—is an orthodox masculine tribal. But it is unclear whether his (mostly) admirable character derives from his orthodoxy. Certainly, other traditionalists/tribals, such as Sakhi, are far from admirable in their brutal maleness. However, Sakhi has come to maturity facing the cultural threat of urbanized/Westernized Pakistan. He is, perhaps, better characterized as a reactionary traditionalist and masculinist—and he does in fact manifest the properties most often associated with these categories. Indeed, his behavior resembles that of the Westernized Farukh far more than it does that of Qasim.

In *Cracking India (Ice-Candy Man)*, Sidhwa does not as closely conjoin concerns of traditionalism with concerns of gender. However, she does present some striking images of the contrast between orthodoxy and reactionary traditionalism, showing very clearly the rigid and sectarian character of the latter in contrast with the former. While there is, perhaps, a hint of romanticism in her portrayal of original intercommunal harmony, the general contrast is no doubt valid. As the narrator, Lenny, describes the change: "One day everybody is themselves—and the next day they are Hindu, Muslim, Sikh, Christian. People shrink, dwindling into symbols" (101). This reduction to symbols is, in effect, definitive of reactionary traditionalism, and it simultaneously prevents both orthodoxy and synthesis.

Meena Alexander's *Nampally Road* provides a variation on the motifs we have been considering. The synthetic male protagonist, Ramu, is contrasted with two other male figures: Limca Gowda, the corrupt, pseudo-traditionalist chief minister of Andhra Pradesh, who promulgates rape and murder; and Swami Chari, the open-minded orthodox traditionalist, who is willing to see Hinduism grow and change (see, for example, p. 86), but who is ineffectual in the face of Gowda's brutality. Gowda is reactionary traditionalist/mimetic and reactionary masculine (with hints of degenerate effeminacy). However, Ramu is much closer to orthodox masculinity than to androgyny.

Turning to women characters, we find many of the same patterns, with some predictable differences. Among male writers, it is not entirely uncommon to find a self-effacing woman—the hero's mother or the mother of his child—standing as a romanticized portrait of orthodox femininity. For example, in Ahmed Ali's *Twilight in Delhi*, Bilqeece, an ideal wife and mother, is treated reprehensibly by her husband Ashgar, but loves him until her death, even though this final suffering too is in part the result of his neglect.

As we have already noted, women writers tend to be more sceptical of women's roles and women's selflessness in traditional patriarchal societies. In *Sunlight on a Broken Column*, for example, Hosain presents a range of traditional women. Some are oppressive, some oppressed, some rebellious. "The Begum," for example, is a sinister figure whose mission in the novel is to arrange a marriage for her son, and thereby condemn some unwilling young woman to strict confinement and servitude, "sentenced to a life of luxurious incarceration," as Hosain puts it (166). In contrast, Aunt Abida is a strong, independent woman who is able to value Islamic traditions and at the same time work within traditional structures to secure intellectual freedom and a degree of familial authority—until she marries. Meera's grandmother from Bhattacharya's *A Goddess Named Gold* provides another case of a powerful and more or less orthodox woman, in this case one who combines personal authority with political skill. Interestingly, she too is, in effect, unmarried, for her husband is a wandering musician who visits home only for a day or two once in a great while. Relevant also is Godmother from *Cracking India*—a strong, unattached (widowed) woman, sternly matriarchal in her dealings not only with members of her family, but with outsiders as well. (On the other hand, it must be admitted that these last two characters at times shade into syncretism—a predictable result of their open attitude toward the dynamics of tradition.)

Occasionally, a writer will simply fall back on colonialist stereotypes of the complete passivity and entirely maternal character of traditional Indian women. We find this, for example, in

Bharati Mukherjee, as when she writes, with only partial irony, of "docile Indian girls," and the "Old World wife who knew her place and would breed like crazy" (143). Similarly, in *Baumgartner's Bombay*, Anita Desai refers to "Indian women in shapeless garments squatting passively with their baskets or babies," part of "one restless, heaving mass" (83; elsewhere she extends this to other stereotypes, for example Indian ahistoricism, as when she refers to rural women living "lives so primitive, so basic and unchanging" in the "absence of...history" [111]).

Rushdie has been particularly interested in the reactionary traditionalist woman character, presenting us with several cases of women who have accepted the strictest Islamic codes and combined this with murderous violence. In the case of Jamila Singer, of *Midnight's Children*, this is indirect; her voice becomes "a sword for purity...a weapon...[to] cleanse men's souls" (376) and sing "troops to their deaths" (405). However, in the case of Sufiya Zinobia (*Shame*: "The woman in the veil: a horror story" [238]), the violence is unmediated and leads to a series of brutal murders. This sort of violence is found in some works by women as well—for example, in Sidhwa's *The Bride*, the mountain women are as harsh in their reactionary traditionalism as are the men. Thus, when a battered wife flees her husband, one of the women calls on the men to "be back soon with that bitch's corpse" in order that the husband's "honour" may be "vindicated" (191). And Meena Alexander clearly characterizes Indira Gandhi as a brutal reactionary traditionalist. Interestingly, Gandhi is similar to the male reactionary traditionalist characters in being corrupt and covertly mimetic as well ("our khadi-clad, iron-fisted Prime Minister—she of the immaculate lineage and Swiss schooling, who on her New York trips made small type in the *Times* by buying her mascara from Bergdorf's," 3).

A wide range of writers link sexual license with Westernization here as well. Mukherjee often does this, as does Mira Nair in *Mississippi Masala*, though neither sets out to criticize the women for promiscuity (one common aim of such characterization). Tagore too draws in part on this idea when he has Bimala seduced by Sandip shortly after leaving purdah. While he does not find her sexual openness unobjectionable—as would, perhaps, Mukherjee or Nair—he does place the blame on the Westernized and hypocritical Sandip, rather than on Bimala herself. Moreover, he carefully criticizes the masculinist romanticization of tradition which is frequently associated with this type of characterization.

Nikhil has second thoughts about the deviations from traditional practice which led to Bimala's abandonment of purdah and subsequent relation with Sandip. He says: "How I should love, Sister Rani, to go back to the days when we first met in this old house of ours." His widowed sister-in-law responds firmly: "No, brother dear....I would not live my life again—not as a woman! Let what I have had to bear end with this one birth. I could not bear it over again" (190).

Alexander links mimeticism with dissolute behavior more broadly. When Mira goes to England, she systematically rebels against traditional practices. In a particularly striking instance, she eats food with her left hand—despite the fact that she is right-handed—precisely because eating with the left hand is traditionally forbidden (29). In keeping with this thorough-going reactionary assimilationism, she "had been forcing [herself] to go out each night with a different fellow...to drink more than [she] felt comfortable doing, and to smoke until [her] throat hurt" (31). Subsequently, she turns away from mimeticism only to find herself now alienated from both India and the West, a "modern woman" (2) in search of an identity, trying to "make up a self that had some continuity with what [she] was" (30; see also 69).

Hosain also considers mimeticism, and carefully links Westernization with reactionary traditionalism. Characters such as Zahra and Mrs. Wadia are not particularly dissolute, but they are able to shift between reactionary traditionalism and mimeticism with shocking ease. Referring to Zahra, Hosain writes: "She was now playing the part of the perfect modern wife as she had once played the part of a dutiful purdah girl....Just as she had once said her prayers five times a day, she now attended social functions morning, afternoon and evening" (140).

Influenced by the socialist views of the Progressive Writers Movement, Kamala Markandaya takes up the figure of a sexually promiscuous Westernized woman and analyzes it in economic, rather than cultural or moral terms. In *Nectar in a Sieve*, Irawaddy literally becomes a prostitute when Western business enters her village. This is not due to dissolution, however, but to the economic situation which colonialism creates, as well as the constraints of her own traditional patriarchal culture.

Contrasted with all of these types, we have the synthetic characters. These would include Hosain's Laila, who is critical of both traditional marriage and Western dissolution; Lenny's mother in *Cracking India*, a woman comfortable at the Parsee temple and at European-style dinner parties; and the socialist activist village girl, Meera, in *A Goddess Named Gold* (though Bhattacharya's Gandhism makes it somewhat unclear if she is more synthetic or more flexibly orthodox). Durgabai, an elderly physician in *Nampally Road*, is a particularly interesting example because her syncretism is based on universalism: "For [Durgabai] there was no gap between Krishna's world and ours. The earth, however dry and racked with heat, was the same for all creatures" (18). (As we shall see, a number of writers—for example, Bessie Head and Ngũgĩ wa Thiong'o—base their valorization of synthesis on universalism.) Like their male counterparts, these characters combine strength and intelligence with sensitivity and gentleness, and they interweave ideas and practices from their own traditions with those from the West.

Turning to African literature, we find in Ngũgĩ's *The River Between* a good example of the tripartite structure of characterization found in *Ulysses*, *The Home and the World*, and other works. Though the assimilated Joshua is not degenerate or effeminate, the other major characters of this novel follow our general principles quite closely. Thus the hero, Waiyaki, is a synthesis of Gikuyu tradition and English education, as well as orthodox masculine and feminine virtues—strength and conciliation, abstract thought and sensitivity, and so on. In contrast, Kabonyi is an aggressive masculinist, a sectarian, and quite explicitly a reactionary traditionalist, for he first converted to Christianity and then violently reacted against this conversion. Finally, orthodox tradition and masculinity are represented in the novel by the figure of Chege the prophet.

The opposition between Dan and Sello in Head's *A Question of Power* is relevant here also. Dan is hypermasculine and nationalist (see, for example, 104–5), whereas Sello is androgynous and internationalist (see, for example, 11). Both show traits of sexual degenerescence inconsistent with this characterization (see, for example, 144 and 148). But this inconsistency is unsurprising, and perhaps unrevealing, given the more general inconsistency of Elizabeth's schizophrenic delusions. In any event, the broad typological orientations of Dan and Sello are clear. Indeed, here they are particularly suggestive because they are presented as part of a delusion, and thus as having deeper roots in colonial subjectivity than might a mere literary convention.

More distant from the Irish and Indian examples are the cases of Achebe and Soyinka, in some of whose works orthodox tradition and orthodox masculinity appear to be valued over synthesis, even when the possibility of genuine orthodoxy is questioned. For example, in *Things Fall Apart*, Okonkwo is a clear example of a reactionary masculinist and reactionary traditionalist—though he is reacting to threats of femininity and degenerescence which he saw in his father, not in European culture. The less violent, less rigid Obierika, in contrast, appears to represent Achebe's vision of genuine masculinity and genuine tradition. Nwoye is ambiguously situated between synthesis and reactionary assimilation; both the character, and the differences between these two responses to colonialism, are downplayed in the novel (despite the obvious "hybridity" of the novel itself, its highly ambivalent portrayal of colonial contact, Christianity, etc.).

In *The Strong Breed*, Soyinka similarly contrasts the synthetic and androgynous Eman with his masculine and orthodox father, as well as with the reactionary Jaguna, who fails to follow tradition because of his excessive aggressiveness. In *The Lion and the Jewel*, Soyinka establishes a similar contrast between the emasculated and assimilated school teacher, on the one hand, and the masculine and traditional Bale on the other. Indeed, there is some sort of conflict along these lines in almost every play by Soyinka—even a play such as *A Dance of the Forests*, which, like many of Soyinka's works, indicates that indigenous tradition was always already corrupt, always already irrecuperable.

Beyond those already named, African literature presents a wide range of Westernized and dissolute characters, many of whom are corrupt and duplicitous as well. Thus we have Soyinka's Jero, a scheming Christian preacher with a penchant for philandering. Or, more significantly, Koomson, in Armah's *The Beautyful Ones Are Not Yet Born*, a supposed nationalist leader who mimics European manners and covertly collaborates with European neocolonialists. Okot P'Bitek's Ocol is a case of this sort as well, in this instance criticized by his traditional wife Lawino; in P'Bitek's account, Lawino's African "naiveté" is more considered, reflective, and admirable than her husband's European "sophistication." Obi Okonkwo, in Achebe's *No Longer at Ease*, is a sympathetic variation of this character schema. Inserted into the Westernized subculture of the Nigerian bureaucracy, he is gradually drawn into corruption, duplicity, and dissolute behavior, in many ways contrary to his own preferences and character.

Women characters follow the pattern we would expect from our discussion of Indian literature. African women writers tend, unsurprisingly, to advocate synthesis. However, their works sometimes hold only the most ambiguous hopes for the future. For example, both Tambu (in *Nervous Conditions*) and Elizabeth (in *A Question of Power*) are synthetic characters who seem to represent an authorial advocacy of synthesis. Elizabeth repeatedly appeals to universalism, and Tambu tries to avoid both the reactionary traditionalism and reactionary assimilationism of members of her family. But both Dangarembga and Head emphasize the other form of "hybridity," to which such synthesis may be dangerously close: the alienating and unsynthesized collocation of indigenous and colonial properties, practices, and identifications which leads to a complete loss of cultural identity and even psychological disintegration. Tambu is paired with Nyasha, an offensive hybrid (as Nyasha herself puts it, 78), who is alienated from Shona culture, but unable to become fully European or to reconcile these different aspects of her identity. The result of this double alienation is psychological disintegration, manifest in a severe eating disorder which is not cured by the end of the novel. Elizabeth too is doubly alienated. Half European and half African by birth, she is accepted by neither community; exiled from her country and ignorant of indigenous traditions in Botswana, she has no culture. In part as a result of this, she suffers a complete mental collapse. And though she appears cured at the end of the novel, she does not so much achieve a new synthesis as merely hope for one.

Predictably, a number of writers present somewhat romanticized portraits of traditional women. However, it is important to note that even traditionalist male writers tend to see traditional women as strong, competent, and to a degree independent. (Put differently, when compared with the Indian works, it appears that both male and female characterization in the African works is shifted toward "masculinity.") A figure such as Alu in Soyinka's *The Swamp Dwellers* is a patient and loving mother, but she is neither timid nor subservient. And P'Bitek's Lawino, while chaste and devoted even in neglect, does not suffer her ill-treatment in silence. Similarly, characters such as Sunma in Soyinka's *The Strong Breed* are willing to take action and defy social authority. Aunt Lucia in Dangarembga's *Nervous Conditions* is a character in some ways parallel to Hosain's Aunt Abida—a powerful unmarried woman in a traditional context. However, Lucia's power is more a matter of sexuality and physical self-assertion. Nyakinyua of Ngũgĩ's *Petals of Blood* is a (more or less) traditional character also. She too is powerful and unmarried (or, rather, widowed). Her strength comes more directly from her connection with the past, both history and traditional practices.

The association of Westernization with loose sexual morals may be found in such characters as Rola, a Westernized prostitute in Soyinka's *A Dance of the Forests*, and Igwezu's unfaithful wife in *The Swamp Dwellers*. (Though in Soyinka the situation is made more complicated by the fact that Rola reincarnates a precolonization figure of similar promiscuity and dissoluteness. In this sense, Soyinka seems to think of the character type as gravitating toward European culture, rather than European culture creating the character type.) In *Petals of Blood*, Wanja's prostitution and Westernization are closely linked as well. However, for Ngũgĩ, this is not due to some moral degeneration on Wanja's part. Rather, it is the direct result of the political economy implied by neo-colonial Westernization. (In this way, Ngũgĩ's approach is similar to that of Markandaya.)

Dangarembga has taken up this character type in order to criticize its ideological presuppositions. Specifically, she characterizes Nyasha in terms stereotypically associated with a "loose" Westernized woman: Nyasha smokes, reads sexually explicit European literature (D. H. Lawrence), speaks aggressively and "out of turn," talks freely with men, and so on. In light of this, Nyasha's father accuses her of "behav[ing] like a whore" (114). However, it is clear that this is a baseless accusation, and thus that Dangarembga is criticizing the stereotype and those who employ it, not the women it is used to denigrate.

Caribbean anglophone literature has many similarities with Indian, African, and Irish writing and thus it is worth devoting a few words to this body of work before concluding. The first thing to note in this context, however, is a difference between the Caribbean situation and the situations of Ireland, India, and Africa. Due to the physical displacement of their ancestors, the loss of indigenous languages, and the mixing of cultures, Caribbean writers cannot have the same relation to tradition as do these other postcolonization societies. Caribbean writers, and Caribbean people more generally, have a much more attenuated connection with the beliefs and practices of their ancestors. Indeed, the longing for a full and fully present tradition, the dream of being rooted in a tradition, is a recurrent theme in Caribbean literature. The sense of rootlessness which underlies this dream has several implications for the creation of character. Most importantly, traditional characters—orthodox or reactionary—appear with relative infrequency in Caribbean literature. There are, of course, exceptions. For example, Lestrade, the "straddler," of Walcott's *Dream on Monkey Mountain* is a reactionary assimilationist who abuses blacks in a vicious and racist manner before he is transformed in a dream into a reactionary traditionalist who calls for the execution of whites.

However, the most interesting aspect of Caribbean characterization in this context concerns the loss of identity and the resultant descent into madness. This often despairing view of the individual's relation to tradition appears to be unusually common in Caribbean writing, no doubt because of the absence of a full sense and experience of indigenous tradition. One explicit treatment of this idea is in the character of Makak in Walcott's *Dream on Monkey Mountain*. Makak goes mad from a sense that he has no cultural identity whatsoever, that everything of value is part of a white culture to which he has no access (due to the impossibility of genuine assimilation). And, while dreaming or delusional, he returns to Africa and acts out a reactionary traditionalism by destroying everything—both in his world and in his mind—that is connected with white culture. In *Omeros*, Walcott varies this theme by sending Achille back, in a fevered dream, to precolonial Africa, in this case seeking genuine tradition, rather than enacting a reactionary traditionalism. Though less explicit than either of these works, the emotional disintegration of the houseless Mr. Biswas in Naipaul's novel is clearly related to Naipaul's sense of the rootlessness of Caribbean culture as well (a sense literalized in the image of the floating tree in *Mimic Men*).

Women characters suffer similar psychological devastation. The emotional collapse of Leila in Caryl Phillips' *The Final Passage* provides a good example. Leila's psychological breakdown follows her exile to England and is linked with the death of her mother. Overwhelmed by the ubiquitous racism of English society, she needs a sense of positive cultural identity, but has none. Having lost the home and the family which might have substituted for that tradition, she sinks into mental illness. Annie John's temporary illness, in Jamaica Kincaid's novel, suggests a similar complex of social and mental factors—if more distantly—in part through its association with Annie's alienation from her mother.[12]

VIOLENCE AND UNIVERSALISM

There is of course more to every one of these characters than their basis in gender attitudes and cultural relations. However, this basis is important, sometimes crucial to our understanding of these characters and of the connections between them. For the patterns of culture and gender identity form a set of cognitive structures which are widespread in post-colonization thought, and thus post-colonization writing. Though we should not reduce Bloom, Waiyaki, and Laila to figures of androgyny and cultural syncretism, we will invariably misunderstand them if we fail to recognize this connection; the same holds for the Citizen, Sandip, and Jamila Singer with respect to reactionary traditionalism and masculinity/femininity, and so forth.

Colonialism—and most particularly European colonialism of the nineteenth and early twentieth centuries—entails the systematic ideological degradation of colonized people and their cultures. It leaves these people with few options for response—the options outlined at the outset of this essay. The issues implicit in these options are not merely conceptual or academic. They are, in fact, critical to the future, not only of the developing world, but of the advanced capitalist countries as well. To take a banal, but revealing example, this essay was originally written to be delivered in Cairo. However, the sharpening conflict between the corrupt, neocolonial (reactionary assimilationist) elite of Egypt, and the militant, fundamentalist (reactionary traditionalist) rebels made the trip, not so much dangerous, as pointless: a group of university professors discussing anglophone literature in a Western hotel which they cannot leave. The idea would be comic, were it not for the great human suffering which surrounds it. Moreover, Egypt is far from unique in this regard. Indeed, there are parallel conflicts—as of now more localized and less intense—throughout even Europe and North America. As Samir Amin has argued, "Without a truly universalist perspective [of the sort we have noted in several writers]...enriched by the contribution of all peoples [i.e., synthetic, in the above sense], the sterile confrontation between the Eurocentrism of some [i.e., colonialism and reactionary assimilationism] and the inverted Eurocentrisms of others [i.e., reactionary traditionalism] will continue, in an atmosphere of destructive fanaticism" (146). The importance of this conflict is clear. But equally clear is the difficulty of achieving a universalistic synthesis rather than an alienating hybridity, a synthesis which preserves diversity, which is, in Ngũgĩ's term "rooted" (*Moving the Centre*, xvii; in urging this goal, Ngũgĩ characterizes himself as "an unrepentant universalist," in a passage echoing Fanon's well-known call for universalism [see Fanon, 197]). These difficulties are only rendered more consequential and more urgent by the fact that the ideologies of colonialism have been linked with the equally brutal ideologies of gender, and thus ultimately with the relations of men and women as well as former colonizers and former colonies.

These are, then, issues which we must consider and investigate economically, politically, and—what is most relevant for students of literature—ideologically. Moreover, they are issues which have already been analyzed and debated, not only in theoretical texts, but implicitly and recurrently in literary texts. Recognizing the insistent attention to these issues in post-colonization literatures, and their systematic appearance in patterns of characterization, is important not only for our understanding of the literature, but also and more significantly for our continuing analysis and critique of colonial ideologies, ideologies of patriarchy, and the reactionary ideological responses to both.

NOTES

1. I use "post-colonization" rather than the more usual "postcolonial" for two reasons. First of all, much of the work I will discuss was written prior to the independence of the countries in question. Secondly, and more importantly, the structures I am setting out to isolate and examine are the result of colonialism and its continuing operation. A term such as "postcolonial," which seems to imply that colonialism is done with, may occlude this operation.

2. It would be valuable to explore the similarities and differences between anglophone, francophone, and other europhone post-colonization literatures, and even more valuable to study the similarities/differences between these and noneurophone post-colonization literatures, such as those in Tamil, Urdu, Arabic, or Yoruba. Such a study, however, would require much more than a single essay, not to mention a remarkable breadth of erudition on the part of its author.

3. Fundamentalism is perhaps best conceived of as a form of dogmatic textual literalism linked with coercive force. It is thus confined to religions with definitive sacred texts, primarily Judaism, Christianity, and Islam. Reactionary traditionalism does, of course, frequently take the form of fundamentalism.

4. In order to avoid confusion, it is important to note that "hybridity"—a popular term in contemporary discussions—is sometimes used to refer to something along the lines of our final category, "synthesis or universalism." However, it is used with equal frequency to refer to the sort of unsynthesized, alienating collocation which defines the fifth category.

5. The patronizing liberalism of European women toward colonized women is repeatedly portrayed in post-colonization works, especially works by women. We find examples of the patronizing white woman in Mrs. Martin from Hosain's *Sunlight on a Broken Column*, Camilla from Bessie Head's *A Question of Power* (see, for example, 77–79), Mrs. Simpson in Buchi Emecheta's *The Slave Girl* (see, for example, 104), Vanessa in Meena Alexander's *Nampally Road*, and so on. Some white women have also created and criticized such characters—Mittee of Daphne Rooke's novel, and Maureen Smales of Nadine Gordimer's *July's People* come to mind.

6. It is, however, important to emphasize that it could do this only in conjunction with other factors—for example, the separate assimilation of blacks to animals, a topic beyond the bounds of the present essay.

7. Some readers of this essay have taken the definition of this category to imply that conceptions of gender vary widely across cultures. I do not mean to imply anything of the sort. Indeed, the fact that gender concepts are ideologically functional indicates that they will be quite similar across patriarchal cultures, for the concepts must do much the same ideological work. This is especially true of gender ideals. For example, female chastity tends to be valued in a wide range of patriarchal and, perhaps especially, patrilineal societies. In contrast, the Western belief in female illogic—now, bizarrely, purported to be a feminist view—is far more variable, both within and across societies (see, for example, Faludi [325] on historical changes in the Western view, and Borthwick [84] for some contrasts in the Indian view).

8. I do not mean to imply that men have reactionary views by nature and that the spontaneous consciousness of women is a critical or non-ideological consciousness (indeed, this view is associated with pseudo-progressive forms of reactionary femininity). On the contrary, I am a firm believer in the Marxist dictum that class origin does not determine class stance. However, it does appear to be the case that colonized women who have pursued the (nontraditional) career of professional writing are, on the whole, more sensitive to issues of patriarchal oppression than are men. On the other hand, many of these women seem less sensitive to the colonial racism directed at men.

9. Indeed, the structures we have been isolating have direct parallels in colonial thought. Thus one could profitably analyze such works as *Kim, A Passage to India, Heart of Darkness*, and so on, in terms of orthodox Englishness, reactionary Englishness, synthesis, the relation of these to gender types, and so on. There are no doubt other contexts in which such an analysis would prove valuable as well.

10. I do not mean to denigrate homosexuality, but merely to point out the scope of these characters' sexual characterization.

11. It would be valuable to consider Irish literature at more length, for it provides as central a case of post-colonization literature as do Africa and South Asia. For example, in Ireland reactionary traditionalism and reactionary masculinity are frequently represented by the common figure of a dogmatic priest, reactionary traditionalism and reactionary femininity by a widowed and sexually repressive mother, and so on.

12. A parallel instance from a European writer may be found in Jean Rhys's *Wide Sargasso Sea.* Antoinette's final madness is the result of her almost complete loss of a sense of personal identity. This loss resulted from many factors, not the least of which was her deep feeling that she belonged neither to the black Caribbean culture (to which she felt herself drawn) nor to the white English culture (in which she found herself imprisoned). Like so many colonized people, she was irreconcilably alienated from both cultural alternatives.

WORKS CITED

Achebe, Chinua. *Things Fall Apart.* New York: Astor-Honor, 1959.

———. *No Longer At Ease.* London: Heinemann, 1963.

Alexander, Meena. *Nampally Road.* San Francisco: Mercury House, 1991.

Ali, Ahmed. *Twilight in Delhi.* Karachi: Oxford University Press, 1984 [1940].

Amin, Samir. *Eurocentrism.* Trans. Russell Moore. New York: Monthly Review Press, 1989.

Armah, Ayi Kwei. *The Beautyful Ones Are Not Yet Born.* London: Heinemann, 1968.

Bhabha, Homi K. "Of Mimicry and Man: The Ambivalence of Colonial Discourse." *October* 28 (1984): 125–33.

———. "Signs Taken for Wonders: Questions of Ambivalence and Authority under a Tree Outside Delhi, May 1817." *Critical Inquiry* 12. 1 (Autumn 1985): 144–65.

Bhattacharya, Bhabani. *A Goddess Named Gold.* Delhi: Hind Pocket Books, 1967 [1960].

Borthwick, Meredith. *The Changing Role of Women in Bengal 1849–1905.* Princeton: Princeton University Press, 1984.

Dangarembga, Tsitsi. *Nervous Conditions.* Seattle: Seal Press, 1988.

Desai, Anita. *Baumgartner's Bombay.* New York: Penguin, 1988.

Emecheta, Buchi. *The Slave Girl.* New York: George Braziller, 1977.

Faludi, Susan. *Backlash: The Undeclared War Against American Women.* New York: Doubleday, 1991.

Fanon, Frantz. *Black Skin, White Masks.* Trans. Charles Lam Markmann. New York: Grove Press, 1967 [1952].

Gordimer, Nadine. *July's People.* New York: Penguin, 1981.

Head, Bessie. *A Question of Power.* London: Heinemann, 1974.

Hosain, Attia. *Sunlight on a Broken Column.* New York: Penguin, 1988 [1961].

Joyce, James. *Ulysses.* Ed. Hans Walter Gabler. New York: Vintage Books, 1986 [1922].

Kincaid, Jamaica. *Annie John.* New York: Plume, 1985.

Lamming, George. *In the Castle of My Skin.* Ann Arbor: University of Michigan Press, 1983 [1953].

Markandaya, Kamala. *Nectar in a Sieve.* New York: New American Library, 1984 [1954].

Mukherjee, Bharati. *The Middleman and Other Stories.* New York: Grove Press, 1988.

Naipaul, V. S. *A House for Mr. Biswas.* New York: Vintage, 1961.

———. *The Mimic Men.* New York: Penguin, 1969 [1967].

Nandy, Ashis. *The Intimate Enemy: Loss and Recovery of Self Under Colonialism.* Delhi: Oxford University Press, 1983.

Narayan, R. K. *The English Teacher.* Chicago: University of Chicago Press, 1980 [1945].

Ngũgĩ wa Thiong'o. *The River Between.* London: Heinemann, 1965.

———. *Moving the Centre: The Struggle for Cultural Freedoms.* London: James Curry, 1993.

———. *Petals of Blood.* New York: Penguin, 1977.

P'Bitek, Okot. *Song of Lawino & Song of Ocol.* London: Heinemann, 1984 [1966].

Phillips, Caryl. *The Final Passage.* New York: Penguin, 1985.

Rao, Raja. *Kanthapura.* New York: New Directions, 1963 [1938].

Rhys, Jean. *Wide Sargasso Sea. In The Complete Novels.* Ed. Diana Athill. New York: W. W. Norton, 1985 [1966].

Rooke, Daphne. *Mittee.* New York: Penguin, 1991 [1951].

Rushdie, Salman. *Midnight's Children.* New York: Avon Books, 1980.

———. *Shame.* New York: Vintage, 1989 [1983].

Sidhwa, Bapsi. *Cracking India: A Novel.* Minneapolis: Milkweed Editions, 1991.

——— *The Bride.* New York: St. Martin's Press, 1983.

Soyinka, Wole. *A Dance of the Forests.* In *Collected Plays I.* New York: Oxford University Press, 1973 [1963].

———. *Jero's Metamorphosis.* In *Collected Plays II.* New York: Oxford University Press, 1974 [1973].

———. *The Lion and the Jewel.* In *Collected Plays II.* New York: Oxford University Press, 1974 [1963].

———. *The Strong Breed.* In *Collected Plays I.* New York: Oxford University Press, 1973 [1964].

———. *The Swamp Dwellers.* In *Collected Plays I.* New York: Oxford University Press, 1973 [1964].

———. *The Trials of Brother Jero.* In *Collected Plays II.* New York: Oxford University Press, 1974 [1964].

Said, Edward. *Orientalism.* New York: Random House, 1978.

Sidhwa, Bapsi. *The Bride.* New York: St. Martin's Press, 1983.

Singh, Khushwant. *Delhi: A Novel.* New Delhi: Penguin, 1990.

Tagore, Rabindranath. *Gora.* London: Macmillan, 1910 [1907].

———. *The Home and the World.* Trans. S. Tagore. London: Macmillan, 1919 [1916].

Walcott, Derek. *Dream on Monkey Mountain.* In *Dream on Monkey Mountain and Other Plays.* New York: Noonday Press, 1970 [1967].

———. *Omeros.* New York: Farrar, Straus and Giroux, 1990.

Woolf, Virginia. *Mrs. Dalloway.* New York: Harvest, 1953 [1925].

5

FRANÇOISE LIONNET

"*Logiques métisses*": Cultural Appropriation and Postcolonial Representations

> If this weird, upside-down caricature of a country called America, if this land of refugees and former indentured servants, religious heretics and half-breeds, whoresons and fugitives—this cauldron of mongrels from all points on the compass—was all I could rightly call home, then aye: I was of it.
>
> —Charles Johnson's *Middle Passage* (179)

> Cependant, il n'y a pas de choix: il faut apprendre et avec ce dont on dispose: un savoir colonisé et un langage truqué.
>
> —Claudine Hermann

Francophone women writers in Africa, the Caribbean, and the Indian Ocean, as well as within France, where they or their families immigrate for various personal or economic reasons, have given us unique insights into what Renato Rosaldo has called the "border zones" of culture.[1] In those areas on the periphery of stable metropolitan cultural discourses, Rosaldo explains, there is an incessant and playful heteroglossia, a bilingual speech or hybrid language that is a site of creative resistance to the dominant conceptual paradigms. In border zones, all of our academic preconceptions about cultural, linguistic, or stylistic norms are constantly being put to the test by creative practices that make visible and set off the processes of adaptation, appropriation, and contestation that govern the construction of identity in colonial and postcolonial contexts.

These processes are the ground upon which contemporary global culture can begin to be understood, defined, and represented, as postcolonial writers encode the everyday realities and subjective perceptions of a numerical majority whose cultural contributions are still considered to be the products of minority voices. By reproducing the changing cultural practices of this majority as it negotiates the conflicts between tradition and modernity, writers create a space for themselves within the dominant discourses while simultaneously articulating a problematic that is increasingly becoming accepted as a quasi-universal process. The global mongrelization or *métissage* of cultural forms creates hybrid identities, and interrelated, if not overlapping, spaces. In those spaces, struggles for the control of means of representation and self-identification are mediated by a single and immensely powerful symbolic system: the colonial language, and the variations to which it is subjected by writers who enrich, transform, and creolize it.

Writers such as Maryse Condé from Guadeloupe, Assia Djebar from Algeria, and Leïla Sebbar, a Franco-Algerian, are part of an increasing number of astute interpreters of the postcolonial condition whose works, published in the 1970s and 1980s, have been redefining francophone history and literature. They create new paradigms that represent, through innovative and self-reflexive literary techniques, both linguistic and geographic exile, displacements from the margins to a metropolitan center, and intercultural exchanges.

In order to understand the cultural and literary praxis of those writers, I want to make a brief incursion into the field of cultural anthropology, which has established some of the parameters within which we commonly understand negatively coded terms such as "acculturation" and "assimilation." My purpose in this paper is to develop, first of all, a theoretical argument about postcolonial culture. This argument is an eminently political one, and on one level it does address the current academic polemics about various forms of cultural fundamentalism. But my approach tends to be indirect. A term like "multiculturalism" takes on different valences in different linguistic and geopolitical contexts, that is, in countries where the relative power of hegemonic and subaltern groups shifts according to factors altogether different from the ones that obtain in the United States. That is why, in the latter part of the paper, I draw my examples from the works of contemporary postcolonial francophone women whose perspectives on multiculturalism differ from the ones we are most familiar with in this country. These writers' concerns and perspectives are an important contribution to these debates, because they echo and often predate those of cultural anthropologists whose theoretical approaches are nonetheless very useful for analyzing the processes at work in the women's novels.[2] My interest in using these novels to understand cultural configurations studied by social scientists is grounded in my belief that literature allows us to enter into the subjective processes of writers and their characters, and thus allows us better to understand the unique perspectives of subjects who are agents of transformation and hybridization in their own narratives, as opposed to being the objects of knowledge as in the discourse of social science.

Let me start with some simple, common sense definitions: "acculturation," Webster's Dictionary tells us, is "the transfer of culture from one ethnic group to another," whereas "assimilation" is "the act of bringing or coming to a resemblance; the merging of diverse cultural elements." Or, as the Oxford English Dictionary would have it, to assimilate is "to make like, to cause to resemble, to incorporate...to become conformed to." Already, we can see some liminal uncertainty in the semantic fields of these terms: is the "transfer...from one ethnic group to another" only a one-way process that causes one culture to erase another? Or could we infer that the transformation of both—or all—of the cultures in contact is extremely likely, if not inevitable, through this process of "acculturation" of one (or several) culture(s) to the other(s)? Is "the merging of diverse cultural elements" to be understood as the inevitable erasure of one element by another? Might it not also suggest that a more intricate and complex phenomenon is in fact taking place, as in those "border zones" where a complex syncretic cultural system comes to replace two or more ostensibly simpler cultures? In such a case, acculturation would not simply be the means of making one element conform to another, assimilate to it, in order to become like that other, but would more truly be a process whereby all elements involved in the interaction would be changed by that encounter. Dominant systems are more likely to absorb and make like them numerically or culturally "weaker" elements. But even then, these "inferior" or subaltern elements contribute to the evolution and transformation of the hegemonic system by producing resistances and counter-discourses.[3]

It has of course been ideologically and politically convenient for the dominant cultures to entertain the fiction of "assimilation" as a means of incorporating—"civilizing"—those cultures viewed as too different and "inferior" to be comfortably accepted and integrated into their norms.[4] But in the long run, the more powerful system does incorporate elements of the weaker one, often to the point where certain of its patterns and practices become indistinguishable from those of the imported or inferior culture. Kwame Anthony Appiah has recently said, "there is, of course, no American culture without African roots" (354). But while it is commonly accepted that African-Americans are "more or less" assimilated and acculturated to "white" American culture, we rarely hear the reciprocal formulation discussed in academic or popular circles.[5] As Toni Morrison forcefully puts it:

> Afro-American culture exists and though it is clear (and becoming clearer) how it has responded to Western culture, the instances where and means by which it has shaped Western culture are poorly recognized or understood. (3)

Similarly, South African anthropologists study the Westernization of blacks in Southern Africa, but not the Africanization of whites who adopt the culinary or musical tastes of blacks. Singer Johnny Clegg, the "White Zulu," and the white Southern African youths who have assimilated (into) black culture have not yet, to my knowledge, become the object of the anthropologist's scrutiny.[6] Here in the United States, a white rap singer named Vanilla Ice has been called "the Elvis of rap," whereas the black rap singer named L. D. Shore rose to fame as "the Black Elvis." But, as Patricia J. Williams recently pointed out, this is "divinely parodic: Elvis, the white black man of a generation ago, reborn in a black man imitating Elvis" (and one might add, reborn in Vanilla Ice, a white man imitating the black rapper imitating Elvis: a dizzying thought [see Bernard]). In all of these cases the point of reference remains "white culture," even if it is an already "mongrelized" white culture, to use Charles Johnson's formulation in the epigraph to this essay.

My quarrel, then, with terms such as "assimilation" and "acculturation" when used in the (post)colonial context, is a quarrel with history: the terms have acquired a negative connotation because they underscore the relation of subjugation that exists between the colonized culture and the hegemonic system. Rosaldo points out that "metropolitan typifications suppress, exclude, even repress border zones," that

> the model for cross-cultural understanding that produces immigration as a site of cultural stripping away is the academic version of the melting pot: theories of acculturation and assim-

> ilation. In this view, immigrants, or at any rate their children and grandchildren, are absorbed into the national culture. Above all, the process involves the loss of one's past—autobiography, history, heritage, language, and all the rest of the so-called cultural baggage.... The theory of assimilation appears to have the inevitability of a law of history. If it doesn't catch up with you this generation, it will in the next. ("Ideology," 87, 82)

In this view, the "assimilated" are seen as existing passively, not as creative agents capable of transforming the practices that they come to adopt. The message proclaimed by contemporary art and literature from Africa and the Caribbean, however, is quite different: it is not assimilation that appears inevitable when Western technology and education are adopted by the colonized, or when immigration to the metropole severs some of the migrants' ties to a particular birthplace. Rather, the move forces individuals to stand in relation to the past and the present at the same time, to look for creative means of incorporating useful "Western" tools, techniques or strategies into their own cosmology or *Weltanschauung*.[7]

What is needed, then, is a new vocabulary for describing patterns of influence that are never unidirectional. Since the influence is usually mutual and reciprocal, however much that fact might have been occluded from the political consciousness and modes of self-representation of metropolitan cultures, a more appropriate term for describing this contact of cultures would be "transculturation." The Cuban poet Nancy Morejón has used this neologism (*transculturación*) to describe a process of cultural intercourse and exchange, a circulation of practices that creates a constant interweaving of symbolic forms and empirical activities among the different cultures that interact with one another. As she puts it, "*reciprocal* influence is the determining factor here, for no single element superimposes itself on another; on the contrary, each one changes into the other so that both can be transformed into a third" (23).[8] Rejecting the binarism of self and other, nationalism and internationalism, Africa and Europe, women writers like Morejón point to a third way, to the *métissage* of forms and identities that is the result of cross-cultural encounters, and that forms the basis for their self-portrayals and their representations of cultural diversity.

Cross- or transcultural exchange has always been "an absolute fact" of life everywhere, even if, as Edouard Glissant has pointed out, "the human imagination, in Western tradition, has always wished to deny or disguise" it (*Caribbean*, 251; see also Lionnet, *Autobiographical*, 9). The realization that "the melting pot" is no theory of social reality, but a necessary myth, or perhaps an enabling metaphor in the construction of an American national identity, is opening the way for a more cautious understanding of the dialectical and complex phenomena of ethnic interactions that have existed in this country since the beginning of colonial times. Similarly, French theories of cultural assimilation that aimed at turning colonized peoples—or, at any rate, the educated elites of the colonies—into acculturated *évolués* who could speak perfect French corresponds only to one aspect of a complex colonial picture: although the colonial linguistic enterprise is alive and well in the "départements d'outre-mer," it now coexists with a strong movement in favor of *créolité*, a movement that does not aim at the outright rejection of French, but at valorizing the multilingual and multiethnic character of creole cultures.[9]

That is why the concept of transculturation proves so useful: the prefix "trans-" suggests the act of traversing, of going through existing cultural territories. Its specifically spatial connotations demarcate a pattern of movement, across cultural arenas and physical topographies, that corresponds more accurately to the notion of "appropriation," a concept more promising than those of acculturation and assimilation, and one that implies active intervention, rather than passive victimization. It is easy to establish how useful this concept can be for our analysis. Abdelkebir Khatibi has shown, in his novel *Amour bilingue*, and his collected essays entitled *Maghreb pluriel*, that for francophone writers whose mother tongue may be Arabic, Berber, Wolof, or Creole, the French language is a means of translating into the colonizer's language a different sensibility, a different vision of the world, a means therefore of transforming the dominant conceptions circulated by the more standard idiom (see also Lionnet, "Of Mangoes"). To write in French is thus also to transform French into a language that becomes the writer's own: French is appropriated, made into a vehicle for expressing a hybrid, heteroglot universe. This creative act of "taking possession" of a language gives rise to the kind of linguistic *métissage* visible in many contemporary francophone works.[10]

Acts of appropriation will produce a greater degree of cultural complexity than the standard anthropological categories (metropolitan vs. colonial, developed vs. primitive, or civilized vs. aboriginal) would tend to suggest. Indeed, the notion of culture has itself become quite controversial among some anthropologists. Rosaldo contextualizes and summarizes the issues:

> Anthropologists hold contradictory notions of culture. The discipline's official view holds that all human conduct is culturally mediated. In other words, people act in relation, not to brute reality, but to culture-specific modes of perceiving and organizing the world.... No domain of culture is more or less culturally mediated than any other.... [But] if official [anthropological] view holds that all cultures are equal, an informal filing system, more often found in corridor talk than in published writings, classifies cultures in quantitative terms, from a lot to a little, from thick to thin, from elaborate to simple.... Culture in this view is defined by difference. Difference...makes culture visible to observers. (78)

If "difference" is what makes culture visible to observers, then the emphasis on difference has the merit of underscoring specificities which would be muted and ignored otherwise. But an overemphasis on dissimilarities is likely to lead from racial and biographical determinism into an essentialist impasse. In this erroneous view of culture wherein difference is rigidly valorized for its own sake, or for the sake of identifying authentic and "pure products" (see Clifford, 1–17), any process of acculturation or transculturation (however real, inevitable, and reciprocal it may have been) is automatically labeled as merely assimilationist. Hence, assimilation is (mis)construed by the dominant system as the elusive means of retaining or creating a fictive purity and authenticity within which the colonized "people without culture" can be absorbed; in opposition to this tendency, the subaltern group, on the other hand, will seek to retain a sense of its own cultural authenticity by advocating a return to precolonial traditions, thus contrasting the past to the present and mythifying its own original ethnic or cultural purity. Difference then becomes—on both sides of this binary system—the reason for exoticizing, "othering," groups that do not share in this mythic cultural purity.

The issue of defining identity in a colonial context has always been a highly charged one: the first generation, represented by Aimé Césaire, Frantz Fanon, Albert Memmi (*Portrait*), and Edouard Glissant (*Le Discours*), has examined with some anxiety the processes through which the colonized internalize a vision of themselves projected by the colonizer, a vision which promotes a form of mimetic idealization of, and identification with, the colonizer. To a degree, these formulations remained dependent upon a Hegelian view of the master-slave dialectic, and of the importance of recognition as the means of self-validation for both colonizer and colonized. By contrast, during the last two decades, writers have largely engaged in a painstaking redefinition of the paradigms of decolonization, thus seeking to undermine any simplistic understanding of the process of assimilation, and the concurrent presuppositions regarding "authenticity" in either dominant or native cultures. As Rosaldo points out,

> the view of an authentic culture as an autonomous internally coherent universe no longer seems tenable in a postcolonial world. Neither "we" nor "they" are as self-contained and homogeneous as we/they once appeared. All of us inhabit an interdependent late 20th century world, which is at once marked by borrowing and lending across porous cultural boundaries, and saturated with inequality, power, and domination. ("Ideology," 87)

The texts and voices of francophone women map out and interpret for us the complex interweavings of traditions that philosophers and anthropologists are beginning to theorize and propound in their own disciplines. As Appiah puts it, "if there is a lesson in the broad shape of this circulation of cultures, it is surely that we are already contaminated by each other, that there is no longer a fully autochtonous *echt*-African culture awaiting salvage by our artists" ("Is the Post- in Postmodernism," 354). He is echoed by Swedish anthropologist Ulf Hannerz, who has pointed out that "the world system, rather than creating massive cultural homogeneity on a global scale, is replacing one diversity with another; and the new diversity is based relatively more on interrelations and less on autonomy" (quoted in Clifford, 17). What these writers and thinkers—"from all points on the compass"—increasingly underline is the dialectical tension that exists between local variations and a worldwide system of interdependent cultures, between diversity and resemblance, between relativism and universalism.

In a controversial book, *Logiques métisses: Anthropologie de l'identité en Afrique et ailleurs*, French anthropologist Jean-Loup Amselle echoes some of the statements made above, and goes a step further in arguing that even before colonial times, the interrelations of cultures was the norm, and that it is the Western anthropologist who has "invented" separate ethnic groups as his objects of study. Arguing against ethnological reason, and in favor of a form of originary indistinction or syncretism, he critiques the anthropological bias towards cultural relativism, and attempts to define a universalist "logique métisse":

> Les anthropologues culturalistes américains tout comme Lévi-Strauss ont eu raison, face à toutes les philosophies de l'histoire et autres sagas du progrès de mettre l'accent sur les

spécificités et le caractère relatif des valeurs promues par chaque société; mais le corollaire de cette attitude généreuse est l'érection de barrières culturelles étanches qui enferment chaque groupe dans sa singularité.

N'est-ce pas dans le droit fil de l'anthropologie culturelle américaine que se situe la notion de société multiculturelle dont on a déjà souligné les ambiguïtés? Loin d'être un instrument de tolérance et de libération des minorités comme l'affirment ses partisans, cette expression manifeste au contraire tous les travers de la raison ethnologique et c'est à ce titre qu'elle a été revendiquée en France par la "nouvelle droite." Isoler une communauté par la définition d'un certain nombre de "différences" conduit à la possibilité de son confinement territorial sinon de son expulsion. L'assignation de différences ou l'étiquetage ethnique, prophéties autocréatrices, ne traduisent pas seulement la reconnaissance de spécificités culturelles, ils sont également corrélatifs de l'affirmation forcenée d'une identité, celle de l'ethnie française. De la sorte, la problématique de la société multiculturelle conduit tout droit, si l'on n'y prend garde, à un développement séparé analogue à l'Apartheid sud-africain—qui lui-même procède en partie de l'application dévoyée de la notion de culture.

A ce fondamentalisme ethnique ou culturel que certains assimilent à la "défaite de la pensée," il ne s'agit pas d'opposer de façon abstraite les droits de l'homme, ces principes dont personne ne sait au juste de quoi ils sont faits. Il faut plutôt mettre en avant l'idée d'un mélange ou d'un métissage originaire des différents groupes qui se sont formés tout au long de l'histoire de l'humanité. (35)

[Given all the philosophies of history and other sagas of human progress, American culturalist anthropologists along with Lévi-Strauss were right to stress the particularist nature and the relative character of the values promoted by different societies. But the flip side of this generous attitude is the erection of impermeable cultural barriers that imprison each group in its own singularity.

Doesn't the notion of multicultural society, the ambiguities of which have already been emphasized, follow directly from the concepts put forth by American cultural anthropology? Far from being an instrument of tolerance toward, and liberation of, minorities as its proponents like to claim, this notion reveals instead all the wrongs of ethnological reason, and that is why it has been claimed by the "new right" in France. To isolate a community by defining a set of characteristic "differences" can lead to the possibility of its territorial confinement, and its eventual expulsion. Ethnic labeling, and the assignment of differences, are self-fulfilling prophecies. They do not just correspond to the acceptance of cultural specificities, but are also correlative with the coercive affirmation of one identity, that of French ethnicity. This is why, if we are not mindful of it, the problematic of the multicultural society can lead straight into a state of separate development analogous to South African apartheid—itself a consequence of the misapplication of the notion of culture.

> To this ethnic or cultural fundamentalism that some would like to assimilate to the "defeat of thought," one does not need to oppose the abstract notion of human rights, these principles that no one can truly define. Rather, one must support and articulate the idea of an originary mixing or *métissage* of the different groups which were formed all through human history.]

Amselle's remarks force us to rethink some of the fundamental notions that we are beginning to take for granted as literary and cultural critics: the respect for multiculturalism, the vexing questions of separatism and cultural autonomy, and the need for contemporary societies to respect difference without falling into a situation of apartheid. It is thus interesting to note that postcolonial women writers implicitly address identical issues in their recent essays and fictional works: they depict characters whose originality stems from the fact that the authors give them universal appeal, letting them live their *métissage* in the most original, ingenious, and beneficial ways. These hybrid characters exemplify the inevitability as well as the benefits and disadvantages of intercultural exchange. For, as Amselle goes on to add,

> Les cultures ne sont pas situées les unes à côté des autres comme des monades leibniziennes sans porte ni fenêtre: elles prennent place dans un ensemble mouvant qui est lui-même *un champ structuré de relations....*
>
> *La définition d'une culture donnée est en fait la résultante d'un rapport de forces interculturel....*La modification du rapport des forces...ainsi que l'éclosion et la disparition des cultures rendent compte des changements qui interviennent dans chaque système sous-culturel pris isolément. (55; my italics)
>
> [Cultures are not located next to one another, without doors or windows, like the monads of Leibniz: they are situated in a fluctuating context which is *a structured field of relations....*

> *The definition of a given culture is in fact the resultant of a ratio of intercultural forces....*The modification of the ratio of forces...along with the appearance and disappearance of cultures explain the changes that occur in each subcultural system when one looks at them in isolation.]

To follow Amselle is to come to the conclusion that it is not the existence of different cultures that induces a comparative (ethnographical) approach, but rather that the critic's (or anthropologist's) stance as comparatist creates an arbitrary and singular object (be it "Bambara culture" or "francophone studies")—and thus imposes the constraints of a determinate set of particularisms. Although Amselle does not deny the specificities inherent in certain cultural manifestations, he is in fact arguing against all theories of culture that would locate singularity within a restrained space, an enclosed geographical area, a "nation" or a "tradition."[11] Based on Amselle's extensive field research in Africa, *Logiques métisses* opposes his own theorizing of a sociological and historical "*espace métissé*" to the traditional culturalist approach of anthropology, which, according to him, is just another form of fundamentalism, itself the breeding ground for many contemporary forms of fascism and essentialist tendencies, as witnessed by the pre–civil rights Southern ideology of "separate but equal" and the various other forms of apartheid promoted in recent years by Enoch Powell in Britain, Jean-Marie Le Pen in France, and David Duke in Louisiana.

The works of Maryse Condé, Assia Djebar, and Leïla Sebbar make concretely visible the dialectical tensions present in Amselle's or Appiah's theorizing, and shed new light on what previous generations of francophone critics had taught us to regard as an "alienating" contact between cultures, one in which the dominant group names and circumscribes the subjected one, instilling a colonized or victim mentality in the latter. What these writers illustrate instead are the dynamic and creative processes mobilized by subgroups as means of resistance to the "victim" syndrome. They use their transformative and performative energies on the language and narrative strategies they borrow from the cultures of the West. To represent their regional cultural realities, they make use of appropriative techniques that interweave traditions and languages. The way they portray characters transforms the way that *they* themselves see the realities of their worlds, as well as the way *we*—readers who are outsiders to the region or culture—will in turn perceive them: that is, no longer as a radically "other" realm, so different and alien that it could only alienate itself more through contact with the West, but rather as a microcosm of the globe. In other words, these recent works point the way back to a new/old concept: humanism, a word that feminists of different stripes are beginning to revalorize; or to borrow Evelyne Accad's more precise formulation, a "femihumanism," a nonseparatist feminism committed to bringing about a pluralistic society based on the rejection of oppression and domination, whether globally or locally (25–26; see also Kofman). This ethical imperative governs their search for new cultural forms and hybrid languages that better represent the particularisms of the communities about which they write without locking them into idiosyncratic dead-ends.

Thus, for Assia Djebar, the French language leads to an ambiguous situation, because it is the only means through which she can acquire a measure of freedom from the confinement of the harem. Yet, it is also a language in which she suffers from a form of "aphasie amoureuse" (*L'Amour*, 142) [aphasia of love (125)], that is, from the complete inability to express "le moindre élan de mon coeur" (145) [the slightest heart-felt emotion (128)] because it is a language that necessarily creates distance and artificiality. Hence, emancipation is a way of breaking ties that bind, but also ties that create a loving, caring community. For Djebar, then, there is this constant tension between individual emancipation and collective female bonding, autobiography and history, writing and orality, as well as between verbal self-unveiling and the quiet dialogues of bodies and words that the ancient traditions of the harem and the hammam make possible among Islamic women. As she explains,

> Comment dire "je," puisque ce serait dédaigner les formules-couvertures qui maintiennent le trajet individuel dans la résignation collective?...Laminage de ma culture orale en perdition: expulsée à onze, douze ans de ce théâtre des aveux féminins, ai-je par là même été épargnée du silence de la mortification? Ecrire les plus anodins des souvenirs d'enfance renvoie donc au corps dépouillé de voix. Tenter l'autobiographie par les seuls mots français, c'est, sous le lent scalpel de l'autopsie à vif, montrer plus que sa peau. Sa chair se desquame, semble-t-il, en lambeaux du parler d'enfance qui ne s'écrit plus. (177–78)

> [How could she say "I," since that would be to scorn the blanket-formulas which ensure that each individual journeys through life in a collective resignation?...My oral tradition has gradually

> been overlaid and is in danger of vanishing: at the age of eleven or twelve I was abruptly ejected from the theater of feminine confidences—was I thereby spared from having to silence my humbled pride? In writing of my childhood memories I am taken back to those bodies bereft of voices. To attempt an autobiography using French words alone is to lend oneself to the vivisector's scalpel, revealing what lies beneath the skin. The flesh flakes off and with it, seemingly, the last shreds of the unwritten language of my childhood. (156)]

Caught between the urgent need to speak of herself as woman, and the age-old restrictions on self-unveiling, the narrator of *L'Amour, la fantasia* faces a dilemma that is crystallized by the use of French: "L'autobiographie pratiquée dans la langue adverse se tisse comme fiction" (243) [Autobiography practiced in the enemy's language has the texture of fiction (216)]. Djebar can chart the complexities inherent in the problem of domination by suggesting that the construction of self and other, of conqueror and conquered, of France and Algeria, and of the woman as mother/sister/daughter is always mediated by an intricate set of images, words, and spaces that are never univocal. The construction of subjectivity is made possible by means of a complex interweaving of metaphors of imprisonment and liberation that are not set in opposition to one another, but engage as alternating patterns in the fabric of self-portraiture, as well as in the evocation of national and/or female liberation:

> Parler de soi-même hors de la langue des aïeules, c'est se dévoiler certes, mais pas seulement pour sortir de l'enfance, pour s'en exiler définitivement. Le dévoilement, aussi contingent, devient, comme le souligne mon arabe dialectal du quotidien, vraiment "se mettre à nu." (178)
>
> [Speaking of oneself in a language other than that of the elders is indeed to unveil oneself, not only to emerge from childhood but to leave it, never to return. Such incidental unveiling is tantamount to stripping oneself naked, as the demotic Arabic dialect emphasizes. (156–57)]

To bare one's self in the language of the conqueror is at once a form of betrayal and the inescapable consequence of any gesture of female emancipation:

> Or cette mise à nu, déployée dans la langue de l'ancien conquérant, lui qui, plus d'un siècle durant, a pu s'emparer de tout, sauf précisément des corps féminins, cette mise à nu renvoie étrangement à la mise à sac du siècle précédent. (178)

> [But this stripping naked, when expressed in the language of the former conqueror (who for more than a century could lay his hands on everything save women's bodies), this stripping naked takes us back oddly enough to the plundering of the preceding century. (156–57)]

To unveil this elusive female self thus complicates all relations of power and domination, since the female had come to represent the land itself, and the difficulties of conquest and appropriation. But here, emancipation and unveiling come to be the alternating patterns in the palimpsest of history, whereas in *Ombre sultane*, the second volume of Djebar's projected quartet, betrayal and liberation again become intertwined as Hajila and Isma are made to represent two facets of a single female destiny that is emblematic of the same dialectic of seclusion and dispersion, confinement and liberation, individuality and collective integrity that forms the basis of Djebar's continuing reflections on the process of othering, and the problems of being other in one's own culture.

Within the Caribbean context, the focus has been somewhat different, given that writers, ever since Jacques Roumain's *Gouverneurs de la rosée* or Aimé Césaire's *Cahier d'un retour au pays natal*, had been engaged in an enterprise of "creolization" of the French language. Among women writers, Simone Schwarz-Bart and Maryse Condé represent the most interesting examples of this phenomenon, although their respective use of language differs considerably. When it was published in 1972 to great critical and popular acclaim, *Pluie et vent sur Télumée Miracle* did much to revitalize the genre of the Caribbean novel by harmonizing the creole vernacular and a rich and subtle metropolitan syntax. But that was in large part because, unlike Condé's *Traversée de la mangrove*, it did not need to contain a glossary of Creole terms: the French language is appropriated and enriched without apparent syntactic or semantic dislocation. The French reader can approach Schwarz-Bart's text and enjoy its exoticism without feeling too disoriented: s/he can entertain the illusion that the protagonists are from a completely different cultural sphere, but that they are knowable, and the language of the text perpetuates this illusion. The originality of Schwarz-Bart is to have succeeded in translating into French a uniquely Caribbean way of perceiving the world: proverbs and oral tales communicate an ancient wisdom. Her use of narrative devices common to the tradition of oral storytelling, and her deft mixture of genres (fable, legend, historical chronicle, and realist descriptions) give this novel a richness of tone and a depth of meaning that make it a major landmark in Caribbean women's writing. But in many ways, it is also a transitional one. Thematically it is linked, as critic Roger Toumson holds, to the "mythe idéologique de la quête identitaire" [ideological myth of the identitary quest] by its portrayal of male revolt (Amboise), and its emphasis on the painful history of slavery that continues to have a profound impact on the life of its female characters Toussine, Victoire, and Télumée (497). *Pluie et vent* thus corresponds to certain expectations that the non-Caribbean reader has about "traditional" Antillean culture, and that the French have about the natural and timeless beauty of the tropics. The novel also satisfies the convention of the Caribbean "roman paysan," a genre that begins with Jacques Roumain's *Gouverneurs de la rosée.*

Condé's *Traversée* also belongs in that tradition of rural novels, but it is a resolutely contemporary work, without the mythic atemporality of Schwarz-Bart's novel. Condé's characters are multifaceted and live in the present, going about their daily lives, self-possessed, and speaking Creole. They do not live under the gaze of the colonizer, they are self-assured in their difference, and they do not—it seems to me—correspond to any existing metropolitan stereotypes about the Antilles. The text does not mythify them, nor does it reveal traces of nostalgia or discontent about the (pre)colonial past, although the past is present in the person of Xantippe, the former slave and "nèg mawon" (255) [runaway black], and in the figure of Francis Sancher, the former revolutionary and disillusioned intellectual. As Xantippe says, "le temps de la vengeance est passé" (259) [the time for vengeance is now past].

This is indeed the first time that Condé has a truly Caribbean audience in mind: although published in Paris, like her previous books, *Traversée* is not written for a French public. Creole words and expressions are translated at the bottom of each page, but this was done after the fact, as a favor to the French reader, and on the recommendation of Condé's editor. Aside from this linguistic *dépaysement*, the text offers no major cultural surprises: the cast of characters is a familiar one for a rural community, with its conflicts among families, its storytellers and teachers, its village idiot and its healer, its migrant workers and other outsiders who bear the brunt of xenophobic reactions on the part of long-time residents. These characters live, love, and die in Rivière au Sel as do humans everywhere. Because the village is isolated, it is possible to identify particularisms that have disappeared from more urban settings in other parts of the Caribbean—but by the same token, these rural characteristics are not unlike those that might be shared by a similarly isolated village in the heart of France's Berry, for example.[12]

One might surmise, then, that an anthropologist looking for "culture" and difference in Rivière au Sel would initially be disappointed, as were Renato and Michelle Rosaldo when they did their fieldwork among Filipinos who are generally viewed by anthropologists as "people without culture" because, having been "acculturated" by three and a half centuries of (Spanish then American) colonial rule, they are not all that "different": they are "rational, not cultural," and "to the ethnographic gaze, these civilized people appear too transparent for study; they seem *just like us*: materialistic, greedy, and prejudiced."[13] The point, of course, as Rosaldo suggests, is that it is precisely those "zones of cultural invisibility" (78) that pose the most compelling questions for contemporary critics and theorists because that is where the transcultural process, through appropriation and contestation, manifests itself with clarity. It is because "they" appear to be like "us" (Western readers), because "they" are involved in "universal" human problems that the characters of *Traversée* are subversive: they undo that opposition between "us" and "them" which is indispensable to the representation of the exotic other in art, literature, or ethnography.[14] The villagers of *Traversée*, like Rosaldo's Filipinos, are human beings whose cultural production and consumption defy the West's attempt to exoticize them.

To refute the paradigm of exoticism and/or victimization, Condé skillfully depicts a self-sufficient community unburdened by crises of identity. She gives voice to each one of a series of characters with a unique perspective on the events that have caused them all to assemble at the wake for Francis Sancher, the stranger whose presence in Rivière au Sel caused some major changes in the relations among the villagers. As a figure that allegorizes both the colonial process and the fate of nomadic intellectuals such as Maryse Condé herself, he is a cleverly drawn character who enters into a complicated relationship with the local *habitants*. He allows Condé to be self-reflexive about her writing, and about the role of writing in her own cultural context (203). Condé appropriates the technique of the novel within the novel to reflect upon the role of the writer as outsider, and of the outsider as catalyst or *pharmakon*, as both poison and antidote, dangerous supplement, chronicler, and *aide-mémoire* of the community.[15]

The organization of the story follows the classic unities of time, place, and plot. Condé borrows from classical and modernist esthetics to create a novel that represents "créolité" in all of its complexity. The Creole and Indian characters voice their own unique perspectives, and it is through them that Condé the writer achieves a sense of her own humility as a recorder and transcriber of reality, a role very much unlike the heroic and prophetic ones that male writers such as Césaire or Glissant espoused as poets and leaders of the community.

For Leïla Sebbar, who writes from within France, the postcolonial condition is synonymous with exile and nomadism, literary *métissage*, and bicultural identity. The theme of immigration is central to all her works, and she focuses on the *Beurs*, the second generation descendents of Algerian immigrants, on "marginal" types of all sorts (runaways, drug addicts) who live in the "border zones" of French cities, on regional peasant culture, and also on historical or literary characters whose mythic lives as nomads and ex-centrics fascinate her: Rimbaud, Flora Tristan, Isabelle Eberhardt, V. S. Naipaul, Jeanne d'Arc, Phoolan Devi, or the Dahoman amazons of the eighteenth century. Her characters are from nowhere and everywhere, they are emblematic of the shock of societies resulting from the major upheavals of (de)colonization. The very concept of the French "hexagon" and the notion of "francité" are questioned in her novels and essays. She belongs, it seems to me, both to French and francophone literature and her writing undermines our academic distinction between "French" and "francophone" areas.[16]

Her *Shérazade* trilogy consists in a geographic and symbolic journey through the signifying system of French orientalisms. A seventeen-year-old runaway who knows very little about her Algerian heritage, Shérazade embarks on a hitch-hiking trip through the hexagon that will allow her to discover the Orient, and the meeting of East and West, through the paintings of nineteenth- and early twentieth-century artists. She writes in a set of notebooks, the title of which is the same as the one Sebbar gives to the second book in the trilogy: here too, self-reflexive devices allow Sebbar to comment both on the status of writing, and on the social problems faced by her characters. If, as Michel Foucault has argued, "we are in the epoch of simultaneity...of juxtaposition...of the near and far, of the side-by-side, of the dispersed...[an] epoch...in which space takes for us the form of relations among sites" (22–23), then Sebbar's narratives are exemplary of a condition of hybridity that allows different historical and spatial configurations to coexist. By reading texts and images of the past in order to understand her own situation as a postcolonial nomad, Shérazade uses all the means at her disposal to survive and contest the negative representations of oriental women that are embedded in the dominant culture. Sebbar gives her character the opportunity to refuse to be made into an "other": although subjected to the male gaze of Julien or Gilles, who can only perceive her through orientalist codes, Shérazade is able to manipulate those codes, to historicize them, and to point to the historical Arab or Saracen influences on southern France, to the always already hybrid nature of French culture: "Tu sais que les guerriers musulmans arrivaient en Gaule avec leurs familles? Ils venaient de loin, depuis l'Arabie en passant par l'Égypte, l'Afrique, l'Atlas. Il y avaient des Mozarabes, des Juifs, des captifs chrétiens ralliés à l'islamisme, des Berbères islamisés" (*Les Carnets*, 264) [Do you know that Muslim warriors would arrive in Gaul with their families? They came from far away, from Arabia, via Egypt, Africa, the Atlas mountains. There were Mozarabs, Jews, Christian prisoners who had become allies of Islam, and Islamized Berbers].

Contrary to popular views that hold that "la France profonde" of the provinces is the purer, more authentic France (unlike cosmopolitan urban centers), Sebbar stages heterogeneity among rural people as well. There, regional patois reinforce difference and plurality:

> —Je ne sais pas leur langue, dit Shérazade.
>
> —Moi, je sais parler l'alsacien dit Marie, mais c'est pas le patois d'ici. L'alsacien c'est une langue; mon père m'a toujours dit ça et il m'interdit de dire que les paysans parlent en patois; il dit que c'est aussi une langue et qu'on doit pas les mépriser. (168)
>
> [—I can't speak their language, Sherazade said.
>
> —I can speak Alsatian, Marie said, but that's not the same dialect as the one spoken here. Alsatian is a language; my father always tells me this, and he forbids me from saying that peasants speak patois; he says that it is a language, and that they should not be despised.]

Sebbar's emphasis on regional minorities mirrors the postcolonial thematics of diversity. Here, as in *Traversée*, peasant culture is represented in all of its complexity, while it is implicitly contrasted to the appropriative gestures of the young urban *Beurs* whose dress codes reflect their postcoloniality:

> —Bon, alors ils disent que c'est leur look à eux, leur style, que personne peut leur piquer parce qu'ils sont les seuls à oser mettre en même temps une chéchia, tu sais ce que c'est? comme leurs ancêtres de là-bas et un jean comme tous les jeunes de partout, ou un battle dress des stocks américains ou une veste de smoking qu'ils trouvent aux Puces, ou un boléro brodé....Tu comprends...les habits traditionnels de leurs grand-pères turcs, arabes, berbères, africains sont à eux et les habits européens sont à tout le monde et eux, leur look, c'est de tout mélanger, mais pas n'importe comment, c'est très étudié. (159)

> [Well, they say that this look is theirs alone. It is a unique style, and nobody can steal it from them because they are the only ones who dare to wear a chechia, you know what that is? like their ancestors from overthere, along with a pair of blue jeans like young people everywhere, or an American combat uniform or a smoking jacket found at the flea market, and an embroidered bolero....You see...the traditional clothes of their Turkish, Arab, Berber, African grandfathers are theirs, and European clothes belong to everybody, and their look, well, it is to mix everything, but not just any old way, it is a very carefully studied way.]

Dress is a signifying system that denotes not just the global process of neocolonialism and assimilation ("un jean comme tous les jeunes de partout"), but the *Beurs'* own rich construction of their lives and transcultural identities, their sense of how the past and the present, the near and the far, come together in the material things that they use, in the practices that they adopt. Their control over their sense of personal identity is evident in this creative use of the means of self-representation, in the "logique métisse" of their sense of self.

Not surprisingly, Sebbar's text reveals the same conscious control of the means of representation. *Les Carnets* draws a new geography of France from Marseille to the Ile de Ré, from Narbonne to Nantes. In its formal organization, the text integrates the voices and the idioms of regional or immigrant minorities, numerous intertextual references to eighteenth- and nineteenth-century travel narratives as well as to traditional and classical Arabic texts, to film, operatic music, and popular culture represented both by *Carte de séjour* ("un groupe rockarabe, rock-métèque," 148) and by a group of female rappers ("rap arabe," 253) who perform at a Moroccan country wedding near the southern town of Castres. Like the *Beurs*, Sebbar weaves her own tapestry using an esthetics of bricolage that carries over into her style of writing, and into the way she actually puts words on paper, since she often writes in cafés, using bits and pieces of paper, "un morceau de nappe, des papiers-sucre, le dos de la note" [a piece of paper tablecloth, sugarcube wrappings, the back of the bill] (Huston and Sebbar, 9). This image of the unassuming nomad or bohemian writer is also in stark contrast to the heroic and angry voices of Maghrebian male writers of the immediate postcolonial and nationalist periods, whose sense of self and seriousness of purpose is derived from an oppositional nativist ideology, and not from the studied ("C'est très étudié") appropriation of such objects and techniques that can transform the relations Rosaldo designates as "inequality, power and domination" that saturate the social and cultural field but cannot succeed in preventing transcultural exchanges.

Although politically and socially peripheral, francophone women writers share with the Beurs this ability to suggest alternative paradigms that maintain discrete *moments* of opposition (translated in dress codes, music, idioms, etc.) without necessarily becoming a counterideology. Such moments are not part of a rigid system, since each context will generate different practices (the metaphoric link between territorial conquest and the rape of women in Algeria, the use of Creole in the Caribbean, and rap music in France) that make visible both the dominant culture's power to impose meaning, and the social actors' power of agency over configurations that will ultimately undermine those meanings. The practices thus serve to delegitimate the cultural hegemony of "French" culture over "francophone" realities.

What the writings I have briefly surveyed suggest, then, is that the old dichotomies are no longer tenable, that the local and the global are increasingly interrelated, and that one cannot be fully understood without reference to the other. But at the same time, it becomes clear that universality would be an empty proposition without the gendered specificities offered by particular writers representing different cultural configurations. Francophone women novelists offer us rich and varied ways of understanding this contemporary dialectic—and the ways in which it reweaves the problematics of classical European humanism into a new tapestry in which there can be no room for the normative approaches of the past.

NOTES

1. Rosaldo uses this term in reference to areas of Hispanic influence in the United States.

2. For a more developed analysis of the novels discussed here, see Lionnet, "*Traversée*" and "Parcours."

3. I use "discourse" in Foucault's sense. See *Archaeology*.

4. As Albert Memmi has indeed pointed out in *The Colonizer and the Colonized*, "it is the colonized who is the first to desire assimilation, and it is the colonizer who refuses it to him" (125), because to assume "that the colonizer could or should accept assimilation and, hence, the colonized's emancipation, means to topple the colonial relationship" (126). Assimilation is thus a fiction uneasily perpetuated by a hegemonic system that simultaneously fears what it wrongly perceives to be inevitable.

5. One notable exception is the work of historian Mechal Sobel, who analyzes the contributions that African notions of time and space made to the slaveowner's *Weltanschauung*, thus becoming part and parcel of the Southerner's perception of reality.

6. In a recent talk at the Program of African Studies at Northwestern University, Jean Comaroff gave a fascinating account of late nineteenth-century practices of South African blacks who were adopting Western clothing, including Victorian wedding gowns and suits.

7. Appiah notes that the African sculpture, *Man with a Bicycle*, is

> a figure who is...polyglot—speaking Yoruba and English, probably some Hausa and a little French for trips to Cotonou or Cameroon...*Man with a Bicycle* is produced by someone who does not care that the bicycle is the white man's invention: it is not there to be Other to the Yoruba Self; it is there because someone cared for its solidity; it is there because it will take us further than our feet will take us; it is there because machines are now as African as novelists. ("Is the Post- in Post-modernism," 357)

8. My emphasis; all translations are mine unless otherwise noted. I have discussed "transculturation" and its relationship to *métissage* in *Autobiographical Voices* (16). The concept of transculturation was first advanced by Fernando Ortiz, as Morejón explains. However, Ortiz's view of culture promotes a form of transculturation that implies the assimilation of Afro-Cuban culture *into* Hispanic culture. Morejón's *transculturación* is more dialectical, as is my term *métissage*. I should add that the present essay was written long before the publication of Mary Louise Pratt's "Arts of the Contact Zone" (an essay excerpted from her book, *Imperial Eyes: Travel Writing and Transculturation*), in which she makes use of the term "autoethnography" much in the same way that I have used the term in my 1989 book, although the corpus she studies, and her approach, are different from mine.

9. This is true both in the Caribbean (see Bernabé, *Eloge*) and in the Indian Ocean (see Sam-Long).

10. For a discussion of the linguistic originality of some of these works, see Bernabé, "Le travail"; LeClézio; Lionnet, "*Traversée*"; Zimra, "Assia Djebar" and "In Her Own Write."

11. Amselle's work thus intersects with that of Anderson, Hobsbawm and Ranger, and Wagner. For a detailed and thorough examination of some of these issues from a different perspective that emphasizes the importance of relativism as a mode of intercultural critique, see Miller, especially chapters one and two.

12 I mention the Berry because it is a mostly agricultural region of France, noted for its healers and storytellers. Marie-Blandine Ouedraogo, discussing the shortcomings of ethnographic representations and the problems of the women's movement in Upper Volta, makes a similar point:

> On a parfois l'impression que les ethnologues ne s'intéressent pas beaucoup à la vie des femmes...qu'elles cherchent à tout prix à découvrir un autre système tout à fait étranger au leur, qu'elles tiennent à se démarquer de nous.
>
> Moi, je trouve que tu mettrais une Africaine devant une paysanne européenne et tu ne verrais pas tellement de différence. De la même manière, une Blanche urbaine ne me paraît pas très différente d'une Africaine des villes. Quand celle-ci veut entrer en contact avec les femmes villageoises, elle rencontre les mèmes difficultés, la même méfiance que l'européenne. (33)
>
> [Sometimes it seems that female ethnologists are not very interested in women's lives...that they try, at all cost, to discover a system completely foreign to their own, that they insist on differentiating themselves from us.
>
> I think that if you were to compare an African woman with a European peasant woman, you would not see a whole lot of differences. Similarly, a white urban woman does not seem to me to be that different from an urban African woman. When the latter wants to communicate with a village woman, she encounters the same difficulties, the same level of suspicion as a European woman does].

13. The Rosaldos were studying the Ilongots who "lacked the ethnographic staples of the day: lineages, villages, men's houses, elaborate rituals..." (77).

14. Hence, these characters are the counterpart of the Man with a Bicycle as described by Appiah (see note 7 above). For an interesting discussion of the issue of cultural and historical relativism, see Mohanty.

15. I use the term in the Greek sense made familiar by Jacques Derrida: "Le pharmakon est ce supplément dangereux qui entre par effraction dans cela même qui voudrait avoir pu s'en passer" (126).

16. On Sebbar and the Beurs, see Mortimer, Woodhull, and the two works cited by Laronde.

WORKS CITED

Accad, Evelyne. *Sexuality and War: Literary Masks of the Middle East.* New York: New York University Press, 1990.

Amselle, Jean-Loup. *Logiques métisses: Anthropologie de l'identité en Afrique et ailleurs.* Paris: Payot, 1990.

Anderson, Benedict. *Imagined Communities.* London: Verso, 1983.

Appiah, Kwame Anthony. "Is the Post- in Postmodernism the Post- in Postcolonial?" *Critical Inquiry* 17 (Winter 1991): 336–57.

———. "Out of Africa: Topologies of Nativism." *Yale Journal of Criticism* 2:1 (1988): 153–78.

Bernabé, Jean. "Le travail de l'écriture chez Simone Schwarz-Bart." *Présence africaine* 121/122 (1982): 166–79.

Bernabé, Jean, Patrick Chamoiseau, and Raphaël Confiant. *Eloge de la créolité.* Paris: Gallimard, 1989.

Bernard, James. "Why The World Is After Vanilla Ice." *New York Times,* 3 February 1991, sec. 2: 1, 26.

Césaire, Aimé. "Notebook of a Return to the Native Land." *The Collected Poetry.* Trans. Clayton Eshleman and Annette Smith. Berkeley: University of California Press, 1983.

Clifford, James. *The Predicament of Culture: Twentieth Century Ethnography, Literature and Art.* Cambridge, MA: Harvard University Press, 1988.

Comaroff, Jean. *Of Revelation and Revolution: Christianity, Colonialism, and Consciousness in South Africa.* Chicago: University of Chicago Press, 1991.

Condé, Maryse. *La Parole des femmes: Essai sur des romancières des Antilles de langue française.* Paris: L'Harmattan, 1979.

———. *Traversée de la mangrove.* Paris: Mercure de France, 1986.

Derrida, Jacques. "La Pharmacie de Platon." *La Dissemination.* Paris: Seuil, 1972, 71–197. Trans. Barbara Johnson. *Dissemination.* Chicago: University of Chicago Press, 1981.

Djebar, Assia. *L'Amour, la fantasia.* Paris: Lattès, 1985. Trans. Dorothy S. Blair. *Fantasia: An Algerian Cavalcade.* London: Quartet, 1985.

———. *Ombre sultane.* Paris: Lattès, 1987. Trans. Dorothy S. Blair. *A Sister to Scheherazade.* London: Quartet, 1987.

Fanon, Frantz. *Peau noire, masques blancs.* Paris: Seuil, 1952.

Foucault, Michel. *The Archaeology of Knowledge.* Trans. Alan M. Sheridan Smith. New York: Pantheon, 1972.

———. "Of Other Spaces." *Diacritics* 16 (Spring 1986): 22–27.

Glissant, Edouard. *Caribbean Discourse.* Trans. J. Michael Dash. Charlottesville: University Press of Virginia, 1989.

———. *Le Discours antillais.* Paris: Seuil, 1980.

Hermann, Claudine. *Les Voleuses de langue.* Paris: des femmes, 1976.

Hobsbawm, Eric, and Terence Ranger. *The Invention of Culture.* Chicago: University of Chicago Press, 1975.

Huston, Nancy, and Leïla Sebbar. *Lettres parisiennes: Autopsie de l'exil.* Paris: Barrault, 1986.

Johnson, Charles. *Middle Passage.* New York: Atheneum, 1990.

Khatibi, Abdelkebir. *Amour bilingue.* Paris: Fata Morgana, 1983. Trans. Richard Howard. *Love in Two Languages.* Minneapolis: University of Minnesota Press, 1990.

———. *Maghreb pluriel.* Paris: Denoël, 1983.

Kofman, Sarah. *Paroles suffoquées.* Paris: Gallilée, 1987.

LeClézio, Marguerite. "Assia Djebar: Ecrire dans la langue adverse." *Contemporary French Civilization* 9.2 (Spring/Summer 1985): 230–44.

Laronde, Michel. "La 'Mouvance beure': émergence médiatique." *The French Review* 61.5 (April 1988): 684–92.

———. "Leïla Sebbar et le roman 'croisé': Histoire, mémoire et identité." *Celfan* 7.1/2 (1987–88): 6–13.

Lionnet, Françoise. *Autobiographical Voices: Race, Gender, Self-Portraiture.* Ithaca: Cornell University Press, 1989.

———. "Of Mangoes and Maroons: Michelle Cliff's *Abeng.*" *De/Colonizing the Subject: Gender and the Politics of Women's Autobiography.* Ed. Sidonie Smith and Julia Watson. Minneapolis: University of Minnesota Press, 1992.

———. "Parcours narratif, itinéraire culturel." *Esthétique de la déconstruction et création romanesque.* Ed. Jean Bessière. Paris: Lettres modernes-Minard, 1992.

———. "*Traversée de la mangrove*: Maryse Condé et la créolité." *The French Review* 66 (February 1993): 475–86.

Lionnet, Françoise, and R. Scharfman, eds. *Post/Colonial Conditions: Exiles, Migrations, Nomadisms.* Double issue of *Yale French Studies* 82/83 (January 1993).

Man with a Bicycle. Statute exhibited at the Center for African Art, New York. In "Perspectives: Angles on African Art," 1987.

Memmi, Albert. *The Colonizer and the Colonized.* Boston: Beacon, 1967.

Miller, Christopher. *Theories of Africans: Francophone Literature and Anthropology in Africa.* Chicago: University of Chicago Press, 1990.

Mohanty, Satya P. "Us and Them: On the Philosophical Bases of Political Criticism." *Yale Journal of Criticism* 2.2 (Spring 1989): 1–31.

Morejón, Nancy. *Nación y mestizaje en Nicolás Guillén.* Havana: Union, 1982.

Morrison, Toni. "Unspeakable Things Unspoken: The Afro-American Presence in American Literature." *Michigan Quarterly Review* 28 (Winter 1989): 1–34.

Mortimer, Mildred. *Journeys Through the French African Novel.* Portsmouth: Heinmann Educational Books, 1991.

Ouedraogo, Marie-Blandine. Interview with Joele Meerstx. "L'Africaine: Sexes et signes." *Les Cahiers du Grif* 29 (Autumn 1984): 3-35.

Pratt, Mary Louise. "Arts of the Contact Zone." *Profession* 91 (1991): 33–40.

———. *Imperial Eyes: Travel Writing and Transculturation.* New York: Routledge, 1992.

Rosaldo, Renato. "Ideology, Place, and People without Culture." *Cultural Anthropology* 3:1 (February 1988): 77–87.

———. "Politics, Patriarchs, and Laughter." *Cultural Critique* 6 (Spring 1987): 65–86.

Roumain, Jacques. *Gouverneurs de la rosée.* Paris: Ed. Français réunis, 1964. Trans. Langston Hughes and Mercer Cook. *Masters of the Dew.* London: Heinemann, 1985.

Sam-Long, Jean-François. "Créolie: Les premiers problèmes..." *Expressions: Revue culturelle réunionaise* 1 (Octobre 1988): 11–24.

Schwarz-Bart, Simone. *Pluie et vent sur Télumée Miracle.* Paris: Seuil, 1972. Trans. Barbara Bray. *The Bridge of Beyond.* London: Heinemann, 1974.

Sebbar, Leila. *Les Carnet de Shérazade.* Paris: Stock, 1985.

———. *Le Fou de Shérazade.* Paris: Stock, 1991.

———. *Shérazade, 17 ans, brune frisée les yeux verts.* Paris: Stock, 1982.

Sobel, Mechal. *The World They Made Together: Black and White Values in Eighteenth-Century Virginia.* Princeton: Princeton University Press, 1987.

Toumson, Roger. *La Trangression des couleurs: Littérature et langage des Antilles.* Vol. 2. Paris: Ed. Caribéennes, 1989.

Wagner, Roy. *The Invention of Culture.* Chicago: University of Chicago Press, 1975.

Williams, Patricia. "Pre–Old Law, Post–New Man and the Adventures of Everywoman." Unpublished paper presented to Northwestern University Cultural Studies Working Group, 5 February 1991.

Woodhull, Winifred. "Exile." In Lionnet and Scharfman.

Zimra, Clarissa. "Writing Woman: The Novels of Assia Djebar." *Substance* 69 (1992): 68–84.

———. "In Her Own Write: Circular Structures of Linguistic Alienation in Assia Djebar's Early Novels." *Research in African Literatures* 11.2 (Summer 1980): 206–23.

6

PATRICK TAYLOR

Narrative, Pluralism, and Decolonization: Recent Caribbean Literature

Caribbean society bears the legacy of colonial oppression, exploitation, and marginalization.[1] Amerindians, Africans, and Indians were included in Europe's onward march of "progress," but only as performers of predefined roles in the drama of European empire. A culturally and racially divided plural society was created, its hierarchical structure held together by force (Smith, 772–75). If ascribed racial difference was the primary distinguishing feature of colonial domination (Fanon, *Wretched*, 39–42), ethnicity, color, class, and gender differentiation and exclusion were also central to colonial society. These sites of difference often became the basis for scenes of disruption as the colonized struggled to free themselves from their colonizers.

According to the Martinican psychiatrist and political activist Frantz Fanon, literature is important in the realization of new historical possibilities in colonial and postcolonial situations (*Wretched*, 239–41). Modern West Indian literature is written from the point of view of the plural margins of colonial society. It presents the stories of individuals and groups struggling to come to grips with the processes of decolonization and the possibilities of a new emancipatory history. Postmodern cultural theory has begun to question the project of decolonization, however: is the movement to the new nation just one more dependent variant of the totalizing European narrative? Some Caribbean writers have adopted a postmodernist aesthetic emphasizing plurality and fragmentation. However, the main thrust of Caribbean writing has been directed towards reconstructing an emancipatory counter-narrative in opposition to the dominant European discourse.

CONTEMPORARY THEORETICAL CONSIDERATIONS

Postcolonial cultural theory has been influenced in a major way by the postmodern revisioning of modernity in seminal French theorists such as Michel Foucault, Jacques Derrida, and Jean-François Lyotard. In works such as *Power/Knowledge*, Foucault links modern claims to truth to the exercise of power and production of constraint (72–73). Derrida's notion of *différance* subverts narrative closure by emphasizing the plurality and temporality of meaning—the ever present "differences" and "deferrals" which constitute the human endeavor (136, 141). In *The Postmodern Condition*, Lyotard states that we "no longer have recourse to the grand narratives—we can resort neither to the dialectic of Spirit nor even to the emancipation of humanity as a validation for postmodern scientific discourse"; the totalizing narratives of modernity have unleashed "as much terror as we can take" (60, 81–82). Postmodernism sees particularism and exclusion where there was thought to be universality and freedom, fragmentation and plurality where there was unity and totality.

The Palestinian critic Edward Said, who is very much indebted to Foucault, has shown how the Western imagination has produced the "Oriental" other, which it knows, controls, and colonizes: "The Orient existed for the West" (*Orientalism*, 204). Yet Said is critical of Foucault and states that Foucault tends to lose the possibility of relatively successful "counterdiscursive attempts" ("Foucault," 153). Though Lyotard does see some role for provisional mini-narratives, Said argues that by dethroning narrative, both Foucault and Lyotard are in danger of leaving historical actors without future possibilities: "There is nothing to look forward to: we are stuck within our circle" ("Intellectuals," 50). The problem is that Said himself remains very suspicious of the inherent exclusionary structure of narrative and sometimes risks trapping himself in a similar circle in his treatment of counter-discursive strategies. His distinction between nationalist and postcolonial generations of intellectuals, where the nationalist generation was "honorably dependent on the West" while the postcolonial intellectuals "rescue from out of colonial history the suppressed native voice," risks privileging postmodern, ironical readings of colonial historiography over narratives of resistance and national liberation ("Third World," 33, 39–40).

Gayatri Spivak, the self-proclaimed postcolonial critic, argues, along different lines, that Foucault, in his work with Deleuze, valorized the oppressed and so obscured the difficult task of counterhegemonic ideological production. Critically appropriating Derrida, she uses the case of the self-immolation (*sati*) of an Indian woman who was active in the nationalist movement to argue that the intellectual must learn to "speak to" the subaltern rather than pretend to "speak for" her ("Can the Subaltern Speak?," 295). Spivak has stated that there is a "symptomatic blank" with respect to imperialism in contemporary French theory. In response to imperialism, Indian historians have committed themselves to the subaltern as subjects of history. In rather contradictory terms, Spivak excuses this as a politically necessary "strategy," while emphasizing that it is "theoretically non-viable" ("Subaltern Studies," 209–10, 207). By suggesting that only deconstruction is theoretically viable and reducing the political interest to strategic considerations, Spivak, like Said, risks legitimating a new hierarchical logic according to which postmodernism is superior to and more progressive than subaltern politics. Benita Parry has argued that Spivak downgrades anti-imperialist texts, writes out anti-colonial agency, and "restricts...the space from which the colonized can be written back into history" (34–35, 39).

Like Spivak, Homi Bhabha's work in postcolonial cultural criticism has been particularly influenced by Derrida, though he also draws from the Lacanian psychoanalytic tradition. Moving beyond the idea of the colonial "other" as the "different," Bhabha locates the "other" as a site of the play of *différance*. The stereotype that defines the "other" is based on an imaginary white ideal. In a unifying movement (the metaphoric) the stereotype masks human differences (the metonymic). To be human, the colonized must conform to the white ideal. However, the colonized cannot conform to this ideal and, therefore, constantly disrupts it. The colonized is constituted as subject in the ambivalence of this double movement ("The Other Question," 167). Bhabha identifies a similar double movement in the narrative of the postcolonial nation. The nation as a pedagogical concept (the inherited modern Western nation) undergoes a process of "dissemi-nation" in the performative act by means of which postcolonial peoples rewrite the nation's "disjunctive temporality" as "a dialectic of various temporalities—modern, colonial, postcolonial, 'native'" ("DissemiNation," 299, 303). The danger in Bhabha's position is that in rescuing the narrative of the colonial subject and the colonial nation from stereotypes and essentialist impositions, he risks recovering only the ongoing process of fragmentation and plurality. Parry argues that Bhabha, more than Spivak, recognizes that the subaltern has resisted colonialism. However, by focusing on the ambivalence of colonial discourse, she states, Bhabha, too, writes out "the counter-discourses which every liberation movement records" (43).

Said, despite his suspicions about Western humanism, does state that it is necessary to recover the notion of the "human community" to which differential experiences "all belong" ("Intellectuals," 56). In *The Philosophical Discourse of Modernity*, Jürgen Habermas argues that it is essential to hold on to this idea of human community as a regulative ideal and therefore opposes the intersubjectivity of communicative reason and action to both the totalitarianism of Western subject-centered reason and the conservatism of postmodernism. Communicative reason is practical and is oriented towards consensus. Where power mediates social relations, distortions must be critically understood and challenged in the ongoing process of communicative action. Habermas argues that there is a "counterdiscourse inherent in modernity" based on emancipatory practice oriented toward human community (296–302).

Though Spivak rejects Habermas with disdain (*Postcolonial*, 72), the idea of an emancipatory counterdiscourse that would go beyond the fragmentation of postmodernist discourse is held by some contemporary postcolonial critics. Appealing to Fanon among others, Houston Baker argues that the Harlem Renaissance was neither modernist nor postmodernist, but instead specific to the African-American historical experience and thus a "counter-modernist" engagement in an "arts of liberation" ("Modernism," 96; *Modernism*, 95). Likewise turning to Fanon, Parry states that the colonized engage as historical subjects in the counterhegemonic process of "writing a text that can answer colonialism back" (44). Both Said and Bhabha do eventually return to Fanon's emancipatory narrative. This is particularly the case with Said, who argues that Lyotard has chosen to forget "the new and more inclusive counternarrative of liberation." Fanon's work challenges the metropolis "to think its history *together with* the history of colonies awakening from the cruel stupor and abused immobility of imperial dominion" ("Representing," 222–24; see also "Yeats," 83). Bhabha, drawing from Fanon's analysis of the "white mask," argues that the racial stereotype obscures its own impossibility. Paraphrasing Fanon, he states that the colonial subject, caught in the ambivalent authority of the stereotype, is denied "that form of negation which gives access to the recognition of difference in the symbolic" ("The Other Question," 162). In his expanded introduction to Fanon's *Black Skin, White Masks*, Bhabha argues that Fanon offers the "hope of a difficult, even dangerous, freedom" where otherness is recognized rather than denied as the human subject is "socially and psychically authenticated" (120). Rather than simply jettison nationalist movements, Bhabha recognizes Fanon's significance: the narrative of postcolonial people must be written against the linear narrative of the Western nation, in the performative time of people in search of their freedom, without harking back to a "true" past ("DissemiNation," 302–03).

In Fanon's works can be heard the voices of men and women who have been differentially marginalized according to their race, class, and gender, but who have determined to end their exclusion without effacing either themselves or each other. As emancipatory narrative, the anticolonial story provides possibilities for reconstructing distorted communicative processes by enabling subjects to decipher their own historical trajectories and recreate them as incessant movements towards reciprocal human understanding. Fanon's emancipatory narrative, as a counterdiscourse of modernity specific to the colonial situation, is open-ended and plural rather than closed and singular. Fanon emphasizes that anticolonial nationalism will founder if it does not move beyond mere nationalism to social and political consciousness based on the ideal of humanity (*Wretched*, 203–5; Taylor, 93–94).

CARIBBEAN LITERARY DIFFERENCES

Early Caribbean nationalist works such as Aimé Césaire's *Cahier* (1947, 1956) and Victor Reid's *New Day* (1949) are to a large extent "honorably dependent on the West," dependent on Marxist and liberal doctrines respectively. Though starting with an oppositional discourse of excluded Africans in the Americas, they trace a historical trajectory culminating in the entry of the new Caribbean subject into "universal" history. That "there is room for everyone at the convocation of conquest" is the vision of Césaire, the male poet and future deputy to France's National Assembly (76–77). Garth sets the tone for the final movement to independence in *New Day*: "Give us the right to walk hand in hand in the march of the new Commonwealth—not as subjects, but as citizens—in our island we have proven that race is but skin-shallow and that we are brothers in the depths of us" (338).

In sharp contrast is the postmodern, postcolonial novel in the Caribbean, a very good example of which is Michelle Cliff's *No Telephone to Heaven* (1987). Simon Gikandi has argued that Cliff's aesthetics are unique because of "her realization that the fragmentation, silence, and repression" of the colonial subject "must be confronted not only as a problem to be overcome but as a condition of possibility" (234). True to the formulas of postmodern critics, Cliff's work is full of ironic twists and narrative dispersions, and nationalist, Marxist, and feminist constructions are vigilantly parodied even as they are generated. Like earlier works, *No Telephone to Heaven* addresses the colonial situation in the Caribbean, the legacy of racial exploitation and oppression. However, Cliff also deals with a neocolonial situation where the expectations of joining the various European nationalist projects are stillborn. A conflictual and violent class system in which relative lightness of skin is a ticket to conspicuous consumption, and in the case of males, to power, is the legacy of colonialism.

Clare, the light-skinned, middle-class female teacher, has begun to "unlearn her privilege," to use Spivak's terms (*Postcolonial*, 9). She relearns history as told from the point of view of oppressed African West Indians and joins a guerilla movement whose goal is to transform the state: "It is no mystery / We making history" (5). Unlike the euphoric movement to freedom outlined in both *New Day* and *Cahier* the very idea of this struggle for freedom becomes the object of contention in the novel: whose representation of freedom? The Jamaican nation was born out of a long struggle that would leave a legacy of fragmented meanings. The guerilla rebels consider themselves to be the heirs of the Afro-Caribbean Maroon tradition of Nanny and Cudjoe. They will ambush the foreign film crew that has reduced the struggles of the maroons to an exotic story in which Cudjoe rescues Nanny from an evil forest god. In a bizarre about-face, however, it is the destiny of the rebels to be ambushed instead by the soldiers of the neocolonial state.

Commenting on Clare, Cliff states that the novels "describe her fragmentation as well as her movement toward homeland and wholeness." The tragedy is that for both Clare and Cliff wholeness and identity are to be found only in the enveloping "female landscape" into which Clare's body has been etched by gunfire ("Clare," 265–66). Nanny is dead. The grandmother is dead. Clare is dead. In *No Telephone to Heaven* Cliff bewails the loss of the Magnanimous Warrior: "What has become of this warrior? Now that we need her more than ever. She has been burned up in an almshouse fire in Kingston" (164). History is mystery; narrative is betrayal. The subaltern cannot be heard. There is no telephone to heaven; there are no African gods who can bring salvation, no millenarian possibilities of social inversion; there is no restorative truth; only Ogun, once the Yoruban god of blacksmiths, heroic male god of war, now the madness of the violence and counter-violence of the postcolonial situation.

Despite its postmodernist and feminist sensibility, Cliff's aesthetic radicalism converges with the political conservatism of another new Caribbean writer, Neil Bissoondath. Cliff uses post-modern literary devices in her work to deconstruct its own pretensions to narrative closure but arrives at a vision of Caribbean history as enforced fragmentation. Where are the possibilities? Bissoondath's work assumes the "impossibility of possibility" (268) and belongs to the tradition of his uncle and patron, V. S. Naipaul. A comparison of Naipaul's *Guerrillas* (1975) and Bissoondath's *A Casual Brutality* suggests that uncle and nephew share a lack of respect for Third World people and their cultures, reduce social and political change to absurdity, and depict women as objects to be murdered (see also Mukherjee, 86–87). Only in England, writes Derek Walcott in a review of Naipaul's *Enigma of Arrival* (1987), does Naipaul find his salvation, in "the sweet itch of an old wound" (29).

Bissoondath's alienated narrator, a male Indian professional living in a fictitious island that could only be Trinidad, finds his salvation in Toronto: "I go, like my forebears, to the future, to the challenge that lies elsewhere of turning nothing into something, far from the casual brutality of collapse, far from the ruins of failure, across thousands of miles of ocean" (378). And so the irony: betrayal representing itself as expiation. Truth is the recognition from the vantage point of North America that one has spent one's life polishing shadows and producing fictions, that the empire has left behind only despair, terror, lies. If in the work of both Cliff and Bissoondath history is fiction and reality is impossibility, then Bissoondath has revealed the underlying truth in Cliff's work: history is not made in the Caribbean, but it is made in North America. Both Cliff and Bissoondath risk leaving the Caribbean caught in a vicious circle, devoid of any future, destined to imperial subordination.

In *Angel* (1987), a deeply disturbing neocolonial tragedy, Merle Collins also analyses the weaknesses, falsities, and distortions of imposed modern histories. However, she does so without reducing Caribbean history to the fragmentation of eternal ignorance and loss. Whereas in the works of Cliff and Bissoondath American planes are fated to arrive and quell the brutality of the ex-colony, in Collins' work there is no destiny in the history that brings those planes to Grenada. History is fiction, but fiction can be possibility. Collins sets herself the task of using the novel form to render the tragedy of the Grenadian revolution historically meaningful.

Through the female protagonist, Angel, the novel traces the influence of the Black Power movement on West Indian students in Jamaica in the seventies and follows the graduates back to revolutionary Grenada. The teachings of Walter Rodney and the experience of working in the slums of Kingston taught the students about the meaning of independence and modernization for the majority of Jamaicans. In Grenada they would find the opportunity to participate in a process of recovering national dignity through socialist transformation. Popular resistance led by Horizon (the New Jewel Movement) brings down Leader (Gairy) and his repressive neocolonial regime in a carnivalesque moment. A new regime of truth is in formation but it is open, as yet undestined, its story untold.

If on one hand the revolution opens up the historical process, on the other hand it is at the mercy of new forms of totalitarian closure. Collins spends only enough time on the revolutionary period to establish the revolution's popularity. Of particular importance to the structure of the novel is the internal crisis of October 1983. If the truth of the revolution in process is an open possibility (the performative), the truth of the revolution turned to terror is a self-destructive contradiction (the pedagogical). As the Party's triumphal narrative begins to fragment, the assumption of the new Party line by an anguished Angel is subverted by the interwoven comments and actions of the family members who confront her. Adhering to the Party's truth, Angel will not reveal to her family what she knows about the conflict within. She repeats time and time again that the Party will work out its own problems. In contrast, Rupert distances himself from the Party and accuses it of ivory-tower elitism, while Carl calls it a secret society. From the community's point of view, the revolution is theirs, not the Party's. The Party's conception of its omniscience is the ground for its claim to omnipotence. In the name of historical truth, a particular way of representing the world, a particular totalization, takes over from all others, becomes the totality of human experience and unleashes terror. The thousands of Grenadians of all ages who march, free Chief, and head to the fort meet the guns and tanks of the revolution: joyful faces turn to "mouths parted, eyes wide in faces frozen into silent masks of unbelieving terror" (265).

Though *Angel* is written from the point of view of a third-person authorial voice, it is a female genealogy and a female perspective that is highlighted. The female voice has its own history in relation to the independence movement and the critical response to that movement articulated in the Black Power and socialist movements, providing a site of resistance to the dominant male voice in these movements. Ma Ettie, Angel's grandmother, leaves the estate house Allan has acquired through his allegiance to the Gairy regime. Angel's mother Doodsie is suspicious of Gairy from the beginning and refuses to follow her husband's nationalist line. Angel ventures out to become active in the revolution. In the disagreements between Doodsie and Angel, mother and daughter, the female story itself, as a unitary narrative culminating in revolution, explodes into the contradictions that constitute the differential historical locations not only of female subjects but of the revolutionary movement as a whole. From Angel's revolutionary, socialist, and feminist perspective, Doodsie had submitted to a patriarchal system of domination represented in the first instance by her husband Allan: "You could have been the manservant" (189–90). However, Angel herself falls prey to the Party's new claim to truth. As Doodsie points out, "now some of allyou who fight wid us self sayin is because we stupid and we caan see de truth!...If a few of you see it an de res of us don see it, what you go do, tie us down? Is not so it is, Angel" (267). Doodsie supports the revolution, but will not submit to the Party's truth. She joins her friend Melba in that final, fateful march to free Chief; Melba is killed. The revolution is in disarray, however, and the traumatized mother returns to the security of the known and thanks God for the intervention of the Americans. In contrast, Angel picks up a gun to defend herself and her nation against the American troops.

If revolution in the works of both Michelle Cliff and Neil Bissoondath ends in a barrage of bullets, in *Angel* the tragedy of the revolution becomes the basis of a new beginning. This new possibility is presented in an ethical metaphor: "If youall would stay togedder," states Doodsie to her backyard fowls, "the chicken-hawk won come down an do nutting!" (255, 289). No doubt, any idea of unity is always at risk of becoming a new totalizing principle. However, Doodsie does not represent a mythical, foundational, and triumphal Mother. Collins' novel locates the ideal of community in a history of fragmentation and violent struggle. At the same time, distortions, in Habermas' sense, are confronted in a quest for dialogue and consensus. Doodsie holds her family together and they survive their differences. The tenacity of a people who made history as they challenged destructive colonial and neocolonial regimes attests to the reality of a foundational unity that makes possible renewed social interaction across the terror of history. Against the fragmentation of postmodernism, as bell hooks points out in *Yearning*, there is a need to cherish community without essentializing it (38).

Just as the comparison of Cliff's work with that of Bissoondath is quite revealing, a comparison of Collins' work with that of Sam Selvon is no less interesting. In contrast both to dependent, masculinist nationalism and to feminist, postmodern writing is the open-ended emancipatory narrative that characterizes Caribbean writers such as Merle Hodge, George Lamming, Earl Lovelace, and Sam Selvon. At the center of Selvon's work is the experience of creolization, that is, the transformation of traditional cultural patterns (Indian, African, and European) as they made historical contact with each other. Ethnic and social differences in a hierarchical, racially structured, plural society ensure that creolization cannot be reduced to Westernization. Selvon's works expose contradictions in the creolization process and point to historical possibilities beyond India, Africa, or Europe.

Selvon's first novel, *A Brighter Sun* (1952), and its later sequel, *Turn Again Tiger* (1958), are written from the point of view of the experience of Indian peasants and workers and their emancipatory quest in a Trinidad in transition. The rhetoric of nationalism as a unitary discourse is called into question when the popular classes are betrayed by the new Westernized middle class. Tiger finds the truth of a dependent nationalism both in his work for an American building the new highway and in his ironic return as wage laborer and houseboy to a modern plantation run by a white man. His contact with a white Eurocentric world marks a site of struggle symbolized by the seduction/rape of the white manager's wife. Nationalist closure is further undermined by tensions between East Indians and Africans in Trinidad as exemplified by the relationship between Tiger and Joe (see Poynting, 16–17).

At the same time, Selvon shows how women, separated by culture and race but unified by male-centered class oppression, can provide a potential nucleus for social change. When Rita, an African Trinidadian, gives her own bed to Urmilla, an Indian Trinidadian, protects her from an abusive husband, and delivers her baby, a new human foundation is encoded in a unifying, female principle. Selvon may appear to be romanticizing women's relationships, but the finitude of history imposes its limits: the baby is born dead. Indeed, the independent nation is a fiction, and history is the reality of difference and ongoing struggle. However, Selvon never loses the foundation of reciprocity in human interaction even as he shows how history displaces that very foundation.

Selvon's novel *Those Who Eat the Cascadura* (1972) builds on this foundation in a parody of popular romance, adventure, and travel genres that exoticize the West Indies and West Indian women in particular. A cocoa estate owned and managed by an Englishman in an independent Trinidad provides the carefree setting (Sans Souci) for one of those fleeting encounters between an enlightened white visitor and an Indian cocoa worker. Like Said's Westerner surveying "the passive, seminal, feminine, even silent and supine East" (*Orientalism*, 138), Garry feels the orientalist's "shock of wonder" when he first glances at the young Indian woman behind the sari. Sarojini is a character out of a romantic film, a beauty in a grand and awesome world, acting out "the pageant of life, living in a dream of colour and music, flowers and birds and wind in leafy trees" (36–37, 122). Unable to control himself, Garry dances on the cocoa with the estate women, frolics in the woods with Sarojini, and brings her frenzied fertility dance to its utmost conclusion. The romantic illusion threatens to crumble when Sarojini finds Garry's return ticket to England, but there is renewed hope in the Cascadura, the fish that, once eaten, ensures that one will return to Trinidad. Eloisa's African Trinidadian rejoinder to Sarojini puts the romance in perspective: "Crick, crack, monkey break my back, wire bend and the story end" (182).

This romantic attachment "like in the pictures" (122) contrasts with the reality of the colonial relation symbolized by Kamalla's submission to her master Roger, paragon of white civilization: "Suddenly he was on top of her, clawing like a beast, hot and panting for another rape" (121). Kamalla is not the only woman to have suffered the master's conceit: Sarojini, it turns out, is probably Roger's own daughter, and his regard for her is not without an incestuous interest. Nor is it only the white male who desires the forbidden fruit. Prekash, the Indian overseer, attempts to rape Sarojini just as the hurricane wipes out the village huts.

The Hindu divinities have not preserved the community. The Obeahman fears that the African gods and ancestors have turned against him and his people. The romance gives way to a reality of oppression and to a colonial legacy symbolized by the repetition of rape. Through parody, irony, and humor Selvon's novel subverts patriarchy and colonialism as well as racial and ethnic exclusion. But the possibilities of understanding and community are not thrown out altogether. They remain in the interrelationships between Sarojini, Eloisa, Manko, and Dummy, all of them liminal characters. Even in her escapade with Garry, limited though it is by uneven commitment and an orientalist imagination, Sarojini has not been entirely silenced. Between Sarojini's romance and Kamalla's tragedy is the reality of a new world in formation: Sarojini consoles herself with the knowledge that she is bearing a child. Creolization, as the creation of the new, becomes the basis for an open-ended vision of human potential in Selvon's work.

Cliff's work can be contrasted to that of Bissoondath in aesthetic terms as well as in terms of ethnicity and gender, but is the always deferred social and political vision that informs their works really that different? The important contrast is with works such as those of Selvon and Collins: they belong to a tradition of Caribbean anticolonial, nationalist literature that, cognizant of its own historicity and multiple centers, envisions renewed forms of community and social interaction. Rather than romantically ignore the problems of the formative nation as writers like Reid and the early Césaire tended to do, or tragically present its destined failure as do Naipaul, Bissoondath, and Cliff, Collins and Selvon open the wounds of history to possibilities of healing. The rigid oppositions between modern and postmodern, between nationalist and postcolonial, between male and female, between narrative unity and fragmentary irruption, give way to the complexity of the historical process.

Postcolonial criticism risks creating a new totalizing discourse that, dependent on French thinkers such as Foucault, Derrida, and Lyotard, constructs, constrains, and disempowers the literatures associated with decolonization. As some critics recognize, narrative can open colonial history to the possibility of decolonization without excluding or effacing the plurality and differences within the Caribbean experience: Indian, African, and creole; nationalist and postcolonial; male and female. There is no privileged subject—which is to say, all subjects are privileged in relation to their peculiar subject situations. The struggle for modernity in the Caribbean becomes a counterdiscourse of the Enlightenment, grounded on the possibility of mutual understanding. Recognizing the terror of history, its closure is refused. To return to Fanon, decolonization is an open-ended process of entering history without relinquishing its multiple centers.

NOTE

1. I am indebted to Arun Mukherjee, Molara Ogundipe-Leslie, and the students in my Postcolonial Thought course for helpful ideas and suggestions regarding this article.

WORKS CITED

Baker, Houston. "Modernism and the Harlem Renaissance." *American Quarterly* 39.1 (1987): 84–97.

———. *Modernism and the Harlem Renaissance.* Chicago: University of Chicago Press, 1987.

Bhabha, Homi K. "DissemiNation: Time, Narrative, and the Margins of the Modern Nation." *Nation and Narration.* Ed. Homi K. Bhabha. New York: Routledge, 1990, 291–322.

———. "The Other Question: Difference, Discrimination and the Discourse of Colonialism." *Literature, Politics and Theory.* Ed. Francis Barker et al. London: Methuen, 1986, 148–72.

———. "'What Does the Black Man Want?'" *New Formations* 1 (Spring 1987): 118–24.

Bissoondath, Neil. *A Casual Brutality.* London: Penguin, 1989.

Césaire, Aimé. *Cahier d'un retour au pays natal. The Collected Poetry.* Trans. Clayton Eshleman and Annette Smith. Berkeley: University of California Press, 1983.

Cliff, Michelle. "Clare Savage as a Crossroads Character." *Caribbean Women Writers.* Ed. Selwyn R. Cudjoe. Wellesley: Calaloux, 1990, 263–68.

———. *No Telephone to Heaven.* New York: Vintage, 1989.

Collins, Merle. *Angel.* London: The Women's, 1987.

Derrida, Jacques. "Différance." *Speech and Phenomena: And Other Essays on Husserl's Theory of Signs.* Trans. David B. Allison. Evanston: Northwestern University Press, 1973, 129–60.

Fanon, Frantz. *The Wretched of the Earth.* Trans. Constance Farrington. New York: Grove, 1968.

———. *Black Skin, White Masks.* Trans. Charles Lam Markmann. New York: Grove, 1967.

Foucault, Michel. *The Foucault Reader.* Ed. Paul Rabinow. New York: Pantheon, 1984.

Gikandi, Simon. *Writing in Limbo: Modernism and Caribbean Literature.* Ithaca: Cornell University Press, 1992.

Habermas, Jürgen. *The Philosophical Discourse of Modernity.* Trans. Frederick Lawrence. Cambridge: MIT Press, 1990.

Hooks, Bell. *Yearning: Race, Gender and Cultural Politics.* Toronto: Between the Lines, 1990.

Lyotard, Jean-François. *The Postmodern Condition.* Trans. Geoff Bennington and Brian Massumi. Minneapolis: University of Minnesota Press, 1984.

Mukherjee, Arun. *Towards an Aesthetic of Opposition: Essays on Literature, Criticism and Cultural Imperialism.* Stratford, Ontario: Williams-Wallace, 1988.

Naipaul, V. S. *Guerrillas.* New York: Ballantine, 1976.

Parry, Benita. "Problems in Current Theories of Colonial Discourse." *Oxford Literary Review* 9 (1987): 27–58.

Poynting, Jeremy. "African-Indian Relations in Caribbean Fiction: A Reply." *Wasafari* 5 (1986): 15–22.

Reid, Victor S. *New Day.* London: Heinemann, 1973.

Said, Edward. "Foucault and the Imagination of Power." *Foucault: A Critical Reader.* Ed. David Couzens Hoy. Oxford: Basil Blackwell, 1986, 149–55.

———. "Intellectuals in the Post-Colonial World." *Salamagundi* 70/71 (1986): 44–64.

———. *Orientalism.* New York: Vintage, 1979.

———. "Representing the Colonized: Anthropology's Interlocutors." *Critical Inquiry* 15 (Winter 1989): 205–25.

———. "Third World Intellectuals and Metropolitan Power." *Raritan* 9.3 (1990): 27–50.

———. "Yeats and Decolonization." *Nationalism, Colonialism and Literature.* Minneapolis: University of Minnesota Press, 1990, 69–95.

Selvon, Samuel. *A Brighter Sun.* London: Longman, 1979.

———. *Those Who Eat the Cascadura.* Toronto: TSAR, 1990.

———. *Turn Again Tiger.* London: Heinemann, 1979.

Smith, M. G. "Social and Cultural Pluralism." *Social and Cultural Pluralism in the Caribbean.* Ed. Vera Rubin. *Annals of the New York Academy of Sciences* 831 (1960): 763–77.

Spivak, Gayatri Chakravorty. "Can the Subaltern Speak?" *Marxism and the Interpretation of Culture.* Ed. Cary Nelson and Lawrence Grossberg. Urbana: University of Illinois Press, 1988, 271–313.

———. *The Post-Colonial Critic: Interviews, Strategies, Dialogues.* New York: Routledge, 1990.

———. "Subaltern Studies: Deconstructing Historiography." *In Other Worlds: Essays in Cultural Politics.* New York: Routledge, 1988. 197–221.

Taylor, Patrick. *The Narrative of Liberation.* Ithaca: Cornell University Press, 1989.

Walcott, Derek. "The Garden Path." *New Republic,* 13 April 1987: 27–30.

7

JOLINE BLAIS

Hysterical Bodies, Colonial Subjects: La Mére in Duras' *Un barrage contre le Pacifique*

At the center of Marguerite Duras' quasi-autobiographical novel of her childhood in Indochina, *Un barrage contre le Pacifique*, broods the restless, enraged figure of a mother, la mère. After the death of her husband, la mère works for fifteen years as a piano player scraping up enough money to purchase from the colonial agents a plot of land upon which she and her children can just barely eke out a living. But, like her years spent as a piano player, the purchase turns out to be a swindle—most of the land lies below the tidal floodplain—and the survival of her family becomes even more precarious. Duras' novel tells the story of how la mère, suffering from the injustices of colonialism, moves from rage to writing. La mère's rage first takes the form of hysterical symptoms which include insomnia, migraines, paralysis, and seizures. Near the beginning of *Un barrage contre le Pacifique*, for example, la mère has a hysterical seizure as her son Joseph tells a stranger the story of his mother's misfortunes. At the center of these misfortunes is la mère's heroic effort to reclaim her plot of land from the salty floodplain by building dikes to keep out the seawater. Joseph's story describes the collapse of these dikes and of la mère's desperate hopes to save the irreclaimable land. "Je vais avoir une crise" la mère says and her "crisis" is clearly psychosomatic:

> La mère devint rouge, essaya de se retenir mais sans y arriver... la mère rit de toute sa gorge....Elle était vieille, elle avait eu tant de malheurs, et si peu d'occasion d'en rire, que le rire en effet, s'emparant d'elle, l'ébranlait dangereusement. La force de son

> rire ne semblait pas venir d'elle et gênait, faisait douter de sa raison. (48–51)[1]
>
> [Ma turned red, tried to restrain herself but without success... ma laughed with all her heart...She was old, she had been through so many hardships, with so few occasions to laugh, that the laughter swept through her and shook her dangerously. The force of her laughter seemed not to come from her and was embarrassing, made one question her sanity.]

This hysterical seizure is triggered by the ambivalent memory of the construction and collapse of the dikes, just as Freud's patients' symptoms are also triggered by a memory of the source of their symptoms. Behind this memory is a mother's sacrifice of her youth and her body to her children, a sacrifice made vain by the relentless oppression of the corrupt colonial system which profits from her failure. For failing to make the wasted land productive, la mère will be obliged to return it to the agents. Her desperate efforts and her passionate love for her children make their oppression by the colonial agents especially wrenching to her body and her spirit. But strangely, remembering her most painful experiences, la mère's body shakes with laughter. "C'était la grande rigolade du grand malheur" (53). This peculiar fit raises three questions: (1) How can la mère's memory of her own exploitation be both painful *and* pleasurable? (2) What is the connection between the building and collapse of the dikes and her hysteria? and (3) How are la mère's symptoms eventually transformed into political resistance, that is, writing? The answer to these questions can be found in la mère's transformation from hysterical body to colonial subject, a transformation elucidated in overlapping but significantly different ways in the theories of Sigmund Freud and Frantz Fanon.

One of Freud's major contributions to the study of hysteria is his suggestion of a link between the somatic and the symbolic in the hysterical symptom: the symptom can be cured by telling the appropriate story. His theories suggest that it is not the *memory* of the disasters that produces pleasure but the *articulation* of that painful memory. By telling—or in this case hearing—a story about the traumatic event, the symptom is simultaneously activated and relieved. If la mère can laugh at her own misery, she is laughing in a scene in which that misery is being transformed into a story, here told by her son. The problem with Freud's explanation of the hysterical symptom lies in the fact that he links the kind of ambivalence la mère experiences to repressed sexual desires patterned on an Oedipal family arrangement, thus limiting all hysterical symptoms to complex family dramas. I would argue that the transformation of bodily symptom into a story releases laughter not simply because it is a release of sexual tension, but because a traumatic and unarticulated personal experience—the building and collapse of the dikes—has finally acquired an articulated social form—a story told by Joseph. If there is repressed desire at the heart of la mère's symptom, that desire has been ravaged by waves of colonial violence.

If Freud explored the link between the symptom and the narrative which could cure it, he unfortunately resisted the most radical consequences of this insight when he insisted on reading the symptom according to an obsolete plot, that is the myth of Oedipus. How could a story in which the first female is overcome and disappears (Sphinx) and the second is wedded and commits suicide (Jocasta), be useful to a widowed woman and her hungry children? How can the story of a wandering man who confounds the local daemon, kills the local king, and imposes his own rule, explain the tribulations of a mother battling colonial oppression? Oedipus seems a story more fit to describe the experience of the male colonizer than the native of either gender. A colonial figure of sorts himself, Oedipus leaves his childhood home and usurps the kingdom of Thebes by killing the king and marrying the widowed queen. He then brings a curse upon the land—because of the crime of incest in marrying his mother and leaving the death of his father unpunished—and must eventually be banished. In Oedipus we have the colonial story in miniature: kill the local ruler, take over the kingdom, and find yourself banished for crimes against the people. But since Freud was already convinced of the explanatory powers of the Oedipal story, he failed to see the hysteric's resistance to Oedipus as a struggle to articulate another plot. Instead, he read the hysteric's attempt to describe her situation as clumsy and imprecise.

> I cannot help wondering how it is that the authorities can produce such smooth and precise *histories* in cases of *hysteria*. As a matter of fact the patients are incapable of giving such reports about themselves. (16; my italics,)

According to Freud, the hysteric could not produce smooth histories because she was at the mercy of suppressed desires that made her insincere about what she really felt. Since the hysteric was prey to amnesias and paramnesias, the truth about hysteria had to be found in the symptom, which was "the expression of their most secret and repressed wishes" (8). So, when Dora would not corroborate Freud's claim that she was in love with Herr K., his response to her "No" was: "If this 'No,' instead of being regarded as the expression of an impartial judgment (of which, indeed, the patient is incapable), is ignored, and if work is continued, the first evidence soon begins to appear that in such a case 'No' signifies the *desired 'Yes'*" (58; my italics). While this "No" may indicate a repression, not every resistance to the analyst is a case of repression. Perhaps we need to ask *whose* desire is being represented here.

By making the *body* the source of truth in hysteria, Freud could manipulate the hysteric's *discourse* for his own purpose. If Dora, for example, insisted that she was not in love with Herr K., then it was because she could not read her own body. Conveniently, the unconscious source of truth is inaccessible to Dora but available to Freud. Thus, Dora was labeled hysteric precisely because she denied being aroused by her handsome suitor, in other words because she was not seduced into femininity by a compelling marriage plot. When assaulted by Herr K., she failed to respond appropriately. Freud writes: "This was surely the situation to call up a distinct feeling of sexual excitement in a girl of fourteen who had never before been approached" (28). Dora, however had a different response than what Freud expected: "Dora had at that moment a violent feeling of disgust, tore herself free from the man, and hurried past him" (28). The problem with this scene was that it did not conform to the proper Oedipal narrative. Dora ought to have been able to transfer her passionate love for her father onto this substitute. But since she did not, she ruined Freud's plot. And to ruin the Oedipal plot was, in Freud's words, to be hysterical:

> In this scene...the behavior of this child of fourteen was already entirely and completely hysterical. I should without question consider a person hysterical in whom an occasion for sexual excitement elicited feelings that were preponderantly or exclusively unpleasurable. (28)

Dora's primary symptom was disgust, a repudiation of this particular scene of sex. Her explanation echoed her behavior, but Freud chose to ignore her words. If Dora was a proper woman, then her disgust was really suppressed desire, rather than articulation of resistance to her culturally mandated and biologically reinforced role.

Thus if hysteria begins as a woman's somatic and symbolic resistance to a plot against her agency, it is later seized upon by Freudian psychoanalysis as evidence for its theories of repression. Monique David-Ménard suggests this critique when she writes in her study, *Hysteria From Freud to Lacan*, "in the Darstellung of jouissance [the scene of the hysterical symptom], hysterics are struggling directly with the symbolic. In other words, we may wonder what type of man makes a woman hysterical" (182). What David-Ménard highlights here is the hysteric's context: the hysteric is responding to an external situation in which privileged men have not only political and economic hegemony but also symbolic mastery, precisely the situation of Dora and of la mère in *Un barrage contre le Pacifique*. But Freud makes two crucial errors in the Dora case that recur through his work on hysteria: (1) He narrows Dora's "external situation" to the family romance and its psychological manifestations, rather than reading the family as the microcosm of larger political and economic forces like patriarchy or colonialism; and (2) while emphasizing the importance of maternal figures, Freud completely trivializes the importance of Dora's real mother. Thus in Freud's theories we find no plot that can convey the mother's version of her own story.

Only while "writing up" his analysis of Dora was Freud able to hear the "pre-Oedipal" story working through Dora's dreams and statements. But while he recognized that the bond of affection between Dora and Frau K. may have been the most important one, he still insisted on reading this according to an Oedipal configuration. This meant that it was the "little man" in Dora that desired the woman in Frau K., rather than a woman longing for the love of another woman. This blind spot over the homosexual potential between women is consistent with Freud's complete dismissal of Dora's mother from his analysis. Given Freud's attribution of maternal characteristics to Dora, his attention to the Sistine Madonna in Dora's dream, and his interest in Dora's identification with Frau K. which included caring for her children, this dismissal of Dora's own mother in his analysis is peculiar. Dora's fascination with maternal jouissance implicit in her adoration of both the Sistine Madonna and her admiration for Frau K. suggests a much more complex relation to the maternal. This makes Freud's negative and dismissive characterization of Dora's relationship to her mother suspect. "The daughter [Dora] looked down on her mother," he writes, "and used to criticize her mercilessly, and she had withdrawn completely from her influence" (20). When Freud does tackle the issue of inheritance in a long footnote, he briefly alludes to the possibility that "pathological conditions such as her mother's must also imply a hereditary predisposition" (20–21, n. 1). However he quickly dismisses the importance of the mother, and expatiates instead on the increasing correlation he finds between fathers with syphilis and daughters with hysteria.[2] In fact the problem of telling a smooth story while taking the mother into account seems to be more Freud's problem than Dora's. It seems as though Freud can only tell a coherent story himself if he highlights the father/daughter connection—a plot he can read into his Oedipal paradigm—and excludes the mother's story.

This story which Freud had difficulty hearing, the story of the mother and of her relations with her children, is precisely the central story ignored by the Oedipal plot, which centers on the hero's adventure at the expense of the suicidal Jocasta. While there are many parallels between la mère and Jocasta—both lose their husband, both have unnatural bonds with their son, both sacrifice themselves for their children—Duras' mother is the subject of her novel rather than merely the object of some hero's desire. The story of the dikes that triggers la mère's hysterical seizure is the story of her struggle against colonial oppression.

Thus while Freud's theories of hysteria shed light on the ambivalence of la mère's response to her son's story, an understanding of the relation between the episode of the dikes and la mère's hysterical symptoms requires the help of Frantz Fanon's theories of the dynamics of colonial politics and mental illness. In *The Wretched of the Earth*, Fanon explains:

> In the period of colonization when it is not contested by armed resistance, when the sum total of harmful nervous stimuli overstep a certain threshold, the defensive attitudes of the natives give way and they find themselves crowding the mental hospitals. (201)

Fanon explains that the legacy of the imperial project is a trail of mental disorders and "ineffacable" wounds. The natives find it difficult if not impossible to cope with the colonial reality and thus suffer from an extreme sensitivity to nervous stimuli. This occurs when the natives refuse to be properly "pacified," in other words when they will not remain in their proper places. Thus to cure a native means to "make him thoroughly a part of a social background of the colonial type"(200). This cure should make us suspicious of Freud's cure for hysteria. For the Oedipal story that could cure their symptom was precisely the one to make a woman "thoroughly a part of a social background" of the patriarchal type. It should not surprise us that one of the groups Fanon studies, the psychosomatic disorders, exhibits symptoms similar to those found in the hysteric: stomach ulcers, abdominal pains, menstrual troubles, insomnia, anxiety attacks, muscular tics or stiffness. In fact, Fanon makes the connection between the hysteric and the native explicit:

> In the colonial world, the emotional sensitivity of the native is kept on the surface of his skin like an open sore which flinches from the caustic agent; and the psyche shrinks back, obliterates itself and finds outlet in muscular demonstrations which have caused certain very wise men to say that the native is a hysterical type. (44)

Like the hysteric who is forced by her culture into a constricted and unbearable gender role, the native is forced into a constricted and unbearable social role. Furthermore, if the hysteric often exhibits an ambivalence about her identity in terms of gender—Am I a man or a woman?—the native also faces a crisis of identity. Fanon explains:

> Because it is a systematic negation of the other person and a furious determination to deny the other person all attributes of humanity, colonialism forces the people it dominates to ask themselves the question constantly: "In reality, who am I?" (200)

The native's sensitivity, his "hysteria," is the result of an onslaught of deep and persistent wounds to the native's ego.

By focusing at once on the woman and the native, Duras' novel points out inadequacies of both theories—Freud ignores the political context of hysteria, Fanon neglects the gendered implications of colonization—and interrogates the workings of both the colonial government and the patriarchal family as they collaborate in the double oppression of the native woman and her children. Thus Duras' novel points us to a postcolonial theory in which hysteria and history battle in the body of a mother. At stake in la mère's battle is not just her own survival and that of her children, but also the survival of the entire colonial project against which she symbolically builds her dikes.

If la mère's resistance were limited to her hysterical body, it would pose no threat to the colonial government. In *The Newly*

Born Woman, which first highlighted the importance of the hysteric for feminism, Hélène Cixous argues that the hysteric resists the patriarchal status quo, but Catherine Clément claims that her resistance is reincorporated back into the family, unless "there is a crossing over to the symbolic act" (156). La mère eventually recognizes the need to speak out of the injustice which produces her symptoms. Thus in the novel we can trace the four levels of resistance articulated by la mère: (1) symptom, (2) speech, (3) story, and (4) text. At the first level of organization we find the subject of the *symptom*: the "I" is trapped in the body, subject to occasional seizures. At the second level we find the subject of *speech*: "Doctor, I suffer from occasional seizures." At the third level we find the subject of a *story*: "One day, I found myself swindled out of my life savings, stuck with a plot of irreclaimable land, with little prospect of caring for my children. So I decided to X, then Y, then Z." Finally we find the subject of a written *text*: "When I write to you asking for my rights, I know your objection, you will say, 'We cannot make an exception in your case, since the law says,' and I will respond, 'If you understood my case, you would see that it is different, because...'" Thus in *Un barrage contre le Pacifique* Duras shows us the stages of political awareness la mère must pass through in order for her resistance to become effective, or at least disruptive. Each stage becomes more difficult to reduce to the same old Oedipal story. Each stage shows the ways a woman, reduced to the condition of a native, can also denounce and resist the violence of colonial authority.

SYMPTOM: BEATING AND CURSING

Julia Kristeva's definition of the semiotic chora suggests that the infant's early contact with the social, economic, and political context is mediated through the mother's body. A threshold between the somatic and the many levels of the symbolic, the semiotic is the first level of organization of impulses and drives which are produced and experienced in the body, but which are structured according to information received from outside the body, from the social, economic, or political context in which the body operates. Since the semiotic is significant but preverbal, it is not yet bound to the structures and meanings available in language or culturally-mandated stories. The hysterical laughter of la mère when she hears Joseph tell her story is an example of the semiotic. While its meaning is difficult to determine, it does start to communicate the tremendous affect—pain, frustration, and anger, for example—attached to her story. Since Kristeva claims the semiotic is pre-Oedipal, it would be appropriate that we get the first manifestations of it from la mère.

Still, this mother's position within her family is ambivalent since, in the absence of her dead husband, la mère serves as both mother and father figure. On one hand, la mère fills the phallic position left open by the death of her husband. Though not always successful, she represents the law for her family, provides financial support, and links her family to the public world via her transactions with the colonial agents. As a former schoolteacher and the primary educator of her children, she also represents access to the symbolic. Furthermore, she follows, albeit ambivalently, a set of values derived from the patriarchal family model which include obedience to parents ("Il fallait lui [la mère] obéir. C'était son plaisir d'éprouver la patience de ses enfants, c'était sa douceur") (110); privileging of the elder son (after Joseph leaves home, la mère abandons her maternal responsibilities though Suzanne is still home: "Depuis le départ de Joseph, et pour la première fois, la mère se désintéressait enfin totalement de la concession") (318); and control of her own and her daughter's sexuality (speaking about giving away Suzanne, la mère says: "Jamais je ne la donnerai à Agosti") (35). On the other hand, as a passionate maternal figure, la mère becomes the object of a compelling non-Oedipal attachment for her children, and a figure of rebellion within the colonial system which seeks to exploit and subdue her. The conflict between her responsibilities as father and her values as mother (this gender ambivalence is a classic trait of the hysteric) makes her a peculiar, unstable figure, a source of profound and passionate ambivalence for her children, whom she both adores and abuses, and a public threat to the colonial administrators.

While it is tricky to trace a linear path between the social influences that order the semiotic within the body and the ways in which the semiotic emerges from the body into a social space, there are moments in the novel when body rhythms and movements indicate a struggle with the symbolic. Michèle Montrelay describes the working out of repressed drives in the hysteric as a series of preverbal pulsations, a rhythm which carries meaning too repressed to come out in the content of language. One such example occurs in the scene of la mère beating Suzanne when she comes home with a diamond ring given to her by M. Jo. La mère gently takes the ring from Suzanne and hides it. Then, after a tense and silent dinner, la mère beats Suzanne soundly and thoroughly. Mired in the semiotic, this beating plays out both the non-verbal form (rhythm) and the verbal content (meaning) of a typical hysterical symptom. According to Montrelay, this movement is comprised of "moments de flux et de reflux, mouvement circulaire qui s'éloigne d'un point à un autre pour réguliérement y revenir" [moments of flowing and ebbing, circular movements which retreat from one point to another only to return with regularity] (27). This definition describes the beating of Suzanne:

> Il y avait bien deux heures que ça durait. Elle se levait, se jettait sur Suzanne et ensuite elle s'affalait dans son fauteuil, hébétée de fatigue, calmée. Puis elle se levait encore et se jetait encore sur Suzanne. (136–37)
>
> [It had been going on for a good two hours. She rose, flung herself on Suzanne and then collapsed back in her chair, numbed with fatigue, calmed. Then she rose again and flung herself once more on Suzanne.]

Each time Suzanne moves, la mère responds by beating her, as though there were a kind of unconscious body rhythm between the two of them. This suggests a deeper meaning to la mère's impulsive flogging than just repressed anger about M. Jo's ring. This beating of Suzanne suggests a physical replaying of her reminiscences, a semiotic reenactment of her misfortunes, from her body onto her daughter's body. Just as the sea rises up to assault her plot of land, la mère rises up to assault her daughter: la mère (the mother) becomes la mer (the sea).

The rhythmic form of the beating suggests not only the ebb and flow of the tides, but also the ebb and flow of la mère's fortunes—against both of which she has to defend herself as the title of the novel reminds us. La mère is constantly devising plans in which she throws all her energy, only to see herself defeated once again. In fact, her battles against the colonial administrators take on the rhythm and proportion of her struggle against the tides which ruin her crops every year. The metaphoric link is clear when la mère describes her cyclical obsession with the building of dikes with her recurrent desire for revenge for being swindled out of her life savings. Furthermore, in her letter to the Kam agents, she writes "un barrage contre le Pacifique, c'est encore plus facile à faire tenir qu'à essayer de dénoncer votre ignominie" [A sea wall against the Pacific, it's even easier to make that hold firm than to try to denounce your treachery]. By substituting a physical task (building dikes) for an impossible verbal task (denouncing the colonials), la mère can express her anger and sense of injustice. As in a symptom, the body channels a protest that has not yet been fully articulated.

The rhythms which choreograph la mère's rage about her situation and are reenacted in the beating of Suzanne are even more complex than at first appears. Ostensibly, la mère beats her daughter because she is afraid that she has slept with M. Jo, compromising her morality and her marriage value. However, la mère has covertly encouraged the prostitution of Suzanne as a last resort for bringing in income which she hopes will keep her family together. Thus she bears the guilt for her daughter's putative loss of virginity. But la mère is also fascinated by the diamond, greedy for the wealth it represents, and possibly even fascinated by the power of Suzanne's sexuality. Consider her ambiguous words: "Une saleté de fille comme j'ai là," she says, then, "Il n'y a rien de plus dégoûtant qu'un bijou" [such a filthy daughter as I have....There is nothing more disgusting than a jewel here {here, the diamond ring}] (135).

La mère's disgust with the ring becomes linked to her fascination with her daughter's sexuality. The "bijou" which is disgusting, the diamond which she at once rejects and desires, becomes the object of the hysterical ambivalence which Freud considered central to the symptom. In Dora's case, it was the jewel box that Freud interpreted as female genitalia. La mère, like the hysteric, at once represses and desires a forbidden object:

> Elle était malade d'avoir pris la bague comme elle l'avait prise, et de l'avoir gardée. Car il lui était déjà impossible de la rendre, c'était sûr. Elle répétait comme une idiote les mêmes choses, les yeux au plancher, honteuse....Quelle jeunesse, quelle vielle ardeur refoulée, quel regain de quel concupiscence jusque-là insoupçonnée s'étaient donc réveillés en elle à la vue de la bague? (136)
>
> [She was ill from having taken the ring the way she took it, and from having kept it. For it was already impossible to give it back, that was certain. She repeated the same words like an idiot, her eyes on the floor, ashamed...What youthfulness, what old repressed passion, what revival of what lust until then unsuspected was thus awoken in her upon seeing the ring?]

The disgusting ring seems to condense the issues in la mère's long-repressed sexuality, a sexuality which disappeared with the death of her husband and which she relinquishes in order to try to provide for her children. But it also represents her guilt for prostituting her daughter, her awe at the wealth the diamond represents, and her fascination with Suzanne's ability to procure in a few months what she herself has been unable to earn in the long years of trying to provide for her children. In fact, the issue of prostitution is crucial in *Un barrage contre le Pacifique*. Suzanne's only positive role model is the prostitute Carmen who insists that colonial culture is a huge brothel. Furthermore, la mère says that if she cannot hope to rebuild her dikes she may as well send her son away and send her daughter to a brothel (297, 234). Thus the brothel represents the corruption of the colonial regime as well as the tragic destiny of an unprotected daughter. It is no wonder la mère feels such ambivalence at the prostitution of her own daughter, because in one way it is a sign that she is losing the battle to keep her family intact.

However, given the years of poverty which she has had to endure, la mère's ambivalence, the fact that she simultaneously rejects and hoards the diamond which is worth twice the mortgage on her bungalow, suggests a fundamental and violent contradiction in a system in which drudgery and luxury exist side by side. As she beats Suzanne "De toute la force de son droit, de toute celle, égale, de son doute" [With the full force of her convictions, with the full force equally of her misgivings] la mère speaks about all of the misfortunes which cluster around her symptom:

> En la battant, elle avait parlé des barrages, de la banque, de sa maladie, de la toiture, des leçons de piano, du cadastre, de sa vieillesse, de sa fatigue, de sa mort. (136)
>
> [While beating her, she has spoken of the sea walls, of the bank [debts], of her illness, of the roof, of the piano lessons, of the cadastral agents, of her old age, of her fatigue, of her death]

This eruption of the semiotic makes clear that behind la mère's ambivalence about her daughter's—and her own—sexuality lies more than just repressed sexual desires. Behind it lies the whole history of her attempt to keep her family together under a corrupt colonial government. If the diamond is disgusting, it is not only because it represents the power of her daughter's prostituted and la mère's repressed sexuality, but also because it represents the injustice of an economic system which exploits indigenous peoples in order to fatten the pockets of the colonial administrators, "ces chiens du cadastre de Kam" [those dogs of the cadastre of Kam] (295) as she calls them. Indeed, Duras does not let the history of the diamond itself go untold. In describing this ambiguous exchange of labor and wealth, the narrator explains,

> ...pour la première fois depuis que les mains ensanglantées d'un noir l'avait extraite du lit pierreux d'une de ces rivières de cauchemar du Katanga, elle s'élançait, enfin délivrée, hors des mains concupiscentes et inhumaines de ses geôliers. (140)
>
> [for the first time since the bloody hands of a black man had extracted it from the rocky bed of one of those nightmare rivers of Katanga, it had escaped, delivered finally from the greedy and inhumane hands of its jailers.

In making this link to the exploited black Africans whose drudgery produces the luxury enjoyed by the colonizing whites, the narrator not only links la mère's rage with the rage which one would expect the diamond mine-worker to feel, but also links the exploitation of blacks in Africa to the colonial exploitation of women in Indochina, the setting of *Un barrage contre le Pacifique*. La mère's protest that not to take it would be a crime (140) may suggest a sexual ambivalence about the diamond, but a more politically conscious reading would point out the critique of private property implied in this hysterical redefinition of crime. In fact, what makes it so difficult for la mère to articulate her rage is precisely that it is based on a reading of colonialism which considers it a crime, a reading no one—except perhaps her children and possibly her neighbors who share her fate—wants to hear.

For all of these reasons, the beating of Suzanne articulates, at the semiotic level, la mère's struggle against exploitation and injustice. To understand la mère's impulse the reader is forced to question the Oedipal subject concerned with his own adventure at the cost of exploiting others and the accumulation of wealth which is at the heart of the colonial project. In this light, la mère becomes a subject which has begun, if awkwardly and violently, to reject the status quo. But as long as la mère's resistance remains in the semiotic sphere, its cost is high—violence directed at her own body and within her own family—and the effectiveness is low—the articulation and understanding of colonial violence never spreads beyond a single thatched roof. If the children begin to share la mère's gut response to the colonial regime, they pay for it by being subject to the violence which transmits it. Furthermore, the beating of Suzanne has no affect on the neighbors, or on the colonial agents in Kam. In Fanon's model, as long as the violence of colonialism isn't clearly articulated, it is also turned inward so that the enraged native either commits suicide or turns on his neighbor. "In the colonial context," he writes, "the natives fight amongst themselves" (248). Once the native understands that the cause of his deep feelings of injustice lies outside himself and his neighbors, then the violence can be directed at the settler. If Freud's hysterics suspected that the source of the violence they felt was the patriarchal family, Freud told them the source was their own desires, thus the violence could only erupt as symptoms within or upon their own body. But because la mère has no patriarch under her roof to subdue her rage, she acts it out first upon her children, and then increasingly upon the true source of her hardships.

Cursing, or the use of abject language, is an example of semiotic resistance in *Un barrage contre le Pacifique* which has a more direct link with the verbal and thus has a slightly larger sphere of influence. If cursing originates in la mère as one dimension of her semiotic resistance, it becomes especially striking in Joseph. Throughout *Un barrage contre le Pacifique*, Joseph's colloquial idiom is marked by curses and scatological interjections. He uses his favorite, "merde" [shit], to express both general dissatisfaction and specific and directed violence. Describing the land concession on which they live to M. Jo, Joseph says, "C'est de la merde... C'est de la merde parfaitement...Et nous on est là à attendre comme des cons que la merde se retire" (59) ["It's shit...it's pure shit...and here we are waiting like idiots for it to withdraw"]. Joseph startles M. Jo with this remark, which, along with the rest of Joseph's rude manners, disables M. Jo's economic advantage. He may be wealthy, but Joseph has no respect for his wealth. Unfortunately, it's easy for Joseph to do this, since he can appeal to racial prejudice. Although never made explicit in *Un barrage contre le Pacifique*, the "M. Jo" of *L'Amant* is Chinese. In this situation, the racial politics are complex because it is the wealthy Chinese who benefit from the policies of French colonization, buying up land from which native peasants and people like la mère are ejected. The fact that Mr. Jo's wealth comes from his father's exploitation of the indigenous peasants who are Joseph's neighbors only makes his rudeness and foul language more justified. However, Joseph's disdain for Mr. Jo may also be a reflection of the only power he can wield against him: his European ancestry and thus supposed racial superiority.

Joseph often opens his sentences with "merde," especially when the situation calls for an affective response. Announcing his horse's death, Joseph says, "Merde...ce coup-ci, il est crevé" [Shit...this time he's going to die] (36). Fed up with the brutal life on the concession after the death of his horse, he says, "Merde...demain on ira à Ram" [Shit...tomorrow we'll go to Ram] (30). Famished, but disgusted by the thought of eating one more serving of stiltbird, he complains, "Merde, j'ai faim...Toujours cette saloperie d'échassier" [Shit...I'm starved...always this filthy stiltbird] (81). Impressed by Mr. Jo's sportscar, he says, "Merde, quelle bagnolle" [Shit, what a sportscar] (42). Learning that the man next to the woman he picks up in the theater is her husband, he blurts out, "Merde, alors, c'est votre mari?" [Shit, man, that's your husband?] (260). In these and numerous other examples in the novel, the literal meaning of merde is less important than its affective force. It expresses Joseph's grief, his boredom, his disgust, his astonishment, his disappointment. But even beyond this instinctual discharge, Joseph's cursing suggest a defiance of the situation which confronts him, a situation which he is powerless to change. Joseph's curses hint at his profound and complex psychic relationship to the abject and to his mother. Nevertheless, like la mère's hysterical seizures and her beating of Suzanne, Joseph's interjections represent semiotic resistance to an unendurable situation.

The fact that Joseph inherits his mother's propensity for rude speech and for cursing suggests that the bond between la mère and her children still has a semiotic dimension, that he is still connected enough to her body to be able to pick up its unarticulated affective states. But Joseph's cursing exemplifies not only his identification with la mère, but also his need to establish his difference from her. Joseph is in danger of reproducing her hysteria. Put another way, he is in danger of losing his ability to distinguish her pain from his, her life story from his. Two instances support this claim: (1) he says he can never forget la mère no matter which woman he is with, and (2) he fails to post la mère's letter to the colonial agents so he can keep it himself. Kristeva defines the semiotic in close relation to the chora, the maternal cauldron of asocial drives and impulses within and against which the subject must differentiate itself. For Kristeva, this chora is related to the abject, since the abject is the not-I from which the subject tries to differentiate itself, a not-I which includes blood, pus, feces, waste, and terror, for example. It corresponds to the anguish and ecstasy of being without borders, such as the borders between life and death, and between the sacred and the profane. Because the mother is the life-giver and primary caretaker of the child, she comes to stand for the abject. If we accept this explanation of the abject, then Joseph's cursing would also represent a rejection of la mère as abjection, an attempt to maintain boundaries between himself and her. But according to Kristeva, this rejection is predicated on a close connection since the abject, "does not radically cut off the subject from what threatens it—on the contrary, abjection acknowledges it to be in perpetual danger" (9).

Un barrage contre le Pacifique, however, problematizes this chora/abject/mother correlation. La mère may be the primary caretaker, but she is also, in Oedipal terms, a phallic figure and the closest access to the symbolic available to Joseph. According to Kristeva, the mother can also represent the symbolic for her child. This is particularly appropriate in *Un barrage contre le Pacifique* since la mère takes her dead husband's role and also has been a schoolteacher and educates her own children. She is one of the few people on the plain who can read and write. For Joseph, access to the symbolic would not mean an escape from la mère, but another link to her. This may explain why he resists her efforts to educate him. That she could use her knowledge as another way of exercising control over her son is evident when she insists on seeking him in Ram, after he has left home, for the sole purpose of educating him.

This may explain why Joseph is on one hand eager to escape la mère's influence and on the other hand her staunchest supporter in the face of her colonial oppressors. But this ambiguous relation with his mother puts Joseph in a double bind. In danger of spending his whole life in the semiotic and symbolic "merde" which both destroys and represents his mother, Joseph is waiting for the shit/ocean/mother to withdraw from his life—it "est là à attendre que la merde [la mer/mère] se retire" [there he is, waiting for the shit {ocean, mother} to withdraw] (59).

In the case of la mère's beating of Suzanne, the semiotic appears as rhythmic movement between the mother and the daughter's body. They are in direct contact, and few words intervene. In the case of Joseph's cursing, the semiotic erupts through language, and so the bodily connection is less direct. While the beating may give la mère some satisfaction, it has little effect on changing the situation against which she rages. Joseph's cursing is also limited in its effects, but unlike the beating, his curses affect people outside the family. He shocks and insults M. Jo, intimidates the colonial agents, and seduces the woman in the theater. Still, the effect he has on people does not fundamentally change his situation. Because cursing is a performative use of language without representational significance, it packs a dramatic punch in context but carries no meaning outside of that context. If the semiotic expresses resistance, its effective range is narrow and its effects often temporary. The semiotic level represents the most minimal organization of hysterical resistance. Satisfying to the hysteric, it has only mild repercussions on nearby others.

SPEECH: FROM SERVANT TO NATIVES TO COLONIAL AGENT

If the first level of resistance to oppression occurs as a symptom in Freud's hysteric and as mental illness or pathological violence in Fanon's native, the next level of resistance involves some form of verbal articulation. And because language is already a shared, social medium, this level of resistance has the potential to be more effective than the semiotic. Of course, this depends on who controls the language and its meanings. One example of verbal articulation in an analytic context is the case of Breuer's client, Anna O. A remarkably clever and creative woman, she invented what she called her "talking" cure which involved talking out her hallucinations and thereby relieving such symptoms as nervous coughing, headaches, and partial paralysis. At the end of the case study Breuer and Freud (1895) write:

> the astonishing fact that from beginning to end of the illness all the stimuli arising from the secondary state, together with their consequences, were permanently removed by being given verbal utterance in hypnosis. *This was not an invention of mine which I imposed on the patient by suggestion. It took me completely by surprise.* (46, my emphasis)

This "talking cure" worked so well in fact that, while they did not invent it, both Breuer and Freud adopted it as their primary therapeutic technique. Thus psychoanalysis opened up a space in which hysterics could begin to articulate their disaffections, transforming symptoms into words.

But this model had limitations. First, although Freud paid increasing attention to these symbolic expressions, he often did so only when they fit his Oedipal model. This meant that whatever the hysteric said became part of an already written story. Second, in dismissing what his clients said and backtracking to the body, he undid their work of articulating distress (moving from nonverbal to verbal). When the words did not fit Freud's story, he was inclined to reinterpret them by focusing on the body. For example, when Dora began fussing with her reticule (a small purse), Freud dismissed her explanation for wearing it (fashion) and produced his version:

> Dora's reticule...was nothing but a representation of the genitals, and her playing with it was an entirely unembarrassed yet unmistakable pantomimic announcement of what she would like to do with them—namely, to masturbate. (77–78)

Since Dora had just denied Freud's explanation that her leucorrhea was related to childhood masturbation, he could override her resistance and maintain his theory by reading her body instead of listening to her words. He justified his reading by saying, "He that has eyes to see and ears to hear may convince himself that no mortal can keep a secret. If his lips are silent, he chatters with his fingertips; betrayal oozes out of him at every pore" (77). After an attempt to connect Dora's hysterical symptom to masturbation, Freud's explanation is telling: vaginal lips speak for oral ones, betrayal oozes out of the body as vaginal secretions ooze out of Dora, both betraying her desire. By reading his own desire onto Dora's body ("Dora wants sex, but she is repressing her desire so she has symptoms"), Freud could read her hysteria as a sexual problem rather than listening to her complaint of being trapped in an intolerable exchange between her father and Herr K. Instead of also taking into account the economic and political context which trapped Dora within her family and made her resistance gratuitous, Freud reduced her problem to desire—either for Herr K. or in his revised view, for Frau K. Thus, Dora was inadvertently reduced to being a player in a game of sexual desire over which she had little control—the condition which she was fighting—rather than the subject of another story she was trying to articulate. So while psychoanalysis opened a space in which hysterics could begin to articulate their distress, it often appropriated their words in the service of its own Oedipal narrative.

Likewise, in the colonial context an opportunity opens up for articulation of the natives' demands: the formation of political parties. Unfortunately these parties are often made up of the "intellectual and commercial elites" (Fanon, 46). Thus while the party leaders are "violent in their words [they are] reformist in their attitudes. When the nationalist political party leaders *say* something, they make quite clear that they do not really *think* it" (46). In the case of both the hysteric and the native, verbal articulation is compromised as long as control over the narrative context remains in the hands of the more privileged, whether the male analyst or the nationalist politician.

In the case of *Un barrage contre le Pacifique*, la mère's attempt to understand her situation and articulate her troubles meets with mixed success. While she has local control over her discourse, she can only speak it in the context of a narrative of colonization which gives her no legitimate voice. At the local level, la mère's articulations function much like the scene of psychoanalysis. Like the hysteric, la mère has an audience, "le caporal," her servant. On nights when Joseph goes hunting, or when she is particularly troubled, la mère often retreats into her room taking the caporal with her, and talks to him for a good part of the night. This is peculiar since the caporal is deaf. This means that he cannot respond to what la mère says except by occasionally nodding his head. Ironically, he is the only character in the novel who is *not* an audience in the etymological sense of "one who hears." Nevertheless, the ideal (that is, noninterfering) audience he embodies, even if it is only a provisional construct, enables la mère to begin to tell her story. Le caporal is a completely receptive audience, allowing her to talk her way out of her distress without interruption or contradiction, both of which are important in the analytic setting. While this situation gives her more latitude than the scene of analysis, her audience cannot be moved by her words.[3] As long as la mère talks only to the caporal, what she says can have no effect beyond herself. She may become the subject of a new utterance, but this does her little practical good. La mère learns that in order for her articulated knowledge to do any good, she must have an audience outside her family. And so she begins telling all the native people what she knows.

In fact, talking about the corruption, greed, and indifference of the colonial agents becomes an obsession for la mère. Once she begins talking to the natives, her neighbors, she cannot stop:

> Elle leur parlait dans l'enthousiasme, ne pouvant résister à la tentation de leur faire partager sa récente initiation et sa compréhension maintenant parfaite de la technique concussionnaire des agents de Kam. (56)
>
> [She spoke to them with enthusiam, unable to resist the temptation to share with them her recent initiation and her now perfect comprehension of the Kam agents' technique of misappropriating public funds.]

The knowledge that la mère has mastered about the colonial agents is described as an initiation, an initiation which marks the passage from symptom to speech, from mental illness to political discourse. As she writes in her letter to the colonial agents:

> Je sais votre puissance....Je sais aussi que toute la connaissance que j'ai de votre ignominie...ne me servirait à rien si j'étais seule à l'avoir. Parce que la connaissance qu'a un seul homme de la faute de cent autres ne lui sert à rien. (293)
>
> [I know your power....I know also that all knowledge that I have of your treachery...would do me no good if I were the only one to know. Because one single person's knowledge of the misdeeds of a hundred others does him no good.]

In her letter to the Kam agents la mère describes the danger of bearing the burden of knowledge about the brutality of the government alone, that is, of being unable to talk about it: "cette connaissance...seule pourrait me faire mourir, pourrait faire mourir un homme rien que d'en supporter le poids" [this knowledge...alone could kill me, could kill someone just by virtue of having to endure the weight of it] (293). Her solution is to talk and later write about her situation incessantly.

Once she understands the mechanisms of corruption and expropriation, her rage can be justified and her situation can be explained as social injustice rather than merely personal sickness. La mère's understanding, however, takes immense effort, and a whole new language:

> Elle se libérait enfin de tout un passé d'illusions et d'ignorance et c'était comme si elle avait découvert un nouveau langage, une nouvelle culture, elle ne pouvait se rassasier d'en parler. (56)
>
> [She finally freed herself of a whole past of illusions and ignorance and it was like she had discovered a new language, a new culture, she couldn't stop talking about it.]

If her explanation needs new language, this suggests that she did not have access to any available languages which could have described her colonial expropriation. And this explains also why her first resistance is nonverbal.

La mère's impulse to talk is not limited to her encounters with the peasants. When she gets a visit from one of the Kam agents, the same triumph, enthusiasm, and hilarity which marks her dialogues with the peasants reappears. In a marvelously funny scene, Joseph challenges the agent to make a full inspection of the land under a burning sun. The agent has heard that la mère's dikes have collapsed and so he wants to verify her inability to make her land productive so he can expel her from her land. But unwilling to make a full inspection for fear of sunstroke, he depends on la mère and Joseph confirming the reports. They do not. They tell him the dikes have been miraculously successful. By discrediting his information, they get control of the encounter. When la mère begins to describe how well her dikes have withheld, Joseph and Suzanne explode with laughter: "C'était un bonheur inexprimable d'entendre la mère parler comme ça" [It was an inexpressible joy to hear ma talk like that] (313). By hearing their mother verbally confront the agent they are momentarily able to avenge themselves. And once la mère begins, she's unstoppable:

> —Salauds! criait la mère, chiens! voleurs!
> Epanouie de colère, libérée, rajeunie, elle se tourna vers Joseph.
> —Ça fait du bien, dit-elle. C'est moins que des chiens.
> Puis elle se retourna vers l'agent, elle ne pouvait pas s'arrêter.
> —Voleurs! Assassins! (314)

> [—Bastards! cried ma, dogs! thieves!
> Enlightened with rage, freed, rejuvenated, she turned toward Joseph.
> —That does me some good, she said. They're worse than dogs.
> Then she turned back toward the agent, she couldn't stop herself.
> Thieves! Murderers!]

Appearing late in the novel, the scene is exhilarating to read since it redresses the injustices borne by la mère and catalogued from the opening of the novel. Furthermore, talk generates action: a new revelation occurs during la mère's tirade. She blurts out that they are the fourth family ruined by the unproductive concession. And when Joseph discovers this, when he learns that their personal misfortunes are not just la mère's fault but are systematic, he has a revelation. He fetches his gun and drives the Kam agent off the land. So la mère's talk produces not only more talk, but political resistance, albeit on a local scale involving one colonial administrator.

It is because la mère recognizes how important language can be as a weapon, or at least as self-defense, that she takes such a fierce position with regard to her children's education. Referring to Joseph's spelling mistakes, she says:

> ...on m'aurait dit ça...quand ils étaient petits, on m'aurait dit qu'à vingt ans ils feraient encore des fautes d'orthographe, j'aurais préféré qu'ils meurent. J'était comme ça quand j'était jeune, j'étais terrible. (348)

> [...if I'd been told...when they were young, if I'd been told that at the age of twenty they would still make spelling mistakes, I

> would have preferred that they had died. I was like that when I was young, I was terrible.]

After Joseph leaves home she makes a scene about his lack of education and insists on going to find him in the city of Ram to teach him "orthography." On the one hand, this could be just another one of her tricks to try to keep her son close by, just another example that she really is a "crackpot." On the other hand, given her own experiences in Indochina, she also realizes how difficult it is to survive without language skills as a minimum defense. If la mère can begin to articulate some resistance to the colonial plot, it's because her training as a teacher has given her privileged access to the colonial language, a skill the natives lack and which she fears her son may also lack. So when she responds to Joseph's spelling mistakes with violence, one can understand why.

Talking goes beyond giving relief to la mère: it begins to explain her strange behavior—seizures, insomnia, violence, cursing—to her children and to her neighbors. It turns personal misfortune into a social problem. Instead of merely being subject to her symptoms, she becomes a subject of powerful utterances. Furthermore, her words involve others in the problems confronted by plain-dwellers. This means (1) the burden of knowledge about colonial exploitation is shared and (2) once understood and verbalized, exploitation can be more effectively resisted. Speech can only be effective, however, if there is someone who is willing to listen, and that person is within hearing range. Furthermore, speech derives its meanings from the larger cultural context, specifically from the available narratives. Since the dominant narrative is the colonial one, la mère's words have limited impact. While she can explain to the native peasants the structure of their oppression, she cannot convince her superiors of the soundness of her demands for justice. La mère must not only verbalize her resistance but revise the story which can make it intelligible to her oppressors.

STORY: PLOTS AND ACCOUNTS

Roland Barthes claims that "the little human 'invents' at once sentence, narrative, and the Oedipus."[4] That is, once a child begins to speak, her words derive their significance from the stories within which they are articulated. Like Freud, Barthes privileges the Oedipal narrative as the origin myth of human culture. While the Oedipal plot may reflect the patriarchal and colonial structures of the French government and society, it does not describe la mère's real conditions. To begin with, her own husband is dead, so her own family lacks the Oedipal figure. Furthermore, as a female head of her household, as a maternal figure, she resembles neither Oedipus nor Jocasta. To make her experiences intelligible would require the formulation of other plots. Fortunately, la mère is a master plotter. If Barthes is right about the simultaneous articulation of speech, story and Oedipus, then what is at stake in la mère's plots is a challenge or alternative to the Oedipal configuration of desire, of the family, and of the subject, the very subject which is necessary to uphold the colonial regime.

Beyond this, la mère's plots also suggest the inadequacy of Fanon's model for her specific situation of colonial exploitation. If the cure for Freud's hysteric is a story—a narrative plot—then the cure for Fanon's native is violence—a political plot. This is because colonialism "is violence in its natural state, and it will only yield when confronted with greater violence"(Fanon, 48). This political plot, however, sounds remarkably like the Oedipal plot, which describes the self-assertion of the male at the expense of the female. If the Oedipal figure both envies and emulates his father and eventually replaces him in an act of real or imagined parricide, Fanon's native has a similar response to the colonizer. Despite his guilt, the native is "ready at a moment's notice to exchange the role of the quarry for that of the hunter....The native is an oppressed person whose permanent dream is to become the persecutor" (41). Like the envious son, the native plots to take his father's/oppressor's place. Thus, while violence changes the identity of the ruler, the oppressive structure of rule remains unchallenged. Fanon acknowledges this when he describes the rise of the nationalistic bourgeoisie, who simply take the place of the colonizers. But even if the more radical event occurred and the peasants—the poorest of the natives who have nothing to lose and everything to gain and for whom violence is the only solution—overthrew the colonists or the nationalist bourgeoisie, they would still be merely replacing the previous class of rulers. Of course, Fanon believed that the character of the struggle would create a new type of man, and that from these new men a national culture would arise that would redefine the nation. Thus in the end, as Fanon describes in his chapter "On National Culture," narrative plots would be required to create and consolidate the national identity. In Fanon's model, violence as a cure for individual mental pathologies gives way to stories as a cure for the new nation's past ills. Still Fanon's new nation does nothing to challenge the gender roles which contribute to la mère's troubles. Fanon's "people" are still men, his "new humanism" is still fundamentally blind to the oppression of half of the native population. What is conspicuously absent in Fanon's analyses of colonial oppression is the awareness of the way gender oppression can be aggravated in a colonial situation so that native women are doubly oppressed under the colonists and never recover any of their precolonial authority once the new nation is proclaimed. The emergence of women's voices from many African nations—Nawal El Saadawi, Bessie Head, Buchi Emecheta, and Mariama Bâ, for example—which are critical of the gender blindness in the politics of decolonization attests to this oversight in Fanon's work.[5]

Because she is both a woman and, in the eyes of the colonial agents, a native, la mère's plots combine an awareness of colonial oppression with an awareness of gender oppression. Plotting for la mère is a survival strategy and la mère is a relentless plotter, a plotter of lives even before she becomes a plotter of stories. The novel opens with a plan to combat the isolation on the plain and to supplement the family income by buying a horse. This instance of plotting out lives that would otherwise be meaningless, uneventful, and thus intolerable soon becomes traceable to la mère. Throughout the novel we see her fabricating stories to keep up her hope, to have something to live for. She plots Suzanne's marriage to the wealthy Mr. Jo. When that plan fails, she imagines that they can get money, amenities like the phonograph, or even rides to the Kam canteen if Suzanne feigns enough interest in him. When Suzanne gets a diamond from him, this becomes the source of yet another adventure for la mère. She first imagines that Suzanne has had to sleep with him to get it and beats her soundly. Then when she learns that Mr. Jo has two more diamonds, she tries to convince Suzanne to resume her relations with him. When this does not work, she takes the whole family to Ram in order to try to sell the ring. Once sold, she plots a strategy for rebuilding her dikes.

Suzanne and Joseph recognize this incessant plotting, and when they realize la mère is making up stories again they respond to her with the same refrain. After beating Suzanne and taking the diamond, la mère worries about not having a plan. When Suzanne responds, "faut plus que tu t'en fasse comme ça tous le temps" [you must not make something of it {i.e. worry} like that all the time], la mère acknowledges her weakness, "C'est vrai que je m'en fais tous le temps" [It's true I do make something of it {worry} all the time] (163) and immediately launches into a frenetic and contagious family revery about being wealthy amidst their abject poverty. Her fantasies are spontaneous and uncontrollable. When Joseph leaves home, for example, and she is near death, she begins another story of going to find him to teach him spelling. Suzanne reminds her, "Faut que tu t'en fasse toujours pour quelque chose...faut toujours que tu inventes quelque chose" [You have to make something of it no matter what...always, you have to invent something] (348).

Beside all the stories she invents, we have evidence that la mère is an obsessive plotter because she is always retreating to her work place. Each time Joseph goes hunting, each time she has insomnia as a result of ruminating on the latest instance of injustice, la mère corners the caporal, and begins to work on her accounts: elle allait "faire ses comptes" [do the accounts {with a play on comptes/contes: to tell stories}] (34). In French the word for "accounts" and the word for "stories" are homonyms: comptes/contes. This suggests that her finances are related to her stories, that la mère's poverty and her attempts to escape it so her children will stay with her are at the center of her obsessive plotting.[6] Just as Joseph is about to leave home, he makes this connection: "Je suis sûr que toutes les nuits elle recommence ses barrages contre le Pacifique...petits ou grands, elle les recommence toutes les nuits" [I'm certain that every night she rebuilds her Pacific sea walls...large or small, she rebuilds them every night] (281).

All of la mère's plots can be seen as part of the same story: the story of her resistance to the injustice of her lot, and her creative attempts to overcome it. The "plot" of land that is the source of her misfortune was itself part of her "plot" to provide for the welfare of her family after the death of her husband. As a single woman in a colony, she would not have fit the Oedipal model, and thus she would have had no role unless she was able to plot herself one. So she did: for fifteen years she worked as a piano player in a movie house so she could save enough money to buy a piece of land. She brought her life savings to the Kam agents and bought a concession, ignorant of the colonial "plot" behind it. Since she was unaware that good plots only went to those willing to pay a hefty bribe, she was sold a worthless one. To make matters worse the deed stipulates that if she is unable to make the land productive within a designated number of years, she forfeits ownership and the land reverts to the colonial agency. So in order to stay on her plot of land she is forced to do some clever plotting (planning and planting). The idea for the dikes—building a wall against the tide which floods her land and leaves it too salty for planting—is her most brilliant plot. But in order to make it work, she has to enlist the support of the local farmers. She does this by linking the story of her past to the building of the dike.

When she tells the peasants the story of her own exploitation, she links it to theirs and invites them to join in her project. She convinces them to help build the dikes by narrating the denouement even before it happens. She describes the stupefaction of the cadastral agents when they see the dike, when they see the plentiful harvest it will permit, when they see they have been duped at their own game. She tells her story with enthusiasm to the point of making the peasants laugh with her. One powerful passage links her ability to plot to her rage and her ability to articulate it:

> Point par point elle leur racontait son histoire et leur parlait longuement de l'organization du marché des concessions...elle leur expliquait aussi comment les expropriations, dont beaucoup avaient été victimes au profit des poivriers chinois, était aussi explicable par l'ignominie des agents de Kam....Des chiens, disait elle, ce sont des chiens. Et les barrages, c'était la revanche. Les paysans riaient de plaisir. (56)
>
> [Point by point she told them her story and spoke to them at length of the organization of the sale of concessions...she explained to them also how the expropriations, of which many had been victim to the profit of the Chinese pepper growers, were also explainable as the greed and treachery of the Kam agents...Dogs, she said, they're just dogs. And the sea walls, that was their revenge. The peasants laughed with joy.]

What is so powerful about la mère's plot is that she has managed to turn—if only momentarily, in the telling—the tragedy of life on the plain into a comedy at the expense of the colonial agents. Just as she bursts into hysterical laughter when she hears her own story told by her son Joseph, so the natives burst into laughter when they hear her plan to foil the colonial agents. By articulating her rage and resistance, la mère's individual consciousness becomes the source of political consciousness. Indeed her message to the natives upon her deathbed is to kill the colonial agents and then hide all evidence of the murder, denying any personal guilt. In a manner reminiscent of Fanon, she counsels them to act collectively and violently against the colonists. The major difference in la mère's case is that since she is more a peasant than a bourgeois, the revolt she counsels bypasses the compromises of the nationalist parties in the Fanonian model. Thus her stories prepare a more radical revolution than the gradual shift of power Fanon describes.

When la mère's first dike fails, she cannot give them up. "C'était une trop belle idée," says Joseph [It was too good an idea] (281). In her letter to the agents she pleads for the five hectares of land beneath her house so she can mortgage them to refinance a new set of dikes. She explains that if she cannot even entertain the hope that her dikes will hold out, it would be better to give her daughter to a brothel and to have her son assassinate the agents. In other words if she cannot plot another story, then her children will be caught in the Freudian Oedipal plot: her daughter an object of exchange, her son a symbolic parricide. The dikes are both the literal boundaries of her plot of land and the symbolic interface between her refashioned narrative plot and the Oedipal plot which surrounds her and threatens to engulfs her. In her words to the cadastral agents, "un barrage contre le Pacifique c'est encore plus facile à faire tenir qu'à essayer de dénoncer votre ignominie" [a sea wall against the Pacific, it's even easier to make that hold firm than to try to denounce your treachery] (291). Thus, when she can no longer plot, when she can no longer entertain a plan to rebuild her dikes, she lies down on her bed and dies of one of her seizures.

Besides her own incessant plotting, la mère tells Joseph the story of her past, a tale he then relates to Suzanne.[7] It is the story of the sacrifice of her youthful body as she worked for fifteen years as a piano player in a local cinema in order to be able to buy a concession for her children, "comme si de mon corps sacrificié il allait fleurir tout un avenir de bonheur pour mes enfants" [as if from the sacrifice of my body a whole future of happiness for my children would flower] (290). Just as her stories to the natives make them understand her obsessions, this story makes it possible for her children to forgive her violence and her crackpot schemes because they know her story. Her tales absolve her from blame in the eyes of those closest to her, thus she is adamant about her children knowing and understanding her story. But her plea is also a warning. Repeating her story briefly on her deathbed, she tells Suzanne that her life has been a failure and that she should never forget it: "Tu le sais, tu le sais que j'ai travaillé depuis quinze ans....Et tu vois où j'en suis maintenant? Je voudrais que tu le voies bien et que tu ne l'oublies jamais" [You know it, you know that I worked from the time I was fifteen years old...and you see where it's got me now? I would like you to look closely and never forget it] (350). Joseph repeats this warning when he tells Suzanne to remember her mother's story and to do just the opposite. If la mère never escapes her own situation, her attempt to plot her way out of it, and her ability to formulate a story out of her experiences, give her temporary respite and give her children the means to free themselves from her burdens when she dies.

As long as la mère's history remains oral, it depends for its effects on having real, empathetic listeners. Without the real presence of the caporal, the peasants and especially her two children, la mère's life (story) might not ever get told, certainly it would be meaningless in a social sense if no one ever heard it. Joseph and Suzanne are especially crucial listeners, since they are the only ones who fully understand her story. If psychoanalysis provided the hysteric with a listener, it was not always a listener as empathetic as la mère's two children. This may be because the analyst rarely shared his client's experiences the way la mère's children share hers. Since the hysteric was often trying to articulate something outside the status quo, something not yet articulated, she had to cross a large gap of understanding. If that gap could not be bridged, the hysteric faced a choice of two unsatisfactory alternatives: burying her story deep in the unconscious where it could only reemerge as a mute physical symptom, or passively accepting the analyst's story.

TEXT: A MOTHER'S LETTER, A DAUGHTER'S NOVEL

Because a text does not depend on the real presence of an actual listener, it can overcome the limits of real but unsympathetic listeners. At the textual level, resistance to the status quo and the attempt to articulate another subject position incorporates all the previous levels: it is signifying, verbal, narrative, and written. Physically separate from the body after it has been written, a text can travel, can be read by others who are not usually physically present to the writer. Within the novel, la mère's letter to the colonial agents suggests her resistance has achieved the textual level of discourse, while the novel itself, the fictionalized biography of the mother by her daughter, can be read as an example of a textualized hysterical narrative.

La mère's letter is not only textualized but it is also interactive since it inscribes the voice of the colonial other within its own discourse. By incorporating the "other" voice within her own written story, la mère makes her personal tale more compelling and more socially significant to the agents. Once she realizes she has been swindled out of her life savings by the Kam agents, la mère's first response is to march into their office and personally insult and threaten them. But her verbal assaults are easily dismissed by the agents as personal grievance rather than as a legitimate critique of their system. Realizing that her insults and threats are ineffective, she spends night after sleepless night composing letters to the agents in the hope of convincing them to grant her request to keep the only five hectares of the concession that are arable. Seen in this light, la mère's insomnia might be interpreted not as a symptom of her own personal illness, but rather as an effect of her desperate attempt to devise a way to keep her land, an effect of the policy which states that she must return the land to the agents after a few years if she cannot make it productive. As she works on her "comptes/contes," her accounts and her stories, she begins to incorporate the objections of the agents into her own story. Her discourse becomes a hybrid, in the Bakhtinian sense, a double-voiced discourse in which she tries to substitute her story, her interpretation of the facts of her case, for the colonial history which gives her no voice (see Bakhtin, 304).

Bakhtin claims that understanding and response are mutually implicated, that one is not possible without the other (282). La mère seems to know this, for her letters plead for a reading and a response. The lack of response by the Kam agents means that they have not bothered to read her letters. For she believes if they once read her letters, they would not only understand her story, but go back to all the previous letters and read those as well. She writes:

> le seule espoir qui me reste c'est qu'une fois, une seule fois, vous réussisiez à lire une de mes lettres...parce qu'il me semble encore que ma situation, si vous la connaissiez bien, ne pourrait pas vous laisser complètement indifférent. (288)
>
> [my only hope is that for once, just once, you will manage to read one of my letters...because it still seems to me that my situation, if you knew it well, could not leave you completely indifferent.]

Her hope, and her belief, is that her words will be able to convince the agents, not because they will be swayed by some logical argument, but because they will understand her situation. Bakhtin describes this dialogic function of language as follows:

> The speaker strives to get a reading on his own word, and on his own conceptual system that determines the word, within the alien conceptual system of the understanding receiver; he enters into dialogic relationships with certain aspects of this system. (282)

What this passage suggests is that a dialogic relationship is a struggle for gaining another's acceptance of one's own version of events. It is a pleading for one's point of view as legitimate. While Bakhtin is more interested in the kind of dialogue that remains undecidable, la mère is more interested in a dialogue that could have real results for her.

The alien conceptual system in la mère's case is the colonial government. And since theirs is the culturally mandated and enforced story, she is waging an uphill battle. But she is clever enough to figure out that one way for the dialogue to work is if she appropriates their version into her own. By including their point of view, she can at least appeal to their self-interest. She writes:

> pour que vous vous intéressiez à moi il faut que je vous parle de vous. De votre ignominie peut-être, mais de vous. Et si vous lisez cette lettre, je suis sûre que vous lirez les autres pour voir quels progrès a fait en moi la connaissance de votre ignominie. (294)
>
> [so that you will interest yourself in my case, I have to speak about you. Of your treachery perhaps, but of you. And if you should read this letter, I am sure you will read the others to see what progress the knowledge of your treachery has made in me.]

And so she describes their taking of bribes for the good concessions, their ruining of hundreds of families like hers who cannot afford the bribe, the expropriation of land from local peasants to sell to Chinese entrepreneurs, the corruption all the way through the ranks of colonial government, the indifference to the starvation and sickness of children on the plain, and finally the mounting consciousness and indignation of the indigenous people as the result of her explanations. She is convinced that if she can capture their interest by talking about *them*, she can convince them of *her* right to keep the five good hectares of land out of the hundred she originally bought. Her letters become a kind of mirror which she holds up to the agents. She counts on their not being able to resist looking at themselves in her mirror.

La mère's letter incorporates a number of different voices. To begin with, her letter is written as though she is in the presence of the agents. Almost every word she writes is written with her audience in mind. For example, her letter begins with an apology, a direct allusion to her suspicion of their annoyance at receiving yet another letter from her. In other places she paraphrases their questions or objections in her own discourse, creating hybrid, double-voiced constructions. For example, she writes about her demand for the five arable hectares: "je connais toutes vos objections: les cinq hectares du haut ne forment qu'un 'tout' avec les cent hectares du bas" (288) [I know all your objections: the five hectares above form a "whole" with the five hectares below]. While the words are all hers, a colon separates her position from theirs. One way to tell that the words are all hers even though she adopts their point of view is the "tout" that designates their term for the indivisibility of the concession and that is distinguished from her words by quotation marks.

Not only has la mère been able to internalize the objections of the agents, the better to respond to them, she has also been able to reproduce their very words:

> Vous me diriez, s'il vous plaisait une fois de me répondre: "A quoi bon? ces cinq hectares ne vous suffisent pas et si vous les hypothéquez pour faire de nouveaux barrages, ces barrages seront aussi mauvais que les premiers." (296)
>
> [You would tell me, if it pleased you to respond: "To what avail? those five hectares do not suffice and if you mortgage them to make new dams, those dams will be as bad as the first ones."]

The tense she uses is conditional, "diriez," which indicates that she is representing a hypothetical situation. Since she has not yet received a response, she must imagine what one would sound like. The fact that she can imagine not just the content, but the very words of a response suggests the extent to which she has been able to understand her opponents. This understanding could help her since she might be able to seduce the agents with her letter if she writes convincing parts for them within her own version of her situation. If she is very clever, she might even be able to put words into their mouths. If she can devise a double-voiced discourse that represents their views but that also represents an understanding of her case, she might even be able to convince them to let her keep the five hectares. But the effectiveness of la mère's letter depends on having the colonial agents read it. The fact that Joseph keeps it for himself suggests that they will never get her letter. While it may help him to remember the horror of his mother's life, it will not produce the effect la mère hoped. In fact, none of her previous letters have had the effect she hoped.

Like Freud in the scene of analysis, the cadastral agents resist identifying with the marginal position because identification with the marginal position makes their own difficult to maintain. For Freud, the threat was epistemological and economic. Identifying with Dora's version of her seduction would challenge his Oedipal theories. If she really was not aroused by her handsome seducer, the surrogate for her beloved father, then the Oedipus complex which defines heterosexual attraction as the norm, could no longer be the central or only theory of the subject. Freud was in a particularly precarious position since he was a paid employee and economic subordinate. Especially after Dora gave him his two weeks notice—like that for a maid—Freud had to defend his epistemological superiority in the face of his economic insecurity. If he could not control the scene of the analysis, he comforted himself with thinking he knew more.[8]

The cadastral agents are in a similar position, though they are far less sympathetic than Freud was since they do not even want to hear what la mère has to say. For them a whole way of life is at stake. La mère is counting on the fact that if she could show the agents what their actions looked like from her point of view, she could convince them to take her side. But if the agents empathized with the objects of their exploitation they would jeopardize their ability to continue their exploitation. If they understood the effect of their expropriation of land on the peasants, they would jeopardize their profits from land speculation. If they realized the misery of the many families they destroyed with their bogus concessions, they would jeopardize their belief in their right to sell them. And if they could not carry on their work, the colonization of Indochina would come to a standstill. While la mère's strategy is seductive by virtue of incorporating some aspects of the colonial position, it is too disruptive to the status quo to be taken seriously. But if la mère can do little to influence the colonial agents in her favor, if she is never able to make her story public enough to effect change, her resistance does produce a legacy for her children. In her letter to the agents she acknowledges this, though she cannot say exactly what effect her struggle will have: "que mon fils s'en aille pour toujours...instruit comme il est de toutes ces choses sur votre ignominie, c'est déjà peut-être un commencement" (296) [let my son depart forever...instructed as he is in all of these aspects of your treachery, maybe that's already a beginning]. If her son does not have a "proper" education, he does have an education about colonial injustice. Just as la mère does not want her children ever to forget her story, so Joseph does not want Suzanne to forget it either. He tells her the story of la mère's past, and tells her to read la mère's letter. As though he suspects that she is the best repository for the family stories, he also tells her his own story, the story of his meeting with the lover who helps him to make the break from la mère. Indeed, Suzanne does turn out to be the one who makes something of the stories.

In *The Mother/Daughter Plot*, Marianne Hirsch claims that a daughter who disclaims the mother's story in order to identify with the father's power is doomed to repeat her mother's oppression. Knowing her mothers' story and internalizing it permits a daughter[9] to understand her oppression and to escape it. The semiotic tie between mother and daughter is reproduction. Without knowing the mother's story the daughter is bound to reproduce it. But if mother and daughter also share a symbolic tie in the articulation of the mother's story, then the daughter may choose to *represent* rather than *reproduce* the mother's story. Because *Un barrage contre le Pacifique* is focalized through Suzanne, in other words, because we hear la mère's story largely from Suzanne's point of view, it often seems as if she is the narrator. While it is important formally to keep the two distinct, thematically, the illusion that Suzanne is the narrator gives us the impression that she has chosen to represent la mère's history rather than reproduce her symptoms and her oppression. This impression is reinforced by the autobiographical parallel: Duras drew on her own past, and her own memories of her mother, to create la mère and her story. If we were willing to momentarily dissolve the barriers between fiction and real life, we might be able to trace a development from the hysterical symptoms of a French woman in Indochina to the production of a novel by her daughter a few decades later. Dora may have been reabsorbed by the family despite her hysterical resistance, but Duras certainly was not. La mère's struggle from symptom to text in *Un barrage contre le Pacifique* suggests that hysteria cannot be reduced to a personal illness, nor can it be explained merely as sexual repression or sexual maladjustment. La mère's and Duras' legacy is not a case history, but a history of another kind.

While Fanon was a psychiatrist, his analyses of the influences of colonization on the colonized stress not only the psychological but also the political, economic, and social realities that often underlie colonial oppression and exploitation rationalized by insistence on "racial difference." Fanon believed that one eventual solution for the colonized—after a period of violent revolt—

was through the construction of alternative, liberating narratives. Had Freud, on one hand, been as keenly attuned to the social, economic and political circumstances of his hysterical patients, he might have offered a better understanding of the hysterics' deployment of precisely this strategy. Had Fanon, on the other hand, been more conscious of the ways colonial and gender oppression reinforce each other, he might have been able to account for the peculiarities of la mère's struggles. By representing the story of a mother very much like her own, Duras' novel suggests a link between gender and colonial oppression, a link which extends the limits of both Freud's descriptions of hysteria and Fanon's theories of colonial resistance. La mère's story demonstrates that (1) hysteria is not merely a personal or family crisis as Freud might have argued, but a response to the political and economic oppression of women, and (2) colonial oppression and resistance takes a different form for women than for the men who figure centrally in Fanon's model. La mère does not want to take the colonizer's place like the proper Oedipal son, or Fanonian native. She wants to denounce the entire colonial project as a crime. Outside of marriage, outside of colonial protection, Duras' hysterical mother produces an alternative to the hegemonic colonial history. Duras' novel thus revises the history which Fanon claims belongs to the colonist—the history of pillage (40)—so that it includes not only the history of the native—the history of decolonization (40)—but the hysteria which first marks la mère's resistance to the double oppression of gender and colony. If Fanon's *history* is a story of colonial oppression, and Freud's *hysteria* is a story of gender oppression, then only a new story, a *hystery* like *Un barrage contre le Pacifique*, can challenge the limits of the narratives we call colonial theory and psychoanalysis.

NOTES

1. All citations are from the Folio edition of *Un barrage contre le Pacifique.*

2. One phrase of Freud's page-long footnote is devoted to the possible pathological predisposition that may be inherited from the mother, while the rest of the footnote focuses on the father's syphilis and its relation to the daughter's neurosis. Preserving this blind spot over the mother, Jacques Lacan, in "Intervention on Transference," highlights Dora's masculine identifications but never addresses her problematic identification with her mother, or at least with her mother's position.

3. Despite Freud's resistance to some of the hysteric's statements, he was moved by others. For example, he did believe that Dora's father was

lying to her about his affair with Frau K., and he did acknowledge that she was caught in a strange sexual exchange, even if he did not recognize the larger economic and political issues involved.

4. See his introduction to the 1966 issue of *Communications*.

5. For other examples, see the Zed Books' *Third World, Second Sex: Women's Struggles and National Liberation* (London 1983) and *Women in Nigeria Today* (London 1985), as well as Stephanie Urdang's *Fighting Two Colonialisms: Women in Guinea Bissau* (New York: Monthly Review, 1979).

6. Virginia Woolf had theorized the link between sufficient "accounts" and the writing of "stories" in her 1929 essay, *A Room of One's Own*. For Woolf, it was "necessary to have five hundred [pounds] a year and a room with a lock on the door if you are to write fiction or poetry" (109). While ma has neither, she does have a different kind of "account" to trigger her narrative capacity, namely her bankrupted bank account and the way it symbolizes her utter exploitation at the hands of the Kam agents.

7. Joseph repeats this gesture with Suzanne when he tells her about his encounter with the woman who takes him away from la mère. He tells Suzanne, warning her never to forget it.

8. See Bernheimer and Kahane, and the last section of Freud's write-up of the Dora case for arguments and examples of Freud's jockeying for control of the scene of analysis. One can read his anger at Dora for abandoning him in his tone and in his equation of her dismissal with a lover's rejection, which curiously sexualizes what might otherwise have been an economic issue, that is, the dismissal of a maid.

9. What this would require of sons is more complex. On one hand, identifying with his mother would make it difficult for a son to take up a typical masculine position. On the other hand, his identification with his mother does not necessarily nullify his simultaneous identification with a phallic position, nor the benefits he receives for his complicity with a gender hierarchy. Furthermore, a son who champions the mother's cause against a real, bad father may be reinscribing the law of the father rather than subverting it. Both daughters and sons would need not only to identify with their mothers but also to work out the implications of their mother's position in their culture, before either of them can effectively challenge prevailing gender norms. Luce Irigaray's strategy of mimicking the feminine position would allow both daughters and sons to investigate the mother's position.

WORKS CITED

Bakhtin, M. M. *The Dialogic Imagination*. Ed. Michael Holquist. Tr. Caryl Emerson and Michael Holquist. Austin: University of Texas Press, 1981.

Barthes, Roland. Introduction. *Communications*. 1966.

Bernheimer, Charles, and Claire Kahane. *In Dora's Case: Freud, Hysteria, Feminism*. New York: Columbia University Press, 1985

Cixous, Hélène, and Catherine Clément. *The Newly Born Woman*. Trans. Betsy Wing. Minneapolis: University of Minnesota Press, 1986.

David-Ménard, Monique. *Hysteria from Freud to Lacan*. Trans. Catherine Porter. Ithaca: Cornell University Press, 1989.

Duras, Marguerite. *Un barrage contre le Pacifique*. Paris: Gallimard, 1950.

Freud, Sigmund. "Fragment of an Analysis of a Case of Hysteria." Standard Edition, vol. 7. 1905.

Freud, Sigmund, and Joseph Breuer. *Studies on Hysteria*. New York: Basic Books, 1955 [1895].

Irigaray, Luce. *This Sex Which Is Not One*. Trans. Catherine Porter. Ithaca: Cornell University Press, 1985.

Hirsch, Marianne. *The Mother/Daughter Plot: Narrative, Psychoanalysis and Feminism*. Bloomington: Indiana University Press, 1989.

Kristeva, Julia. *Powers of Horror: An Essay on Abjection*. Trans. Leon S. Roudiez. New York: Columbia University Press, 1982.

Lacan, Jacques. *Écrits : A Selection*. Trans. Alan Sheridan. New York: Norton, 1977.

———. "With the École Freudienne." *Feminine Sexuality*. Ed. Juliet Mitchell and Jacqueline Rose. Trans. Jacqueline Rose. New York: Norton, 1985.

Montrelay, Michèle. *L'Ombre et le nom*. Paris: Minuit, 1977.

Sophocles. *Three Tragedies*. Ed. David Grene and Richard Lattimore. Chicago: University of Chicago Press, 1954.

Young-Bruehl, Elizabeth. *Freud on Women: A Reader*. New York: Norton, 1990.

8

Laura E. Donaldson

Launcelot's Feast: Teaching Poststructuralism and the New Mestiza

Recently, my postgraduate school unconscious inflicted a second recurring nightmare upon me. (The first one, in which I found myself mysteriously enrolled in yet another Ph.D. program, caused me to wake up with my heart pounding from anxiety.) The most recent version is intimately connected to my vocation as a teacher of postmodern/poststructuralist theory. In the dream, my "Poetics of Fracture" class sits attentively listening to the instructor's sweeping (and definitive) criticisms of Husserl, Heidegger, Lévi-Strauss, Lacan, Foucault, and Habermas. Suddenly, the students metamorphose before my eyes: their heads swell to gigantic proportions and they display the steely yellow gaze of a predator. The group begins to shout and drown out my voice with a critique of my critiques. I talk louder but cannot make myself heard. In desperation, I leap across the teacher's desk and grab a woman in the front row. As I shake her and try to make her listen, I notice the tiny panel at the base of her neck. Its blinking lights reveal the student's true identity, since she is not a student at all, but a cyborg whose human exterior conceals the fact that she has been programmed to destroy: in this case, conceptual human edifices rather than actual human life. Much to my horror, I realize that I have created her—but how? I awaken, my heart pounding from anxiety.

This dream (which originally occurred when I was teaching Mary Shelley's *Frankenstein* as a critique of masculinist science) might well be the generic nightmare of those who teach post-structuralist theory. While part of our charge as educators includes developing critical capacities within our students, it also encompasses teaching them how to affirm: we want them not only to critique those social and intellectual frameworks which need challenging, but also to embrace that which is positive, both personally and socially. However, because of its propensity toward negative dismantling, or a "placing under erasure," poststructuralism encourages both teacher and student to perform the critical gesture to an often exaggeratedly repetitive degree.

The problem of affirmation in contemporary Euramerican critical theory stems partly from its failure to recognize the diverse forms and rich traditions of theorizing that exist in "other," often historically marginalized cultures.[1] Barbara Christian illuminates this process in her essay "The Race for Theory" when she remarks: "People of color have always theorized—but in forms quite different from the Western form of abstract logic. And I am inclined to say that our theorizing...is often in narrative forms, in the stories we create, in the riddles and proverbs, in the play with language, since dynamic rather than fixed ideas seem more to our liking" (52). In order to perceive these traditions, however, the dominant critical establishment must first transform the very way it defines theory. Indeed, I would argue, Euramerican academicians must engage in a process of decolonization which acknowledges how circumscribing the definition of theory has also suppressed those very models that might offer alternative configurations of critique and affirmation.

My essay will explore the theoretical and pedagogical implications of two models dealing explicitly with this issue: Gayatri Chakravorty Spivak's "affirmative deconstruction" and Gloria Anzaldúa's postcolonial discourse of the "new *mestiza*," or mixed race woman. Spivak's articulation of affirmative deconstruction comprises one term of this debate because it brilliantly dramatizes both the political usefulness and limits of Euramerican poststructuralist theory. Anzaldúa's construct of the new mestiza exists as a "Third World" alternative to this view because it imbricates critique with affirmation in startlingly new patterns. Let me emphasize that the purpose of reading between and within these two discourses is not to choose one over the other, since this would turn their interaction into an all too familiar "race for theory" where one wins and the other loses. I instead wish to juxtapose them in the hopes of producing provocative tensions and insights that might potentially transform not only the way the academy teaches theory, but also its very presuppositions.

ON OPEN-ENDEDNESS, OR THE PRACTICAL POLITICS OF CRITIQUE

> We are suffering from an absolute despot duality that says we are able to be only one or the other.
>
> —Gloria Anzaldúa, *Borderlands/La Frontera*

No stance has embodied poststructuralism's profound distrust of master narratives and totalizing frameworks more than "deconstruction," the interpretive strategy generated by the French philosopher Jacques Derrida. His introduction of such terms as "supplementarity" and "undecidability" to the Euramerican critical lexicon characterizes what one might call deconstruction's "negative" phase. And perhaps nothing illustrates this phase more vividly than an exercise that an former instructor of mine used to teach her bewildered students about the infinite circularity of the signifier. In this exercise, we were asked to look up a word (signifier) in the dictionary. "How," she asked, "do you define this word?" Initially, most of us answered this question by quoting its denotative definition, that is, its representational content. "But," she would counter, "how do you define those words?" The answer, of course, is that one can only define them by looking up other words, that is, signifiers only take on meaning in relation to other signifiers. This dizzyingly unsuccessful attempt to exit the dictionary convinced us that "we cannot get outside it; we can only wander about in it, exposing inconsistencies, patched up rips, and hidden false assumptions concerning the existence of real signifieds designated by signifiers that point to them" (Berman, 202). Or, as succinctly summarized by Richard Rorty, "crosstalk is all that we are going to get" (108). It hardly seems surprising, then, that many academics and nonacademics alike considered Derridean deconstruction as the "Just Say No" campaign of poststructuralist theory.

This perception is exceedingly ironic since, according to Gayatri Chakravorty Spivak, deconstruction's genuine subversiveness consists of the opposite demand to just "say yes to everything" (*Critic*, 47). Spivak describes this "affirmative" turn as the discovery that deconstruction does not insist that we say no to "whatever positive stuff you're doing, that is to say 'keeping the question alive,' but instead obliges you to say...yes to that which interrupts your project" (*Critic*, 47). In other words, deconstruction is not metaphysical or rhetorical nihilism, but rather acts as a detective investigating "authority in language, and the pronouncements of any self-constituted authority for what it is repressing or what it is not saying" (Johnson, 167). Extending this insight, Spivak discerns in what she calls affirmative deconstruction a "practical politics of the open end" that is located between its stalled-out beginnings, or différance, and its endings, or aporias ("Commitment," 283).

It is important to note the emphatic distinction which Spivak makes between her practical politics of the open end and an actual political program. Because a political program founded upon deconstruction says yes to everything, it must inevitably disintegrate into a "wishy-washy pluralism" or "irresponsible hedonism" which would recuperate genuine difference and defuse authentic conflict (Spivak, *Critic*, 104). For this reason, a practical politics of the open end rejects the "massive ideological act" of a political program in favor of a strategic "daily maintenance." In fact, Spivak describes its function through an analogy with one of the most mundane habits known to humankind—the practice of brushing one's teeth:

> For example, when we actually brush our teeth, or clean ourselves everyday, or take exercise, or whatever, we don't think we are fighting a losing battle against mortality, but, in fact, all of these efforts are doomed to failure because we are going to die. On the other hand, we really think of it much more as upkeep and as maintenance rather than as an irreducibly doomed repeated effort. This kind of activity cannot be replaced by an operation. We can't have a surgical operation which takes care of the daily maintenance of a body doomed to die. That operation would be identical with death. (*Critic*, 105)

Although this comparison encourages a somewhat irreverent view of affirmative deconstruction as a kind of political tartar control, it more seriously illustrates that a practical politics of the open end marks the limits of Euramerican poststructuralism because it cannot constitute itself as "a counter-program for the production of knowledge" (Spivak, *Critic*, 47).

If affirmative deconstruction only generates those moments which continually prevent us from lapsing either into fundamentalism or totalitarianism, we cannot subsequently transpose it into a positive sequence capable of producing a desperately needed, nonmaster narrative for cultural transformation. Are we now at a critical impasse? Is there no way to embrace affirmation (of political programs, social agendas, each other) without becoming mired in a totalitarianism from which we need rescuing? I believe that one possible answer to these questions lies just across the postcolonial border.

BORDER THEORIES

> Living on borders and in margins, keeping intact one's shifting and multiple identity and integrity, is like trying to swim in a new element, an "alien" element.
>
> —Gloria Anzaldúa, *Borderlands*

Gloria Anzaldúa's *Borderlands/La Frontera: The New Mestiza* is a postcolonial narrative that achieves ends similar to those elaborated above, yet also allows us to exchange deconstruction's endless instabilities for firmer critical ground. I use the term "postcolonial" advisedly here to identify the mestiza's origins within both historical and discursive colonialism. According to Anzaldúa, the "mixed race woman's" historical origins include the Spanish-American struggle for control over the Southwest and Mexico as well as the continued socioeconomic disempowerment of indigenous communities. Her discursive origins lie in resistance to both the essentialist identity-formations of European humanism and the active oppression of women—especially lesbian women—within the patriarchal organization of Chicano and Euramerican cultures.

While the title signifies those physical "borderlands" of the Southwest Texas/Mexican border, Anzaldúa also notes that its psychological, sexual, and spiritual demarcations are not restricted to geographical regions. Describing her own experience as a mestiza, she poignantly relates:

> I am a border woman. I grew up between two cultures, the Mexican (with a heavy Indian influence) and the Anglo (as a member of a colonized people in our own territory). I have been straddling that tejas-Mexican border, and others, all my life. It's not a comfortable territory to live in, this place of contradictions....However, there have been compensations for this *mestiza*, and certain joys. (Preface)

This paradigm of mestizaje offends not only a biological homogeneity which views "race" in monolithic terms, but also a cultural homogeneity which becomes an instrument of conquest through its imposition of a coercive unity (Harris, *Womb*, xviii).[2]

Like the deconstructor, then, the mestiza proclaims that homogeneity—"the theological motif *par excellence*" (Derrida, *Positions*, 64)—is "decidedly the one to be destroyed" (*Positions*, 64). Further, just as the interminable analyses of différance "inhabit philosophical opposition, resisting and disorganizing it, without ever constituting a third term" (Derrida, *Positions*, 43), the mixed-race woman's "ceaseless dialogue" among her various identities works to undo such hardened racial oppositions as European/Indian without herself constituting a "master narrative" of ethnic identity.

The mestiza's willingness "to make herself vulnerable to foreign ways of seeing and thinking" parallels affirmative deconstruction's radical acceptance of vulnerability, for she also experiences the demand to say yes to everything: "She surrenders all notions of safety, of the familiar. Deconstruct, construct. She becomes a *nahual*, able to transform herself into a tree, a coyote, into another person" (Anzaldúa, 82–83). However, unlike deconstruction's confinement to exposing the limits of power-knowledge, the mestiza's discourse of hybridity gives us "a piece of ground to stand on, a ground from which to view the world" (Anzaldúa, 23). She is not confined to the preventive maintenance of brushing her teeth, since she is figured by an act which combines both critique and affirmation—the kneading of bread:

> *Soy un amasamiento,* I am an act of kneading, of uniting and joining that not only has produced both a creature of darkness and a creature of light, but also a creature that questions the definitions of light and dark and gives them new meanings. (81)

Just as the motion of kneading constantly decenters the (literal) matter at hand, the mestiza intervenes within the rigidities of hierarchical identity. However, kneading produces an end-product, namely bread, and its deconstructive performance likewise produces a fluid and visionary end-product: the counter-narrative of a new, non-essentialist identity. In his essay, "DissemiNation: Time, Narrative, and the Margins of the Modern Nation," Homi K. Bhabha thematizes what he calls "counter-narratives of the nation that continually evoke and erase its totalizing boundaries—both actual and conceptual—disturb those ideological manoeuvres through which 'imagined communities' are given essentialist identities" (300). The postcolonial discourse of the mestiza constitutes such a counter-narrative and, because of this, surpasses the more limited critical potential of affirmative deconstruction:

> As a *mestiza* I have no country, my homeland cast me out; yet all countries are mine because I am every woman's sister or potential lover. (As a lesbian I have no race, my own people disclaim me; but I am all races because there is the queer of me in all races.) I am cultureless because, as a feminist, I challenge the collective cultural religious male-derived beliefs of Indo-Hispanics and Anglos; yet I am cultured because I am partici-

> pating in the creation of yet another culture, a new story to explain the world and our participation in it, a new value system with images and symbols that connect us to each other and to the planet. (Anzaldúa, 81)

In order to fully understand the mestiza's capacity to invoke this "new value system," I will investigate her ability not only to destabilize but also to transform the agonizing opposition of Christian and Jew in Shakespeare's play *The Merchant of Venice.* Reading from a "mixed" perspective produces a powerful counter-narrative to the dominance of Christian over Jew—a narrative that also anticipates how the mestiza might irrevocably change both the way we read texts and the way we teach theory. Indeed, I would argue, the interactions between Shylock, Antonio and Launcelot exist as a profoundly important experimental field for understanding the pedagogical and theoretical implications of deconstruction in an/other language.

ON SELF AND OTHER, CHRISTIAN AND JEW, THE WEST AND THE REST OF US

> Strangely, the foreigner lives within us: he is the hidden face of our identity, the space that wrecks our abode, the time in which understanding and affinity founder. By recognizing him within ourselves, we are spared detesting him in himself.
>
> —Julia Kristeva, *Strangers to Ourselves*

In 1096, an anonymous preacher named Peter the Hermit responded to the call of Pope Urban II by mobilizing a famine-starved European peasantry for what historians now call "the People's Crusade." Of the thousands of poor Christians who marched from Cologne on that fateful Easter Sunday, only a few survived to reach Jerusalem. Not surprisingly, other victims of the desire to expel nonbelievers from Christianity's holy sites included thousands of Jews, who often chose to kill themselves rather than accept the choice of forced conversion or forced execution.

A radical appeal to binary opposition empowered both the Crusades and the preaching of Peter the Hermit, for each depended upon a structuring principle dividing the world into the Christ and Antichrist, with the "good" half, that is, the pure and white half, battling the "evil," that is, the impure and dark, for cosmic hegemony. Thus, one need not wait for Jacques Derrida to inform us about "the conflictual and subordinating structure of opposition" (*Positions*, 41), since it already tragically exists within the text of history. The current resurgence of Christian Aryanism in the United States, neo-Nazism in Germany and pro-white military organizations in South Africa merely repeat the Crusades' dualistic fantasy. Although these contemporary groups often cloak their binarisms in populist rhetoric, they nevertheless promote the lethal supremacy of white over dark, Christian over Jew, man over woman, pure over impure. It is precisely the presence in our world of these new "Peter the Hermits" which illustrates the intractable paradox of poststructuralist theory: the political need to decenter such oppositions and the simultaneous need to move beyond them.

As a trenchant case in point, the late Allan Bloom's objections both to poststructuralism and multiculturalism in *The Closing Of The American Mind* are by now only too well known. However, his own analysis of the paradigmatic positions of Self and Other—which he interpolates through the positions of Christian and Jew in *The Merchant of Venice*—reveals the weakness of his challenge to a dominant Christian culture's deeply embedded anti-Judaism. In an essay first presented as a lecture to the University of Chicago's Hillel Foundation, Bloom observes that, like Othello, Shylock's foreignness produces in some measure an "unhappy destiny": "In other words, Venice did not fulfill for them its promise of being a society in which men could live as men, not as whites and blacks, Christians and Jews, Venetians and foreigners" (65). This ideal of equality, or the coincidence of opposites in the signifier "men," functions as the noncontradictory and homogenous horizon framing Bloom's discussion.

He argues, for example, that our only choice "seems to be a hostile diversity on a high level or a common humanity on the level of the beasts" (74). We can either accept "with manly resolution" the inevitability of conflict or the bastardization of all that is noble and true in each of the separate (Christian and Jewish) points of view" (Bloom 82). Instead of enabling us to move beyond these paralyzing dichotomies, Bloom's analysis actually solidifies a position of lamentation: we can only rue Shakespeare's—and by extension, dominant Christian society's—inability to unite humanity on the level of "its truly human sameness." Bloom's regret of the separate but unequal status of Jews in a Christian world simply resides within, and thereby confirms, their hierarchical opposition.

In addition, his ideal of separate but equal jumps too quickly beyond opposition. Jacques Derrida might observe that in either case, Bloom's critical moves leave us no hold on the dyad

Christian/Jew and no means of effectively intervening in its oppressive political field (*Positions*, 41). It is precisely at this point that Bloom needs a deconstructive reading in order to subvert the oppositions Christian versus Jew and "Christian love versus Jewish law." According to Bloom, *The Merchant of Venice* portrays Shylock and Antonio, respectively, as models of Judaism and Christianity by construing them as prototypes of Moses and Jesus and assigning them the stereotypical values of law and love.[3] Thus, Shylock "holds that respect for and obedience to the law is the condition for leading a decent life," while Antonio "bases his whole life on generosity and love for his fellow man" (Bloom, 69).

This is not a balanced opposition, however, for a dominant Christianity has denounced this alleged Jewish adherence to the law as the perverse distortion of blinded fanatics. Like the Christian audience for whom Shakespeare wrote his play, Antonio subscribes to the view of Shylock and Judaism expressed by the Duke: "Thou art come to answer a stony adversary, an inhuman wretch, uncapable of pity, void and empty from any dram of mercy" (4.1.3–6). The Duke's description of Shylock as "stony" simultaneously denounces both the individual and his religion, for it not only conjures the intractable nature of stone, but also Judaism's founding text, or the "tablets of stone, with the law and commands I (Yahweh) have written..." (Ex 24:12). In seeming contrast to the Christian patience and forgiveness of Antonio, then, Shylock's Jewish intransigence inspires only a bitter contempt.

A deconstructive reading of *The Merchant of Venice* might scrutinize the text's presentation of an authoritative Christianity and "tease out" what it suppresses in the name of love. One seam of self-rupture certainly appears in Bassanio's boast to Antonio that "The Jew shall have my flesh, blood, bones, and all, ere thou shalt lose for me one drop of blood" (4.1.112–13). Portia, whose famous speech touting mercy over justice apparently confirms the opposition between Christian and Jew, in fact rejects Bassanio's more connotative definition of this bond and resorts to a legalistic interpretation that previously characterized only the fanatically literal "People of the Book":[4]

> Tarry a little; there is something else.
> This bond doth give thee here no jot of blood;
> The words expressly are "a pound of flesh."
> Take then thy bond, take thou thy pound of flesh;
> But in the cutting it, if thou dost shed
> One drop of Christian blood, thy lands and goods

> Are by the laws of Venice confiscate
> Unto the state of Venice. (4.1.304–11)

No blood, no bones, and precisely one pound of flesh. Although Portia's intolerable hermeneutics of the law forces Shylock to admit defeat, it also belies the Duke's assertion that the reader, like Shylock "shalt see the difference of our spirit" (4.1.367). In this context, "Spirit" invokes not only the spirit of forgiveness, but also the essence of Christianity as defined by the apostle Paul: "He has made us competent as ministers of a new covenant—not of the letter but of the Spirit; for the letter kills, but the Spirit gives life" (2 Cor: 6).

Portia's discourse in *The Merchant of Venice* disallows Christianity's claim to a transcendently pure love, for it sets into motion "the displaced and equivocal passage of one different thing to another, from one term of an opposition to the other. Thus one could reconsider all the pairs of opposites...on which our discourse lives, not in order to see opposition erase itself but to see what indicates that each of the terms must appear...as the other different and deferred in the economy of the same" (Derrida, "Différance," 17). To paraphrase Derrida, this play of *différance* between Christian and Jew, love and law, transgressively deconstructs their opposition through displacing—and even reversing—their explicitly stated textual positions and definitions. Christianity's suppression of this moment also legitimates the suppression of its own theological hybridity and allows it to cast Judaism as the wholly demonic other.

Our deconstructive intervention in the opposition Christian/Jew does not equal affirmation, however, because it fails to construct an effective counter-narrative to the ravages of anti-Semitism. The question now becomes how the kneaded (and needed) discourse of the new mestiza provides an alternative perspective through which to interpret the "dough" of Antonio and Shylock. In Shakespeare's play, one site of mixedness resides in the single character who literally and metaphorically straddles the border of both Jewish and Christian worlds—Launcelot Gobbo, the trickster and clown. Bloom's analysis predictably belittles Launcelot's position by foregrounding "the ridiculousness of the man who tries to live in the worlds of Antonio and Shylock at the same time; everything is so different that he is like someone who wants to stand on his head and his feet at the same time" (70). This statement cleanly maintains the antagonistic separation of Christian and Jew and, like those who also condemned Salman

Rushdie's *The Satanic Verses*, promulgates the belief that intermingling with a different culture inevitably degrades one's own (Rushdie, 4).

In contradiction to this stance, I interpret Launcelot Gobbo as a figure who is so threatening that readers privileging homogeneity and segregation must necessarily remain blind to the way he generates other constellations of meaning within the play. The key to Launcelot's subversiveness lies, I believe, in Shylock's rather curt and dismissive description of him as "that fool of Hagar's offspring" (2.6.43). For those unfamiliar with biblical history, "Hagar's offspring" is none other than Ishmael, the illegitimate son of the Hebrew patriarch, Abraham, and his wife Sarah's Egyptian serving woman. For most Jewish commentators, Ishmael exists as a palpable obstacle to establishing the covenant between the Israelites and Yahweh, whereas for Christians, he signifies Abraham and Sarah's unbelief in God's promise to send them a line of descendants. Each of these interpretations ignores the most salient fact of Abraham's liaison with Hagar: it is an act of miscegenation which traverses ethnic, cultural and religious boundaries, and which irrevocably establishes Judeo-Christian monotheism as an "absolutism of the Pure" (Rushdie, 4) through the rejection of its progeny.

We glimpse a return of the repressed Ishmael and all that he represents in the guise of the trickster, Launcelot. This association with Ishmael invests Launcelot's role as messenger to those in power (his most important act is to notify the aristocracy of their mail) and emigrant from Jewish to Christian spheres (from Shylock's service to Bassanio's) with new meaning. However, Launcelot's movement does not so much connote immigration as infiltration. Indeed, his displacement from the textual territory of the subordinate to that of the dominant imbues the Christian sphere with "a kind of bastard hope" of "hybridity, impurity, intermingling, the transformation that comes of new and unexpected combinations of human beings, cultures, ideas, politics" (Rushdie, 4). Launcelot and Lorenzo's (who is, not coincidentally, one of the play's most explicitly anti-Jewish characters) discussion of dinner preparations becomes especially significant in this context.

This particular scene turns on the double meaning of the word "cover": simultaneously to cover the table with food and the head with a hat. Lorenzo responds to Launcelot's penchant for verbal punning by expressing discomfort with this hermeneutic double-voicedness and a desire for literal interpretation: "I pray thee understand a plain man in his plain meaning: go to thy fellows, bid them cover the table, serve in the meat, and we will come in to dinner" (3.5.57–59). But to attend the feast of Launcelot, which surely recalls the Eucharist, that other feast of Christendom, is precisely to accept the mixing of these meanings and to negotiate ceaselessly between them—just as it means to accept the mixing of Christian and Jew and to negotiate *their* meaning. Confronted with its own *mestizaje*, Christianity can no longer base its identity on the theological negations of anti-Judaism or the social perpetuation of anti-Semitism;[5] instead, it must positively define itself in relation to the multiplicitous production of the signifiers "Jew" and "Christian" from the same texts of the Book.

The affirmative deconstruction articulated by Derrida and Spivak is unable to create such a counter-narrative; instead, it can only immerse us in the heady and seductive experience of critique. The discourse of mestizaje, on the other hand, not only critiques the structures of binary opposition, but also provides the enabling conditions for a nontotalitarian affirmation. The importance of the postcolonial mestiza for reconfiguring Euramerican notions of theory and the teaching of poststructuralism can hardly be underestimated.

The interweaving of autobiography, play with multiple languages, historical essays and poetry within *Borderlands/La Frontera* suggest a new theoretical paradigm. The new mestiza elaborates theory indirectly, through the intimacies of her life and the starkness of her poetry. She teaches us to read by beginning with the *différance* of the text, but never stagnating within this open-ended deferral and difference. She forces us to vacate a process of critique which, since it is by definition parasitic upon an external framework, often becomes too literally reactionary to be revolutionary. Last but not least, she demands that both students and teachers live in the borderlands. In the words of Anzaldúa:

To live in the Borderlands means you

> are neither *hispana india negra española*
> *ni gabacha, eres mestiza, mulata*, half-breed
> caught in the crossfire between camps
> while carrying all five races on your back
> not knowing which side to turn to, run from;

To live in the Borderlands means to

> put *chile* in borscht,
> eat whole wheat *tortillas*,
> speak Tex-Mex with a Brooklyn accent;
> be stopped by *la migra* at the border checkpoints;

To survive the Borderlands

> you must live *sin fronteras*
> be a crossroads

Not only to survive, but to survive more freely and humanely, we must live in the theoretical frontier and become a crossroads where critique and affirmation meet and transform each other.

NOTES

1. I take the issue "the problem of affirmation in critical theory" from a Society for Critical Exchange project which originated during 1988–89. This paper was originally presented in somewhat different form for an SCE panel at the Modern Language Association meeting in Chicago, 1988. It was further refined for a weekend meeting of project participants at Case Western Reserve University in the spring of 1989. I wish to acknowledge the both the intellectual and economic support of the SCE in developing the ideas in this essay.

2. I do not wish to suggest here that *mestizaje* is always and everywhere revolutionary or subversive. Harris speaks within the specific context of Caribbean colonialism, with its highly structured racial definitions and an underlying privileging of homogeneity. However, in Central America, for example, it has historically been the Mestizos who have most directly oppressed indigenous peoples. In Cherokee culture, the mixed offspring of Tsalagi-white marriages were often those who most actively directed the nation toward assimilation and its disastrous culmination in the Trail of Tears. For a more extended discussion of these issues, see my forthcoming essay, "Mixed Messages?: Rethinking postcolonial Hybridity."

3. The common Christian notion that Judaism is primarily a religion of "the law" involves a reductionist view of the Torah, which means any oral or written "teaching" or "instruction" derived from the Mount Sinai encounter of Moses and Yahweh.

4. While Terry Eagleton moves in a very different direction, I am grateful to his invigorating discussion of *The Merchant of Venice* for inspiring these thoughts. See *William Shakespeare* (Oxford: Basil Blackwell, 1986), 35–48.

5. Gavin I. Langmuir makes a valuable distinction between Christian anti-Judaism, which negatively values Judaism because it denies the divinity of Christ, and anti-Semitism, which is based on complete fabri-

cations such as Jews eating Christian children or obscenely defiling the Eucharist. See *Toward A Definition of Antisemitism* (Berkeley: University of California Press, 1990).

WORKS CITED

Anzaldúa, Gloria. *Borderlands/La Frontera: The New Mestiza*. San Francisco: Spinsters/Aunt Lute, 1987.

Berman, Art. *From the New Criticism to Deconstruction: The Reception of Structuralism and Post-structuralism*. Urbana: University of Illinois Press, 1988.

Bhabha, Homi K. "DissemiNation: Time, Narrative, and the Margins of the Modern Nation." *Nation and Narration*. Ed. Homi K. Bhabha. New York: Routledge, 1990, 291–322.

Bloom, Allan. "On Christian and Jew: *The Merchant of Venice*." *Giants And Dwarfs: Essays 1960–1990*. New York: Simon and Schuster, 1990, 64–82.

Christian, Barbara. "The Race for Theory." *Cultural Critique* 6 (1987): 51–64. Ed. Abdul R. JanMohamed and David Lloyd.

Derrida, Jacques. "Différance." *Margins of Philosophy*. Trans. Alan Bass. Chicago: University of Chicago Press, 1982, 1–28.

———. *Positions*. Trans. Alan Bass. Chicago: University of Chicago Press, 1981.

González, Justo. *The Crusades: Piety Misguided*. Nashville: Graded, 1988.

Harris, Wilson. *The Womb of Space: The Cross-Cultural Imagination*. Westport: Greenwood, 1983.

Johnson, Barbara. "Interview with Imre Salusinszky." *Criticism in Society*. Ed. Imre Salusinszky. New York: Methuen, 1987, 150–75.

Rorty, Richard. "Philosophy as a Kind of Writing: An Essay on Derrida." *Consequences of Pragmatism (Essays: 1971–1980)*. Minneapolis: University of Minnesota Press, 1982, 90–109.

Rushdie, Salman. "In Good Faith." *Imaginary Homelands: Essays and Criticism 1981-1991*. New York: Viking Penguin, 1991, 393–414.

Spivak, Gayatri Chakravorty. "Political Commitment and the Postmodern Critic." *The New Historicism*. Ed. H. Aram Veeser. New York: Routledge, Chapman and Hall, 1989, 277–92.

———. *The Post-colonial Critic: Interviews, Strategies, Dialogues*. Ed. Sarah Harasym. New York: Routledge, Chapman and Hall, 1990.

9

TERESA L. EBERT

Subalterity and Feminism in the Moment of the (Post)modern: The Materialist Return

Several years ago, in the course of a discussion on what has happened to the political left in the West, especially in the United States, Robert Fitch observed that one of most visible changes has been the left's preoccupation with questions of the "Third World" or (post)coloniality. The left, as he said, "having gotten rid of those nineteenth-century heirlooms" of socialism

> needed to replace them with something to avoid the embarrassment of empty space—preferably something without sharp edges. Third World workers and peasants fit in quite well. Didn't they deserve our attention more than the workers in our own society? In absolute terms, weren't they even poorer and even more oppressed? Besides, relationships with them were easier to maintain. They were located in convenient out-of-the-way places so you hardly ever saw them. And if asked why we didn't support workers in our own communities, we could always answer that we were anti-imperialists and that the truly deserving workers were outside our reach. So the new internationalism of the left meant that support for Third World struggles gradually tended to replace, rather than reinforce involvement in struggles at home. (18–19)

In other words, this new preoccupation with (post)coloniality is far from being the mark of the left's internationalization and growing involvement in the plight of the working class in the world. Instead it is a strategy of evasion and containment of social struggle.

In fact, Fitch goes on to say that:

> by and large, special concern with labor, class and the transformation of society has been displaced intellectually by the "posts-." With the advent of postindustrialism, postmodernism, postMarxism or whatever, the assumption appears to be that here in the U.S. we are all bourgeois, or could be with suitable government programs and affirmative action. (19)

The important point here is that the left, by and large, feels defeated in the capitalist world and has succumbed to the prevailing logic or ideology of the bourgeoisie. It has thus lost the initiative to deal with the "home" problems (rampant sexism, racism, economic devastation, and its global exportation) and has instead turned to the safely distant "Other"—particularly the "subaltern."

This shift and the "pleasure" the "other" often generates for the left as an escape from the "home" difficulties of labor and class is vividly demonstrated by New York City's 1993 Labor Day parade. According to *The New York Times*, the parade

> celebrated cross-dressing and Caribbean ethnicity with much more gusto than it showed for working men and women or union solidarity.
>
> At a time when wages are stagnant or falling and when practically every politician recognizes the big issue to be jobs, jobs, jobs, what does the perfunctory marching mean? Is class struggle truly over?...Or is it simply a case that drag queens and West Indians throw much better parties? (Kaufman)

In the face of such contradictions we need to ask whether the growing interest in the academy at the present time with issues of coloniality/postcoloniality[1] is a mark of international activism and a global retheorization of the understanding of exploitation or merely a means of running away from the problems at home. This is a question of what Foucault has called power/knowledge and the politics of truth—however, it is articulated largely as a matter of discourse. The issue for us at this moment is whether we should attend to the (discursive) politics of truth and explore the axes of power/knowledge relations—particularly regarding the "Other"—or whether, as Marx argued, we should engage the *economics of untruth* involving ourselves?

In other words, at the present time there are, to my mind, two fundamentally different ways of understanding postcoloniality. The first, and by far most prevalent, mode engages postcoloniality as a regime of power/knowledge relations and foregrounds the problems of representation; it is, therefore, part of the project exploring the discursive politics of truth.[2] In contrast, the second mode does not take postcoloniality to be simply a problem of cultural politics, as Foucauldian genealogy proposes, but instead understands it as basically an economic issue that has to be explored in the context of the international division of labor and poses the problem of the economics of untruth in the relations of metropolitan and periphery.[3]

While postcoloniality understood as cultural politics is necessary, it is, to my mind, a very limited project. The more productive and politically effective undertaking is, I believe, one that sees postcoloniality as the articulation of the international division of labor. To say this does not mean I am dispensing with the problems of representation, knowledge or truth, but rather I am arguing that these cannot be understood separate from the political economy of labor. This is an especially pressing issue for feminism, since feminist theory in postmodernity is increasingly substituting discourse for political economy. Such a move is all the more problematic when we note that not only is feminism one of the primary sites for inquiry into postcoloniality but that issues of "Third World Women," "Women of Color," and postcoloniality are becoming one of the predominant arenas of Western feminist concerns. Prominent feminist theorists—from Donna Haraway and Elizabeth Meese to Gayatri Spivak—increasingly focus their recent work on issues of postcoloniality.[4] The major anthologies of feminist theory in the last few years—such as Marianne Hirsch and Evelyn Fox Keller's *Conflicts in Feminism*, Elizabeth Weed's collection from the Pembroke Center, *Coming to Terms: Feminism, Theory, Politics*, and Judith Butler and Joan Scott's *Feminists Theorize Politics*, all have significant discussions of Third World women, and a number of anthologies such as Chandra Mohanty, Ann Russo, and Lourdes Torres's *Third World Women and the Politics of Feminism* and Sidonie Smith and Julia Watson's *De/Colonizing the Subject* are entirely devoted to these issues.

My concern here is to ask some difficult and, for many, quite discomforting questions about the political and social effects of the way postmodern feminist theorists are engaging the postcolonial, specifically the "subaltern." I will be carrying out this inquiry through a "critique" of several exemplary texts, notably Gayatri Spivak's "Can the Subaltern Speak?"—which an interviewer in *Socialist Review* called her "most famous (or notorious) work" and a "major contribution to this discussion" (Winant, 83)—as well as Elizabeth Meese's turn from—or what she calls the "ex-tension" of—poststructuralism to postcoloniality in her recent book *(Ex)Tensions: Re-figuring Feminist Criticism.*

Feminist and postmodern encounters with the Third World/ postcolonial see themselves as postimperialist but what is the status of this claim? I want to begin by situating the question in relation to a nonfeminist text, but one that raises troubling issues for us. The essay, "Postcolonial Culture, Postimperial Criticism," was recently published by W.J.T. Mitchell, the editor of *Critical Inquiry*, in what is one of the major journals of postcolonial discourse, *Transition*. Even here the economic geopolitics of postcolonialism are at work. The journal *Transition*, according to its frontispiece, "was founded thirty years ago in Uganda by Rajat Neogy." However, the journal we are reading is a "new series" no longer from Uganda, but from the metropolitan heart where it is edited by two Harvard professors, Kwame Anthony Appiah and Henry Louis Gates, Jr., and published by Oxford University Press. In one of the leading "Position" papers opening issue no. 56, Mitchell claims that we are in "the process of 'decolonization,' a term that suggests as its necessary corollary some related transformations in the corresponding centers of empire, a 'deimperialization'" (13). But such an assumption is little more than an ahistorical postulation of an automatic reflex and confuses the end of one specific stage of imperialism (nineteenth-century territorial colonialism) with the end of imperialism as a global system of exploitation. In fact, imperialism—that is, the international division of labor and appropriation of economic and natural resources benefiting First World countries at the expense of Third World societies—is thriving under new guises and by other means, such as the international debt structure, "free trade" or "export processing" zones and the practices of multinational corporations, creating what Annette Fuentes and Barbara Ehrenreich have called the "global factory." Nor has the West abandoned direct military coercion and territorial occupation—witness the continued military occupation of both the Northern and Southern regions of Iraq. In fact, at one point in the postwar "peace," the United States was carrying out such an intensive campaign of military overflights in Southern Iraq—one every four minutes—that the machinery (the jets and aircraft carriers) could not hold up under the strain.

The automatic assumption of the deimperialization of the Center is itself an act of concealed imperialism. However, beginning from this assumption, Mitchell goes on to argue that there is a "cultural reconfiguration...overwhelmingly evident in the global cultural relations of the First, Second and Third Worlds" (14): a "reconfiguration and relocation of cultural and critical energy, reversals of center and margin, production and consumption, dominant and emergent forces, reversals in traditional divisions of cultural labor such as 'criticism' and 'creative writing'" (13). And what is this profound reversal? "The commonplace," he says, which "is simply this: the most important literature is now emerging from the former colonies of the Western empires...the most provocative new criticism is emanating from research universities in the advanced industrial democracies, that is, from the former centers of the 'Western empires'—Europe and the United States" (14). If this is "the commonplace," as Mitchell claims, of current knowledges, that the creative energies and articulations of experience are to be found in the former colonies, but that the theories, interpretations and criticisms—the master knowledges—we use to make sense of them are the products of the research centers of the former empire, then there is little if any de-imperialization going on. Instead, we have the concealed "commonplace" that the old power-knowledge relations of domination and exploitation are reproducing themselves in new forms.

They are able to do so through two moves that have serious implications for postmodern feminist theory, which is often complicit in these strategies. The first is to read "contemporary criticism"—by which Mitchell means postmodern "anti-foundationalist" discourses such as "pragmatism and deconstruction" that "come to the Third World from the First"—as "subvert(ing) the imperial economy that supports it, 'decentering' the very structure of discursive authority" (16). But this claim for the "postimperialist subversiveness" of anti-foundational discourses is itself an essentializing notion that erases their specific historical uses and effects. For instance, the deconstructive insistence on rhetorical indeterminacy is not postimperialist in its effect when it puts under erasure the certainty and truth-value of the political principles distinguishing the discourses of the African National Conference and those of neo-Nazi and apartheid white supremacists. Second, such a concept of "postimperialist criticism" or knowledge can only be maintained by restricting the arena of subversive intervention to that of the discourses or representations of empire, in short, to cultural politics. This requires that we follow Mitchell's injunction "to resist," as he says, "the notion that this relationship"—"between First World Critical movements and literary developments in the Second and Third Worlds"—"reflects the traditional economic relations of imperial centers and colonial peripheries" (17). In short, what Mitchell calls a "rhetoric of decolonization from the imperial center" is only possible if we suppress the global economic realities of the international division of labor and its articulation through the construction of significations, representations, and subjectivities.

Most feminist inquiries into the postcolonialism and the subaltern, see themselves, like Mitchell, to be participating in post-imperialist knowledges and producing a subversive "rhetoric of decolonization from the imperial center." But in doing so, many feminists frequently participate in the same uncritical and ahistorical notion of de-imperialization maintained by essentializing the political effects of discursive performances and, more important, at the cost of suppressing the economic relations—in short, the labor relations—between center and periphery, between overdeveloped and underdeveloped countries,[5] and, not least, between Western feminists and the subalterns they study.

Gayatri Spivak seems well aware of this issue in her essay "Can the Subaltern Speak?," in which she insists on situating the possibility/impossibility of postimperialist knowledges in the West within the international division of labor, for as she says, "Western intellectual production is, in many ways, complicit with Western international economic interests" (271). In current postcolonial discourses, particularly concerning the subaltern, "the first-world intellectual," according to Spivak, "masquerad(es) as the absent nonrepresenter who lets the oppressed speak for themselves" (292). In other words, the seemingly compassionate gesture to let the subaltern speak, to give voice to the other, is not only paternalistic but relies on an illusory transparency that occludes the continuing historical privilege and economic collaboration of the "benevolent Western intellectual" in the international division of labor. Spivak's concern in the essay is, thus, to deconstruct the way "the intellectual is complicit in the persistent constitution of the Other as the Self's shadow"—and by Self, with a capitalized "S," she means the continued perpetuation of the sovereign subject of Western imperialism in which the Other, the subaltern, is repeatedly re-constituted as the different/the Other of the United States/Europe (280). "This S/subject," according to Spivak, "belongs to the exploiter's side of the international division of labor" (280). These efforts to give voice to subaltern subjects operate, Spivak argues, through a ruthless dislocation of "motives (desires), and power (of knowledge)" from the economic situation, which is put "under erasure" by Western intellectuals (280).

In developing this argument, Spivak devotes much of her critique to a deconstruction of the interview between Michel Foucault and Gilles Deleuze called "Intellectuals and Power."[6] Her interventions in this text are of considerable importance to feminist and postcolonial critics in the U.S. academy since most of their discourses on the empowerment of the Other are heavily indebted to this text. In the interview, Foucault and Deleuze propose what is, in effect, a new theoretical model for deconstructing the idea of theorist as universal intellectual—that is, for displacing the relationship between the intellectual, who traditionally would articulate theoretical knowledges for the masses, who would then follow these knowledges. As Foucault said, "the intellectual discovered that the masses no longer need him to gain knowledge: they *know* perfectly well, without illusion; they know far better than he" (Foucault and Deleuze, 207). And Deleuze states, "a theorizing intellectual, for us, is no longer a subject, a representing or representative consciousness. Those who act and struggle are no longer represented.... Representation no longer exists; there's only action" (Foucault and Deleuze, 206). The point of this retheorization and the project of empowerment following from it tries to establish an equal relationship between the intellectual and the people, specifically, the subaltern.

But it is illusory. For, as Spivak argues, the intellectual's rewriting of theory as a "relay of practice" in which "the oppressed can know and speak for themselves" reintroduces an irreducible "Subject [capital 'S'] of desire and power" and a

> self-proximate, if not self-identical, subject of the oppressed. Further, the intellectuals who are neither of these S/subjects, become transparent in the relay race, for they merely report on the nonrepresented subject and analyze (without analyzing the workings of (the unnamed Subject irreducibly presupposed by) power and desire. (Spivak, "Can the Subaltern Speak?," 279–80).

In short, the efforts to give voice to the subaltern not only reinstate an essentialized Subject of power but also "romanticiz[e] the subaltern," as she says in a *Socialist Review* interview, constituting them as "unified subjects" immune from "all of the complications of 'subject production' [that] apply to us" but do not "apply to them" (Winant, 90). Moreover, this "transparency" of the intellectual marks for Spivak the place of economic "interest" and "is maintained by a vehement denegation"—by which she means the intellectual's refusal to acknowledge his/her own economic interestedness.

This blindness is especially apparent in her critique of Foucault's notion of power which underlies this postcolonial theory of empowering the Other. In his discussion with Deleuze, Foucault invokes a "geographical discontinuity" to displace the Marxist notion of "exploitation"—and the corresponding necessity of collective economic struggle—with his own notion of diffuse power that allows for multiple resistances based on alliance politics. But such a notion of decentralized power, Spivak quite rightly argues, not only erases "the real mark of 'geographical (geopolitical) discontinuity' (which) is the international division of labor," but it is itself "made possible by a certain stage of exploitation...and is geopolitically specific to the First World" ("Can the Subaltern Speak?," 289). Foucault's argument that a new mechanism of power emerges in the seventeenth and eighteenth centuries—one that he says is "absolutely incompatible with the relations of sovereignty...and is more dependent upon bodies and what they do than upon the Earth and its products" (Power/Knowledge, 104)—is, Spivak contends, "secured *by means* of territorial imperialism—the Earth and its products—'elsewhere'" ("Can the Subaltern Speak?," 290). In other words, the very ground of this new diffuse, asystematic mechanism of power put forth by Foucault and grounding most postcolonial politics of empowering the subaltern is, in fact, historically dependent on a sovereign and systematic exercise of economic and military coercion elsewhere and not just then but also now. For Foucault is blind, Spivak maintains, not only to the "first wave of 'geographical discontinuity'"—and here she points out that the "real mark of 'geographical (geopolitical) discontinuity' is the international division of labor" ("Can the Subaltern Speak?," 289)—but Foucault also "remain[s] impervious to its second wave in the middle decades of our own century" (290)—by which she means the global economic and military domination of American imperialism that ushered in, as she quotes Mike Davis, the "new era of commercial liberalism" (290). It is this imperialist based commercial liberalism that supports contemporary bourgeois notions of discursive freedom.

Spivak's deconstruction of the concealed, ongoing imperialist politics of Western representations of the subaltern is an important critique. The outcome of such a project is a necessary one for feminist/postcolonial critics: as Spivak says, "to confront (the subaltern) is not to represent...them but to learn to represent ourselves" ("Can the Subaltern Speak?," 288–89), or as she also says, "the task of the first-world subject of knowledge in our historical moment is to resist and critique 'recognition' of the Third World through 'assimilation'" (292).

But Spivak's text also has its own blindspots or aporias, and I want to engage some of the more important ones for feminist theories of subalterity. First, for all her emphasis on the international division of labor, Spivak posits a crucial omission. In discussing the woman subaltern—"the woman...doubly in shadow"—she also raises the issue of the "heterogeneous Other," which she claims is "Outside (though not completely so) the circuit of the *international* division of labor.... Here are subsistence farmers, unorganized peasant labor, the tribals, and the communities of zero workers on the street or in the countryside" ("Can the Subaltern Speak?," 288). According to her own logic this "outside" of subalterns should also include women's subsistence labor—their unpaid domestic work. Spivak's exclusion of subsistence workers and other subalterns from the circuit of the international division of labor derives from a rather orthodox Marxist notion of labor as only wage-labor—as the production of surplus value—and excludes all other forms of labor. But materialist-feminists, specifically the German School associated with Maria Mies, have radically retheorized the issue of labor.[7] For Mies, subsistence labor—especially women's production and reproduction of the means of life, that is, use value—is not outside the international division of labor and appropriation, but rather is the very basis of the historical accumulation of capital. In other words, as Mies argues, "the capitalist production process [is] one which comprises...the *superexploitation* of non-wage laborers (women, colonies, peasants) upon which wage labor exploitation is then possible" (*Patriarchy*, 48). Extremely important for our analysis, Mies goes on to note that this superexploited, subsistence labor "is not compensated for by a wage... but is mainly determined by force or coercive institutions. This is the main reason for the growing poverty and starvation of Third World producers" (48). This relation of subsistence labor and capital accumulation is, in short, the basis of the *difference* constituting the subaltern as "different," as "other." Moreover, we need to recognize that the very privilege of the Western intellectual and feminist depends on, or rather is an economic effect of, the *superexploitation* of subsistence workers, even what Spivak calls the "zero communities of workers," and women by global capitalism.

Spivak's blindness to this relation of subsistence labor and capital accumulation leads, I believe, to a serious slippage in her analysis of the representation of the subaltern woman—in which she herself occludes the political economy, the labor relations of representation by substituting a discursive politics that textualizes the subaltern.[8] Thus we find Spivak's analysis of "*sati* or *suttee*," that is, "widow self-immolation" or widow burning in India, as, what she calls, the "exemplum of the woman-in-imperialism" almost entirely confined "within discursive practice" ("Can the Subaltern Speak?," 305, 306). She posits the "other woman," the subaltern as a silent, unrepresentable excess outside the labor relations and circulating instead in a discursive circuit in which "the figure of the woman disappears," according to Spivak, "into a violent shuttling which is the displaced figuration of the 'third-world woman' caught between tradition and modernization" (306) and concludes "there is no space from which the sexed subaltern can speak" (307); "the subaltern cannot speak" (308).

Such a conclusion, however, is the result of her reinscribing, in the end, the very discursive politics and problematic notion of empowerment that she effectively critiqued earlier in her text. For the question she asks, "Can the Subaltern Speak?," and then answers in the negative, is itself a misplaced question for a materialist postcolonial critique. To pose the problem of the subaltern in the terms, "Can she speak?," is simply to reify the project of giving a voice to the Other as the primary political agenda and to mistake a discursive empowerment for a social and economic enablement. This displacement, however, is widely shared in feminist and postcolonial discourses. As Bell Hooks writes, the process of gaining a voice is "a metaphor for self-transformation... for women of oppressed groups...coming to voice is an act of resistance. Speaking becomes both a way to engage in active self-transformation and a rite of passage where one moves from being object to being subject. Only as subjects can we speak" (12). Without denying the importance of these struggles to speak, we need also to recognize that such an agenda reinscribes the autonomous individual of bourgeois ideology in which "speaking," "coming to voice," is largely understood as a voluntaristic act of free will and consciousness, presupposing a coherent, self-identical subjectivity. The discourse of empowering voice, in short, reduces the struggles for emancipation and the end of exploitation to a discursive freedom that equates democracy with speaking, with free speech. In doing so, it displaces *material democracy*—the equal access of all to social and economic resources—and substitutes verbal empowerment for economic and social enablement; individual expression for collective social struggle to transform existing social relations.

The question "Can the Subaltern Speak?" blocks the more pressing questions for the subaltern: what are the historical, material conditions for "hearing" the subaltern and, more important, what are the effective knowledges and modes of collective subjectivity the subaltern needs to transform the economic and political conditions of her life—to intervene in the international division of labor? If we examine the "anecdote," as Spivak calls it, that provoked her despairing conclusion, "the Subaltern cannot speak," we find the subaltern speaking all along. The incident as originally described by Spivak is as follows:

> A young woman of sixteen or seventeen, Bhuvaneswari Bhaduri, hanged herself in her father's modest apartment in North Calcutta in 1926. The suicide was a puzzle since, as Bhuvaneswari was menstruating at the time, it was clearly not a case of illicit pregnancy. Nearly a decade later, it was discovered that she was a member of one of the many groups involved in the armed struggle for Indian independence. She had finally been entrusted with a political assassination. Unable to confront the task and yet aware of the practical need for trust, she killed herself. ("Can the Subaltern Speak?," 307)

Our political understanding of her "puzzling" suicide—that it was an alternative to carrying out a political assassination for the anti-colonial struggle—is the result of a letter she had left. As Spivak says—revising her view of the incident in the *Socialist Review* interview—"this woman took good care to speak, and look at what happened.... She left a letter that was discovered...even when, whether showing her political impotence or her political power, she tries to speak and make it clear, so that it would be read one way, the women in the family—radical women—decide to forget it" (Winant, 89). In other words, the subaltern is not mute, as Spivak claims, although her speaking is suppressed.

Spivak reads this as "an unemphatic, ad hoc, subaltern rewriting of the social text of *sati*-suicide" (308), but if we move beyond the bounds of "discursive practice" in which Spivak has confined her analysis, we find that this incident raises other issues for us. Not the least of these, is the question of the historical subjectivities and knowledges available to Bhuvaneswari and which would enable her to intervene to transform the economic and political relations of imperialism—that would enable her, in short, to participate in the armed resistance of the anti-colonial struggle. Her suicide would suggest that these collective subjectivities and new frames of understanding were not fully available to her and/or that the social and ideological contradictions of her specific situation did not allow her to fully take up this new position. *Why not?* That is the question. The emphasis on her "voice," her autonomous, self-evident, voluntary speaking, or on the other hand, a discursive suppression of her free speech, cover over and conceal the material and ideological issues of her struggle to build and enact a revolutionary subjectivity for herself and to actively transform the colonial relations of exploitation.

The problematic of her failed struggle is all the more apparent when we contrast this incident to the "Telangana People's Struggle" in Hyderabad a decade or so later when subaltern women—illiterate peasants, bonded laborers, and even middle-class women like Bhuvaneswari—joined in armed resistance against the extremely oppressive feudal social and economic conditions under the princely reign of the Nizam, kept in power as "subservient allies" by British colonial rule and the imperialist economic regime (Stree Shakti Sanghatana, 1). These struggles enabled the women to collectively unite in their villages to oppose the atrocities of the landowners and their police; to fight with the guerrilla squads and even to become squad commanders and barefoot doctors. The question for these women, these "subalterns," is not simply one of "coming to voice" (although many did), nor of "voice" as an unmediated expression of an already given consciousness and experience. Rather the question is what has enabled these women to struggle on their own behalf, to engage in the revolution to transform the division of labor and the limited access to social resources oppressing them? In short, what has enabled them to become collective subjects in the social and economic struggle for emancipation.

A crucial part of this answer, I believe, is the collective development of materialist "explanatory critiques"—by which I mean those practices and "struggle concepts" (the term is from Maria Mies, *Patriarchy*, 36) through which the subject develops historical knowledge of the social totality and her own subjectivities.[9] She acquires, in other words, an understanding of how the existing social institutions (such as, "motherhood," "family," "poverty") have in fact come about and how they can be changed. Critique, in other words, is that knowledge-practice that historically situates the conditions of possibility of what empirically exists under patriarchal-imperialist-capitalist labor relations and, more importantly, points to what is suppressed by the empirically existing: what *could be* (instead of what actually *is*). Critique indicates that what "is" is not necessarily the real/true but rather only the existing actuality which is transformable. The role of critique in postcolonialism and what I call resistance postmodern feminism[10] is exactly this: the production of historical knowledges that mark the transformability of existing social arrangements and the possibility of a different social organization—an organization free from exploitation. Quite simply then, critique is a mode of knowing that inquires into what is not said, into the silences and the suppressed or missing, in order to uncover the concealed operations of power and underlying socioeconomic relations connecting the myriad details and seemingly disparate events and representations of our lives. It shows how seemingly disconnected zones of culture—including the privileges of Western intellectuals and the suffering of subalterns—are in fact linked through the highly differentiated and dispersed operation of a systematic logic of exploitation and international division of labor informing all practices in societies globally under imperialist late-capitalism. In sum, materialist critique disrupts that which represents itself as what is, as natural, as inevitable, as the way things are, and exposes the way "what is" is historically and socially produced out of social contradictions and how it supports inequality. Critique enables us to not only *explain* how class, race, gender and imperialist oppression operate so we can change it, but also to collectively build the emancipatory subjectivities we need to carry out the revolutionary struggle.

While there were serious limits on the forms of historical critique available to the women in the "Telangana People's Struggle," especially regarding issues of gender, the social and political enablement of these women is deeply indebted to the knowledges and subjectivities made available to them through collective practices of critique, particularly as disseminated in political education classes. According to members of the feminist collective, Stree Shakti Sanghatana, which has written the history of these women and their resistance, "All the women refer to the (Communist) Party or the Sangham as the basis and the cause of their liberation" (Kannabiran and Lalitha, 186).

> They were taught to read and write and discuss political questions. Political classes were held for them.... The knowledge they gained as a result of these classes gave them the tools to understand their own social reality.... [T]he ideological framework provided by the Party helped the women to analyze their situation, process their knowledge and make sense of their

> surroundings.... The opportunity to act, the power to fight for control over their own lives gave the women an identity, a sense of enormous strength and wisdom. (Kannabiran and Lalitha, 185)

As was the case for the subalterns in the "Telangana Uprising," the Marxian tradition of materialist critique has been one of the most productive sites for developing a historical explanatory critique, but it is not necessarily the only site. If we resist romanticizing the subaltern, we find that the conditions of exploitation and their situation in the division of labor have led them to produce forms of materialist critique. This is quite evident in Rigoberta Menchu's autobiographical history of the struggles of subalterns in Guatemala—the collective struggle of "Indians," peasants, and Ladinos—against the landowners.[11] Menchu is a revolutionary leader of the Peasant Unity Committee (CUC) and a Nobel Peace Prize winner. In discussing the Indians' tradition of centuries of resistance to the colonial domination of Whites (the Spanish) in Guatemala, she points to, at the very least, a nascent materialist critique informing that tradition: a fundamental understanding of the division of labor and colonial exploitation based on it. When an Indian child is forty days old, she/he is initiated into the community in a collective ceremony that locates her/him in the history and knowledges of the people. First, according to Menchu, the "parents make a commitment. They promise to teach the child to keep the secrets of our people," then toward the end, the people say "Let no landowner extinguish all this, nor any rich man wipe out our customs. Let our children, be they workers or servants, respect and keep their secrets" (Burgos-Debray, 12). And again when the child is ten years old, another ceremony, according to Menchu, "reminds them that our ancestors were dishonoured by the White Man, by colonization" (Burgos-Debray, 13). Such traditions clearly mark not only a critique of the class and labor relations of colonialism, but also its cultural politics: for the subaltern to speak, to reveal the secrets of her identity *to the colonizer, to us*, is to make these vulnerable to the colonizers', to our, appropriation and assimilation, even commodification of them.

This critique was even more strongly developed out of the specific material conditions of exploitation of her family and village at the hands of the landowners, so that Menchu repeatedly tells how her father—an illiterate peasant who helped found and lead the CUC—would say, "my children there are rich people and there are poor. The rich have become rich because they took what our ancestors had away from them, and now they grow fat on the sweat of our labour. We know this is true because we live it every day, not because someone else tells us" (Burgos-Debray, 121). But this is not a self-evident, transparent experience. What Menchu calls "seeing things more clearly" or having "clarity of thought" comes from the long painful struggle of what she specifically identifies as "criticism and self-criticism" (Burgos-Debray, 166) from days and nights of discussion among the *companeros*. It is through such critique and discussion that she and other members of the CUC are able to overcome the historical barriers of racial oppression and discrimination between the Indians and *ladinos* (those of mixed Spanish and Indian blood) and to see as Menchu says that "our poverty united us...the root of our problems lay in the ownership of the land. All our country's riches are in the hands of the few" (Burgos-Debray, 166).

I want to return here to the problem of how Western feminists engage these discourses of the subaltern by critiquing Elizabeth Meese's "benevolent" and "compassionate" reading of Rigoberta Menchu's "story" in her book *(Ex)tensions*. Meese's reading is located in what she calls "feminism's double bind...that it cannot speak 'for' other women, nor can it speak 'without' or 'apart from' other women." Instead, she says, "it must create a space where women who are not these white, middle-class Anglo-American or European feminists can speak or write" (98). The unsaid of this postmodern project of empowering the Other, the subaltern to speak, is not to empower them to speak *for themselves*—for as Menchu makes clear, the subaltern *already* speaks *for* herself and *to* other subalterns—the hidden agenda is to empower the subaltern to speak to *us*. Is this just another form of imperialist appropriation masquerading as a decolonizing gesture? For all Meese's thoughtful and compassionate care—and she is both caring and careful—the end result of her encounter with the subaltern is the reinscription of the Western feminist as the sovereign subject of imperialism. This is not a personal inadequacy of Meese, but rather the historical effect of the postmodern discourses of empowerment she employs: her project is firmly located in the discursive politics of desire and power Spivak so severely critiqued in Foucault, and is thus subject to the same limitations.

Meese's aim is to "recuperate the experience of the feminist project's desire for writing the other woman" (101), or more specifically to write herself and Western feminism in a benevolent or, as she says, "compassionate" relation to the subaltern. She thus ends her writing by declaring "my own desire for feminism and (with) a Quiche Indian woman...if she can grow to love the *ladino companero*, might she someday learn to love the feminist theorist?" (128). But why should she? For as Meese quickly acknowledges and passes over at the beginning of her text:

> The undeniable complicity of the United States government in Guatemala's ongoing regime of political murder and oppression cannot be separated from my position as writer and my production of the Quiche Indian as both the tragic victim and the courageous opponent of my country. (100)

Meese and we ourselves exist, in other words, in a relation of complicity with the imperialist political and economic exploitation of Menchu and her people in the international division of labor. However, rather than critically interrogate and intervene in that systematic circuit of labor relations and exploitation, Meese completely displaces it by substituting a circuit of discursive desires and differences. Colonialism, thus, becomes largely a discursive arena from which the economic and certainly the international division of labor almost entirely disappear.

In a deconstructive move Meese repeatedly tries to put under erasure the binary oppositions of Western/Third World feminism; Self/Other; feminism/*machismo*; Indian/*ladino*; rich/poor. She sees Menchu as exemplary in "crossing over the oppositions, contradicting the contradictions" (113). She is especially concerned with Menchu's relation as an Indian/Indianist to the *ladinos* who have historically exploited and racially discriminated against Indians—the crossing over, in short, of barriers of racial discrimination. For Meese the "structural position (of the *ladino*) resembles (that of) the feminist theorist." She thus enacts a textual transfer: if Menchu can "cross over" and learn to "love the *ladino*," she can learn to "love the feminist theorist"—Meese, you, and me, thereby absolving us of our complicity and privilege in the concealed circuit of the imperialist division of labor and economic appropriation. Thus Meese claims that

> Rigoberta Menchu's struggles to liberate the racial or ethnic term from economic and moral connotations of the opposition are instructive to feminist criticism as it negotiates other (con)-founding oppositions such as masculine/feminine, political/personal. Her contribution to the discussion of *ladinos* is the retrospective awareness ("afterwards we realized") that *ladinos* can be human (like Indians) good and bad depending on how they behave rather than on any essential (blood) nature. This is

> a profoundly un/settling awareness for the revolutionary who needs to be clear about who the enemy is. (116)

But there is an equally unsettling aporia here on the part of the feminist desiring not to be complicit with the enemy: *after what* did Menchu change her understanding of *ladinos*? For Menchu, the man who taught her "to love *ladinos* a lot" (165) was "a teacher, who worked with the CUC," and taught her Spanish; he was "an intellectual," "a companero who had taken the side of the poor, although I have to say that he was middle class. He was someone who'd been able to study, who had a profession and everything. But he also understood clearly that he had to share these things with the poor, especially his knowledge" (165, 166). But, unlike Meese, whose discursive desiring erases her understanding of her position in the international division of labor, Menchu's *ladino companero* is an intellectual who has recognized and broken with his own class position and joined in solidarity in the struggle to overthrow the system producing his own privilege and exploiting Menchu. And like her he has educated himself and others into the struggle through critique, for it is in the context of discussing her relation to *ladinos*, in general, and this *ladino companero*, in particular, that Menchu stresses the "lengthy discussions" and "times for criticism and self-criticism" (166).

It is the historicity of this economic and revolutionary reality and the necessity for materialist critique that Meese's textual substitutions occlude. For Meese the "crossing over" of the boundaries of Indian and *ladino*, marked by the "*ladino/companero* opposition," is a "shifting nominalization" in which the "definitions of the oppositional terms refuse to stay put, to stay on the respective sides of the divide" (116–17), and later she again states that the "'unwieldy,' confounded category of the *companero ladino*...[is] neither strictly one nor the other, terms and identities which refuse to stay put in the very space of [Menchu's] own speaking" (119). Such rhetorical slippages finally allow her to claim these "odd hybrids, the *ladino companero*, the feminist man, the (com)passionate U.S. feminist theorist—each an instance of being neither one thing nor the other, somehow both in an uncanny identity of man and woman, enemy and friend" (121–22). The uncanny, rhetorical indeterminacy of these binary oppositions, may discursively "free" the "(com)passionate U.S. feminist theorist" from the material realities of the imperialist division of labor with its binary oppositions of exploiter and exploited, but it will do little to emancipate Menchu and other subalterns from the real conditions of starvation, torture, and death that they face in their real material struggles against the landowners and global capitalism supporting them.

Where, then, does my critique leave those of us who seek to join in solidarity with the struggles of the subalterns—with those exploited by the international division of labor—and who do not wish to appropriate them for our own desires? By way of a partial answer I would like to recall the comments of Nawal El Saadawi, the Egyptian feminist, who has said:

> As a writer, I am often invited to international conferences, and I must say that I hate this division between Eastern and Western feminists. Because, in fact, many women in the West are quite backward and many women in the East are very progressive, and vice versa, so the division between East and West is ambiguous and misleading. And when I attend such international meetings I am frequently asked a question by Western women that I know is well intentioned but, even so, is grounded in assumptions that are quite racist: "You have come from an impoverished, backward country. How can we help you?" It is always assumed that we women of color need assistance and that so-called First World women must help us. And so we often hear, "How can we help you?" We usually respond by saying, "Well, you can help us by fighting here in your country against the same system that is oppressing us all." (155)

In other words, the struggle against the exploitation of the subaltern in the international division of labor begins at home—it begins with the critique and intervention in the knowledge practices, subjectivities and social relations here at the "center" that sustain the global economic relations of postmodern, late-capitalist imperialism.

NOTES

1. The current engagement with issues of coloniality/postcoloniality is deeply indebted to the work of Fanon although Fanon often becomes the "unsaid" of these discourses. For some of the recent articulations of the concept of postcoloniality see, Vijay Mishra and Bob Hodge, "What is Post(-)colonialism?"; Kwame Anthony Appiah, "Is the Post- in Postmodernism the Post- in Postcolonial?"; Bill Ashcroft, et al. *The Empire Writes Back*; Spivak, *The Post-Colonial Critic*; and special issues of journals such as *Social Text* 31/32 (1992) and *Polygraph* 4 (1990).

2. The genealogy of postcolonialism as discourse or cultural politics traces itself to the earlier works of Fanon while the materialist understanding of postcoloniality is shaped in part by the later works of Fanon.

For discussions of the relation of cultural politics to Fanon, see especially Benita Parry, "Problems in Current Theories of Colonial Discourse"; Homi Bhabha, "Remembering Fanon: Self, Psyche, and the Colonial Condition" and "'What Does the Black Man Want?'"; Stephan Feuchtwang, "Fanonian Spaces"; and Barbara Harlow, "Narratives of Resistance." Also of importance is Memmi's *The Colonizer and the Colonized.* Some of the key texts addressing coloniality/postcoloniality in terms of dicourses or cultural politics include those of Bhabha and Trinh Minh-ha; much of the writings of Spivak as well as many of the essays in Mohanty et al., *Third World Women and the Politics of Feminism*; Eagleton, Jameson, and Said, *Nationalism, Colonialism, and Literature*; Niranjan, *Siting Translation*; JanMohamed, *Manichean Aesthetics*; Gates, *"Race," Writing and Difference*; JanMohamed and Lloyd, *The Nature and Context of Minority Discourse*; Anzaldúa, *Making Face, Making Soul*; Parker, *Nationalisms and Sexualities*; Petersen and Rutherford, *A Double Colonization*; Alcoff, "The Problem of Speaking for Others"; and such special issues of journals as "NeoColonialism," *The Oxford Literary Review* 13.1–2 (1991); "Third World Literary and Cultural Criticism," *South Atlantic Quarterly* 87.1 (1988); "Discourse of the Other: Postcoloniality, Positionality, and Subjectivity," *Quarterly Review of Film and Video* 13.1–3 (1991); "New Americanists 2: National Identities and Postnational Narratives," *Boundary 2* 19.1 (1992); "Writing after Colonialism," *Social Text* 13/14 (1986), and "Colonial Discourse," *Social Text* 19/20 (1988); "Identities," *Critical Inquiry* 18.4 (Summer 1992). A neoconservative exemplar is Pascal Bruckner's *The Tears of the White Man.*

3. Materialist critiques of coloniality and postcoloniality (although they rarely use the term) begin with Marx, *On Colonialism*; are developed by Lenin in *Imperialism: The Highest Stage of Capitalism*, and are continued more fully in such Marxist critiques as Vakhrushev, *Neocolonialism: Methods and Manoeuvres*, and Woddis, *An Introduction to Neo-Colonialism.* More recent materialist critiques include such texts as Amin, *Eurocentrism and Empire of Chaos*; Mies, *Patriarchy and Accumulation on a World Scale*; Mies et al., *Women the Last Colony*; Magubane, *The Political Economy of Race and Class in South Africa*; Fuentes and Ehrenreich, *Women in the Global Factory*; Enloe, *Bananas, Beaches and Bases*; as well as such special journal issues as "Reflections on Racism," *Thesis Eleven* 32 (1992) and "New World Order?" *Socialist Register 1992.*

4. See, for instance, Haraway, "A Manifesto for Cyborgs" and *Primate Visions*; Meese, *(Ex)tensions*; and Spivak's work since 1985.

5. I am using Maria Mies' terms here to signal not simply geospatial relations, but the historical, material relations of exploitation and unequal development (Mies, *Patriarchy*, 39–40).

6. Published in Foucault's *Language, Counter-Memory, Practice.*

7. For a discussion of "the German school," see Omvedt and for exemplary texts see Mies, *Patriarchy* and Mies et al., *Women: The Last Colony*.

8. This slippage from the economic to discourse, from a materialist critique to a tropological reading informs most of Spivak's writings, see not only the texts and interviews collected in *In Other Worlds: Essays in Cultural Politics* and *The Postcolonial Critic*, but also "Imperialism and Sexual Difference," "Naming" (Interview), "Three Women's Texts and a Critique of Imperialism," and "Woman in Difference: Mahasweta Devi's 'Douloti the Beautiful'." Spivak especially thematizes and textualizes the economic in her reading of Devi's stories.

9. For a critical discussion of critique and its uses for emancipatory politics and social struggle, see my essay, "Ludic Feminism, the Body, Performance and Labor: Bringing *Materialism* Back into Feminist Cultural Studies," and my book, *Ludic Feminism and After*, University of Michigan Press, 1995.

10. For my development of the concept of resistance postmodernism, see my texts "Writing in the Political: Resistance (Post)modernism" and "The 'Difference' of Postmodern Feminism." Also see Peter McLaren's deployment of this concept in his essay "Multiculturalism and the Postmodern Critique: Towards a Pedagogy of Resistance and Transformation."

11. *I...Rigoberta Menchu*, ed. Elisabeth Burgos-Debray.

WORKS CITED

Alcoff, Linda. "The Problem of Speaking for Others." *Culture Critique* 20 (Winter 1991–92): 5–32.

Amin, Samir. *Empire of Chaos*. New York: Monthly Review Press, 1992.

———. *Eurocentrism*. New York: Monthly Review Press, 1989.

Anzaldúa, Gloria, ed. *Making Face, Making Soul: Haciendo Caras: Creative and Critical Perspectives by Women of Color*. San Francisco: Aunt Lute Foundation, 1990.

Appiah, Kwame Anthony. "Is the Post- in Postmodernism the Post- in Postcolonial?" *Critical Inquiry* 17 (Winter 1991): 336–57.

Ashcroft, Bill et al. *The Empire Writes Back: Theory and Practice in Post-Colonial Literatures*. London and New York: Routledge, 1989.

Barrios de Chungara, Domitila. *Let Me Speak! Testimony of Domitila, a Woman of the Bolivian Mines*. New York: Monthly Review Press, 1978.

Bhabha, Homi. "The Other Question..." *Screen* 24.6 (1988): 18–36.

———. "Freedom's Basis in the Indeterminate." *October* 61 (Summer 1992): 46–57.

———. "Remembering Fanon: Self, Psyche, and the Colonial Condition." *Remaking History*. Ed. B. Kruger and P. Mariani. Seattle: Bay Press, 1989, 131–48.

———. "'What Does the Black Man Want?'" *New Formations* 1 (Spring 1987): 118–23.

Bruckner, Pascal. *The Tears of the White Man: Compassion as Contempt.* New York: Free Press, 1986.

Burgos-Debray, Elisabeth, ed. *I...Rigoberta Menchu: An Indian Woman in Guatemala.* London and New York: Verso, 1984.

"Colonial Discourse." Special issue of *Social Text* 19/20 (Fall 1988).

"Discourse of the Other: Postcoloniality, Positionality, and Subjectivity." Special issue of *Quarterly Review of Film and Video* 13.1–3 (1991).

Eagleton, Terry, Fredric Jameson and Edward Said. *Nationalism, Colonialism and Literature.* Minneapolis: University of Minnesota Press, 1990.

Ebert, Teresa. "The 'Difference' of Postmodern Feminism." *College English* 53.8 (December 1991): 886–904.

———. *Ludic Feminism and After.* University of Michigan Press, 1995.

———. "Ludic Feminism, the Body, Performance and Labor: Bringing *Materialism* Back into Feminist Cultural Studies." *Cultural Critique* 23 (Winter 1992–93): 5–50.

———. "Writing in the Political: Resistance (Post)modernism." *Legal Studies Forum* 15.4 (1991). Special issue, "Transformative Discourses in Postmodern Social, Cultural and Legal Theory": 291–304.

El Saadawi, Nawal. Untitled. *Critical Fictions: The Politics of Imaginative Writing.* Ed. Philomena Mariani. Seattle: Bay Press, 1991, 15556.

Enloe, Cynthia. *Bananas, Beaches and Bases: Making Feminist Sense of International Politics.* Berkeley: University of California Press, 1990.

Fanon, Frantz. *Black Skin, White Masks.* New York: Grove Weidenfeld, 1967.

———. *A Dying Colonialism.* 1965. New York: Grove Weidenfeld, 1967 [1965].

———. *Toward the African Revolution.* New York: Grove Press, 1969 [1967].

———. *The Wretched of the Earth.* New York: Grove Press, 1968.

Feuchtwang, Stephan. "Fanonian Spaces." *New Formations* 1 (Spring 1987): 124–30.

Fitch, Robert. "What's Left to Write?" *Voice Literary Supplement*, May 1989: 18–22.

Foucault, Michel, and Gilles Deleuze. "Intellectuals and Power." *Language, Counter-Memory, Practice.* Ed. and trans. D. Bouchard. Ithaca: Cornell University Press, 1977.

———. *Power/Knowledge.* Ed. C. Gordon. New York: Pantheon, 1980.

Fuentes, Annette, and Barbara Ehrenreich. *Women in the Global Factory.* Boston: South End Press, 1984.

Gates, Henry Louis, ed. *"Race," Writing, and Difference.* Chicago: University of Chicago Press, 1985 and 1986.

Guha, Ranajit, and Gayatri Chakravorty Spivak, eds. *Selected Subaltern Studies.* New York: Oxford University Press, 1988.

Harlow, Barbara. "Narratives of Resistance." *New Formations* 1 (Spring 1987): 131–36.

Haraway, Donna. "A Manifesto for Cyborgs: Science, Technology and Socialist Feminism in the 1980s" and Commentary. *Coming to Terms: Feminism, Theory, Politics.* Ed. Elizabeth Weed. New York and London: Routledge, 1989, 173–217.

———. *Primate Visions: Gender, Race, and Nature in the World of Modern Science.* New York: Routledge, 1989.

Hooks, Bell. *Talking Back: Thinking Feminist, Thinking Black.* Boston: South End Press, 1989.

"Identities." Special issue of *Critical Inquiry* 18.4 (Summer 1992).

JanMohamed, Abdul. *Manichean Aesthetics: The Politics of Literature in Colonial Africa.* Amherst: University of Massachusetts Press, 1983.

JanMohamed, Abdul, and David Lloyd. *The Nature and Context of Minority Discourse.* New York: Oxford University Press, 1990.

Kannabiran, Vasantha, and K. Lalitha, "That Magic Time: Women in the Telangana People's Struggle." *Recasting Women: Essays in Colonial History.* Ed. Kumkum Sangari and Sudesh Vaid. New Delhi: Kali for Women, 1989. (Rpt. Rutgers University Press).

Kaufman, Michael T. "Of Parades and Union Spirit and a Handful of Spectators." *New York Times* 8 Sept. 1993: New York Pages, B12.

Lenin, V.I. *Imperialism: The Highest Stage of Capitalism.* New York: International Publishers, 1939.

Magubane, Bernard. *The Political Economy of Race and Class in South Africa.* Rev. ed. New York: Monthly Review Press, 1980.

Marx, Karl and Frederick Engels. *On Colonialism.* New York: International Publishers, 1972.

McLaren, Peter. "Multiculturalism and the Postmodern Critique: Towards a Pedagogy of Resistance and Transformation." *Cultural Studies* 7.1 (January 1993). Special issue on "The Politics of Pedagogy/The Pedagogy of Culture(s), 118–46.

Meese, Elizabeth. *(Ex)tensions: Re-Figuring Feminist Criticism.* Urbana: University of Illinois Press, 1990.

Memmi, Albert. *The Colonizer and the Colonized.* 1965. Rpt. Boston: Beacon Press, 1967.

Mies, Maria. *Patriarchy and Accumulation on a World Scale: Women in the International Division of Labour.* London and Atlantic Highlands, NJ: Zed Books, 1986.

Mies, Maria et al. *Women: The Last Colony.* London and Atlantic Highlands, NJ: Zed Books, 1988.

Minh-Ha, Trinh T. *When the Moon Waxes Red: Representation, Gender and Cultural Politics.* New York: Routledge, 1991.

———. *Woman, Native, Other: Writing Postcoloniality and Feminism.* Bloomington: Indiana University Press, 1989.

Mishra, Vijay, and Bob Hodge, "What is Post(-)colonialism?" *Textual Practice* 5.3 (Winter 1991): 399–414.

Mitchell, W. J. T. "Postcolonial Culture, Postimperial Criticism." *Transition* 56 (1992): 11–19.

Mohanty, Chandra et al. *Third World Women and the Politics of Feminism.* Bloomington: Indiana University Press, 1991.

"Neocolonialism." Special issue of *The Oxford Literary Review* 13.1–2 (1991).

"New Americanists 2: National Identities and Postnational Narratives." Special issue of *Boundary* 2 19.1 (Spring 1992).

"New World Order?" *Socialist Register 1992.* Ed. R. Miliband and L. Panitch. New York: Monthly Review Press, 1992.

Niranjana, Tejaswini. *Siting Translation: History, Post-Structuralism, and the Colonial Context.* Berkeley: University of California Press, 1992.

Omvedt, Gail. "'Patriarchy': The Analysis of Women's Oppression." *Insurgent Sociologist* 13.3 (Spring 1986): 30–50.

Parry, Benita. "Problems in Current Theories of Colonial Discourse." *Oxford Literary Review* 9.1–2 (1987): 27–58.

Petersen, Kirsten Holst, and Anna Rutherford, eds. *A Double Colonization: Colonial and Post-Colonial Women's Writing.* Mundelstrup, Denmark and Oxford, England: Dangaroo Press, 1986.

"Post-Colonial Cultures of Resistance." Special Issue of *Polygraph* 4 (1990).

"Reflections on Racism." *Thesis Eleven* 32 (1992).

Smith, Sidonie and Julia Watson, eds. *De/Colonizing the Subject: The Politics of Gender in Women's Autobiography.* Minneapolis: University of Minnesota Press, 1992.

Social Text 31/32 (1992). Special issue on "The Question of Post-colonialism and the Third World."

Spivak, Gayatri Chakravorty. "Can the Subaltern Speak?" *Marxism and the Interpretation of Culture.* Ed. C. Nelson and L. Grossberg. Urbana: University of Illinois Press, 1988, 271–313.

———. *In Other Worlds: Essays in Cultural Politics.* New York and London: Methuen, 1987.

———. "Imperialism and Sexual Difference." *Oxford Literary Review* 8.1–2 (1986): 225–40.

———. "Naming" (Interview). *Stanford Humanities Review* 1.1 (Spring 1989): 84–97.

———. "The Political Economy of Women as Seen by a Literary Critic" and Commentary. *Coming to Terms.* Ed. Elizabeth Weed. New York and London: Routledge, 1989, 218–39.

———. *The Post-Colonial Critic: Interviews, Strategies, Dialogues.* Ed. S. Harasym. New York and London: Routledge, 1990.

———. "Three Women's Texts and a Critique of Imperialism." *Critical Inquiry* 12 (Autumn 1985): 243–61.

———. "Woman in Difference: Mahasweta Devi's 'Douloti the Beautiful'." *Nationalisms & Sexualities.* Ed. A. Parker et al. New York and London: Routledge, 1992.

Stree Shakti Sanghatana. *"We Were Making History": Women and the Telangana Uprising.* London: Zed Books, 1989.

"Third World Literary and Cultural Criticism." Special issue of *The South Atlantic Quarterly* 87.1 (Winter 1988).

Vakhrushev, Vasily. *Neocolonialism: Methods and Manoeuvres.* Moscow: Progress, 1973.

Winant, Howard. "Gayatri Spivak on the Politics of the Postcolonial Subject" (Interview). *Socialist Review* 90.3 (1990): 81–97.

Woddis, Jack. *Introduction to Neo-Colonialism.* New York: International Publishers, 1967.

"Writing after Colonialism." Special issue of *Social Text* 13/14 (Winter/Spring 1986).

10

AMITAVA KUMAR

Postcolonial Tour 93 (All Major U. S. Cities)

Postcoloniality is the jewel in the crown of the United States academic-cultural empire.

The raw materials most often come from the fertile and economically depressed regions of the South, are processed and profitably packaged in the lit. crit. industry here, and then quickly sold to consumers in the North and, with considerably less success, elsewhere. The reality, of course, is more complex than that but only slightly so.

One has to note, for example, that postcolonial studies under the broader rubric of multiculturalism is hailed as a response to the darkening demographics, so to speak, of this part of the North American continent. By the end of the century white folks will only be a minority in this country. But, the crucial question is: will they not be a dominant minority? The answer, by all accounts, is yes. And in the context of this piece, it is worth asking whether the constitution of what is being described as postcoloniality doesn't foreclose the advancement of colored people "here" and certainly "there"?[1]

Please think of what follows as a personal guide to what one might with false cheerfulness call the Postcolonial Tour 93. I'd like to map partially here the emergence of "emergent literatures" in the United States, mainly through visible and influential presentation in journals and special issues over the past several years.

On the subject of tours, consider the proposition that the teaching of postcolonial literature in this country is quite a bit like holding a Band-Aid concert for the starving Ethiopians in a stadium in New

York, London, or Paris. After all, concerts will not help unless the debilitating policies of food production imposed by the IMF and the World Bank are reversed—according to one economist, only about 6 percent of Ethiopian agriculture is modern, and almost all of it produces coffee for export rather than food for the people (Sehdev Kumar, 48–49).

In a way similar to the postcolonial economist commenting on Ethiopia, Henry Louis Gates, Jr., writing about African-American studies, serves caution to those who have been celebrating the introduction of multicultural curricula: "It sometimes seems that blacks are doing better in the college curriculum than they are in the streets" (*Loose Canons*, 19). This is true also of the widely burgeoning postcolonial courses in U. S. universities. In the case of India—during the same time that more books by writers of Indian origin were being published here in the United States, a journal was launched here, and at least three anthologies of Indian writing were announced—the government of the Indian elite put into effect its IMF and World Bank–directed New Economic Policy that inaugurated a new era of bondage for the Indian poor under the heel of U. S. corporate interests. Expenditures on essential development and social welfare programs were slashed and (academics please note!) research and development expenditure further declined from the already low $2.76 per capita compared to $100–600 per capita in more prosperous countries (Bidwai, *Times*, 14; quoted in *People's Front*, 14). As the noted journalist Praful Bidwai put it: "The earlier conjunction between non-alignment and the pursuit of national interest is dead. India, which for so long—under the irrepressibly moralistic, left-inclined Jawaharlal Nehru, the implacable Indira Gandhi, the maverick Morarji Desai and the unreliable Rajiv Gandhi—defied U. S. tutelage, has finally come around" ("India's Passage," 50).

I invoke this depressing scenario not to posit any simple relation between the growth of the postcolonial studies enterprise and the greater exploitation of the people living in those countries designated as postcolonial. Instead, my purpose is to underline my search to understand the extent or degree to which, if at all, these asymmetries have been addressed by the many journals that have sought to define and enrich the field of postcolonial studies.

In the fall of 1986, when I arrived from India to join the graduate program at Syracuse University, the special issue of *Critical Inquiry* on "'Race,' Writing, and Difference" had come out the previous year and was about to be joined by a companion volume of rejoinders. This set of special issues (12.1 [1985] and 13.1 [1986]), later published by the University of Chicago Press, quickly became a benchmark for scholars around me working on issues of race and postcoloniality. Henry Louis Gates, Jr., the editor of *"Race," Writing, and Difference*, presented the object of the volume's collective inquiry in terms of "the curious dialectic between formal language use and the inscription of metaphorical racial differences" (6). It was in relation to this declared focus on the language-based construction of Otherness that later volumes would define their interest and emphasis.

Hence, in his preface to a special issue of *Modern Fiction Studies* dealing with "narratives of colonial resistance," Timothy Brennan declared that "in contrast to the excellent and varied work published recently in mainstream journals under the rubric of 'minority' or 'colonial' discourse—I felt that specific attention should be paid to the social upheavals underlying the renewed interest of minority discourse itself" (3). Although the difference that Brennan was seeking to establish was more of degree than of kind, it is certainly worth noting that there was an explicit attention in this volume to go beyond the use of the Third World as a base to transform literary studies in the United States. In fact, one of the contributors to that volume, John Beverley, concluded his analysis of testimonial narratives in Latin America with the question whether attempts to set up alternative canons do not, in reality, "preempt or occlude a vision of an emergent popular-democratic culture that is no longer based on the institutions of humanism and literature" (28).

The other season-opener at that time, in the spring of 1989, was a special issue of *Discourse* in whose pages the editor, Trinh T. Minh-ha, extended Gates's interest in the linguistic inscription of difference by drawing attention to the "crises of meaning, subject, and structure...inherent to the signifying function." For Trinh, it was language, poetical language to be more precise, where "the social code is undone, decomposed, desedimented, expanded, and renewed, hence, the focal point for cultural consciousness and change" (5). The contributors to that collection acknowledged the indeterminacy of language, not only in poetry or literature but also in popular culture and film. What was being "unnamed" here was not so much the divisions of the world or even the divisions into disciplines; instead, it was the traditional anthropological-theoretical practice of imposing divisions, and the habit of naming them, that was being critiqued or undone.

Of course, the schematic opposition I have set up between two trends in the configuration of postcolonial studies has, to an extent, only the false excitement of pop-criticism: should the Oscar go to *Gandhi* or to *E.T.*? Where this opposition does become useful is in trying to discern how the tension of this binary—a tension that has been present in the debates around postcoloniality, informed as they have been by the productive differences of Marxism, poststructuralism, feminism, gay and lesbian studies—has been played upon in several analyses and what the consequences have been of such interrogations. In 1987, the twin issues of *Cultural Critique* devoted to the elaboration of minority discourse performed the early service of suggesting the complex tasks awaiting the growth of postcolonial studies. Abdul R. JanMohamed and David Lloyd helpfully insisted on the need for disciplinary as well as institutional transgressions ("Introduction: Toward a Theory" and "Introduction: Minority Discourse"). If we examine the journals that were produced in the years that followed, then, in that outbreak of interest in postcolonial studies we witness the fulfillment of the first part of JanMohamed and Lloyd's appeal, but hardly ever the second. In other words, the consolidation of postcolonial studies has largely been a function of its engagement with other fields of study (history, anthropology, film studies), but very little with groups, organizations, or peoples united in struggles outside the walls of the academy.

A good example of productive, disciplinary cross-hatching is the recent debate in the pages of *Public Culture* (4.2 [1992] and 5.1 [1992]) on the function of pomp and power in postcolonial Africa.[2] That debate, which "brings together" historians, political scientists, anthropologists, specialists in literature, and cultural theorists, is significant because it demonstrates that the chief benefit of a dialogue across disciplines is that one is more likely to escape the trap of generalization and produce specific, more accurate knowledge. Earlier, in 1987, Aijaz Ahmad's polemical and influential rejoinder to Fredric Jameson in the pages of *Social Text* generated the amount of attention it did not only because it provided fodder for the anti-Marxist opponents of Jameson (see Ahmad, "Jameson's Rhetoric" and Jameson, "Third World Literature"). Rather, Ahmad forcefully brought home to West-based academics that the particularities of the so-called Third World nations couldn't be subsumed under false generalizations, however well-intentioned.

Much before Ahmad's text, Chandra Talpade Mohanty had critiqued the Western feminist scholarship that produced the singular and monolithic subject called the "Third World Woman" only to perpetuate a discourse that remains colonizing. More recently, the previously mentioned essays by McClintock and Shohat put a much-needed stress on a finely differentiated and historically responsible production of analyses. And yet, in spite of this healthy demand, these debates for many readers signify only a call to perform better readings rather than to perform readings for better ends. Thus, for example, in an attempt to "go further" than what usually goes on in academic debates, V. Y. Mudimbe concludes his article in *Public Culture* by firmly establishing, beyond the conventions of criticism, the common goal of the betterment of Africa: "I believe that the masochist period has lasted long enough. Let us remain critical and, at the same time, try to balance our critiques with concrete and programmatic projects" (61–62).

Why has there been a general absence, an absence quite glaring in the prestigious journals and hyped-up offerings of university presses, of broad efforts and initiatives aimed at interrupting interpretation and introducing change? To my mind, it is linked both to the preservation of the institution of literary studies and to the limits of the class and broadly cultural alliances of academics dealing with the postcolonial question. Moreover, among the scholars of postcoloniality, the guilt, but also the pain, of not providing what Mudimbe calls "concrete and programmatic projects" finds its expression and sublimation through the interminable interest in the figure of the intellectual. Not entirely without a sense of irony, let me retrace some of that discussion for you, dear reader, my *yaar*.

It's difficult to discern clearly the features of a ghost, but methinks it's Salman Rushdie in the darkness out there. It's not very scholarly to name a phenomenon after an apparition, but let me risk giving the problem of the postcolonial intellectual the unseemly title of "the Rushdie Syndrome." Therein lies a perverse tale of magical realism.

When Rushdie published *Midnight's Children* in 1981, the *New York Times* described the event as "a Continent finding its voice," a comment which presumed, as Aijaz Ahmad caustically put it, that "one has no voice if one does not speak in English" (3). A few years later, after his novel *The Satanic Verses* was banned in India, Rushdie wrote an "Open Letter to Rajiv Gandhi" and published it in the *New York Times* (where else but in the pages of the *Times* could one possibly address the Indian prime minister!). It was now Rushdie's turn to be presumptuous. He glibly turned the ban and its withdrawal into the touchstone of Indian democracy: "The question raised by the book's banning is precisely whether India, by behaving in this fashion, can any more lay claim to the title of a civilized society." And one wanted to ask: "Where were you, Mr Rushdie, when the Sikhs were butchered and burnt during the November 1984 riots in Delhi?"[3]

The point I'm trying to narrativize here is that selective, self-serving logic that thrives on ignorance sustains much of what is valorized as postcolonial. In the special issue of *The South Atlantic Quarterly* entitled "Third World Literary and Cultural Criticism," Timothy Brennan rightly argued that Rushdie was the Westernized, cosmopolitan intellectual, who because of his ideological proximity to the metropolitan centers, could be readily accepted as the proud mascot of postcolonial cultural production. But Rushdie, Brennan went on, was a far cry from those intellectuals, like the Nicaraguan poet José Coronel Urtecho, who were fashioning a literature and a community of resistance outside the prestige-economy of the West and its contempt for national-popular cultures.[4] Even now, our opposition to the Iranian theocracy's *fatwa* against Rushdie shouldn't be allowed to obscure the fact that postcolonial celebrities do not share the condition of the masses of Asia or Africa, and even if they sometimes do, they are rarely sighted in the service of postcolonial studies in the U. S. academy.

Middle- and upper-middle class immigrants in the West, with little or no history of involvement in organized or even unorganized struggles, are today, Rushdie-like, assuming the voice of entire continents and their silenced masses (see Ahmad, *In Theory*). It is this isolation, very much supported by the dominant ideology here, that I must fault for the regular inability to move beyond the function of reading—while often reproducing a rhetoric replete with the language of radicality and change.[5]

There is a recognition, sometimes, of the limits of reading. For instance, Gayatri Chakravorty Spivak has persistently critiqued all complacent assumptions about the accessibility of displaced subjectivities: "[T]he subaltern is the name of the place which is so displaced from what made me and the organized resister, that to have it speak is like Godot arriving on a bus" (81). But such has been the complacency on the part of much of Spivak's audience that such criticism, instead of lending greater momentum to self-reflexive actions directed at dismantling those structures that engender subalternity, has often provided occasion for endless self-agonizing about the goals—indeed, the very possibility—of critical acts.[6]

The hostile current intellectual climate is well revealed in the words of a Republican nominee to the National Endowment for the Humanities advisory council when he promises that he is "going to adopt a West Point approach and sound the guns against those in the humanities who want to destroy the greatness of our intellectual past" (Winkler, A5). This kind of conservative belligerence has had the unfortunate consequence not only of retarding the legitimation and growth of multicultural syllabi, but also, more seriously, keeping scholars locked in the limited gesture of only demanding more inclusive curricula—and then basking in the victory of having achieved that hard-fought but hollow goal.

The tragedy of the Rushdie syndrome is that it is unable to address or explain the crisis of readership. Who are our readers and what are the limits of the readings we propose? Eduardo Galeano has written eloquently about the "indirect censorship" through the illiteracy that pervades the so-called Third World. If, like Galeano, we note the difficulties that attend our writings, we will be drawing attention to the socioeconomic and ideological structures that overdetermine our cultural production.

Further, postcolonial intellectuals, rather than remaining satisfied with the transparent positivity of a curriculum that includes names beautifully inflected with other accents and colors, are especially poised to introduce radical doubt even in the liberal heart of the American academy. My departmental colleague, John Mowitt, has written of the horizon that lies beyond the antinomy of the "political correctness" debate: "This is much more than a matter of anticipating, and to that extent identifying with, the others' position. It is a matter of inscribing within one's own position the possibility and necessity of a position which is obscured by what one opposes" (221). The general ambivalence that Mowitt is here proposing translates, in what I have been very generally calling the postcolonial context, into a continual reassessment of claims and concepts.

I want to conclude by briefly examining or reassessing the term "difference," which is perhaps the privileged first entry in the lexicon of multicultural studies.

Winifred Woodhull, in her article in the recent *Yale French Studies* double-volume on "Post/Colonial Conditions," quotes the North African writer Tahar Ben Jelloum, who, calling for a rhetoric of integration in the anti-racist struggles, points out that the right to difference is now "a hollow and dangerous gimmick [which has been] prostituted and above all appropriated by the opportunism of advertising to the point that it will have to be left to the unimaginative politicians and the peddlers of cigarette lighters" (7).

Ben Jelloum's argument could not have had greater pertinence in the context of the present moment. At the time of the writing of this article, more than 1.8 million people in Germany are demanding recognition as citizens and protection from murderous racist attacks. The Turkish "guest worker" invited to Germany during the boom years of the earlier decades continues to be the "auslander" [foreigner]. In late May, the banner with the words "Born Here, Burned Here," hung in front of the house where five women and children were fire-bombed, was aimed at contesting the logic of imposed difference. In that context, as well as in other, parallel cases of discriminatory separations, whether of African-Americans in the United States or of Palestinians at the hands of the Israelis in the Occupied Territories, the discussion cannot be limited to a bland celebration of difference. Rather, as Ben Jelloum indicates, we have to recognize as a necessary step the rejection of any adherence to essentialized difference or a fixed understanding of integration.[7] That necessary step allows us to get farther away from vague idealisms and false, ahistorical illusions.

It also brings us—or will bring us—closer to critical practices where we can imagine postcolonial intellectuals organizing around the issue of economic low-intensity conflict or the complete devastation of the education system in our countries of origin. Those who undertake the production of the next special issue on postcoloniality must also face urgent questions of announcing forums or associations for forging unities that will lead to such critical practices—words and actions that will make visible in new and more challenging ways than I can do here with these photographs, the fight of the workers inside the United States for a radically different global order, the dreams of the struggling peoples in India or Brazil or anywhere else, and the demands for food, housing, and a decent wage made by those outside the academy's walls right here.

PERFORMING POSTCOLONIALITY

Right-wing tracts written in recent years by the likes of Roger Kimball and Dinesh D'Souza have had the dubious virtue of containing answers to questions that George Bush was perhaps too smart to ask Rush Limbaugh. However, the new emphasis on

multicultural pedagogy, which is the ostensible target of Kimball and D'Souza, finds its more productive critique in the writings of other, more committed, left-inclined scholars.

In the course of his presidential address at the 1992 Annual Meeting of the Modern Language Association, Houston Baker self-critically denounced the false and hypocritical universalism that underlies the bland invocation of the familiar holy trinity of cultural analyses: "[O]ur resolute inclusiveness amounts to no more than a thoughtless pandering to high-flown, abstract ideals. 'PC' might then signify a 'pandering calculus'—a rhetoric of limits designed to standardize variations of 'race, class, gender' for normal multicultural classroom settings" (404). In opposition to a normative and homogenizing teaching, Baker called for "a new, local pedagogy for a new day of freedom" (409). This pedagogy, in its attention to the particular, and, moreover, in opening a process of dialogue with it, is distinguished by its interest in the concrete and the contextual.

Baker presents a scenario from one of his lectures. Today, in his Black Women's writing class, Professor Baker is going to deal with the poetry of Phillis Wheatley. In class, the discussion among most students and the teacher on topics like the neoclassical literary conventions in Wheatley's poetry is carried on with considerable intellectual fervor. When a black female undergraduate, sitting in the corner in his lecture-room, asks why the class isn't discussing the question of Wheatley's importance for the black community, Professor Baker points out that the class was intended to develop "reading skills." The professor proclaims with some gravity that "we are going to learn to be sophisticated readers of black expressive-cultural texts" (403). In retrospect, chastened by the poor performance of his students and speaking as a reformed pedagogue, Baker admits that the only fit reading "for a course devoted to black women's writing was a cultural-political one emphasizing local geographies": "Such a reading would have recognized the undergraduate voice from the corner not as a multicultural abstraction of 'race and gender' but as an actual black woman's voice rife with narrative potential" (404). The teacher is not a poor learner. As a redemptive gesture, Baker takes us on a critical tour of the immediate environs of his lecture-room, to the street lined with white-male fraternity houses whose occupants threaten the lives and peace of black, female, lesbian and gay, and other minority students.

This attentiveness to the particular shares obvious qualities with struggles elsewhere that are marked by the refusal to be obliterated by the general idea. For example, when the eighties ended in India, the decade closed its eyes on a steadily declining political climate marked by the violent lumpenization of public culture and institutions. Amidst that bloody transformation, the People's Union for Democratic Rights, a Delhi-based human rights organization, continued its work of recording and protesting abuses suffered by the common people at the hands of the state and the powerful. A report released by the organization, on the struggles of refugee women workers in Delhi, ended with a piece of verse in Hindi: "We don't have to fight for some symbol/ for some name/for some grand program/We have to fight a rather small fight/for the small people/for small things."

This ambition to address the local, the immediate, and the urgent is rooted in the open solidarity shared with those who are often dropped out of the results of huge, magnificent schemes and the grand slogans for social change. The activism of the Delhi human rights workers is akin to a type of pedagogy that, as Houston Baker puts it, creates "an inescapably shared situation" which, in turn, "produces an inescapable sense of immediate responsibility" (405). And yet, when you invoke Delhi or Dhaka, Nairobi or Johannesburg, San Salvador or Saigon, particularly in the U. S. academy, how do you provoke that shared response that we have so far been describing as a feature of the pedagogy of the local?

The artist who among all the names that one usually encounters in the lists of (post)colonial intellectuals best epitomizes the insurgent significance of the local is the Kenyan writer, Ngũgĩ wa Thiong'o. Ngũgĩ attained rebellious importance—and success as a mobilizer, which ultimately earned him a stay in the prison of the repressive Kenyan state—by abandoning English and adopting Gikuyu and Kiswahili, the primary languages of the people around him, as the languages for his writing. His interest in theater, for instance, was motivated by the situational understanding that drama was an inherent part of any Kenyan's existence: "it was part and parcel of the rhythm of daily and seasonal life of the community" (see especially the chapter on "The Language of African Theatre").

It was not simply the relation to the ritual and ceremonial practices of song and dance, common among the populace, that gave theater its active force in Kenya. Rather, as Ngũgĩ makes clear, it was its relation to the lived histories and struggles of the people that allowed theater to stage communal dialogue and social change. The vital relevance of the experiment at the Kamiriithu Community Education and Cultural Centre lay in the type of preeminently pedagogical exchanges among the people, described in fascinating detail by Ngũgĩ.[8] As definitely as they make shoes for the Canadian corporation, we find the Kenyan workers giving shape to the changing conditions of their understanding. The workers, in Ngũgĩ's narrative, begin to account—in several senses of that word—for the circumstances of their lives. They ask why they are paid only a pittance, they count the number of comrades who have died in those factories. When a worker removes his shirt to show the marks of the burns, he dramatizes his own struggles and the broader struggle between capital and labor. "'Gases,' he said. 'And what did I get as compensation? Dismissal. Laid off. Without even a watch for my faithfulness in service'" (55).

This terrible meaningfulness, the import of the local, cannot unproblematically bear transfer to a classroom in a North American university. In fact, while the didactic model of exchange among the Kenyan workers might have great value here as a method of collective inquiry, its plain invocation here, without bringing the lessons home, as it were, is not going to be altogether different from the business-as-usual purveying of the exotic, the merely different, the Other. Two texts that in my own experience have been useful in helping students perceive their own locality by making visible the relations between "here" and "there" are Jamaica Kincaid's *A Small Place* and Paul Smith's "Visiting the Banana Republic." Both of these essays, in their different ways, use the figure of the "tourist" to explicate the exploitative relation that binds the North American to the countries of the South. I might mention as an aside that the "North American" in these essays is a construct that leaves aside the indigent populations here that do not go to Antigua for their vacations or even shop at Gap or Banana Republic. And, although the possibility of engaging the inhabitants of "the Other America"—to use Michael Harrington's famous phrase—is a part of the larger story I'm telling here, it is worth noting that Kincaid's book and Smith's essay entertain no delusions about the poor in this country being necessarily free from the effects of capitalism and advertising, levitating in some pure realm of politically conscious nirvana. In that sense, therefore, these texts challenge students to confront what they think and what they know about the so-called "Third World."

Kincaid's marvellously polemical piece, which opens with the words, "If you go to Antigua as a tourist, this is what you will see..." remaps the Third World and locates its geography in the wasteland of Western, multinational control and a greedy, racist ignorance. Her prose, remarkably candid in its confrontational address, repeatedly presses on the Western reader-tourist "visiting Antigua" the lesson of global inequities and contradictions—sometimes, in twenty-five words or so: "When you sit down to eat your delicious meal, it's better that you don't know that most of what you are eating came off a plane from Miami. And before it got on a plane in Miami, who knows where it came from? A good guess is that it came from a place like Antigua first, where it was grown dirt-cheap, went to Miami, and came back" (14).

In Smith's essay, the local in the sense that I have been describing it, as the weight of subjective involvement and responsibility, is engendered through an innovative, two-fold critique. An analysis of the U. S. clothing industry's exploitative role in Asia is interwoven with a witty critique of the representational strategies used by that industry to produce a laundered history of imperial loot and neocolonial plunder. What does it mean for you to wear a Banana Republic shirt? For undergraduates in your class on postcoloniality or cultural studies, this question becomes a helpful way to approach what Smith, in his reading of the Banana Republic sales catalog, calls an attempt "to simply satirize or to evacuate antagonism from the actual history and to install that history as the origin of contemporary and readily available benefits" (144). At the same time, as Smith shows, the question also opens the way for building an understanding of the global economic order based on the production of "free production zones (FPZs) and export processing zones (EPZs) in the third world" (132). At the level of the economy and also at the level of culture, the local Self is shown to be implicated in the production and impoverishment of that seemingly distant Other.

For students in the West, and certainly for the people at large held in the smothering embrace of the commercial culture, the following exchange between Donald Duck and an African witch doctor (whatever the referent might be of that phrase) is a window to the understanding as well the representation of the postcolonial spaces:

> Donald (talking to a witch doctor in Africa): "I see you're an up to date nation!
> Have you got telephones?"
> Witch doctor: "Have we gottee telephones!...All colors, all shapes...only trouble is only *one* has wires. It's a hot line to the world loan bank." (Quoted in Dorfman and Mattelart, 48)

The excellent "handbook of decolonisation" (John Berger's praise) in which this exchange is quoted, Ariel Dorfman and Armand Mattelart's *How to Read Donald Duck*, is one of the very few texts that employ trenchant critiques of mass culture representations to demystify colonial exploitation and anti-colonial struggles.[9] It is on the terrain of mass culture, however—because it is the ground of increasingly more knowledge and experience—that the shared response will have to be sought, from students as well as other public citizens. It is in that spirit that I now introduce a brief newspaper piece I wrote as a response to the hysteria surrounding the so-called Dream Team during the 1992 Barcelona Olympics—and the repetition of the Gulf War Syndrome, this time as farce.

There is only one thing wrong with the U. S. basketball "dream team": Gen. Norman Schwarzkopf isn't its coach.

In the opening minutes of the game against Angola, the NBC commentators could hardly control their feelings of silly triumph—against a country which has only two modern indoor gyms and whose professional basketball is still sustained entirely through its absorption in the markets of its former colonial master, Portugal. And I couldn't help but think that the only missing touch in this triumphalist celebration was Stormin' Norman's directing hand, explaining to the servile press and the public the broad mechanism of the attack marshaled by Magic Johnson, the striking power of Michael Jordan, and the broadly admired aggressivity of Charles Barkley.

If you, like me, had already had your lunch that Saturday afternoon when the game began, the feeling of belligerent well-being that oozed out of the television screen would have made your stomach heave. What made it worse was that viewers were held prisoners by the equally nauseous advertising, which also shamelessly touted worldwide U. S. hegemony as a pleasant fact: "Coca Cola, the One Taste the Whole World Shares." Yes? If Randy Travis, the country singer collecting megadollars for being the Coke spokesperson, were to be plucked from his studio-ranch and put in a Third World slum, the only thing he'd probably be prepared to eat would be his words.

Why do we continue to be given pleasures wrapped in the national flag? This question is all the more painful in a context where we have witnessed in the parade of nations the appearance of teams in tattered flags, like waifs enshrouded in the smoke of a house that has been burnt down. Think, for example, about Croatia and, if you dare, about Palestine.

The point is not to evoke sympathy for new or weak nations; instead, let's reflect on the inadequacy of nationalism as a doctrine to lead us to war or even our games. We need to face the inescapable questions of history, of colonial plunder and continuing neo-exploitation today, so that we realize that national configurations are at best problematic. Nations differ from each other or, more accurately, most nations have been held hostage to the whims and the needs of the powerful ones through most of recent history. Let me make this point clearer by appealing to basketball and one of its most fetishized images: the Nike Air shoe.

According to the latest *Harper's* magazine, it will take an Indonesian worker who makes a Nike shoe 44,492 years to earn the $20 million endorsement fee that Michael Jordan gets paid for endorsing it. If you hasten to point out that the Indonesian worker will be quite unlikely to execute any of the masterful slam-dunks that Jordan repeatedly produces in the air enroute to the basket, let me remind you that one of the chief reasons why

Indonesia is unable to boast of Jordans and Johnsons is that for every Nike shoe that sells for $80 in the United States the Indonesian worker who produced it gets only 12 cents.

Sportsmen and women are not produced in a vacuum. The next time you hear NBC commentators go gaga over a victory in a game against yet another small Third World nation, remember to ask preliminary questions, like: when was the last time Bush bombed that country, or Reagan imposed an embargo against it, or whoever else named Rockefeller or Guggenheim stole copper from its shores.[10]

I have quoted my journalistic writing because I need to make an additional point. That our students should examine the general aspects of mass and popular culture also has as its emphatic partner the argument that teachers should be active participants in public, nonacademic cultures. Addressing literary critics and cultural theorists, Edward Said has written that "instead of noninterference and specialization, there must be interference, crossing of borders and obstacles, a determined attempt to generalize exactly at those points where generalizations seem impossible to make" (157). The first among the interferences that Said recommends is the crossing from literature to journalism. His thinking is fuelled by a clear-sighted understanding of what he deems required of a social, critical consciousness. And my own appreciation for Said's argument is as much motivated by the wish to redefine U. S. academic professionalism and tenure requirements as it is by what is clearly the greater need of constructing (in Homi Bhabha's phrase) "a migrant or postcolonial public sphere."

Let me sketch out, albeit a bit schematically, some of the concerns that might inform a theory of postcolonial pedagogy, particularly its reliance on past disciplinary or institutional transgressions in other, emergent fields of inquiry like feminist studies and queer theory. I have tried to organize these meditations around the trope of "border crossings."

1. For Henry Giroux, postcolonial theory serves as one of the primary conditions that produces what he calls "border pedagogy":

> The terrain of learning becomes inextricably linked to the shifting parameters of place, identity, history, and power. Border pedagogy shifts the emphasis of the knowledge/power relationship away from the limited emphasis on the mapping of domination toward the politically strategic issue of engaging the

> ways in which knowledge can be remapped, reterritorialized, and decentered in the wider interests of rewriting the borders and coordinates of an oppositional cultural politics. (30)

Giroux's rather general statement is certainly acceptable as a programmatic sentiment; the task of rewriting and coordination he recommends, however, must necessarily inhabit the grain of specific national, regional, and sometimes local, differences. Among other questions, it is pertinent to inquire whether Giroux assumes this refashioning to be undertaken "here" in the United States or "there" in the so-called Third World. An attention to specific contexts might redefine one's optimism and also the particular ends of any pedagogical program. Let me provide a brief example.

In *Liberation* (New Delhi), a journal that represents the opinion of the parliamentary as well as extraparliamentary left in India, the attempt to instigate what Giroux calls "an oppositional cultural politics" has included the recovery of a history that is different from the one being popularized by the religious right. Thus, in a recent issue of that journal (April 1991), the portrait of a militant leader of the early 1900s, Bhagat Singh, is printed on the back cover, with his name, and the titles "Rashtra Nayak" [National Leader], Shaheed-e-Azam [Martyr of the Nation], and, in English, "Harbinger of New India, Symbol of Clarity and Confidence for a Nation in Confusion and Crisis." This is not very different from the discourse of a bourgeois-nationalist party like the Congress (I), which would almost certainly have appealed to a different persona from Indian history but employed a similar rhetoric! A different approach would involve the border-crossing into ordinary culture, where the Indian leftists would discover, on the doors of the lorries and on calendars sold in stores on the streets, portraits of Bhagat Singh—drained of all historical content, of revolutionary Marxist politics, of radical differences from many of those in the bourgeois-nationalist pantheon with whom he is indiscriminately lumped. In other words, oppositional cultural politics in India, certainly in the context of radical revision of history by the left, will have to take note that the displacements are often only returns—and a more lasting break will have to involve the idiom of quotidian culture and its contradictions.

2. Since so much of the discussion around postcoloniality is paradoxically focused only on developments in the U. S. academy, and for the most part on one discipline in that institution, it is crucial that we learn more about the struggles for learning that

are going on in various parts of the world. Decades ago, the Chilean poet Pablo Neruda wrote in his *Memoirs*: "Our Latin American countries have millions of illiterates; this cultural lag survives as a heritage and privilege of feudalism. In the face of this stumbling block of seventy million illiterates, we can say that our readers have not yet been born. We must speed up the birth, so that we and all poets will be read" (296). It does not cease to surprise and shock me that discussions in critical theory, especially postcolonial theory, blithely go on without mentioning illiteracy—warmly complacent with the assured readership within the profession. The politics of (non)education and its relation to the general political economy become clear in this statement by Steve Whitman, quoted in a recent article by Henry Giroux: "[O]ne out of every four Black men will go to prison at some point in his life....Furthermore, it costs about $20,000 a year to send a person to prison, about what it would cost to send that person to Harvard." Giroux provides further details:

> Additionally, 45% of all minority children live in poverty while the drop-out rate among minority students has attained truly alarming proportions, reaching as high as 70% in some major urban areas. The problems are compounded by an unemployment rate among black youth that is currently 38.4%. (18–19)[11]

In the face of this incredible disenfranchisement in the United States and certainly elsewhere, it is vitally important to note the achievements of an educator like Paulo Freire who, in working with unlettered peasants in Brazil or Guinea Bissau, describes for us a process of coming into consciousness of the word and the world.[12] The process of acquiring literacy in Freire's technique of education has been described by Abdul JanMohamed as a "shift from existence in a sedimented state of society or subjectivity to a reactivated examination of that society or subjectivity" (112–13). JanMohamed names these peasants "border intellectuals." A more generalized application of that nomenclature, still faithful to the character of Freire's pedagogy, would apply to those intellectuals who question the boundaries of their professional knowledge or expertise and contribute to general literacy—of the peasant as well as the professor.

This is not simply a romanticization of manual labor. Rather, it is an invitation to consider, on the one hand, the problem of illiteracy, and, on the other, the prospect of ending it through what Freire would call "dialogism"—the process of mutual learning and correction. When someone like Che Guevara asks intellectuals to "become black, mulatto, a worker, a peasant; go down among the people, respond to the people, that is to all the necessities of all of Cuba," his appeal is not a dismissal of intellectual labor. It is something more, it is a definition of intellectual labor (45). Said has written that "critical consciousness is awareness of the resistances to theory, reactions to it elicited by those concrete experiences or interpretations with which it is in conflict" (*The World, the Text*, 242). It is my contention that the issue of the unavailable constituency, the giant body of illiterate and disenfranchised readership, should be critically recognized as one of the chief resistances to all theory, and most certainly postcolonial theory.

3. "Cross-dressing" as a form of border crossing cannot be metaphorically invoked, Michael Moon and Eve K. Sedgwick have argued, without naming its tacit, homosexual subject, and without "incurring many of the punitive risks of openly gay enunciation in a homophobic culture" (13). We cannot—should not—talk of border crossing, while pretending that people trying to cross borders don't get arrested, put into camps, shot to death, or simply run over by speeding cars on the highway.

And yet, when Moon and Sedgwick later offer the thought that "there *is* such a process as *coming out as a fat woman*" (27), one cannot but be struck by the border crossing of a metaphor, cross-hatching live, contradicting meanings, organizing meaning in groups that will help carry the banner of protest. Making meaning is risky business. The critical effort is properly critical when vulnerable to change. And, especially in postcolonial theory, criticism has to make connections that would seem to destroy the singularity of objects, events, histories—but only to restore to them a wholeness in a global sense, by linking a variety of effects in a social analytics that eschews provincialism. Once again I would like to introduce a newspaper article I wrote, this one connecting the ban on gays in the U. S. military to the photograph of a destitute woman sitting at a bus-stop in New Delhi.

Even though he's not the most photogenic of this nation's senators, Sam Nunn didn't let that thought stop him from sending from his brief vacation on the naval submarines a postcard to the American people with his own picture on it.

You probably received it too, in your morning newspaper on 11 May. The photo shows Nunn crouching with his colleague Sen. John Warner in front of three sailors who are lying on their bunks. On 16 May, in another article appearing beneath the same picture, someone was quoted as saying that this photograph taken aboard the submarine Montpelier had done more to retain the ban on gays in the military than "a thousand generals testifying against it."

Now, why is that so? What could possibly be so powerful about an image where a sailor, prostrate on his bunk, is holding his right hand out as if he were directing the senators' probing looks to the submarine's faulty roof which only that morning had sprung a leak? (These things can be dangerous in a sub, you know!)

I do not believe that the power of this image is that it brought home to the land-locked public of the United States the first image of close living in the subs and ships. Instead, the photograph's presumed power lies in its presentation: in the unusual image of the senators squatting in the cramped quarters on the frontlines of this debate, the combatant Nunn looking more knotted than his tie and hence, also more real, and then in the story's headline, which declares with absolute and unchallenged finality: "Senators board ships, told gay ban must remain." The equally tendentious subheading, ignoring the contrary views of other sailors, offers the words of a (really) Petty Officer: "I will refuse to serve."

The distortion here is not of the kind where I can shrilly claim that the sailor was actually complaining that the bunks gave so little space for maneuvering it was impossible to entertain any ideas of sex involving another person, male or female. Rather, I want to appropriate briefly the sailor's place and voice another complaint: why do we so drastically reduce the immense complexity of reality, its wide heterogeneity and scope of dissent, by what we so quickly accept as the singular truth presented in the shallow frame of an image?

Susan Sontag has written: "Photographs furnish instant history, instant sociology, instant participation." Instead of critically building diverse contexts for a photograph with words and other images, every morning we allow newspapers to stir a spoonful of information in a cup and slide it beneath our nose. But, that's not how we are going to wake up.

Take a look at the woman in the following photograph, which was taken by me at a bus-stop in my homeland, India, one August afternoon two years ago. We could fix the meaning of this photograph in the static reproduction of a stereotype: Indian poverty. The viewer stares into the starving mouth of an entire nation and its unchanging history in the Western psyche.

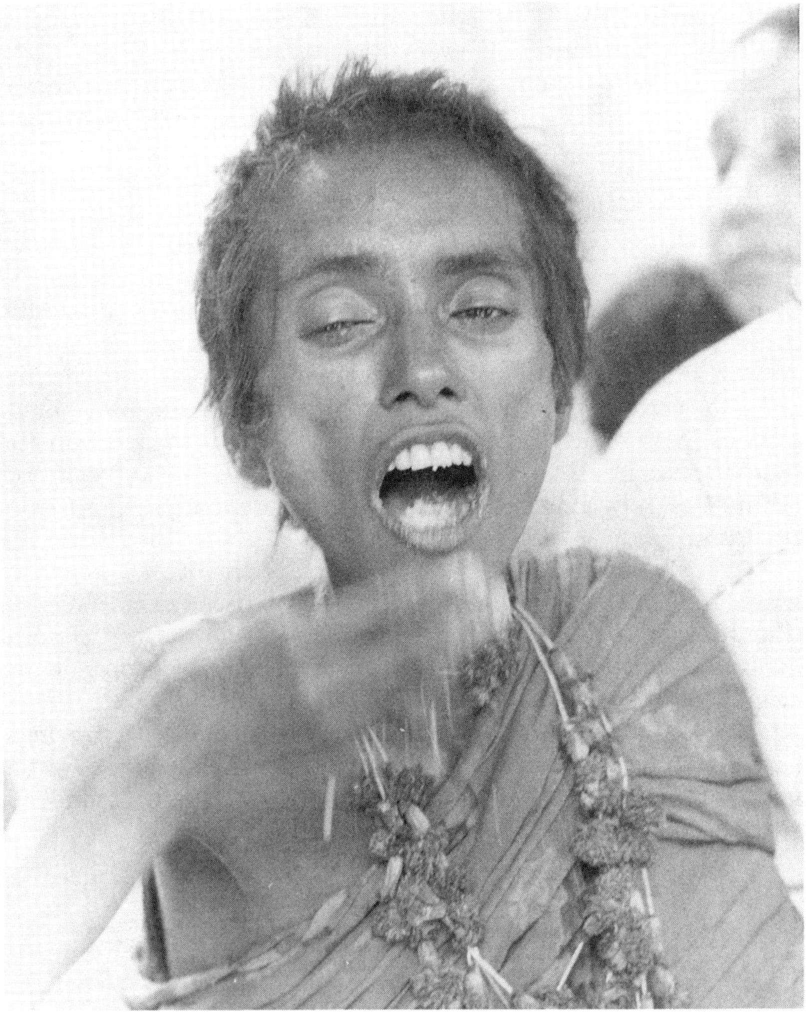

Alternatively, however, we can build another practice of receiving and understanding images. As a photographer presenting this image to North American viewers, for example, it might make sense to juxtapose this image with the following caption: "Alice Walker has written of the poet Jean Toomer's journey in the early '20s into the American Deep South where he encountered black women with work-worn, sexually abused bodies and an intense, almost unconscious, spirituality: 'These crazy Saints stared out at the world, wildly, like lunatics—or quietly, like suicides; and the "God"

that was in their gaze was as mute as great stone.' I have looked at the faces of some of the men and women in India, the land of my birth, and found only evacuation zones, abandoned, cleared even of memories. For me these are not nameless sites, however; in them I recognize the political geography of postcolonial histories and well-remembered struggles."

Free speech is only another name for advertising unless it involves interpretation. We need to interrupt received narratives and draw new relations between different realities. I would very much like to have seen beside the reports of the senators' impassioned concern about people living and working in proximity, other images from the sweatshops and the tenement houses showing folks stifled in claustrophobic conditions and eliciting never a word from these few good men. The sexist and homophobic sections of the U.S. Army might already have won the mother of all battles here, at home, if Sam Nunn's campaign brochure was so gullibly consumed as a documentary report from the front.[13]

4. In the journalism that we produce, in the other borders we cross, in the pedagogy we perform, we could heed Brecht's dictum that the "great and complicated things that go on in the world cannot be adequately recognized by the people who do not use every possible aid to understanding" (73).

We need to assemble our words, our diverse images, our songs. I offer you, beside the photograph of the pockmarked faces of the founding fathers of the crumbling college in a small town in India, a small poem written for my young sister entering school:

History
(For Divya Singh)

They caught the peasant
walking home from the field.
On the dark road
they gagged him
and cut off his nose.
This they took to the museum
and stuck to the king's
noseless statue.
Thus was born the history
that is taught in schools.

The assemblage of forms that I propose, you will have recognized, owes a great deal to Brecht's ideas about the political and didactic uses of montage and collage. But, apart from the usefulness of these techniques in producing critiques of mimetic representation or granting a better-theorized insurgent agency to the cultural worker, there is also an urgent way in which this fact of reinventing writing-effects impacts on the the role of the postmodern theorist and academic:

> Will the collage/montage revolution in representation be admitted into the academic essay, into the discourse of knowledge, replacing the "realist" criticism based on the notions of "truth" as correspondence to or correct reproduction of a referent object of study? (86)

For Greg Ulmer, this question serves as the point of departure for the innovations of writers like Roland Barthes and later, Jacques Derrida, who Ulmer rightly sees as protesting the divisions of literature and criticism, along with the assumptions those divisions entail. The necessity of the task of reorganizing language seems well expressed to me in the quote of Derrida's that Ulmer cites:

> The deconstruction of a pedagogical institution and all that it implies. What this institution cannot bear, is for anyone to tamper with language....It can bear more readily the most apparently revolutionary ideological sorts of "content," if only that content does not touch the borders of language and of all the juridico-political contracts that it guarantees. (87)

To encourage students to write *otherwise* is to inspire them to assemble their truths, to frame realities, and to juxtapose and work through contradictions. In the postcolonial setting, this task is all the more important because it means negotiating through conflictual cultural narratives as well as the traps of both colonialist and nativist presumptions, languages, and identities. But more immediately, in my own classrooms here in the United States I have found that the impulse to play with alternative modes of writing has translated into an interrogation and critical presentation of expressive self-identities. In the face of instrumentalized learning found elsewhere, students respond eagerly to this challenge of defining their selves and spinning out for themselves the web of alliances in terms of who it is that they are speaking for, or, perhaps, speaking with. This pleasure that my students feel—and I feel—also has to be a part of the elaboration of postcolonial pedagogy. As Brecht said, "the pleasure of learning depends on all sorts of things; but none the less there is such a thing as pleasurable learning, cheerful and militant learning" (73).

NOTES

1. My immediate interest is not in detailing the problems that inhere in the term "postcolonialism"; instead, I want to examine what is made (im)possible through the extant constructions of the subject in the U. S. academy. For helpful elucidations of the inconsistencies and contradictions that make any generalizable use of the term "postcolonialism" difficult, see the excellent articles by McClintock and Shohat. Also relevant is the essay by Mishra and Hodge.

2. A different sort of permeation through institutionalized, disciplinary boundaries can be found in an anthology that dissolves the line between *critical* thinkers and creative *writers* to present to readers what it announces in its title as "critical fictions." See Mariani, *Critical Fictions*.

3. Rushdie's "Open Letter" was reprinted in *The Patriot* (New Delhi), 27 November 1988, alongside my own "Open Letter" to Rushdie expressing, in part, what I broach here.

4. Timothy Brennan, "India, Nationalism, and Other Failures," *The South Atlantic Quarterly* 87.1 (Winter 1988): 131–46. A more elaborate version of this essay was published in the *Race and Class* special issue entitled "Literature: Colonial Lines of Descent," 31.1 (1989): 1–19.

5. For a broad critique of what she calls "the exorbitation of discourse and a related incuriosity about the enabling socio-economic and political institutions and other forms of social praxis," see Parry.

6. A notable exception to this practice is Zakia Pathak's and Rajeswari Sunder Rajan's "Shahbano," which heeds Spivak's warning in order to document the multiple dislocations of a subaltern subject and also her willed resistance in alliance with a feminist collectivity.

7. In his wonderfully nuanced article "An Ideology of Difference," Edward Said has called for the construction of a "creative difference" that will challenge the tyranny of "mere difference."

8. The workers were keen that the details of the exploitation and the harsh conditions of life in the multinational companies be laid bare. I remember for instance how one group who worked in a particular department at the nearby Bata shoe factory sat down to work out the process and quantity of their exploitation in order to explain it all to those of us who had never worked in a factory. Within a single day they would make shoes to the value of all the monthly wages for the entire work force of three thousand. So they worked for themselves for one day. For whom were they working for the other twenty-nine days? They calculated *what* of *what* they produced went for wear and tear of the machinery and for the repayment of initial capital, and

because the company had been there since 1938 they assumed that the initial investment had been repaid a long time ago. To whom did the rest go? To the owners in Canada. What about entrepreneurial skills—the brainpower—which regulated the entire system though seated in offices in Nairobi or far away in Canada? What about the shareholder whose money made the entire system work? Ah, well. They had never seen that brainpower and that shareholder once lift a hammer to make a shoe. If they could make guns and set up armament factories in the harsh conditions of the forest and mountains without the brainpower and money-power of any shareholder from abroad, could they not run a shoemaking factory ? The discussion would go on....(Ngũgĩ, 55)

9. For a persuasive argument in favor of using popular culture as a legitimate subject of investigation which will also be urgently taken up by students, see Aronowitz.

10. This section was published in *The Star Tribune*, Minneapolis-St. Paul, 4 August 1992.

11. At this point, I want to show you—with no higher motivation than simply making visible what is seldom remembered in discussions of critical theory—children in schools, in eastern India with students sitting on the ground in the open air, and in the Midwestern United States with two black students watching their teacher write out their punishment which says: "Write: I will be in control."

12. In *Pedagogy in Progress*, I was also struck by passages like the following one for reasons other than the one I mention above, chiefly the description of an extant, politicized viewpoint:

> During my visit I stayed in the home of the president of the cooperative. I took part in one of those seminars for the urban population. I was not at all surprised by the lucid manner in which the peasants spoke on the various themes of the seminar: their criticism of individualism, opportunism and personalism; their emphasis on the necessity of cooperative work; their repudiation of vertical solutions; their defense of their right to have a voice in what happens; the manner in which their political practice had radicalized them; their insight that the causes of their most fundamental problems could not always be found in the few acres they cultivated. They had come little by little to a vision of the whole, overcoming a localized version of their situation. (Freire, 142)

13. This section was published in *The Star Tribune*, Minneapolis-St. Paul, Sunday, 27 June 1993.

WORKS CITED

Ahmad, Aijaz. *In Theory*. New York: Verso, 1992.

———. "Jameson's Rhetoric of Otherness and the 'National Allegory.'" *Social Text* 17 (Fall 1987): 3–25.

Aronowitz, Stanley. "Mass Culture and the Eclipse of Reason." *The Crisis in Historical Materialism.* New York: 1981. 281–88.

Baker, Houston A., Jr. "Local Pedagogy; or, How I Redeemed My Spring Semester." *PMLA* 108.3 (May 1993): 400–409. MLA Presidential Address, New York, December 1992.

Beverley, John. "The Margin at the Center: On *Testimonio* (Testimonial Narrative)." *Modern Fiction Studies* 35.1 (Spring 1989): 11–28.

Bidwai, Praful. "India's Passage to Washington." *The Nation*, 20 January 1992, 50.

———. *The Times of India*, 19 August 1992.

Brecht, Bertolt. *Brecht on Theatre: The Development of an Aesthetic.* Ed. and trans. John Willett. New York: Hill and Wang, 1964.

Brennan, Timothy. "India, Nationalism, and Other Failures." *The South Atlantic Quarterly* 87.1 (Winter 1988): 131–46. A more elaborate version of this essay was published in the *Race and Class* special issue entitled "Literature: Colonial Lines of Descent," 31.1 (1989): 1–19.

———. Preface. *Modern Fiction Studies* 35.1 (Spring 1989): 3–8.

D'Souza, Dinesh. *Illiberal Education: The Politics of Race and Sex on Campus.* New York: Free Press, 1991.

Dorfman, Ariel, and Armand Mattelart. *How to Read Donald Duck.* Trans. and intro. David Kunzle. New York: International General, 1975.

Freire, Paulo. *Pedagogy in Progress: The Letters to Guinea-Bissau.* Trans. Carman St. John Hunter. New York: Seabury, 1978.

———. *Pedagogy of the Oppressed.* Trans. Myra Bergman Ramos. New York: Continuum, 1984.

Galeano, Eduardo. "In Defence of the Word." *They Shoot Writers, Don't They?* Ed. George Theiner. Boston: Faber and Faber, 1984, 188–99.

Gates, Henry Louis, Jr. *Loose Canons: Notes on the Culture Wars.* New York: Oxford University Press, 1992.

———, ed. *"Race," Writing, and Difference.* Chicago: University of Chicago Press, 1986.

Giroux, Henry A. *Border Crossings: Cultural Workers and the Politics of Education.* New York: Routledge, 1992.

———. "The Politics of Insurgent Multiculturalism in the Era of the Los Angeles Uprising." *The Journal of the Midwest Modern Language Association* 26.1 (Spring 1993): 12–30.

Jameson, Fredric. "Third World Literature in an Age of Multinational Capitalism." *Social Text* 15 (Fall 1986): 65–88.

JanMohamed, Abdul R. "Some Implications of Paulo Freire's Border Pedagogy." *Cultural Studies* 7.1 (January 1993): 107–17.

JanMohamed, Abdul R., and David Lloyd. "Introduction: Minority Discourse—What is to Be Done?" *Cultural Critique* 7 (Fall 1987): 5–17.

———. "Introduction: Toward a Theory of Minority Discourse." *Cultural Critique* 6 (Spring 1987): 5–12.

Kimball, Roger. *Tenured Radicals: How Politics has Corrupted Higher Education.* New York: Harper & Row, 1990.

Kincaid, Jamaica. *A Small Place.* New York: Plume, 1988.

Kumar, Amitava. "Open Letter to Salman Rushdie." *The Patriot* (New Delhi), 27 November 1988.

———. Letter. *The Star Tribune*, 4 August 1992: 12 A.

———. Letter. *The Star-Tribune*, 27 June 1993: 21 A.

Kumar, Sehdev. "The Third World Toils for the First." *World Press Review*, July 1988: 48–49.

Limbaugh, Rush H., III. *The Way Things Ought To Be.* New York: Pocket Books, 1992.

Mariani, Philomena, ed. *Critical Fictions.* Seattle: Bay Press, 1991.

McClintock, Anne. "The Angel of Progress: Pitfalls of the Term 'Post-Colonialism.'" *Social Text* 31–32 (1992).

Mishra, Vijay, and Bob Hodge."What is Post(-)Colonialism?" *Textual Practice* 5.3 (Winter 1991: 399–414.

Mohanty, Chandra Talpade. "Under Western Eyes: Feminist Scholarship and Colonial Discourses." *Boundary 2* 12.3/13.1 (Spring/Fall 1984): 333–58.

Moon, Michael, and Eve Kosofsky Sedgwick. "Divinity: A Dossier/A Performance Piece/A Little-Understood Emotion." *Discourse* 13.1 (Fall/Winter 1990–91): 12–39.

Mowitt, John. *Text.* Durham: Duke University Press, 1992.

Mudimbe, V. Y. "Save the African Continent." *Public Culture* 5.1 (Fall 1992): 61–62.

Neruda, Pablo. *Memoirs.* Trans. Hardie St. Martin. New York: Penguin, 1978.

Ngũgĩ wa Thiong'o. *Decolonising the Mind.* Portsmouth: Heinemann, 1981.

Parry, Benita. "Problems in Current Theories of Colonial Discourse," *Oxford Literary Review* 9.1/2 (1987): 27–58.

Pathak, Zakias, and Rajeswari Sunder Rajan. "Shahbano." *Signs* 4.3 (Spring 1989): 558–82.

People's Front. Publication of Indian People's Front September/October 1992.

People's Union for Democratic Rights. "Sadda Hak, Ethey Rakh." *A Report on Refugee Women Workers of Delhi.* April 1989. Trans. Amitav Kumar.

Retamar, Roberto Fernandez. *Caliban and Other Essays.* Trans. Edward Baker. Minneapolis: University of Minnesota Press, 1989.

Rushdie, Salman. "Open Letter to Rajiv Gandhi." *The New York Times*, 19 October 1988. Rpt. in *The Patriot* (New Delhi), 27 November 1988.

Said, Edward W. "An Ideology of Difference." *"Race" Writing, and Difference.* Ed. Henry Louis Gates, Jr. New York: Oxford University Press, 1992, 38–58.

———. "Opponents, Audiences, Constituencies and Community." *The Anti-Aesthetic: Essays on Postmodern Culture.* Ed. Hal Foster. Seattle: Bay Press, 1983.

———. *The World, the Text, the Critic.* Cambridge, MA: Harvard University Press, 1983.

Shohat, Ella. "Notes on the 'Post-Colonial.'" *Social Text* 3.1/2 (1992).

Smith, Paul. "Visiting the Banana Republic." *Universal Abandon? The Politics of Postmodernism.* Ed. Andrew Ross. Minneapolis: University of Minnesota Press, 1988, 128–48.

Spivak, Gayatri. "Gayatri Spivak on the Politics of the Subaltern." Interview by Howard Winant, *Socialist Review* (North-South Relations in the New World Order) 20.3 (July–September 1990): 81–97.

Trinh T. Minh-ha. *Discourse* 11.2 (Spring-Summer 1989): 5–17.

Ulmer, Greg. "The Object of Post-Criticism." *The Anti-Aesthetic: Essays on Postmodern Culture.* Ed. by Hal Foster. Seattle: Bay Press, 1993, 83–110.

Winkler, Karen J. "A Conservative Plans to 'Sound the Guns' at NEH." *The Chronicle of Higher Education*, 16 October 1991: A5.

Woodhull, Winifred. "Exile." *Yale French Studies* 82 (1993) (Post/Colonial Conditions, vol. 1): 7–24.

Part II

PEDAGOGY

Terminologies, Problematics, Readings

11

RAJESWARI MOHAN

Dodging the Crossfire: Questions for Postcolonial Pedagogy

From the start, the project of teaching postcolonial literature has had to negotiate between varied discursive and institutional practices serving competing pedagogical and political interests. Forged out of the postcolonial world's peculiar circumstances and historical antagonisms, much of the literature tries to break free of the narrative structures and tropes that have long dominated Euro-American representations of the Other. This goal is inspired by the belief that in order to move towards a truly egalitarian and free society, culture itself has to be decolonized because of its shaping effect on postcolonial experience and consciousness. As such, postcolonial writers and critics largely accept the importance of taking charge of narratives and discourses in a manner that maintains the oppositional edge if not the semi-autonomous status of postcolonial knowledge. In turn, these commitments entail certain pedagogic imperatives, not the least of which is that postcolonial texts cannot be incorporated into an aesthetic and critical tradition determined by the Euro-American canon. Under the anti-foundationalist regime of postmodernism, this insistence on difference lends itself to being read as a reactionary nostalgia for an imagined precolonial innocence. Postcolonial writers have, in turn, responded with a ringing critique of the formalism implicit in the critique and call for a renewed attention to the politics and history of their texts.[1]

This exchange is a minor skirmish in the larger battle over multiculturalism, under whose auspices postcolonial literature and culture are usually studied. We are by now familiar with the various charges made by critics of multiculturalism—its polarizing or contentious stance, its alleged lack of intellectual rigor, its supposed potential for reverse discrimination, and its "exaggerated and preferential" treatment of a "minority" point of view. The energies of proponents of multiculturalism have been so thoroughly absorbed in responding to these criticisms that they have been effectively distracted from vigorous analysis of the theoretical questions and pedagogic challenges posed by the entry of postcolonial texts into the discursive circuits and institutional arenas of literary study. As arguments for multicultural education become compelling in the context of shifting demography in the United States and its contested place in global affairs, multiculturalism is being deployed increasingly as a reformist strategy that contains the transformative potential of social heterogeneity. With multiculturalism being recuperated as an ahistorical and depoliticized knowledge, it is ever more important that discussions of pedagogy take up the question of how postcolonial texts get mediated in the classroom rather than simply engage with questions of what texts to teach and why.

As an upshot of contestations over literature, theory, and politics, most of us professing literature today agree that canons and texts gain their importance and currency from the work they perform of advancing particular interpretations of historically urgent issues. Texts have come to be seen as terrains of conflicting interpretations that attempt to subvert or consolidate the distribution of power and wealth in a social formation that, in our times, spans the globe. Foregrounding the historical and political context as well as the theoretical framework within which a text becomes meaningful, then, makes visible the interests it serves at particular historical conjunctures. The theoretical arguments of Michel Foucault have been crucial to the elaboration of this process by drawing our attention to the ways systems of nomenclature and taxonomic grids shape and direct our investigations and their effects. Taking Foucault's arguments as its starting point, this essay will examine the global politics of nomenclature and the micropolitics of literary study in the American academy insofar as they guide the study of postcolonial texts. In so doing, the essay recognizes the need to attend to recent theoretical developments mediating postcolonial literature into the Western academic and scholarly circuit for their own implication—as mystification *and* critical knowledge—in the global distribution of power, prestige, and wealth. Consideration of such issues impress upon us the need for a mode of reading that is attentive to the shifting meaning and ideological effectivity of a text as it circulates between Western metropolises and postcolonial peripheries.[2] Postcolonial texts are caught up in the regional dynamics of Third World politics and American culture wars as well as the global negotiations demanded by the New World Order and multinational capitalism. In other words, they are recruited to serve varying ideologies and are involved in the work of producing first as well as Third World subjects. These multiple commitments prevent the emergence of a single authoritative interpretation in any given instance. In teaching these texts, it is not enough merely to acknowledge their polyphony and indeterminacy. It is even more important to situate and understand their multiple inflections in the context of the contradictory ideologies that speak through them. This would involve setting up the diachronic and synchronic structural coordinates of the various ideologies traversing a given text. That is, a thick reading of the text's thematic complexity and narrative form has to draw upon colonial history and indigenous aesthetic traditions, as well as the synchronic structures of domestic politics and international economic and political arrangements.

In large part, the political context for the study of postcolonial literature was created in the American academy by feminist and Afro-American critiques of the literary canon, critiques that were echoed in the international scene by writers such as Chinua Achebe and Ngũgĩ wa Thiong'o. These writers insisted upon the role of their literature in decolonizing the mind, fostering a sense of collectivity, and thereby creating the basis of an egalitarian society. Implicit in their discussions is an understanding of narrative as a socially symbolic mediation of the frustrations and hopes informing experiences of postcoloniality, and consequently they demand that the teaching and reading of their texts be guided by the goal of transformative political action. Accommodating this demand requires a reunderstanding of the classroom not as a space of cosmopolitan instruction but as a site of contestation over what comes to be counted as the real and the truthful. As counter narratives that challenge, interrupt, or undercut colonial discourses—such as primitivism, orientalism, and underdevelopment—postcolonial texts make visible the ideological supports of global economic and political arrangements. Their strangeness to Western readers, sometimes augmented by strategies of defamiliarization, encourages a focus on alterity as a category continually constituted by (neo)colonial practices. In the classroom, therefore, they discourage an antiquarian or exoticized interest in constructions of Otherness, drawing attention instead to the psychological and political investments of the hegemonic Subject in these constructions. But while postcolonial texts emerge as objects of study inextricably yoked to politics, the terms of these politics have not been specified adequately. Whether a text is qualified as Commonwealth, Third World, or postcolonial makes all the difference to its meaning and status, the prefixes activating different genealogies, emphases and, inevitably, politics.

Historical and political reference has been almost completely suppressed in contemporary uses of the term "Commonwealth literature." When the Commonwealth was inaugurated by the Balfour Declaration of 1926 and legalized in 1931 by the Statute of Westminster, it was only the "white colonies" (a designation which suppresses the history of genocide and marginalization of indigenous populations in those territories) that were recognized as "autonomous communities within the British Empire, equal in status [to UK], in no way subordinate to one another" (quoted in Lloyd, 295). Later, as other parts of the British empire in Asia, Africa, and the Caribbean gained independence, they joined the Commonwealth as well. By now, the economic and political preferences ensured by the Commonwealth were largely defunct, and it was acknowledged that the organization mainly served a sentimental purpose: "The nerves of the British were soothed in the two decades of decolonization which followed [1949] by the thought that they were gaining new members of the Commonwealth rather than losing colonies" (Lloyd 330). The fact that sentiment did not blunt politically canny manipulation of the Commonwealth is best exemplified by British immigration and visa politics since the 1960s, whereby, through a series of legislations, the Commonwealth is effectively divided as the "old" and the "new", the latter comprising all the erstwhile British colonies other than Australia, New Zealand, and Canada. On this division rests the selective continuation of privileges to the "old" Commonwealth (Couper).

This hierarchy of privilege is, of course, not visible in the usage "Commonwealth literature," with its nostalgia for a shared history and its myth of free exchange among equals bound by the rituals and codes of Queen's English and cricket. Furthermore, as Salman Rushdie points out in his essay, "Commonwealth Literature Does Not Exist," the assurance that the Commonwealth is made up of members "equal in status and in no way subordinate to one another" has proven to be false in the study of Commonwealth literature as well, for "it would never do to include English literature, the great sacred thing itself, with this bunch of upstarts, huddling together under this new and badly made umbrella" (62). To the extent that "Commonwealth literature" is used as if it were a neutral, descriptive category, it is ideologically misleading.

Conceptually, as well, the category lacks versatility, heuristic value, and analytical focus. "Commonwealth literature" thus cannot provide a conceptual handle on a body of texts as diverse as Anita Desai's novels of manners, Ngũgĩ wa Thiong'o's Marxist-inspired critiques of neocolonialist elites, and Wilson Harris' abstract syncretism. And what does one do with emigres like Salman Rushdie, V.S. Naipaul, and Buchi Emecheta? As British citizens, these writers cannot technically be considered Commonwealth writers. What of Nadine Gordimer, Alex La Guma, J.M. Coetzee, and other South African writers whose country was expelled from the Commonwealth for its apartheid policies? Perhaps Ngũgĩ's later writings in Gikuyu cannot be counted even though his early English writings have set the terms of the debate on teaching non-Western literatures. This would be one consequence of the outrageous assumption that the most influential, imaginative, and compelling writings from the postcolonial world are those in English. Teaching a course under the rubric of Commonwealth literature would also necessitate the exclusion of Francophone and Latin American texts which add considerable range, depth, and complexity to discussions of postcolonial texts, particularly in the classroom. One particularly intriguing line of inquiry enabled by a comparative analysis of francophone and anglophone texts is the argument made by Abiola Irele and Es'kia Mphahlele, among others, that "Africans have since the beginning been thinking the same thoughts and putting them in the same words, whatever colonial flag has been waved over [their] heads" (Ogede, 181). As well, such comparisons illuminate the distinctive features of the cultural politics of settler colonial as opposed to assimilationist contexts, and highlight the specific strategies of resistance emerging out of Islamic, Christian, or Akan traditions, to name but a few. Latin American texts bring these investigations closer to home, so to speak, dwelling as they do on the consequences of the changing of the guard from European to U.S. imperialism.

More favored in the United States than "Commonwealth" is the term "Third World." This term has for long been critiqued for implying that the non-Western world is a monolithic entity and thereby disregarding the profound differences among the various national and social formations comprising the Third World. While the advantage of this perspective has been to show the uniformity and ferocity of the battles each society has had to wage for survival against First World imperialisms, the enormous variety of national and religious cultures in the Third World and vital differences in their histories are papered over.[3] Reading texts as of the Third World, then, participates in the epistemic violence documented by postcolonial intellectuals such as Fanon, Césaire, and Ngũgĩ.

With its increasing popularity, the term "Third World" has all but lost the historical and political distinctions it was meant to signify when it was embraced as an identity by newly decolonized nations at the Bandung conference in 1955. At that time, the urgency of the term derived from the need to forge an economic and political alliance that would help these nations articulate their agendas of growth and cultural decolonization in a world dominated by Cold War rivalries. The current loose usage of the term "Third World literature" continues to carry some of this genealogical burden albeit without its critical edge. Indeed, largely as a legacy of area studies and development theories, "Third World" stands at the head of a chain of signifiers that include underdevelopment, oppressive tradition, high illiteracy, rural and urban poverty, religious fanaticism, and overpopulation. The depoliticization of the term is implicated in an understanding of geopolitics that continues to carve up the world and arrange the resulting segments in a hierarchy of First World (capitalist), Second World (socialist), and Third World. Significantly, while the first two worlds are defined in terms of mode of production, the defining feature of the Third World seems to be an absence of determinate economic or political systems. The three-world schema thus sets up the Third World as a vacuum to be filled up by the economic and political maneuvering of the first two worlds. More significantly, this hierarchical taxonomy has underwritten a discursive modality and an accompanying power-knowledge grid that enable an intellectual agenda in the academy complementary to the ideological agenda of the Cold War (see Pletsch). With the collapse of the Iron Curtain and the Second World's enthusiastic turn to capitalism, it is time we reconsider the label "Third World literature" if only for reasons of historical relevance.

A more complex version of "Third Worldism" is advanced by Fredric Jameson in his definition of Third World texts as national allegories:

> All third-world texts are necessarily...allegorical, and in a very specific way: they are to be read as what I will call national allegories...particularly when their forms develop out of predominantly western machineries of representation, such as the novel. ("Third World," 69)

According to Jameson, the ideological split between the public and private that is fundamental to the constitution of Western societies blocks the emergence of a politically informed culture. As a consequence, politics has been regarded in the West as extraneous and disruptive to art, like a "pistol shot in the middle of a concert" (69). Third World literatures, on the other hand, are national allegories premised on entirely different relations between the public and the private: "The story of the private individual destiny is always an allegory of the embattled situation of the public third-world culture and society" (69).

Jameson's formulation has the advantage of expanding the range of oppositional positions available in a non-Western text to include not just resistance to global (neo)imperialism, but also to oppressive and exploitative domestic arrangements. However, his schema still depends on a simplifying binary opposition between the first and the Third World in which, contrary to usage, the Third World is the privileged pole. Also implicit in his paradigm of nationalist allegory is a valorization of the Western idea of nationhood which is taken as the norm every country aspires to. At this point, the binary opposition collapses upon itself, since the nationalist allegory of the Third World always-already bears the trace of First World nationalisms, and the formulation lends itself to the imperialist argument that a developed sense of nationhood was one of the cultural benefits of imperialism (see Anderson, for instance). Indeed, in the wake of Jameson's own persuasive theorization of narrative as a socially symbolic act in *Political Unconscious*, the novel, in general, has come to be seen as the exemplary form of nationalist consciousness.[4]

Furthermore, by situating Third World oppositionality only in texts available to the West, Jameson ignores the many and often untranslated narratives of subaltern resistance to imperialism and nationalism. Since the suppression of the subaltern voice has enabled the emergence of the *comprador bourgeoisie* as the nationalist elite, Jameson's articulation participates in the mystification of the transition from imperialism to neo-imperialism as postcoloniality. Most importantly, Jameson oddly ignores the processes by which "feudal" or "precapitalist" practices in postcolonial cultures (which are the bases of "nationalist allegory") are subordinated to or even recruited to serve the interests of global capitalism. As a consequence, the mutations of indigenous and imposed cultural traditions as they are inscribed in postcolonial texts escapes his attention. So too, as Aijaz Ahmed has pointed out in his response to Jameson, does the interesting question about the effects of reading practices and theoretical schemas that "frame" postcolonial novels at their points of reception.

The study of Third World literatures takes place side by side with other modes of studying the Third World—modernization and development theories, for instance—which all too often conveniently explain away the underdevelopment and deprivation in the Third World as prima facie evidence of its cultural inferiority. Such explanations explicitly set up the first world as the model of rationality and planned development that the Third World should strive to emulate (Kofele-Kale, 38). Critics have attempted to alter this view of the Third World by emphasizing the rich array and depth of the folklore, art, and literature of the Third World, but in doing so have been unable to keep at bay the demands of commodity aesthetics, which is forever in search of new ideas to commodify. Cultural productions of the Third World have been equally available to bands like the Talking Heads and to department stores like Bloomingdales in their marketing of funky postmodern sounds and fashions. Similarly, pluralist appropriations of postmodern difference often enlist Third World texts to support an agenda of diversity or benign variation. Thus, it is not always clear whether Third World texts are merely taking their place on the shelves of exotic imports, beside the Colombian coffee and the Darjeeling tea; or whether they do indeed assert radically oppositional narratives that disrupt the discourses—of Orientalism and primitivism, among others—that serve as ideological ground for economic and political maneuvering in the postcolonial world.

Whether texts serve an agenda of commodity fetishism or radical critique (these being but the two most compelling of any number of possibilities) would depend on the discourses that mediate them into the classroom. It could be argued that, given the history and established patterns of its use, the term Third World pulls against the goals of radical pedagogy. As a discursive frame, Third Worldism introduces a number of potential problems into a discussion of texts. To quickly map out some of these trouble spots, Third Worldism brings with it the burden of area studies which encourage a descriptive rather than an interrogative or critical reading of texts. The pressures of multiculturalism further sharpen this tendency into a vacuous pluralism. Constructions of the Third World as a geographical area, as a collectivity defined by its minority status, or as an "imagined community," usually do not allow for a focus on or understanding of the articulation effects on culture of the Third World's shifting position in global economic and political orders.[5]

After this litany of woes, "postcoloniality" seems to provide a promising analytical framework. As a historical and epistemological category, postcoloniality immediately draws attention to the historical and cultural contexts of producing and reading texts in a world riven by political hierarchies, economic manipulations, and hegemonic interests. Historically situating cultural politics in the aftermath of European and American imperialisms of the nineteenth and twentieth centuries, postcoloniality immediately draws attention to the political and economic residues of colonialism. Certain issues become unavoidable within the frame of postcoloniality: the cultural violence of the colonial encounter, the all too frequent failure to keep the promise of an egalitarian society made during national liberation struggles, the establishment of new class and gender elites in postindependence nationalist cultures, the destruction of indigenous traditions and kinship networks, the displacement of local modes of self-government, the erosion of agrarian economies in favor of import-based "cash" economies and urban industrialism, the ongoing economic dependency of postcolonial societies linked structurally and financially to their erstwhile colonizers, the effect of metropolitan practices and institutions such as the church, mass media, and education, to name a few.[6] At the same time, by allowing for the widely variant histories of colonialism, the heterogeneity of the postcolonial context is not overlooked.[7] The range of questions brought into textual analysis by the discursive history of postcoloniality, necessarily broadens the scope of pedagogic strategies. Primarily, these questions enable a discussion of not only the formal and stylistic, but also the thematic and contextual features of postcolonial literature. In so doing, they initiate an interrogation of the conventions of literary study that privilege the aesthetic qualities of a text over its political content, or that do not understand the aesthetic as itself a historically specific and politically fraught category.

Postcoloniality also usefully foregrounds the political and psychological investments of texts by drawing attention to the contradictory position of the postcolonial writer and reader, cunningly figured by Abena Busia as the predicament of Caliban:

> This tongue that I have mastered
> has mastered me;
>
> has taught me curses
> in the language of the master
>
> has taught me bondage
> in the language of the master
>
> I speak this dispossession
> in the language of the master. (3)

This ambivalence is underscored by Gayatri Spivak as the defining instance of postcoloniality, as an "impossible 'no' to a structure, which one critiques, yet inhabits intimately" ("Poststructuralism," 225). Analysis of this ambivalence leads one to explore its formal and rhetorical ramifications as well. Language is an issue that immediately comes to the forefront for as Frantz Fanon remarked, for a postcolonial writer "to choose a language is to choose a world," a world where oppression seems to provide the tools for its undoing. The evolution of patois, the appropriation of Western narrative modes such as the novel, the mutation of conventions of epistolary fiction and *Bildungsroman*, the refiguring of standard European tropes of alterity, are some powerful strategies of resistance that undergo intriguing mutations when worked into indigenous narrative traditions.

The advantages of postcoloniality as a frame of reference have been ably demonstrated in the works of Barbara Harlow and Abdul JanMohamed, and most recently by the Australian writers Bill Ashcroft, Gareth Griffiths, and Helen Tiffin. These critics see postcoloniality neither as a backward-looking attempt to retrieve a lost cultural purity, nor as a clean and complete supersession of colonialism, but as an engagement with the history of colonial oppression. They read the novels of Buchi Emecheta, Chinua Achebe, and Ghassan Kanafani as attempts to understand the effects of colonial occupation on the contemporary problems in their worlds. Tracing the novels' oscillation between an anxious recognition of the inescapable binds of the colonial experience and a cunning orchestration of resistance to colonial hegemony, these critics underline the provisionality and precariousness of the "post" in postcolonial literature, which continually threatens to succumb to a despairing view that the world is still bound under neo-imperialism.

The postcolonial world is neither even, homogeneous, nor monolithic, as the periodic cycles of internal dissent and brutal suppression in places as far-flung and diverse as Lagos and Toronto repeatedly and painfully demonstrate. These cycles mark two significant moments in postcoloniality—displacement of the colonizer and his replacement. Analyses alert to this double rhythm, such as Fanon's *Wretched of the Earth*, caution that the postcolonial project of national reconstruction is always vulnerable to the danger of co-optation by an avaricious national bourgeoisie:

> During the struggle for liberation the leader awakened the people and promised them a forward march, heroic and unmitigated. Today, he uses every means to put them to sleep, and three or four times a year asks them to remember the colonial period and to look back on the long way they have come since then. (169)

Thus even as Fanon emphasizes the importance of a national government that carries out the "popular will," he is acutely aware of the possibility that other interests, national and international, can commandeer the postcolonial state and its socioeconomic agenda. To take postcoloniality as a permanent utopian supersession of colonialism would therefore be a mistake, since exploitation and oppression usually continue within global capitalism retooled as neo-imperialism and aided by an enthusiastic comprador bourgeoisie. This assessment has been supported by recent theoretical investigations into the economic alignments of postcolonial societies, which indicate that while the colonial state was an instrument the metropolitan bourgeoisie wielded unequivocally against the colonized, the postcolonial state is a site of much more complicated maneuvers between the metropolitan bourgeoisie, the bourgeoisie of other advanced capitalist countries, and indigenous classes (Alavi et al.). This makes the economic, cultural, and political practices of postcoloniality open to multiple and contradictory influences.

However, theorizing postcoloniality has run into dead ends in some instances. In one attempt to investigate the ideological status of postcolonial texts, postcoloniality has been defined as the "need, in nations and groups that have been victims of imperialism to achieve an identity uncontaminated by Universalist or Eurocentric concepts and images" (During 33). In this instance, the definition of postcoloniality is explicitly situated as an attempt to satisfy postmodernism's political desire for epistemologically pure grounds of opposition. By displacing a nostalgia for lost origins and absolute presence—a nostalgia that postmodernism has disallowed the West—onto the Third World, During is well within the postmodern tradition of continuing the ideological groundwork for multinational capitalism in the guise of valorizing the Other.[8] Such definitions of postcolonial writing have profound textual and political consequences: for instance, since During's definition freezes the text of alterity in a static relation to a past defined exclusively along the pole of imperialism, it rides roughshod over crucial nuances in the history of erstwhile colonies. The complex interaction of domestic patriarchal, caste, and class hierarchies with the needs of a globally operative system that has evolved forms of exploitation and domination only inadequately explained as "imperialism" is effaced in During's understanding of postcoloniality. Furthermore, in the systematic displacement of the possibility of political engagement and revolutionary action—a possibility that postmodernism puts under erasure—on to the Other constructed as Third World, insurgent nationalities, resisting margins, and so on, a new pattern of unequal demands emerges. The curious similarity between the radical postmodernist's epistemological and aesthetic expectations of non-Western cultures and the economic and political demands made on the postcolonial world by the international circulation of commodities and the balance of power, supports Fredric Jameson's analysis of postmodernism as the cultural logic of late capitalism.

In contrast to the textualized postcoloniality theorized by During, Marxist discourses on colonialism and postcoloniality address the neocolonial relations implicit in postcoloniality. Arguing that imperialism did not disappear with the end of direct colonial rule but merely assumed more insidious forms, postcolonial theorists see their societies as sites of an ongoing capitalist exploitation. As certain productive relations become impossible in the West because of technological innovations, environmental regulations, and changing social arrangements, they are moved out into the sweatshops of poorer countries; as metropolitan markets get saturated, the developing world becomes the target or dumping ground for commodities refused by the West. In this context, studying postcolonial texts often aids intellectuals in their role as market researchers who provide the cultural knowledge necessary for the efficient functioning of multinational agencies and corporations. Gayatri Spivak has forcefully argued that postcolonial texts are caught up in the ideology of neoimperialism and are often read in ways that implicitly serve the interests of multinational capitalism by privileging an aspiring bourgeois elite identified with the postcolonial space as the authentic voice of the margins ("Poststructuralism"). In the face of such recuperative strategies, it is crucial to resist romanticizing the postcolonial world as a pure site of alterity and instead to generate nuanced readings of the implication of its own elites in neocolonial systems.

In arguments such as During's, the status of postcolonial texts, as valorized texts of alterity, derives to a large extent from the intellectual currency of postmodernism. As a historically specific epistemology and aesthetic, postmodernism is committed to producing anti-totalizing, anti-foundationalist, decentered, fragmented, and oppositional narratives. This commitment has been a crucial factor in the installation of non-Western texts within the academic study of literature. With the deconstruction of Western metaphysics and the attendant decentering of the subject, the margin is valorized and alterity becomes a privileged site of intellectual enquiry and political strategy. However, even as postmodernism valorizes alterity for a variety of reasons and resists absorbing the Other into the Self, it is consistently led to the paradoxical recognition that the Other can never speak as Other. As the insoluble precipitate that eludes, resists, and undermines the will of master discourses to be all-inclusive, the Other is always in excess of representation. Put differently, even as postmodern philosophy stages a refusal to contain or assimilate the other, it paradoxically invests certain sites with an exclusive importance and meaning *as other* for a Eurocentric discourse. Not only does this move reinstall, however tortuously, a Eurocentric perspective, but it also shears off from postcolonial texts the urgent political burden they bear. The resulting tensions, often unacknowledged, produce serious conceptual ambiguities in postmodern articulations of postcoloniality, and have recently drawn heavy fire (Shohat).

If postmodern theory has served as the implicit basis of the inclusion of non-Western texts in literary studies, it has also been the predominant conceptual frame within, or in reaction to, which the texts are read and understood. However, the privileging of difference has often been understood as an argument for situating postcolonial texts as a safe haven from the onslaughts of theory. Two points need to be made here: First, novelty is an important factor in guaranteeing the assimilation of these texts into the postmodern canon, not only because "newness" is the absolute mark of value in the capitalist market place, but also because the postmodern privileging of the anti-mimetic ensures an immediate valorization of postcolonial anti-realism as new modes of *self*-fragmentation. Such appropriations often overlook the marked divergence of ludic from political or resistance postmodernism (see Ebert). Second, a decontextualization inevitably takes place during theoretical mediation, whereby politically charged and historically urgent discursive and textual elements are reduced to purely formal and aesthetic properties of the text. Social contradiction becomes ambiguity or deferral; dialogic contestation becomes arbitrary juxtaposition, play, or collage; and interrogation of politically interested narratives becomes self-reflexivity. The political gets aesthetized and resistance becomes a fashionable gesture.

Instead, if one begins with the material contexts of postcolonial literature, it becomes clear that the simultaneous demands of numerous ideological and social pressures produce an epistemology of difference. That is, the sedimented effects of the various concerns and agendas discussed earlier produce an indeterminacy that is somewhat at odds with postmodern aesthetics. Viewed thus, postcolonial literature's frequent focus on liminality and marginality can be seen as a provisional and contingent emphasis rather than as an essential feature; its narrative strategies of resistance and oppositional agency can be seen to be grounded in histories of racism and imperialism rather than as an effect of a decontextualized language. Given the fluctuations of history, the parameters of oppositional agency are themselves seen as something to be constantly negotiated rather than as something given. In this respect, narratives become important as the staging ground of these negotiations, the ground where memory, voice, and vision are constantly reformulated in the press of an ever shifting global context.

Dominant pedagogic practices within the academy often contain the radical implications of these reformulations. Postcolonial texts are most frequently taught and studied within separate canons of non-Western, Third World, or Commonwealth literature. If a desire to disrupt ethnocentricity initiated the study of these texts in the academy, a whole range of institutional and social forces have helped protect most literature departments from serious self-critique. The ghettoization of nontraditional texts within their own canons and sometimes within their own separate departments has severely circumscribed their disruptive effects. Thus while it has become appropriate and even desirable to allow postmodern texts like those of Derrida, Foucault, Lacan, and Lyotard to restructure canonical Western literature and our ways of reading its texts, it is still uncommon for Joyce and Sterne to be read through Rushdie, Evelyn Waugh and Conrad to be read through Chinua Achebe, or Virginia Woolf to be read through Buchi Emecheta.

Ngũgĩ wa Thiong'o suggests that such encounters may be productive for the study of Western canonical texts as well, by drawing attention to the slippages and silences in European texts, particularly those centered on the modernist moment of anxiety about "man without history—solitary and free—with unexplainable despair and anguish and death as the ultimate truth about the human condition" (78). A study of postcolonial literature suggests that this stance may arise out of a partial vision of a world riven by social changes or out of a dimly apprehended investment in the social order threatened by the changes. In fact, one of the joys of reading postcolonial writers such as Salman Rushdie, Ngũgĩ wa Thiong'o, Jamaica Kincaid, Wilson Harris, and J.M. Coetzee is tracking their irreverent appropriation and mimicry of colonialist tropes. By critically appropriating and rearticulating signifying structures of Western culture, these writers encourage a reunderstanding of the aesthetic modes and thematic concerns of canonical texts.

If we have spent so much time in charting the discursive field in which postcolonial texts are read, it is only to demonstrate that these texts are always already situated in hegemonic Western discourses, such that reading them involves, from the start, a delicate negotiation through a minefield of contesting interpretive claims and contradictory political effects. My point in discussing these levels of mediation is not to argue for a rigorously positivist mode of reading which would amass enough contextual detail to flesh out the meaning of the text. Postmodern theory has taught us that the text can never be an unmediated presence to us despite our best efforts; feminist and postcolonial critics continue to challenge familiar and comfortable reading practices that impose Euro- or phallocentric readings as the unproblematic meaning of a text. What I am arguing against is an uncritical valorization of alterity that ignores the specific and contingent historical and political pressures—both global and regional—within which alterity is articulated.

What Ngũgĩ has to say about one much discussed pole of alterity, race, is especially pertinent here:

> Often we [African writers and their readers] never moved beyond blackness, beyond the racial aspect of the struggle for national liberation from colonial rule, to see what was basic to colonial oppression: the fact that we were part and parcel of a worldwide system of production called capitalism: the fact that the colonial, political and cultural invasion was to make conquest in the economic sphere more entrenched and permanent: and therefore that the African people's anti-colonial struggle was more than a racial struggle. It was also, and more fundamentally, a struggle against that system that for four hundred years had devastated a continent. (7)

If we are to understand the full implication of Ngũgĩ's argument, our encounter with postcolonial texts cannot come to rest on authenticity, "that respectable child of old fashioned exoticism" (Rushdie, 67). It is true that, with increasing scholarly activity in the area, we have come to see European and American involvement in Africa, Asia, and South America as but one twist in the unfolding of indigenous cultural processes. But even the recovery of these processes, exciting as it may be, takes its urgency from its role in providing counter-discursive strategies to cultural imperialism. We must therefore follow the shifting lines that link the struggle over representation to the struggle for political and economic rights waged in different sectors of the worldwide system to which Ngũgĩ refers. It is precisely the historical situatedness of postcolonial texts and their complex articulation within postmodern, nationalist, and oppositional discourses that make them subversive—and interesting—in a multipronged fashion.

Needless to say, the pedagogic challenge of facilitating such readings in the class room gains a new order of complexity around the issue of postcolonial feminisms. Even as I was putting together this paper, my class on postcolonial women writers was reading Bessie Head's *Collector of Treasures*. The first response of most of my students to this text was an awed and respectful silence. Being politically correct liberal arts students, they know too well the dangers of imposing their expectations on the text and therefore wait for the text to reveal itself, if only through its proxy their teacher, a woman marked "other"wise. But there were others in the class, strong feminists who had come to that point in their development when they were questioning the homogeneity of the construct "woman" in feminist discourses. For them the course provided an opportunity to explore the differences and hierarchies between communities of women, and to learn about the widely divergent priorities implicit in narratives of feminine experience in the postcolonial world. We had read selections from Maria Mies's *Patriarchy and Accumulation on the World Scale*, where the sexualization of the Western bourgeois woman in the nineteenth century and the liberation of the professional woman in the twentieth century are shown to be enabled directly by the economic benefits and ideological imperatives of Western imperialism and neo-imperialism. We had read the introduction to Kumari Jayawardena's *Feminism and Nationalism in the Third World*, which provided a historical ground for understanding the complex negotiations between feminist and nationalist agendas in the postcolonial world. We had also read Jennifer Wicke's essay, "Postmodernism: The Perfume of Information," which establishes the connection between the lifestyle of today's postfeminist woman and the superexploitation of postcolonial women in the Free Trade Zones. These considerations made it difficult, if not impossible, for the course to become a safari of the intellect.

The problem of maintaining the polyvalence of the text in relation to the different cultural and political contexts it straddles was the trickiest. For instance, in one of Head's stories, "Witchcraft," the main character Mma-Mabele is a staunch Christian who disdains the superstitious practices of her village. Christianity seems to set up an empowering distance between her and her community. The Church and the Christian hospital impart to her the ability to rationalize, "to sort out the true from the false in the everyday round of village life, but not immunity from strange forms of assault" (48). But because she refuses to accommodate male desire—constructed as freely roaming and irresponsible—her sexuality is called into question, and she comes to be known as a "he-man." While Mma-Mabele feigns disinterest in her reputation, she seems to realize that this marginalization of her sexuality threatens her place and membership in the community. For she develops a mysterious ailment that everyone around her recognizes to be caused by witchcraft. Faced with social ostracism that attempts to erase her as a sexual subject, Mma-Mabele displays symptoms that situate her firmly within the superstitious communal circle. Having withdrawn herself from sexual circulation, she inserts herself into the circuit of the *baloi* who dispense charms and cures. In suffering, she becomes part of the village.

My attempts to analyze Mma-Mabele's ailment and her subsequent cure made me painfully aware of the analytical suppleness demanded of postcolonial readers. For one thing, Mma-Mabele's reliance on Christianity was complexly inflected by the historical position of evangelism as the right arm of imperialism, by the disruption of gynocentric religious traditions by the Western church, by the hybridization of Christianity in Africa, and by the empowering role played by the discourse of Christian humanism during anti-colonial struggles. Indeed, this history is repeatedly alluded to in many of the stories in *Collector of Treasures*. While Africans in the diaspora are trying more and more to reconstruct a precolonial spiritual and cultural identity, the African Christian church is still a strong site of resistance in Botswana and South Africa. To complicate matters further, religious identity is a contentious point in ongoing rivalries in Africa. The pedagogic challenge, then, is to keep in sight this shifting genealogy of Christianity in Africa, while trying to understand Bessie Head's reliance on religion as an exemplary instance of saying "the impossible 'no'."

A similar problem presented itself when we tried to understand women's roles and privileges within a sex-gender system informed by traditional and Western patriarchal values. Mma-Mabele attributes her miraculous recovery by the end of the story to her sense of maternal responsibility saying, "I am too poor [to be ill] and there is no one else to feed my children" (956). This was a vexed point for the feminists in my class, who were dissatisfied with what seemed like a cop-out to a patriarchal system powerfully critiqued in the story. While Mma-Mabele resists her heterosexist positioning as sexual object, she accedes willingly to her position as mother within a gender system integral to the heterosexual order. While rationality and religion seem to give her an oppositional agency, they fail to support her at her time of greatest need, in the process disclosing their implication in the social arrangements that cause her illness in the first place.

In U.S. classrooms, Head's valorization of motherhood enters a historically and theoretically fraught contestation. The predicament of Mma-Mabele resonates powerfully with ongoing sociological discussions of the pauperization of women compounding the problems posed by rising numbers of female-headed single-parent households. Theoretically, the question of motherhood has drawn profoundly ambivalent responses from feminists in the West. Early feminists like Shulamith Firestone have argued that motherhood is the very bane of women's empowerment, while recent theorists like Kristeva have sought to inflect motherhood differently, as both continuous pain and inherent basis of an alternative, woman-centered knowledge. As with the issue of religion, understanding the significance of the family in Bessie Head's stories would involve looking at the ways the institutions of marriage and family functioned in precolonial societies and studying the effects of colonialism, migrant labor, and urbanization on indigenous kinship systems. Such an analysis, besides drawing out the contextual density of the story may also bring into contemporary discourses on motherhood an understanding of the complex, globally articulated structures shaping various experiences of maternity.

There are also enough hints in the story that Mma-Mabele's affliction may be caused by vitamin deficiency. We are also told of a shadowy but "benevolent" employer who gives her time off when she falls ill, but who obviously does not pay her well enough to sustain a healthy diet. One wonders if this employer is a member of the native elite or of the settler colonial class. These hints push us to look at the structural causes of hunger, malnutrition, and the absence of health care facilities, and their effect on gender ideologies. In turn, these investigations allow us to explain the ambivalences and contradictions in the story as arising out of the complex positioning of women as subjects desirous of freedom in difference, that is to see their agonistic consciousness of the need to articulate their struggles as women to the daily battle for survival under grossly adverse conditions that consumes the energies of most members of their community, including their adversaries in the gender system.

It goes without saying that such an enquiry will have to look outside of literary criticism or history for its answers. A rigorous study of postcolonial texts does make intellectual demands of a transdisciplinary nature, entailing as it does a scrupulous tracing of historical contexts and discursive inflections. And in the most successful instances, reading a postcolonial text involves keeping in sight three questions simultaneously: How does the text construct the world for postcolonial readers in all their heterogeneity? How does it construct the "other" world for equally heterogeneous Western readers? and what does it tell Western readers about their own world?

NOTES

1. For an early critique of simplistic applications of Western aesthetics to postcolonial texts, see Soyinka. For critiques of poststructuralist theory from postcolonial standpoints, see Parry, Sangari, and Shohat.

2. "Ideological effectivity" is a shorthand reference to the enormous body of work on ideology inaugurated by Louis Althusser. For the purposes of this paper, it is important to remember that ideology—working principally through the institutional apparatus of education—serves to "interpellate" or produce the subjects necessary for the maintenance of existing relations of exploitation and domination.

3. In this context, Kofele-Kale's remark that the Third World is not confined to the geographical territories designated as such, but includes the dispossessed of the First World such as the "Amerindians, Appalachians, and Black America, and Latinos of North America" (38) is an important intervention in the benign assignment of names and attributes that have for long taken up the energies of First World liberal scholars. A similar insistence by the women of color caucus at the National Women's Studies Association further inflects the essentialist construction of "woman of color" by drawing attention to the economic and political consequences of racism as well as to the heterogeneous positions occupied by Third World women (Sandoval).

4. This is the organizing premise of the collection of essays edited by Homi Bhabha, *Nation and Narration.* In a recent lengthy critique of the Jameson-Ahmad exchange, Madhava Prasad suggests that Jameson's attempt to formulate a separate and distinct theory of postcolonial literature is unproductive largely because he overlooks the point that all reading and interpretation takes place within a theory, if only implied, connecting literature to nationalism.

5. A notable exception to pluralist constructions of the Third World is Chandra Mohanty's discussion of the category in "Cartographies of Struggle: Third World Women and the Politics of Feminism." However, I draw support for my argument in favor of postcoloniality as a stronger analytical category from Mohanty's assessment that the "common context of struggle" in the third world is directly related to its colonial and neocolonial history (8–9).

6. Select texts that bring up these questions are Ngũgĩ wa Thiong'o's *Devil on the Cross*, Ayi Kwei Armah's *The Beautyful Ones Are Not Yet Born*, Bessie Head's *Collector of Treasures*, Chinua Achebe's *Things Fall Apart*, Leila Abouzeid's *Year of the Elephant*, Buchi Emecheta's *Joys of Motherhood*, Earl Lovelace's *Wine of Astonishment*, Tsitsi Dangarembga's *Nervous Conditions*, Salman Rushdie's *Satanic Verses*, Yambo Ouloguem's *Bound to Violence*.

7. This, unfortunately, is not always the case in discussions of postcoloniality, witness the argument advanced by Ashcroft, Griffiths, and Tiffin, in their otherwise valuable study, for overriding important differences in international and domestic positions of postcolonial societies and emphasizing instead their common anti-imperialist histories. Like any category, "postcolonial" is not immune to overgeneralizing and dehistoricizing uses. Shohat's and McClintock's critiques usefully problematize the unfounded optimism sometimes implicit in such instances, but they overstate their case by attributing the problems they identify to intrinsic flaws of the category.

8. A more striking instance of postmodernism's displacement of the nostalgia for lost presence on to the non-European world may be found in Jacques Derrida's "The Ends of Man" where he argues that the epistemological and military-economic violence of the West has so completely co-opted Western knowledge that a "radical trembling can only come from the outside." In "Can the Subaltern Speak?" Gayatri Spivak critiques a similar tendency in the work of Lyotard, and Deleuze and Guattari. Her argument is that the subject of knowledge presumed by postmodern anti-foundationalism is deeply implicated in the global arrangements of power and exploitation under late capitalism.

WORKS CITED

Achebe, Chinua. *Morning Yet on Creation Day*. New York: Anchor Doubleday, 1976.

Ahmad, Aijaz. "Jameson's Rhetoric of Otherness and the 'National Allegory.'" *Social Text* 6.2 (1987): 3–27.

Alavi, Hamza, et al. *Capitalism and Colonial Production*. London: Croom Helm, 1982.

Anderson, Benedict. *Imagined Communities: Reflections on the Origin and Spread of Nationalism*. London: Verso, 1983.

Appiah, Anthony. "Is the Post- in Postmodernism the Post- in Postcolonial?" *Critical Inquiry* 17 (1991): 336–57.

Ashcroft, Bill, Gareth Griffiths, and Helen Tiffin. *The Empire Writes Back*. London: Routledge, 1989.

Bhabha, Homi, ed. *Nation and Narration*. New York: Routledge, 1990.

———. "Signs Taken for Wonders: Question of Ambivalence and Authority under a Tree Outside Delhi, May 1817." *Critical Inquiry* 12.1 (1985): 144–65.

Busia, Abena. *Testimonies of Exile*. Trenton, NJ: Africa World Press, 1990.

Couper, Kristin. "Immigration, Nationality and Citizenship." *New Political Science* 16/17 (1989): 91–100.

Derrida, Jacques. "The Ends of Man." *Margins of Philosophy*. Trans. Alan Bass. Chicago: University of Chicago Press, 1982. 134–35.

Dorfman, Ariel and Armand Mattelart. *How to Read Donald Duck*. New York: International General, 1971.

During, Simon. "Postmodernism or Postcolonialism Today." *Textual Practice* 1.1 (1987): 32–47.

Ebert, Teresa. "The 'Difference' of Postmodern Feminism." *College English* 53.8 (1991): 886-904.

Fanon, Frantz. *Wretched of the Earth*. Trans. Constance Farrington. New York: Grove Press, 1963.

Foucault, Michel. *The Archaeology of Knowledge*. Trans. A. Sheridan Smith. New York: Pantheon, 1972.

Head, Bessie. *Collector of Treasures*. London: Heinemann, 1977.

Harlow, Barbara. *Resistance Literature*. New York: Methuen, 1987.

Irele, Abiola. "The African Scholar." *Transition* 51 (1991): 56–69.

Jameson, Fredric. *The Political Unconscious: Narrative as a Socially Symbolic Act*. Ithaca: Cornell University Press, 1981.

———. "Postmodernism or the Cultural Logic of Late Capitalism." *New Left Review* 146 (1984): 53–92.

———. "Third World Literature in the Era of Multinational Capitalism." *Social Text* 5.3 (1986): 65–88.

JanMohamed, Abdul. *Manichean Aesthetics: The Politics of Literature in Colonial Africa*. Amherst: University of Massachusetts Press, 1983.

Jeyawardena, Kumari. *Feminism and Nationalism in the Third World*. London: Zed Books, 1986.

Kofele-Kale, Ndiva. "Common Issues in Third World Studies." Keynote Address delivered to the Third World Studies Workshop, Governor's State University, Park Forest, Illinois, 26 April 1975.

Lloyd, Trevor Owen. *The British Empire 1558–1983*. Oxford: Oxford University Press, 1984.

Mies, Maria. *Patriarchy and Accumulation on a World Scale: Women in the International Division of Labor*. London: Zed Books, 1986.

Mohanty, Chandra. "Cartographies of Struggle: Third World Women and the Politics of Feminism." *Third World Women and the Politics of Feminism.* Ed. Chandra Mohanty, Ann Russo, and Lourdes Torres. Bloomington: Indiana University Press, 1991, 1–47.

McClintock, Anne. "The Angel of Progress: Pitfalls of the Term 'Post-Colonialism'." *Social Text* 31/32 (1992): 84–98.

Nelson, Cary. "Against English: Theory and the Limits of Discipline." *Profession* 87: 46–52.

Ngũgĩ wa Thiong'o. *Decolonizing the Mind: The Politics of Language in African Literature.* London: James Currey, 1986.

———. *Writers in Politics.* London: Heinemann, 1981.

Ogede, Ode S. "The Offal Kind." *Transition* 55 (1992): 179–84.

Parry, Benita. "Problems in Current Theories of Colonial Discourse." *Oxford Literary Review* 9.1-2 (1987): 27–58.

Pletsch, Carl. "The Three Worlds, or the Division of Social Scientific Labor, circa 1950–1975." *Comparative Studies in Society and History* 23.4 (1981): 565–90.

Prasad, Madhava. "On the Question of a Theory of (Third World) Literature." *Social Text* 31/32 (1992): 57–83.

Rushdie, Salman. "'Commonwealth Literature' Does Not Exist." *Imaginary Homelands.* London: Granta, 1991, 61–70.

Sandoval, Chela. "Feminism and Racism: A Report on the 1981 National Women's Studies Association Conference." *Making Face, Making Soul.* Ed. Gloria Anzaldua. San Francisco: Aunt Lute Foundation, 1990.

Sangari, Kum Kum. "The Politics of the Possible." *Cultural Critique* 7 (1987): 157–86.

Shohat, Ella. "Notes on the 'Post-Colonial'." *Social Text* 31/32 (1992): 99–113.

Soyinka, Wole. *Myth, Literature and the African World.* Cambridge: Cambridge University Press, 1976.

Spivak, Gayatri Chakravorty. "Can the Subaltern Speak?" *Marxism and the Interpretaton of Culture.* Ed. Cary Nelson and Lawrence Grossberg. Urbana: University of Illinois Press, 1988, 271–313.

———. "Poststructuralism, Marginality, Postcoloniality and Value." *Literary Theory Today.* Ed. Peter Collier and Helga Geyer-Ryan. Ithaca: Cornell University Press, 1990.

Wicke, Jennifer. "Posmodernism: The Perfume of Information." *Yale Journal of Criticism.* 1.2 (1988): 145–60.

12

STEPHEN SLEMON

Teaching at the End of Empire

> The school never forgot the day when big Bob Fraser "answered back" in class. Before the words were well out of his lips, the master, with a single stride, was in front of him, and laying two swift, stinging cuts from the rawhide over big Bob's back, commanded, "Hold out your hand!" in a voice so terrible, and with eyes of such blazing light, that before Bob was aware, he shot out his hand and stood waiting the blow. Never, in all its history, did the school receive such a thrill as the next few moments brought; for while Bob stood waiting, the master's words fell clear-cut upon the dead silence: "No, Robert, you are too big to thrash. You are a man. No man should strike you—and I apologize." And then big Bob forgot his wonted sheepishness and spoke out with a man's voice, "I am sorry I spoke back, sir." And then all the girls began to cry and wipe their eyes with their aprons, while the master and Bob shook hands silently. From that day and hour Bob Fraser would have slain anyone offering to make trouble for the master. Archibald Munro's rule was firmly established.

The passage is from Ralph Connor's "The Spelling Match," but my quotation is from *The Canada Book of Prose and Verse, Book One*, a school primer edited by Lorne Pierce and Dora Whitefield for Ryerson Press in Toronto, and authorized in 1927 for school use in British Columbia, Alberta, Saskatchewan, Manitoba, Ontario, Nova Scotia, Prince Edward Island, and Newfoundland. The date is significant; for at the historical moment that big Bob Fraser is made once again to stand up tall in his colonial schoolhouse—the subject-to-be-educated at the outpost or end of the British Empire—so too does the nation, having taken its blow from global war, now insist upon its own arrival in adulthood, its own coherent individuality, its power to regulate at the level of affect, its power to speak in a voice of its own. Authority calls; the subject answers; and in the process what begins as an oppositional practice—big Bob "answering back"—returns as the completed formation of a subject position in which the condition of adult male individuality is undivided and undying loyalty to the "master's" authority, unending continuation of the master's rule. The interpellation of big Bob Fraser is thus an allegory not only of nation-making within the apparatus of colonial control, but also of the formation of the identified colonial subject: a subject, I want to argue, which has been fashioned *in the first instance* as the effect of colonialist education as it circulates and regulates the valency of literary meaning.

This claim, of course, is by no means a new one. Ever since Althusser identified education itself as a primary state apparatus for producing the work of ideology, an enormous amount of archaeological research has come forward on the frontline role that literary education—especially English studies—has played in the manufacture of hierarchical social relations. D. J. Palmer and Chris Baldick, for example, have shown that in Britain, English studies was first instituted in women's and working men's colleges as a "soft" or "civilizing" object of study, and so has its national roots in gender and class control. In the British colonial context, Gauri Viswanathan's recent study of British literary education in India has shown that English studies as a formal discipline actually began in India—that "English literature appeared as a subject in the curriculum of the colonies long before it was institutionalized in the home country" (3)—and more importantly, that it did so as a technology for the manufacture of consent to colonial domination.

These findings, needless to say, constitute a remarkable disturbance in the discipline, but it is one that most teachers of postcolonial national literatures will have encountered immediately, and this at the thematic level of the texts they discuss in the classroom. For one of the most insistent arguments made by postcolonial writing—and in this context George Lamming's *In the Castle of My Skin* or Jamaica Kincaid's *Annie John* are just two of what are literally hundreds of examples—is that colonialist literary learning is at the primal scene of colonialist cultural control, and that a pedagogy of the book plays a necessary and material role in the strategic production of willing subjects of empire.

Given this wide range of critical studies that expose the embeddedness of English studies within British colonialism, however, and the repeated gesture to the scene of literary learning that takes place in postcolonial writing, I find it surprising that relatively little work has as yet come forward on the specific strategies that might underpin a *post*colonial literary pedagogy, an oppositional or counter-colonialist pedagogy for literary teaching itself. I need to be precise here, for of course a great deal of sociological analysis has followed on from Paulo Freire's work on pedagogical resistance; there have been all *sorts* of studies on the purchase of educational institutions on literary pedagogy; and a spectacular controversy has erupted over the politics of canon and *content* within various English studies curricula. But what I mean here is that except for some scattered articles on postcolonialism and the classroom—Gayatri Spivak's article on "The Making of Americans," for example, or Arun Mukherjee's important piece on "Ideology in the Classroom"—and outside of an engagement with postcolonialism as a pedagogical vector within a general cultural theory, surprisingly little seems to have been written about the frontline exigencies of postcolonial literary teaching at the level of immediate classroom engagement.[1] My project in this paper is to present an argument about *one* reason why this might be so.

But before I do that I need briefly to acknowledge some of the *other* reasons why pedagogical models for postcolonial literary teaching are less than thick upon the academic ground. First, and simply: the field of postcolonialism is relatively new, and thus it is one to which the publishing industry has not yet entirely offered its profit-taking embrace. Second, the question has been raised as to whether a genuinely postcolonial critical perspective can take place *within* the apparatus of English studies: the place where "postcolonialism," whatever that is, usually gets taught. The moment in which we infiltrate Third World "knowledges" into Western literary education, Spivak argues, we become complicitous with the information-retrieval systems of imperialist custodianship, and thus we become complicitous in the founding of a "new orientalism" on the site of what we had hoped would function as an agent of resistance (see "Poststructuralism," "Making"). Third, postcolonialism has all sorts of reasons to suspect that a practicable approach to literary teaching under the aegis of the Western liberal "humanities" is already an exercise in postcolonial self-defeat. Most important here is the argument, made by Barbara Harlow and many others, that like the prison system, the humanities are inescapably committed to the manufacture of responsible, culpable individuals whose position in a world economy is entirely a matter of their own self-fashioning—clearly a thesis incompatible with most of the arguments that take place within postcolonial political critique. And fourth—perhaps most importantly—the whole enterprise of pedagogical research at present seems to be located very much at the "soft option" end of disciplinary engagement. Pedagogy, that is to say, is discursively in the feminine, in the "service" ranks of professional engagement, beneath the purview of intellectual advancement, and far from the rugged masculinity of the theoretical frontier. Who, then, actually *wants* to work on the immediate exigencies of postcolonial pedagogy, when postcolonialism as an institutionalized discipline circulates as a theatre for naked careerism and for professional self-emplacement?

My argument in this paper, however, is that another complexity underpins the general invisibility of a practical postcolonial literary pedagogy. And in order to unpack this structure, I want to offer three historical moments, three scenes of literary learning, which in my argument are meant to function paradigmatically as the three separate terms of a rhetorical syllogism.

The first of these scenes is again that Canadian school primer from 1927, *The Canada Book of Prose and Verse*. This is a work that places itself against the generation of imperial readers which preceded it in the colonial curriculum—readers such as *The Queen's Primers* and Nelson's *Royal Readers*, which hammer messages of imperial duty home at every turn. And this reader opposes those earlier imperial primers directly at the level of content by quite consciously foregrounding the work of about thirty avowedly *Canadian* writers. What comes across, unmistakably, is the idea that the Canadian landscape is indeed a fit subject for literary expression, and that Canadian writers can stand cheek-by-jowl with their British counterparts in every literary genre and at every literary theme. All "Commonwealth" national literatures have witnessed a similar kind of editorial intervention in literary curriculum: it marks a politics of repatriation at moments of administrative independence, and it practises an important interruption in that English literary monologue that has hitherto stood in for the complete apparatus of literary expression (see Odejide, for example). At the level of *content*, that is, this school reader presents itself as a *post*colonialist document, and it does so quite consciously. In fact, its acknowledgments page actually lists the Canadian authors whose work can be found in the volume.

But at the level of what Michael Apple calls "the hidden curriculum," *The Canada Book of Prose and Verse* is in contradiction with itself, and in a way that structurally undermines its conscious postcolonial cultural agenda. The text begins with a repetition of that greatest of colonialist tropes, the literary work as appropriative traveler, in Emily Dickinson's "There is no frigate like a book To take us leagues away"; and then sails on to articulate a remarkably coherent teleology of progressivist arrival through chapters on "Books and Reading," "Heroes and Adventure," "Enjoying Life," "The Out-of-Doors," "The School Theatre," "Home Life," "School Days," "Workers and Their Work," "The Young Citizen," and finally "The Spirit of the North," to arrive at last at an astonishingly clear articulation of monolithic nationality in Marjorie Pickthall's "Star of the North," the closing selection in the volume. Subtitled "A Hymn," Pickthall's poem reads as follows:

> Out of the dust God called new nations forth,
> The land and sea made ready at His voice;
> He broke the barriers of the North
> And bade our plains rejoice;
> He saw the untrodden prairie hold
> Empire of early gold.
> Star of the North,
> He bade thee shine
> And prove once more the dreams of men divine.
>
> Ask of the seas what our white frontiers dare,
> Ask of the skies where our young banners fly
> Like stars unloosened from the hair
> Of wild-winged victory.
> God's thunder only wakening thrills
> The ramparts of our hills.
> Star of the North,
> No foe shall stain,
> What France has loved, where Britain's dead have lain!
>
> Dark is the watch-fire, sheathed the ancient sword,
> But sons must follow where their sires have led,
> To the anointed end, O Lord,
> Where marched the mighty dead.
> Firm stands the red flag battle-blown,
> And we will guard our own,
> Our Canada,
> From snow to sea,
> One hope, one home, one shining destiny!

"One hope, one home"—everywhere in this reader, the nation functions as a boundary text which denies ethnicity and the play of cultural difference. Indigenity, when recognized, is relegated to the picturesque and the retreating past; and as for the present state of the nation, it is figured agriculturally: Canada as the bread-basket of the Empire, and thus readable as part of the machinery of economic, if not administrative, colonialism. The reader, structurally, tells a growing-up story for *both* the nation and the child subject, and it makes that story monolithic, exclusionary, appropriative, and imperially contingent. Structurally, that is, *The Canada Book of Prose and Verse* calls down its own interruptive content, and what emerges here—as Homi Bhabha has argued in an article entitled "DissemiNation"—is that the "cultural construction of nationness" is made to function discursively, *within* colonialism, "as a form of social and textual affiliation" to the Imperium (292). The Canadian nation, that is, marks out a *topos*, a field for identification, which through the educational process is made to move inward into the student: an affect and an internalization of the Real. The figure of the emergent "nation," which begins as an interruptive marker in a discourse of empire, structurally figures itself as the site upon which the interpellated subject-to-be-educated in the colonial schoolhouse becomes coterminous with the book—a narrative of formation, self-fashioning, and completion, whose condition of possibility is a continuing affiliation to the imperialist text.

And so the object-lesson of my first scene of learning is that postcolonial opposition, when pitched solely at the level of nationalist *content*, can actually function as a topic of colonialist *address*. In this instance at least, the *topos* of postcolonial nationalism becomes one of the ways in which an affiliation to colonialist narratives of containment is promulgated and internalized. And when a postcolonial textual critique actually reads this content-based postcolonialism against the grain of its own self-fashioning, it finds its oppositional claims nugatory, and its postcolonialism—as *pedagogy*—hopelessly compromised.

The second scene of learning—the second term in the general syllogism that structures this paper—takes place within Erna Brodber's important West Indian novel *Myal*, published in 1988. The novel opens with the figure of imperialism's docile body at the moment of learning—Ella O'Grady, aged 13, reciting by heart, and before the whole class, the entire text of Kipling's poem "Oh, where are you going to all you Big Steamers"—and then traces her progress into adulthood, where she has grown up to become the literary teacher in the same schoolroom at the book's end. This time her text is a child's tale about Percy the chick, Master Willie, Mr. Dan, and the other animals on Mr. Joe's farm—animals who have bolted for freedom only to discover that no one will care for them so deeply as Mr. Joe does, and so they come home. Ella has now learned to read this text as a *colonialist* fable—an allegory that robs its student readers of possible alternatives to imperialist management—and her work is to find a way of teaching the story against its grain. Her project is to make an oppositional teaching practice genuinely postcolonial, and for this, her way of teaching the text has to be culturally effective. If it is not, her students—subjects-to-be-educated into the ends of Empire—will remain not only economically but also cognitively enmeshed within colonialist representations, and the cycle of domination through the manufacture of consent will continue for yet another generation.

Myal tells the story of how Ella succeeds, and it does so through a narrative that might in itself encode a theory of postcolonial or counter-hegemonic teaching within the compromised apparatus of an imperialist English studies. To get started, Ella has to have learned how to read oppositionally; she has to have acquired the formal and theoretical skills that underlie the practice of textual critique. But to *teach* against colonialist hegemony, Ella needs to accept her provisional and possibly compromised status as a worker who struggles against the imperium from within—that is, she needs to address colonial power from within the schoolhouse, because if she doesn't teach this text and try, as she says, "to correct images from the inside" (110), somebody else will teach this story, and will likely do so without her oppositional clarity. And to reach her students with this oppositional energy, Ella needs communal support at the level of local, anti-colonialist resistance—in this case a group of characters who have taken on the animal names of the children's story (Mr. Dan, Master Willie, and so on), as ironic internalizations and as code names, and who maintain a coherent, subterranean telepathic conversation between themselves, one that the text suggests has been going on, in the guise of colonialism's allegory of control, for centuries.

Myal's postcolonial lesson, then, is that anti-colonialist textual critique needs culturally specific and local knowledges, and needs to function from within the ideological machineries for colonialist control. For if literary education itself actually is the "end" or aim of Empire—the place where ideology works to secure dependency and affiliation, and thus economic control—the project of an oppositional pedagogical postcolonialism is to stay at this end of Empire, but to try to reverse the temporal and positional vector in the preposition. Teaching *at* the end of Empire: Ella *at* this end has to transfigure "at" into an active prepositional marker and find ways to teach "at" or *against* the end of Empire—an "end" that is interpellative and ideological, and an "at" that needs to be grounded immediately in a space of subaltern agency, a space of oppositional action and of cultural self-knowledge.

My third scene of learning is an anecdotal one, but before adducing its lesson I want to say something about the ramifications for teaching that inhere from the first two. The lesson of *The Canada Book of Prose and Verse* suggests that an inculcation of local and nationalist knowledges goes nowhere as a postcolonial pedagogy unless it enters into specific negotiations with the practices and methods of an anti- or counter-colonialist theoretical critique. The telos of Brodber's *Myal*, however, suggests that a postcolonial textual critique only takes ground when embedded in local knowledges, subterranean voices: those "authentic," expressivist voices of Otherness to which the imperialist interloper never has pure access. To teach the lesson of the first requires critical theory: that is, it requires a negative hermeneutics, a hermeneutics of suspicion, against the voices of authority, against the embodiments of nationhood, against expressivist theories of full cultural presence, and against the textual possibility of literary identification. To teach the lesson of the second, however, requires anthropology: it requires a positive hermeneutics, a recognition of cultural authenticity in the vocalizations of the Other, and a reading for cultural presence, for local and oppositional knowledges, within the structure of postcolonial textual expression.

Needless to say, these two currents within postcolonialism are profoundly at odds with one another at the level of theory, and so, characteristically, my third scene of learning is a compromised one: it is myself, teaching "Commonwealth" literature to third-year students in a full-year course in the Department of English at the University of Alberta in Canada. "Commonwealth" literature, says Timothy Brennan, is a "fictional entity created by scholars in the provinces and depending on the imaginary coherence of tea time" (xiii). It is politically outdated, grounded in an ethos of global spatialization and monolithic nationhood, and embedded in a pedagogy of nativist recuperation (see also Bhabha, Interview). But whatever its inception, this "Commonwealth" space of categorical compromise is the one place in my department where post-colonialism of any kind takes place formally at the undergraduate level. And so I begin the course theoretically, with what I hope represents a politically vigilant, oppositional, and deconstructive assault on the ideological underpinnings to one of the great master texts of European colonialist control: Defoe's *Robinson Crusoe.* Later, however, the text before us is R. K. Narayan's *The Guide,* and in complete violation of the kind of critical theory I began with—specifically, of the oppositional, deconstructive, anti-ethnographic critique advanced by exemplary theorists such as Trinh T. Minh-ha and James Clifford—I explain in positivist terms, however weakly, the principles of Hindu *advaita vendantin* metaphysics, and let the students think about the ways in which these principles might structure a reading of the text. What happens, pedagogically, I think, is instructive. The process of metaphysical, anthropological unpacking for reading *The Guide* produces a destabilizing effect in the students: they are troubled by their lack of knowledge, by the radical *otherness* of a non-Western organizing script; they find themselves a little more suspicious of Western cultural naturalization, of universalist generalizations, or the idea of purely recuperable meanings. What starts to emerge is a powerful motive for experiencing a sense of genuine cross-cultural respect. The deconstructive energetics of reading against *Robinson Crusoe,* however, taken in isolation at the beginning of this course, actually underscore what turns out to be a "feel good" exercise for the students: an exercise that lends them a sense of textual mastery and interpretive control. I end up worrying that what the students have really learned from their isolated exercise in anti-colonialist textual critique is a sense of superiority, and a renewed investment in the claims of global modernity over the semiotic excesses of the past.

It would be deeply uncritical to overread this experiential encounter at two pedagogical moments within one university-level course, but the third term in my syllogism nevertheless suggests—and this is my thesis in this paper—that postcolonialism, whatever its engagement at the level of pure theoretical reading, needs to accommodate contradictory critical projects at the level of its undergraduate pedagogy. Two vast—and vastly different—kinds of critical projects mark the general field of postcolonial literary studies in its present moment: one positivist and anthropological, the other sceptical and deconstructive, one exemplified in Benita Parry's expressivist appeal for a reading of "an/other" knowledge on the part of the colonized, the other exemplified in Gayatri Spivak's deconstructive claim that "there is no space [within textual representation] from where the subaltern...subject can speak." In the theatre of critical publishing, where postcolonialism as a theory of reading is displayed most visibly as a contemporary cultural practice, there seems to be little attempt to negotiate between these mutually suspicious and usually hostile critical methods: in this space, postcolonialism resembles a post-Darwinian universe in which theoretical critique is an ascendent species, and knowledge-based research into other cultural systems is in the last throes of extinction. But in a postcolonial pedagogical practice—a space of teaching at the end of Empire, and thus a space of direct political engagement with the continuing ravages of neocolonialism—there must be a space that allows the claims of both modalities of reading to take place. At the level of pedagogy, there can be no oppositional critique without a grounding in the thick materiality of other knowledges, other systems of interpretation. And there can be no effective oppositional content without the anti-referential clarity of an anti-colonialist critique.

There are implications for such a thesis, and I want to end this paper by meditating on two of them. First, a pedagogy that embraces a significant order of contradiction or *difference* at the level of its foundational methodologies for textual reading has to give away the idea that a practicable postcolonialism can ever found itself on a pure and unproblematized notion of top-down political instruction at the level of its content. Here, as elsewhere, postcolonialism has to recognize the profound extent to which it is situated within the ambit of a continuing neocolonialism, which means that it needs to accept that its politics are interventionary at best, never simply expressivist, and never fully arrived. Gayatri Spivak's claim that a pedagogy for Third World knowledges within an English Studies curriculum *necessarily* produces a "new orientalism" of cultural affect, Timothy Brennan's wholesale dismissal of a "Commonwealth" literary agenda because its roots run strikingly into a Eurocentric spatializing technology for proclaiming the "end of Empire"—these, I think, are critiques which can circulate as purist doctrines within the cultural institution of literary studies, and which can appeal in practice to a space outside the continuing circulation of neocolonialist power, where the last flag at the last outpost of Empire really has been taken down. But as Ella O'Grady discovered, the untranscendable urgency of a postcolonial project is a redress of power at the level of its *local* oppressions, and for this its pedagogy needs to sustain its frontline interventionary work of "correct[ing] images from the inside." Peter Elbow's theory of a pedagogy that embraces contraries at the foundational level, W. J. T. Mitchell's avowal of a critical method of "dialectical pluralism," Gerald Graff's exhortation to teach the conflicts within literary learning: these approaches are sometimes read as blandly liberal ones within the discipline of literary studies, but I want to suggest that they may in fact be enormously useful to the description of a postcolonial pedagogy based on an incoherent and constantly renegotiated set of reading strategies. For if, in Gramscian terms, an oppositional or counter-hegemonic practice can be seen to secure a politics of oppression simply by recognizing that its dominant binaries remain in place, a processive pedagogy of thinking through methodological contradiction can also be redirected toward real social change at the level of the local. And it can begin that redirection by opening within English Studies itself—the place of colonialist management—a cognitive space in which the subject-to-be-educated reads the effects of ideology in both personal and political dimensions, and finds within that space, to use Ross Chambers' terms, something that functions as a "room for manoeuvre."

If such a room actually can be opened at the site of neocolonialist ideological production, then there will also be implications for the way in which we read the question of agency under power—which leads me to the second and last of my closing meditations for this paper. For if a postcolonial pedagogy reproduces English Studies as a site for both a power and its resistance, and if it also works locally to produce some genuine order of social change, then we must give away the idea that hegemony is absolute and infinitely capable of recuperating its oppositions. Homi Bhabha has claimed that colonial authority, under the necessary logic of its own ambivalence, is always partial, disjunctive, and fragmented, that it is open to textual analysis, and that it can be disarticulated—and because this is so, he argues, "the subject of culture" needs to shift away from negative dialectics towards "an attention to the place and time of *enunciative* agency" ("Postcolonial Authority," 57, my emphasis). If such a shift is to take place, there would seem to be two primary locations towards which a pedagogical postcolonialism would need to direct its attention: the subject by or for whom the postcolonial text claims to speak—that is, the colonized—and the subject to whom the text is addressed within the circuit of postcolonial pedagogy: that is, the student subject within the discipline of organized literary studies. Seen in this way, the colonized is a subject who can always claim an aporetic and contingent self-knowledge and enunciative agency, even when the processes of imperial subordination seem never more totalizing and the possibilities for knowing resistance seem never more abject.[2] And the student can only be a subject whose disjunctive and contradictory emplacement at the ambivalent "end" of Empire is also a necessary place for this subaltern textual opposition, a necessary agent in the construction of anti-colonialist social change.

Both orders of agency, of course, remain architecturally ambivalent and difficult to address. But if postcolonial literary pedagogy does indeed need to give away methodological coherence in order to work strategically, it may well turn out to be that the place where critical theory needs to turn, in the post-colonial first instance, is again to the scene of classroom learning. For if literary learning is there, at the primal scene of colonialist management, then a dialectics of Empire and its oppositions would suggest that literary learning will have to remain at the foreground of a postcolonialism as the inescapable place for the articulation of its resistances. Unless, of course, the cognitive technologies of contemporary neocolonialism somehow crumble under a radical relocation of the Self-and-Other dialectic that characterizes Western modernity. Unless the unimaginable happens politically, and the end of Empire actually arrives, at some future, utopian, and historical moment.

NOTES

1. I gave an earlier version of this paper in March 1992 at the "Post-Colonialism: Theory and Practice" conference, sponsored by the Comparative Literature program at the University of British Columbia, and organized by Eva-Marie Kroller. There I learned that Jim Greenlaw, a Ph.D. candidate in the Faculty of Education, is writing his dissertation on the pedagogy of postcolonial literatures. My thanks to participants at this conference for their helpful comments and suggestions.

2. For a detailed examination of the question of a displaced agency for colonial subjects, see Bhabha's "Postcolonial Authority."

WORKS CITED

Althusser, Louis. "Ideology and Ideological State Apparatuses (Notes Towards an Investigation)." *Lenin and Philosophy and Other Essays.* Trans. B. Brewster. New York: Monthly Review Press, 1971.

Apple, Michael. *Ideology and Curriculum.* London: Routledge and Kegan Paul, 1979.

Baldick, Chris. *The Social Mission of English Criticism 1948–1932.* Oxford: Clarendon, 1983.

Bhabha, Homi K. "DissemiNation: Time, Narrative, and the Margins of the Modern Nation." *Nation and Narration.* Ed. Homi K. Bhabha, 291–322.

———. Interview with David Bennett and Terry Collits. "The Postcolonial Critic—Homi Bhabha Interviewed." *Arena* 96 (1991): 47–63.

———. "Postcolonial Authority and Postmodern Guilt." *Cultural Studies.* Ed. Lawrence Grossberg, Cary Nelson, and Paula A. Treichler. New York: Routledge, 1992, 56–68.

Brodber, Erna. *Myal.* London: New Beacon, 1988.

Chambers, Ross. *Room for Manoeuvre: Reading (the) Oppositional (in) Narrative.* Chicago: University of Chicago Press, 1990.

Clifford, James. *The Predicament of Culture: Twentieth Century Ethnography, Literature, and Art.* Cambridge, MA: Harvard University Press, 1988.

Doyle, Brian. *English and Englishness.* London: Routledge, 1989.

Elbow, Peter. *Embracing Contraries: Explorations in Learning and Teaching.* New York: Oxford University Press, 1986.

Freire, Paulo. *Pedagogy of the Oppressed.* Trans. Myra Bergman Ramos. New York: Seabury, 1970.

Graff, Gerald. "Teach the Conflicts." *South Atlantic Quarterly* 89.1 (Winter 1990): 51–67.

Hulme, Peter. *Colonial Encounters: Europe and the Native Caribbean, 1492–1797.* London: Methuen, 1986.

Hunter, Ian. *Culture and Government: The Emergence of Literary Education.* London, Macmillan, 1988.

Mitchell, W. J. T. *Iconology: Image, Text, Ideology.* Chicago: University of Chicago Press, 1986.

Mukherjee, Arun. "Ideology in the Classroom: A Case Study in the Teaching of English Literature in Canadian Universities." *Dalhousie Review* 66.1/2 (Spring/Summer 1986): 22–29.

Odejide, Abiola. "Education as Quest: The Nigerian School Story." *Children's Literature in Education* 18.2 (1987): 77–87.

Palmer, D. J. *The Rise of English Studies.* London: Oxford University Press, 1965.

Parry, Benita. "Problems in Current Theories of Colonial Discourse." *Oxford Literary Review* 9.1/2 (1987): 27–51.

Pierce, Lorne, and Dora Whitefield. *The Canada Book of Prose and Verse, Book One.* Rev. ed., 1935. Toronto: Ryerson, 1927.

Spivak, Gayatri Chakravorty. "Can the Subaltern Speak?: Speculations on Widow-Sacrifice." *Wedge* 7/8 (Winter/Spring 1985).

———. "The Making of Americans, the Teaching of English, and the Future of Cultural Studies." *New Literary History* 21 (1990): 781–98.

———. "Poststructuralism, Marginality, Postcoloniality and Value." *Literary Theory Today.* Ed. Peter Collier and Helga Geyer-Ryan. Cambridge: Cambridge UP, 1991. 219–44.

Trinh T. Minh-ha. *Woman, Native, Other: Writing Postcoloniality and Feminism.* Bloomington: Indiana University Press, 1989.

Viswanathan, Gauri. *Masks of Conquest: Literary Study and British Rule in India.* London: Faber and Faber, 1989.

13

Allen Carey-Webb

Heart of Darkness, *Tarzan*, and the "Third World": Canons and Encounters in World Literature, English 109

Exclusion

> Unlike the classical stage of national or market capitalism, then, pieces of the puzzle are missing; it can never be fully reconstructed; no enlargement of personal experience (in the knowledge of other social classes, for example), no intensity of self-examination (in the form of whatever social guilt), no scientific deductions on the basis of internal evidence of First World data, can ever be enough to include this radical otherness of colonial life, colonial suffering, and exploitation, let alone the structural connections between that and this, between absent and daily life in the metropolis.
>
> —Fredric Jameson

Inclusion

> The mere addition of Afro-American texts to the present canon without any explicit and persuasive account of how this addition leads us to see the canon anew reveals the worst of academic pluralist ideology. Serious Afro-American canon formation cannot take place without a wholesome reconsideration of the canon already in place.
>
> —Cornel West

These two citations point to the peculiarly redundant status of *Heart of Darkness* as a canonical text. The first is from a recent essay on "Modernism" by Fredric Jameson, where he argues that the determining condition of modernism is a sensed "missing piece," specifically the way in which an international economic system separates the citizens of the colonizing power from the experience of the colonized. As an established classic text of modernism, *Heart of Darkness* could be seen as an attempt to provide this suppressed knowledge—or at any rate to narrate its absence: indeed we might think of Jameson's "missing piece" as the secret of the barbarity of the ivory trade that Marlow keeps from Kurtz's Intended. Yet *Heart of Darkness* can also be taken as an exemplary text within the developing canon of anglophone and francophone "Third World" literature: inverting and renarrating this paradigmatic tale of a colonial encounter has become a recognized strategy of postcolonial writers. Conrad is often alluded to directly or indirectly and the disturbing journey to the Land of the Other is a recurrent narrative pattern in postcolonial fiction from Camara Laye's *Enfant Noir* to Ama Ata Aidoo's *Our Sister Killjoy*.[1] While Jameson writes of what modernism excludes, Cornel West warns against merely including Afro-American texts within an established canon whose premises remain otherwise unquestioned. The place of *Heart of Darkness* in two canons or "traditions" that are still for the most part kept separate by our governing pedagogical conventions points up the tendency, even in the postcolonial world, to keep cultures and identities isolated and self-contained. *Heart of Darkness* seems the perfect test case for West's assertion that to take postcolonial writing seriously is not merely to include it among traditionally established literature, but to engage in "a reconsideration of the canon already in place."

I approached a required introductory course at the University of Oregon with Conrad's novella and West's advice in mind. Following a strategy familiar to postcolonial literature teaching, I paired the reading of *Heart of Darkness* with a number of "Third World" texts including Achebe's *Things Fall Apart*, Kane's *Ambiguous Adventure*, Paule Marshall's *Praisesong for the Widow*, and Rigoberta Menchú's testimonial. In complex, interesting ways each work could be seen as a narration of colonial encounter and each explored the problematics of cultural "crossing over." What made the course unusual, and, I believe, particularly effective, was starting it with Edgar Rice Burrough's *Tarzan of the Apes*. *Tarzan* led students to fundamental questions about what literature is, who defines the canon and why. *Tarzan* also turned out to be a useful text for thinking about *Heart of Darkness*. Contrasting the works pointed to shortcomings, lacks, "missing pieces" in Conrad's critique of imperialism. Indeed, the problem of "missing pieces" seemed to haunt the class, first moving us toward the "Third World" texts to "fill in" absent voices, and then, in turn, troubling and decentering our understanding of "Third World" literature as well.

RACISM AND THE CLASSICS: THE CASE OF *HEART OF DARKNESS*

Before discussing *Tarzan*, it is worthwhile to situate a bit more carefully the issues that arise when teaching *Heart of Darkness* in the 1990s. *Heart of Darkness* has long been a staple of the introductory course. In my first year of college, decades ago and in a different era of literature studies, class discussion centered on the immanent symbolic and psychological complexity of the novella and Conrad's unique linguistic style. At that time the narration of a passage through holocaust was not at the front of our awareness. We didn't know or weren't interested in the history of the Congo, the fact that

> as many as 6,000,000 persons may have been uprooted, tortured, and murdered through the forced labor system used to extract ivory and what reformers called "red rubber" from "the heart of darkness." (Brantlinger, "*Heart*," 365)

Neither Conrad's attack on Belgian colonialism nor his parody of romantic colonial fiction were the focus when I was in school, yet, it now seems critical to consider *Heart of Darkness* in its social, historical, and literary context and to do so in a way that both highlights its anti-colonial stance and explores the ambiguities and contradictions in its treatment of Africa and Africans.

Of course, the attack on the developing imperial system in Africa is everywhere present in the novella. There is the corruption of the Trading Society, the forced labor and the grove of death, the depopulation of the countryside, the indiscriminate murder of the natives, the senseless firing into the bush, the Eldorado Exploring Expedition, the Society for the Suppression of Savage Customs, corrupt administrators, and Kurtz himself. Attending to *Heart of Darkness*'s portrayal of imperialist practices is primary to teaching the novella in context, yet to read *Heart of Darkness* as a purely anti-colonial text leaves out the recent debate over Conrad's complicity in colonialist assumptions and philosophy. Bringing these more difficult matters into the classroom suggests ambiguities and equivocations not only in Conrad but in attitudes we and our students may hold as well.

Chinua Achebe's 1975 lecture "An Image of Africa: Racism in Conrad's *Heart of Darkness*" and Frances B. Singh's 1978 essay "The Colonialistic Bias of *Heart of Darkness*" initiated a still-running discussion in Conrad circles about the representation of Africans and the anti-colonial politics of the novella.[2] Achebe believes that Conrad's condemnation of Belgian colonialism sidesteps admitting equality between white and black people, and portrays Africans as lacking the power of expression, devoid of recognizable humanity, in short, as cannibals who should stay in "their place." Achebe argues that the peculiar power of *Heart of Darkness* is located in an appeal to a racist fear of equality:

> Herein lies the meaning of *Heart of Darkness* and the fascination it holds over the Western mind: "What thrilled you was just the thought of their humanity—like yours...Ugly." (254)

While Achebe calls *Heart of Darkness* "permanent literature," something which is "read and taught and continuously evaluated by serious academics," he maintains that it cannot be "great art" because it

> parades in the most vulgar fashion prejudices and insults from which a section of humanity has suffered untold agonies and atrocities in the past and continues to do so in many ways and many places today...[it] celebrates the dehumanization [of Africans and]...depersonalizes a portion of the human race. (257)

More disturbing for Achebe than Conrad's novella per se is the way in which Achebe sees *Heart of Darkness* pointing to the pervasiveness of racism in Western thought. As a case in point, he discusses a highly detailed psychoanalytic biography of Conrad that doesn't even touch on Conrad's attitude toward black people, "Which only leads one to surmise that Western psychoanalysts must regard the kind of racism displayed by Conrad as absolutely normal" (259).

In her essay Frances Singh maintains that even though *Heart of Darkness* may be "one of the most powerful indictments of colonialism ever written" its critique is profoundly compromised by an acceptance of nineteenth-century anthropology that considered African tribes "primitive" and "savage," by a failure to distinguish between the metaphors of evil blackness and black skin, and by an endorsement of English colonialism over Belgian on the grounds of greater "efficiency." Singh calls Marlow's sympathy for Africans "superficial":

> He feels sorry for them when he sees them dying, but when he sees them healthy, practicing their customs, he feels nothing but abhorrence and loathing, like a good colonizer to whom such a feeling offers a perfect rationalization for his policies. (272)

She believes that Marlow's (and Conrad's) attitude toward the Africans reflects a colonialistic bias:

> He may sympathize with the plight of blacks, he may be disgusted by the effects of economic colonialism, but because he has no desire to understand or appreciate people of any culture other than his own, he is not emancipated from the mentality of a colonizer. (272)

Singh concludes that the limitations of Conrad's perspective reduce the significance of his work and, ironically, turn "a story that was meant to be a clear-cut attack on a vicious system into a partial apology for it" (280).

In the 1980s articles and studies in response to Achebe and Singh appeared in rapid succession. "Third World" writers who sought to temper Achebe's views were soon published. In 1982 *Conradiana* devoted an issue to the discussion. As if to refute the charge that Conrad scholars had by their silence colluded in the alleged racism of the text, a long bibliography of writing on the general topic of Conrad and colonialism was included.[3] The issues raised by Achebe and Singh preceded Benita Parry's critical analysis, *Conrad and Imperialism*, and Patrick Brantlinger's significant work on nineteenth-century British attitudes toward Africans, and it seemed to inspire Bette London's feminist and Reynold Humphries' poststructuralist discussions of Conrad. The significance of the debate is signalled by Robert Kimbrough's radically revised 1988 Norton Critical Edition of *Heart of Darkness*, which includes the Achebe and Singh essays and critical responses.

It is Achebe's charge of racism that draws the attention of Conrad enthusiasts. Unfortunately, some of their comments are more reactive than thoughtful. J. M. Robertson asks, "What can it be but a form of political jingoism that pushes Achebe into this anti-creative stance" and makes him "so perniciously wrong about a fellow writer and truth-teller?" (107). He believes Achebe "undermines his credibility and spoils the magnificent contribution he has made as a novelist." Reinhardt Kuesgen describes Achebe's judgment of the novella as "obviously erroneous" (28) and hopes that "modern literary scholarship will reduce the need for Achebe's aggressiveness" (32). Ian Watt emphasizes that unlike "many modern anthropologists and their followers" we should join Conrad's moral rejection of African cannibalism.[4]

Some Conrad scholars take Achebe's condemnation of Conrad's racism as an accusation from which the great artist must be exonerated. They argue that Conrad may have used racist expressions or held racist ideas but that he was less racist than his contemporaries (Sarvan, Hawkins, Watts, Watt).[5] They assume that unlike those deluded or "racist" nineteenth-century contemporaries of Conrad, today's critics can make their judgments objectively. This effort to excuse, apologize, or explain for Conrad because his understanding was "limited by his time" still avoids directly confronting the questions Achebe and Singh raise about the text and misses their broader point that the issue is not just *Heart of Darkness*, but the possible existence of pervasive racist and colonialist perspectives in a broader context. What is at stake is not really Conrad himself or the essential guilt or innocence of his text, but the way we understand *Heart of Darkness* and our own society.

The responses of the "Third World" writers are more to the point. They are willing to entertain Achebe's fundamental argument, but hesitate to go as far as Achebe does in criticizing the text. Peter Nazareth claims that rather than narrating the "us" of the West and the "them" of Africa, *Heart of Darkness* equivocates on cultural identity and "erodes the solid walls of personality" (179). While sharing the concern about Western attitudes toward the "Third World," Wilson Harris believes Achebe's judgment of *Heart of Darkness* misses Conrad's "crucial parody of the proprieties of established order that mask corruption in all societies" (265). (Nonetheless, Harris believes that Conrad failed to move beyond a purely nihilistic viewpoint and thus can be read as supporting liberal complacency.) C. P. Sarvan argues that the emphasis in Conrad "is on continuity, on persistence through time and peoples, and therefore on the fundamental oneness of man and his nature" (283). While Nazareth, Harris, and Sarvan do not dismiss Achebe's charges, they do read Conrad with a view to what he reveals about a transhistoric, universal "human nature." Their humanist perspective is attractive, though while it should not be dismissed, it is not unproblematic. In attempting to define a universal human nature one needs to ask, whose definition of "human nature" is called upon to serve for everyone else? It is pertinent to recall Wole Soyinka's warning to beware the neocolonial wolf who comes dressed in the sheep's clothing of "universality" (see Gates, "Talkin'," 408).

Without traveling further into the complex and interesting arguments that arise in the discussion, it is evident that to charge one of the established "great works" with "racism" is, in the academic context at least, to commit a serious act. At times, defenders of Conrad reveal more about the institutionalization of Conrad as an object of study than about nineteenth- or twentieth-century colonialism or racial philosophy. Underlying some responses to Achebe appears to be the anxiety that if Conrad's writing is indeed racist, *Heart of Darkness* would somehow be less worthy of analysis and the Conrad scholar would be therefore reduced in stature. Yet why should this be so? The intellectual complexity and artistic sophistication of the novella, and particularly its evident attack on colonialism, make understanding possible racism in the work all the more urgent. In *The Political Unconscious*, Jameson argues that

> The restoration of the meaning of the greatest cultural monuments cannot be separated from a passionate and partisan assessment of everything that is oppressive in them and that knows complicity with privilege and class domination. (299)

To cease paying attention to a text, or to minimize its importance, because it is "racist" is to suggest that racism is not an important object of investigation, that literature is to be uncritically venerated, and that the authority of the literature scholar or teacher emanates from the superficial truth of the literary text.[6]

If we are willing to entertain the arguments of Achebe and Singh we may want to examine *Heart of Darkness* with our students in order to explore colonialist and racist ways of knowing and to pursue possibilities for overcoming them. Toward this end we may need more than the text itself. Other depictions of Africans, both contemporaneous with Conrad and from our own time, would be relevant. A study of the novella from a critical postcolonial perspective ought to draw connections between literature and broader discourse. We may want to ask about why *Heart of Darkness* in particular has such a revered place, and what it signifies, that to accuse it of racism should bring a covey of Conradophiles down on your head.

"HE HAD FILED TEETH TOO": THE POPULARITY OF *TARZAN*

The questions are not elementary, and the teacher who hopes to have her or his students investigate colonialist discourse in the work by a once-through reading of Conrad confronts an uphill battle. *Heart of Darkness* is not an easy book for college students to read, and situating it is notoriously difficult to do. I found teaching *Tarzan* alongside *Heart of Darkness* an effective way for students to investigate Achebe's charges, and gain a more complicated understanding of *Heart of Darkness*. Rather than impose a "politically correct" view, comparing the texts allowed the students to make an analysis and draw their own conclusions.

For a start, there are remarkable similarities between *Heart of Darkness* (1899) and its less respected—but far more popular—American cousin.[7] Both texts chart the journey of aristocratic European men to the "savage" jungles of Africa. Sent by the English colonial office, John Clayton, Lord Greystoke, has a mission similar to Marlow's. He is to

> make a peculiarly delicate investigation of conditions in a British West Coast African Colony from whose simple native inhabitants another European power was known to be recruiting soldiers for its native army, which it used solely for the forcible collection of rubber and ivory from the savage tribes along the Congo and the Aruwimi. (2)

The main characters of both books are cast as the cultural and racial embodiment of the best of Western civilization. If "all Europe went into the making of Kurtz," Greystoke is

> the type of Englishman that one likes best to associate with the noblest monuments of historic achievement upon a thousand victorious battlefields—a strong, virile man—mentally, morally, and physically. (2)

In both the novel and the novella the hero returns to the West, Marlow to Brussels and Tarzan, son of Greystoke and wife Alice, to Wisconsin. *Heart of Darkness* ends with Marlow withholding the dark knowledge of Kurtz's last words from his intended. *Tarzan* ends with Tarzan withholding the secret of his parentage from Jane. The similarities between the two works goes beyond a coincidence of setting, plot, character, and event. Thematically, politically, and philosophically, there is much in common. In both, the jungle is portrayed as a disturbing and threatening force and the Africans as primitive, racially inferior types lower down the scale of social evolution.[8] Marlow's vision of the natives, his recognition of "remote kinship with this wild and passionate uproar" (38), his discovery of Kurtz's participation in "unspeakable rites," resonates with Burroughs' depiction of the "Dum-Dum" of the apes:

> Many travelers have seen the drums of the great apes, and some have heard the sounds of their beating and the noise of the wild, weird revelry of these first lords of the jungle, but Tarzan, Lord

> Greystoke, is, doubtless, the only human being who ever joined in the fierce, mad, intoxicating revel of the Dum-Dum. From this primitive function has arisen, unquestionably, all the forms and ceremonials of modern church and state, for through all the countless ages, back beyond the uttermost ramparts of a dawning humanity our fierce, hairy forebears danced out the rites of the Dum-Dum to the sound of their earthen drums, beneath the bright light of a tropical moon in the depth of a mighty jungle which stands unchanged today as it stood on that long forgotten night in the dim, unthinkable vistas of the long dead past when our first shaggy ancestor swung from a swaying bough and dropped lightly upon the soft turf of the first meeting place. (52)

Or a scene that Tarzan observes later among the Africans:

> The circle of warriors about the cringing captive drew closer and closer to their prey as they danced in wild and savage abandon to the maddening music of the drums....The women and children shrieked their delight. The warriors licked their hideous lips in anticipation of the feast to come. (81)

Lacking Conrad's highly "literary" language, Burroughs' colonialist and racist images of Africans are more immediately on the surface. In both, the "savagery" and "primitiveness" of the Africans is disturbing precisely because their difference is appropriated, in a conventional orientalist gesture, to an earlier stage of Western development.

In *Tarzan* there may be greater admiration for the athleticism of the hero, but the response to the encounter with African "savagery" is very similar to that of *Heart of Darkness*. In the confrontation with the "dark continent," only "an honest concern for the right way of going to work" (Conrad 39) can provide salvation. Abandoned by a mutinous crew, Lord Greystoke and his pregnant wife Alice determine to face the "primeval" African jungle teeming with "prowling beasts of prey":

> "Oh, John," she cried at last, "the horror of it. What are we to do? What are we to do?"
>
> "There is but one thing to do, Alice," and he spoke quietly as though they were sitting in their snug living room at home, "and that is work. Work must be our salvation. We must not give ourselves time to think, for in that direction lies madness." (16)

Despite their critique of colonial rapacity, in confrontation with "the horror" there is a willing blindness, a capitalist devotion to mechanical work that takes the place of any critical analysis. While *Heart of Darkness* and *Tarzan* oppose the brutalities of Belgian colonialism, both seem to accept and perhaps even admire the more "restrained" and "effective" British version. Marlow distinguishes the British from the Romans, describing the Romans in terms that would appear to apply to the Belgians: "What saves us is efficiency—the devotion to efficiency. But these chaps were no account really. They were no colonists, their administration was merely a squeeze, and nothing more" (10).[9] Burroughs describes King Leopold of Belgium as an "arch hypocrite" whose officers practice "still crueler barbarities" than even the Africans themselves (175). Yet neither text questions that Kurtz or Tarzan would, "alone" in the jungle, come to rule over "savage" Africa and Africans. As Europeans this much is merely to be expected.

The depiction of women in both texts is organized by the boundaries established by the colonial enterprise. For Conrad and Burroughs white women do not belong in Africa and must be protected by white men even from knowledge of it. Marlow lies to the Intended about Kurtz's last words. For Greystoke, "It was the thought of taking this fair young girl into the dangers and isolation of tropical Africa that appalled him" (2). While in *Tarzan* white women do visit the "dark continent," it is Jane's presence in Africa that rushes the story forward. An ape with a "great hairy body" and a "snarling hideous mouth" captures Jane and threatens to make her "the first of his new household" (153). Tarzan rescues her, safeguards her, and returns her to civilization. For Conrad there is an unbridgeable distance between the "fair," "pale," and "pure" Intended and the "savage and superb, wild eyed and magnificent" African mistress. Moreover, "They—the women I mean—are out of it—should be out of it. We must help them to stay in that beautiful world of their own lest ours gets worse" (49). Burroughs' main female character, though simple and stereotypical, is less culturally fixed. At least Jane, like the white men, has a "civilized" exterior and a "primitive" and "passionate" heart:

> The veil of centuries of civilization and culture was swept from the blurred vision of the Baltimore girl...it was a primeval woman who sprang forward with outstretched arms toward the primeval man who had fought for her and won her. (156)

Even though it is entirely physical, Jane's affection for Tarzan would not be possible, of course, if he were not of European ancestry. In both texts, keeping white women safe from Africa seems connected to an unstated but profound anxiety about miscegenation.

The texts do have different effects and invoke different audiences, but remain, in their difference, curiously connected. *Tarzan* is both a paean to class distinction and inequality and an expression of the unfettered freedom of its superhero. The middle- or working-class reader is given a utopian fantasy of strength, identity with nature, and liberation of the passions while all along being fed a strongly patriotic line. *Heart of Darkness* is more scandalous and more intellectual. The sophisticated irony and sensuous vision of Marlow reveals darkness and corruption not just in Africa but in the institutions of European colonialism. The "elite" readers of the "sophisticated" *Heart of Darkness*—who may have less reason to want to challenge social hierarchy seriously, I suppose—may find it easy to contain the subversion of the text precisely because of its irony and sensuousness. Conrad's literariness, his "impressionism," heightens the scandal of the content but can also override it, especially when *Heart of Darkness* is taught without a simultaneous investigation of colonial atrocity or the tradition of the colonial romance—a tradition of which it is both a part and a criticism.[10] As much as *Tarzan* can help to reveal a colonialistic bias in *Heart of Darkness*, it can also, by comparison, bring out Conrad's anti-imperialist message.

The students loved *Tarzan*, but it is not a simple matter to sort out the aesthetic appeal of the novel. For many *Tarzan* was "great literature" because they couldn't put it down; they were delighted by the fast-paced plot linked with the "exotic" and "adventurous" story. My students soon recognized the racism of *Tarzan*, but the enjoyment of reading the story didn't seem to be dissonant with racist depictions. In fact, there seemed to be pleasure at the site of both sexual domination and racial exoticism:

> Jane—her lithe, young form flattened against the trunk of a great tree, her hands tight pressed against her rising and falling bosom, and her eyes wide with mingled horror, fascination, fear, and admiration—watched the primordial ape battle with the primeval man for possession of a woman—for her. (155-56)

> Their yellow teeth were filed to sharp points, and their great protruding lips added still further to the low and bestial brutishness of their appearance. (64)

> He had filed teeth too, the poor devil, and the wool of his pate shaved into queer patterns, and three ornamental scars on each of his cheeks. He ought to have been clapping his hands and stamping his feet on the bank. (Conrad, 38)

Investigating the class's reactions to these passages revealed not only the offensive stereotyping in the texts but the way sexist, racist, and colonialist perspectives deeply pervade ways of reading and are bound into even the production of pleasure and desire. Discussing the class's reaction to passages such as these brought Achebe's reading of Conrad close to home: "Herein lies the meaning of *Heart of Darkness* and the fascination it holds over the Western mind: 'What thrilled you was just the thought of their humanity—like yours...Ugly'" (254).

With an obviously "popular" text like *Tarzan* students were automatically disposed to a socially, politically, and culturally critical stance. Even though this was an introductory course, my students seemed already to understand that while we are supposed to criticize "popular" fiction, in "great art" we "willingly suspend disbelief." *Tarzan* served not so much to level the aesthetic complexity of *Heart of Darkness* as to help students recognize different modes of reading and, simultaneously, to put those modes of reading in question. In understanding Conrad this may be especially important. Jameson argues that Conrad is relevant to the formulation of twentieth-century mass culture:

> In Conrad we can sense the emergence not merely of what will be contemporary modernism (itself now become a literary institution), but also, still tangibly juxtaposed with it, of what will variously be called popular culture or mass culture, the commercialized cultural discourse of what, in late capitalism, is often described as a media society. (*Political Unconscious*, 206)

It was easier to see that there are such things as reading "regimes" when we tried to read "against the grain," when we tried to consider *Heart of Darkness* sociologically and *Tarzan* as high literature.[11] I discovered that by applying a literary mode of reading to *Tarzan* students became aware of how a "literary approach" differs from others, its advantages and limitations, and this, it seems to me, is exactly what an "introductory" course ought to do.[12] Looking for the "literary" in Tarzan, my students noticed the chapter titles echoing the title of Conrad's "symbolic" work: "Out to Sea," "The Light of Knowledge," "The Call of the Primitive," "The Height of Civilization," and so on. These titles suggested various metaphorical and allegorical possibilities for reading the novel, many of them just the sort of thing that has been done for so long with *Heart of Darkness*. The application of this "literary" mode of reading to *Tarzan* pointed up that an immanent approach to literary texts skirts sociological, political, and ideological questions. What happens then when we take *Tarzan* seriously as literary text? Might it change how we view literary quality?[13]

Applying the "popular" mode of reading to "literary" works, and vice versa, tends to raise questions about the nature and purposes of the way we organize our teaching. *Tarzan* revealed a distance between the global sweep of the class title, "World Literature," and the more limited course description of the introductory series, English 107/109: "Literary and cultural foundations of the Western world; an analysis of selected masterpieces of literature read in chronological order from ancient to modern." Such gaps create "teachable moments." Rather than simply demarcating a field of study, this course description attempts to maintain borders between who is "Western" and who is not, between what is "ancient" and what is "modern," between which texts are "masterpieces" and which are not, and so on.[14] As students started the class reading *Tarzan*, they were from the beginning asking questions like: What is "world literature" anyway? Who defined it? Are some cultures or certain texts missing from "World Literature"?[15] At the "survey" level in particular the sweeping titles and syllabi of genre, geographical, and historical courses produce and reproduce both the canon and "Western civilization" as natural and self-contained. In this situation a postcolonial pedagogy is especially relevant.

Using *Tarzan* made it possible to render problematic words like "complex," and in so doing interrogate assumptions about "literariness." If the characters are in some ways "simple," the plot of *Tarzan* is not. The action is rapid and intricate. *Tarzan* is a hard book to put down (evidenced by the fact that it was followed by more than twenty highly profitable sequels). Comparing *Tarzan* and *Heart of Darkness* raises the question of why complexity of plot should have less "literary value" than complexity of symbolism. The notion of the literary value of plot challenges the Kantian aesthetic that underlies the justification of the exclusion of the popular. Can the "popular" Tarzan not only provide "enjoyment arising from mere sensation" but also give "the pleasure of reflection" Kant associates with fine art (173)? Can we really maintain the integrity of Kant's distinctions? Does a Kantian aesthetic play into the question of whose culture is "better" or "best"?

The students' sheer enjoyment of *Tarzan* and the difficulty many of them had reading the much shorter *Heart of Darkness* led some to wonder if "good" books were simply "hard to read" books. This is a risky train of thought to have your students pursue in front of you. It can link the authority of the canon to that of the teacher, and may elucidate for students John Guillory's observation that "in teaching the canon, we are not only investing a set of texts with authority; we are equally instituting the authority of the teaching profession" (351). It raises questions it might be easier—but less interesting—to avoid than to confront. Does analyzing a culture's texts have a subtle "promotional" effect? Is the process of teaching the literature class, regardless of the texts we choose, an inevitable establishing of inequality on the basis of an invidious "refinement" of taste? Is Pierre Bourdieu correct that cultural knowledge is just a way to maintain social distinctions?

"THIRD WORLD" LITERATURE: FINDING A "PLACE" FOR *THINGS FALL APART*

A solution to some of these problems might appear to be teaching "Third World" and especially African texts along with *Heart of Darkness*. Reading *Things Fall Apart* after Conrad and Burroughs in our class did indeed establish a sort of dialogue that added to our understanding of the novels we read earlier and opened into the issues involved in an "African" perspective and in "Third World" literature more generally.[16] Abdul JanMohamed describes the importance of the "dialogue" between "First" and "Third World" texts:

> This dialogue merits our attention for two reasons: first in spite of the often studied attempts by ethnocentric canonizers in English and other (Western) language and literature departments to ignore Third World culture and art, they will not go away; and second as this analysis of colonialist literature (a literature, we must remember that is supposed to mediate between different cultures) demonstrates, the domain of literary and cultural syncretism belongs not to colonialist and neocolonialist writers, but increasingly to Third World artists. (104)

As I noted at the beginning, *Heart of Darkness* is one of the best-known stories of the colonial encounter in English and has been drawn on by postcolonial writers. It is certainly part of the dialogue JanMohamed describes and one of the key texts for a postcolonial pedagogy. There are, however, risks involved in organizing a reading of postcolonial literature framed by *Heart of Darkness*, or using *Heart of Darkness* or *Tarzan* as the jumping off point for reading *Things Fall Apart* or any other postcolonial text. Rather than directly discussing the experience of teaching *Things Fall Apart* or the other "Third World" literature on my syllabus, it is this problem of the reception and contextualization of "Third World" literature that came up in my class and that I would like to address.

The significance of *Things Fall Apart* for a Western understanding of Africa is widely recognized. Taught in conjunction with texts of the colonial encounter, the depiction of the pre-contact Ibos in Achebe's novel reveals a complexity and richness in African tribal society completely missed in the writing of Burroughs or Conrad. Portraying Africans as reasoning individuals holding varying positions toward colonial domination, the novel explodes the racist conception of the "primitive savage." Furthermore, as a novel that unsettles distinctions between literature, ethnography, and history, *Things Fall Apart* challenges Western definitions of the "literary." The famous last line of the novel ironically turns Western imperialist discourse against itself. Using a phrase that could have been borrowed from Kurtz's report to the International Society for the Suppression of Savage Customs in *Heart of Darkness*, the colonial administrator in *Things Fall Apart* trivializes the events of the story, encapsulating them as "the pacification of the primitive tribes of the Lower Niger." Twenty years before Said's *Orientalism*, Achebe connects the language of "the student of primitive customs" to the administrator of colonial law.

Despite the power of *Things Fall Apart*, it is hard to know how to teach the novel so as to unsettle established ways of reading rather than once again reinforcing them. Achebe's novel is often used as a companion to Sophocles' *Oedipus Rex*. Yet, in exploring the tragic hero's hubris and the universality of fate, the African text may be valorized precisely because it expresses themes we associate with Western high art. With "literary artistry" as the exclusive focus of attention, *Things Fall Apart*'s evocation of a people in crisis and its critique of colonialist discourse may be missed. Conversely, as "Third World literature" the novel may be taught solely for its "politics," and interpreted by students simply as a reaction to Western imperialism.

The question of how to read *Things Fall Apart* was something I wanted the class to address. I decided to approach the issue by examining with the students the covers of the various used editions on our class shelf in the book store. The first Fawcett cover (1969) is a collage of images of violence, tribal costumes, and pith-helmeted white men. It recalls the association of the text with the Nigerian independence struggle.[17] The second cover is more symbolic: a half-dressed black man with a knife confronts a flaming cross. The cover of the latest edition (1988) appears to invoke a tradition of "primitive" folk art: a brightly colored rooster is shown hanging upside down in front of a black background. It is clear that these covers represent at least one trajectory of "Third World" literature in the West: a recuperation of the politically unsettling by the symbolic and aesthetic. Although we should take care not to collapse the relationship of "First" and "Third World" into one of class, Pierre Bourdieu's description of the differential responses by class to photographs of an old woman's hands comments significantly upon the progression of the covers:

> Everything takes place as if the emphasis on form could only be achieved by means of neutralization of any kind of affective or ethical interest in the object of representation which accompanies (without any necessary cause-effect relation) mastery of the means of grasping the distinctive properties which this particular form takes on in its relations with other forms (i.e., through reference to the universe of works of art and its history). (44)

We had our discussion of the different covers before we read the novel, and this allowed my introductory students to further investigate the way they were supposed to see African literature and how they were being "cued" to bring particular modes of reading into operation.

As any frame of reading would tend to bring out certain features of the text, my framing of the novel with *Tarzan* and *Heart of Darkness* tended to focus attention on *Things Fall Apart* as speaking back to European discourse. It could also have been framed in an "African" context, which we would have had to think of, as I hope we do a European one, as hybrid and multilayered, involving, in the African case, African oral traditions, African contact narrative, and anglophone and francophone literary practices and invention. As an investigation of "postcoloniality," a consideration of *Things Fall Apart* ought not rest with a "speaking back." The postcolonial should not be merely an inversion of the terms of the colonial, but should include also a self-consciousness about the crossing over, the complexity and the entanglement of identity. Thus, effective as *Things Fall Apart* is for the exploration of colonialist discourse, it is not somehow "representative" of "the" African viewpoint, nor in itself an expression of the range of postcolonial understanding.[18]

In his response to Fredric Jameson's well-known contention that "Third World" literature is "national allegory," Aijaz Ahmad points out the danger of letting the few texts that have come to stand for "Third World" literature in the West be overvalorized. In a recent article Anthony Appiah goes further. He argues that the African novel is actually a hybridized construction, produced and circulated in an international market of cultural commodities dominated by the West. Thus the particular position of the African intellectual writer must be considered before taking the African novel as able to "speak for" an African population. Appiah points out that the first generation of African novels, which includes *Things Fall Apart*, were part of a modernist and realist effort to legitimate nationalism as an anticolonial project. (Thus we might also ask about the existence of the "missing piece" in *Things Fall Apart*. Which "Nigerian" stories are not told here? and so forth.) He argues further that the second stage of African writing, the current one, represents a critique of the first stage, and "identifies the realist novel as part of the tactic of nationalist legitimation." This is a critical step, because in the present era, the African nation-state founded in anti-colonial struggle is often despotic, corrupt, and not at all postcolonial despite a change in the composition of the ruling class.

Rather than taking African writing as Other, Appiah believes, it is important to investigate the interrelationship of cultures:

> If there is a lesson in the broad shape of this circulation of cultures, it is surely that we are all already contaminated by each other, that there is no longer a fully autochthonous *echt*-African culture awaiting salvage by our artists (just as there is, of course, no American culture without African roots). And there is a clear sense in some postcolonial writing that the postulation of unitary Africa over against a monolithic West—the binarism of Self and Other—is the last of the shibboleths of the modernizers that we must learn to live without. (354)

In this "circulating" and "contaminated" view of culture any investigation of modern identity cannot avoid the colonial encounter, and can no longer interpret this encounter as effecting only the non-West. Nor does Modernism extend uniformly or exclusively over the "First World." The valorization of *Heart of Darkness*—a text that is inescapably about colonial contact—as a formative text of Western Modernism is simply one indication of cultural entanglement.[19] Moreover, the colonial encounter should not be seen by our students or by us as something in the distant past.

In a 1986 article on intellectuals in the postcolonial world Edward Said points out:

> The colonial encounter continues, as much in the drawing of lines and the defending of barriers, as in the enormously complex and interesting interchange between former colonial partners. ("Intellectuals," 50)

In this light, our own self-consciousness about the literary canon may be related to increased contact with "other" cultures both "internally" and via an expanding and increasingly pervasive European and North American colonialism and neocolonialism. Yet the drawing of borders Said refers to is everywhere around us, even when, as with the canon, we might think they are breaking down. It is in this space of interchange, of interpenetrated identity, that a postcolonial pedagogy takes its place.

It is not surprising that in the response to Achebe's comments on *Heart of Darkness* several scholars suggest reading *Things Fall Apart* (see Robertson, 110–12; Hawkins, 163; Watts, 205–7). What is interesting is that this suggestion is made persistently by those critics who find it most difficult to entertain Achebe's view of Conrad as racist. They would seem to approve the inclusion of "great" literature from "different traditions" in our scholarship and teaching, but in a way that simultaneously ratifies the canon and underscores established notions of literary quality. In other words, as Cornel West warns, *Things Fall Apart*, or any other postcolonial or minority text, may be easily included in a superficial "multiculturalism" that actually legitimates a monocultural perspective. A meaningful postcolonial pedagogy needs to come with a critical agenda, one that is not satisfied by a simplistic or good will incorporation of difference. We need to recognize cultural diversity and difference, yes, but more than that we need to understand that such differences—and even the way we understand such differences—are political, tied to opposing interests and ongoing exploitative relationships.[20] What must be recognized is the relational nature of "Third World" writing and the putting into question of "Western" texts and established ways of reading. The problem of pluralism is that it offers acceptance of the presumedly "Other," on the terms of the "Self" and in a way that legitimates the "Self" as contained and independent. The alternative is a serious analysis of institutions and an openness to changing them. S. P. Mohanty points to the simultaneous reconstitution of cultural frames that must take place in any cultural encounter that seeks authentic knowledge: "Two systems of understanding encounter each other to the very extent that both are contextualized as forms of life; this encounter leaves open the possibility of a fundamental change in both" (16). Thus a meaningful postcolonial analysis must put the study of canon together with that of colonial encounter. The integration of "postcolonial," "emergent," "minority," and "Third World" literature into the curriculum of English, and other, literature departments should be neither easy nor comfortable. A truly postcolonial way of teaching requires that literature courses, to some degree at least, investigate themselves.

NOTES

1. Peter Nazareth borrows Gates's term "signifying" to describe the relationship between Conrad and a dozen "Third World" novels, including *Season of Migration to the North, A Grain of Wheat, Palace of the Peacock, A Bend in the River, Scorpion Orchid, Flight to Canada,* and his own *The General Is Up.*

2. Achebe's piece was given as a lecture at the University of Massachusetts and was first published as the "Chancellor's Lecture at the University of Massachusetts," Amherst, 18 February 1975. It was later reprinted in *Massachusetts Review* 18:4 (Winter 1977), 782–94. It is also found in Chinua Achebe, *Hopes and Impediments* (New York: Doubleday, 1989) and in amended version in the 1988 Norton Critical Edition of *Heart of Darkness.* See also Chinua Achebe, "Viewpoint," *Times Literary Supplement,* 1 February 1980, p. 113. (Quotations here are from the Norton version for Achebe, Singh, Harris, and Sarvan.) Responses include: Hawkins, Watt, Watts, Harris, Sarvan, Nazareth (especially "Out"), Hamner, Robertson, Kuesgen, Blake, Brantlinger (Achebe is mentioned in both, but is the focus of "*Heart*"), Humphries, and London. Although not strictly responses, Mahood, Singh, Parry, and JanMohamed are also immediately relevant.

3. Hamner's bibliography, however, seems to do more to further Achebe's point that racism is not an issue in Conrad scholarship. Of the 177 titles listed, not counting the works that respond to Achebe, only thirteen hint that they might address Conrad's attitude toward native peoples, and three or four would appear to take a critical view.

4. Watt's defense of Conrad is confusing. He contradicts the thrust of his earlier argument about cannibalism by claiming that "Both Marlow and Conrad show a real readiness to see that their [the African] way of life has real meaning and value" (8). He clarifies with, "Marlow and Conrad, then, are not fairly to be considered as 'racists,' although they are not in theory wholly opposed to the doctrine" (8).

5. A version of this argument is made in an unpublished Ph.D. dissertation by Doreatha Drummond. She argues that Conrad's attitudes "matured" between the time he wrote *The Nigger of the Narcissus* (1896) and *The Shadow Line* (1917). She sees *Heart of Darkness* as a "transitional" stage.

6. Robert Scholes has pointed out that this is precisely the problem of establishing a canon:

> The trouble with establishing a canon—the great insuperable problem—is that it removes the chosen texts from history and from human actualities, placing them forever behind a veil of pieties. This soulful rhetoric is guaranteed to drain the life out of the texts studied, because it permits only worship and forbids all criticism.

7. According to the fly leaf of the 1979 edition, *Tarzan* has been translated into "32 known languages, including Braille" and has been "known and loved by literally a thousand million or more."

8. It is not necessary to prove that Burroughs read Conrad. Ruppel states, "In nearly all exotic literature of this period, the jungle is a malignant, terrifying antagonist of the Europeans, and the natives are its children and accomplices" (11). Brantlinger also claims that *Heart of Darkness* borrows from the popular and compromises its critique of colonialism: "In simplifying his memories and sources, Conrad arrived at the dichotomous 'manichean' pattern of the imperialist adventure romance, a pattern radically at odds with any realist, exposé intention" ("Heart," 372).

9. Brantlinger makes the argument that "Marlow distinguishes between British imperialism and that of the other European powers: the red parts of the map are good to see, he says, 'because one knows that some real work is done in there.' *Heart of Darkness* is specifically about what Conrad saw in King Leopold's African empire in 1890; the extent to which his critique can be generalized to imperialism beyond the Congo is unclear" ("Heart," 364).

10. An important analysis of the way Conrad attacks colonialism by undermining the assumptions and methods of the colonial romance is found in the unpublished Ph.D. dissertation of David Neale Bunn. Bunn compares *Heart of Darkness* to Rider Haggard's *King Solomon's Mines* and makes a case that the "impressionism" of the novel is a self-conscious parody of the traditional colonial romance: "By delaying Marlow's voyage into the interior, and by lengthening the period of his inactivity, Conrad ends up placing considerable emphasis on description and cognition. This deflection of narration into description is a common tactic in the novel, and a means by which Conrad weans his audience away from expectations inculcated by the African romance" (275).

11. To do so would be to engage precisely in what Tony Bennett considers the nature and function of "criticism": "Whereas theory's concern is to analyze the determinations which are operative in the processes whereby meanings are produced in relation to textual phenomena, criticism's concern is to intervene within such processes, to make texts mean differently by modifying the determinations which bear in upon them—it should seek to detach texts from socially dominant reading formations and to install them in new ones" (71).

12. Of course, there are many "clues" that *Tarzan* is not "great literature" that we could and did discuss in class: the "sensational" cover with its picture of an ape monster grasping by the hair a desperate blond woman in torn clothes while a muscular Tarzan charges with a glinting knife; the fact the book is not found in the "literature" section of the book store but in the "science fiction and fantasy" section; and, our common knowledge of the story from films and comic strips.

13. There are two critical studies of Burroughs by a classics scholar, Erling Holtsmark, where an extensive and earnest examination of the relation between *Tarzan* and Greek and Roman language, literature, and thought is attempted. For me Holtzmark's project does less to "elevate" *Tarzan* than to denigrate the Greek and Roman myths he cites.

14. This description, like most routine catalog descriptions, is remarkably problematic. The phrase "chronological order from Ancient to Modern" establishes notions of periodization and a theory of development, and the metaphor "literary and cultural foundations" suggests a sort of humanist base/superstructure theory of history. The course description collapses "cultural" into "literary" and proclaims literary value. One might ask, what colonial history and/or what struggles for power within the university itself led to "World Literature" being taught in the English department?

Simply examining the latest Norton Critical Edition of *Heart of Darkness* is an interesting way for students to think about what goes into making a canon. There is no question but that *Heart of Darkness* is a "masterpiece": after all, the novella takes up only 69 of the 420 pages of the volume, not counting the 17 pages of introduction to the third critical edition!

15. Gates puts the case for teaching the history of the canon this way: "I agree with those conservatives who have raised the alarm about our students' ignorance of history. But part of the history we need to teach has to be the history of the very idea of the 'canon,' which involves the history both of literary pedagogy and of the very institution of the school. One function of literary history is then to conceal all connections between institutionalized interests and the literature we remember. Pay no attention to the men behind the curtain, booms the Great Oz of literary history" ("Whose," 45).

16. Susan Blake suggests a dialogic approach that pairs *Heart of Darkness* with Ousmane Sembene's *God's Bits of Wood.* Mahood puts together Achebe's *Arrow of God* with *Heart of Darkness.* In a recent "Point of View" piece in *The Chronicle of Higher Education,* Gerald Graff uses Achebe's critique of Conrad as an example of the way in which literary theory can be useful for modifying pedagogical practice.

17. Barbara Harlow points out that the novel was written two years before independence. Her comments on *Things Fall Apart* in the preface to *Resistance Literature* suggest the political sophistication of Achebe's use of African mythology.

18. These issues came up particularly sharply in class discussion during our reading of Menchú's testimonial. For an analysis of the testimonial form and its implications for literary study see Beverley. For a discussion of teaching testimonial see my article, "Auto/Biography."

19. An important matter for those of us in literary institutions is Gauri Viswanathan's argument that English literature as a subject of study was invented first as an effort to control colonial subjects in India, and only later brought to England to achieve the same sort of end with the British working class.

20. Philip Wexler comments on the presentation of difference in school curriculums: "The curriculum which teaches difference as cultural pluralism, reads difference as an attitudinal, cultural misunderstanding. The source of difference in opposing interests is ignored. The silent problem, exploitation, can then be resolved through understanding, good will and common values" (288).

WORKS CITED

Achebe, Chinua. "An Image of Africa: Racism in Conrad's *Heart of Darkness.*" Conrad, 251–62.

———. *Things Fall Apart.* New York: Fawcett, 1969.

Ahmad, Aijaz. "Jameson's Rhetoric of Otherness and the 'National Allegory.'" *Social Text* 17 (Fall 1987): 3–25.

Aidoo, Christina Ama Ata. *Our Sister Killjoy: Or, Reflections from a Black-Eyed Squint.* London: Longman, 1977.

Appiah, Kwame Anthony. "Is the Post- in Postmodernism the Post- in Postcolonial?" *Critical Inquiry* 17 (1991): 336–57.

Bennett, Tony. "Texts in History: the Determinations of Readings and Their Texts." *Poststructuralism and the Question of History.* Ed. Derek Attridge, Geoff Bennington, and Robert Young. New York: Cambridge University Press, 1989.

Beverley, John. "The Margin at the Center: On *Testimonio* (Testimonial Narrative)." *Modern Fiction Studies* 35.1 (Spring 1989): 11–28.

Blake, Susan L. "Racism and the Classics: Teaching *Heart of Darkness.*" *College Language Association Journal* 25.4 (1982): 396–404.

Bourdieu, Pierre. *Distinction: A Social Critique of the Judgment of Taste.* Trans. Richard Nice. Cambridge, MA: Harvard University Press, 1984.

Bunn, David Neale. "Embodying Africa: Description, Ideology, Imperialism, and the Colonial Romance." Ph.D. diss., Northwestern University, 1987.

Burroughs, Edgar Rice. *Tarzan of the Apes.* New York: Ballantine, 1976 [1912].

Brantlinger, Patrick. "*Heart of Darkness*: Anti-Imperialism, Racism, or Impressionism?" *Criticism: A Quarterly for Literature and the Arts* 27.4 (1985): 363–85.

———. "Victorians and Africans: The Genealogy of the Myth of the Dark Continent." Gates, "*Race*," 185–222.

Carey-Webb, Allen. "Auto/Biography of the Oppressed: The Power of Testimonial." *English Journal* 80.4 (April 1991): 44–48.

Conrad, Joseph. *Heart of Darkness.* Ed. Robert Kimbrough. New York: Norton, 1988.

Drummond, Doreatha. "Joseph Conrad's Confrontation with Racism." Ph.D. diss., University of Illinois at Urbana-Champaign, 1986.

Fernando, Lloyd. *Scorpion Orchid.* Singapore: Heinemann, 1976.

Gates, Henry Louis Jr., ed. *"Race," Writing, and Difference.* Chicago: University of Chicago Press, 1985.

———. "Talkin' That Talk." "*Race*," 402–9.

———. "Whose Canon Is It, Anyway?" *New York Times Book Review*, 26 February 1989: 1, 44–45.

Guillory, John. "The Ideology of Canon-Formation: T. S. Eliot and Cleanth Brooks." *Canons.* Ed. Robert Van Hallberg. Chicago: University Chicago Press, 1983. 337–62.

Graff, Gerald. "What Has Literary Theory Wrought?" *Chronicle of Higher Education* 12 (February 1992): A48.

Haggard, Sir Henry Rider. *She, King Solomon's Mines, Allan Quatermain.* New York: Dover, 1979.

Hamner, Robert D. "Joseph Conrad and the Colonial World: A Selected Bibliography." *Conradiana* 14.3 (1982): 217–29.

Harlow, Barbara. *Resistance Literature.* New York: Methuen, 1987.

Harris, Wilson. "The Frontier on Which *Heart of Darkness* Stands." Conrad, 262–67. Also in *Research in African Literatures* 12 (1981): 86–92.

Hawkins, Hunt. "The Issue of Racism in *Heart of Darkness.*" *Conradiana* 14.3 (1982): 163–71.

Holtsmark, Erling B. *Edgar Rice Burroughs.* Boston: Twayne, 1986.

———. Tarzan *and Tradition: Classical Myth in Popular Literature.* Westport, CT: Greenwood Press, 1981.

Humphries, Reynold. "The Discourse of Colonialism: Its Meaning and Relevance for Conrad's Fiction." *Conradiana* 21.2 (1989): 107–33.

Jameson, Fredric. "Modernism and Imperialism." *Nationalism, Colonialism and Literature.* Minneapolis: University of Minnesota Press, 1990. 43–67.

———. *The Political Unconscious: Narrative as a Socially Symbolic Act.* Ithaca: Cornell University Press, 1981.

———. "Third-World Literature in the Era of Multinational Capitalism." *Social Text* 15 (1986): 65–88.

JanMohamed, Abdul. "The Economy of Manichean Allegory: The Function of Racial Difference in Colonialist Literature." Gates, "*Race,*" 78–106.

Kane, Cheikh Hamidou. *Ambiguous Adventure.* Trans. Katherine Woods. London: Heinemann, 1962.

Kant, Immanuel. "On Fine Art." *Critique of Judgment.* Trans. Werner Pluhar. Indianapolis: Hackett, 1987, 172–73.

Kuesgen, Reinhardt. "Conrad and Achebe: Aspects of the Novel." *World Literature Written in English* 24.1 (Summer 1984): 27–33.

Laye, Camara. *The Dark Child.* Trans. James Kirkup and Ernest Jones. New York: Farrar, Strauss and Giroux, 1971.

London, Bette. "Reading Race and Gender in Conrad's Dark Continent." *Criticism* 31.3 (Summer 1989): 235–52.

Mahood, Molly. *The Colonial Encounter.* London: Rex Collings, 1977.

Marshall, Paule. *Praisesong for the Widow.* New York: Obelisk, 1984.

Menchú, Rigoberta, and Elisabeth Burgos-Debray. *I, Rigoberta Menchú.* Trans. Ann Wright. London: Verso, 1983.

Mohanty, S. P. "Us and Them: On the Philosophical Bases of Political Criticism." *Yale Journal of Criticism* 2.2 (1989): 1–31.

Naipaul, V. S. *A Bend in the River.* New York: Vintage, 1980.

Nazareth, Peter. "Conrad's Descendents." *Conradiana* 22.2 (1990): 101–10.

———. *The General Is Up.* Calcutta: P. Lal, 1984.

———. "Out of Darkness: Conrad and Other Third World Writers." *Conradiana* 14.3 (1982): 173–88.

Ngũgĩ wa Thiong'o. *A Grain of Wheat.* London: Heinemann, 1967.

Parry, Benita. *Conrad and Imperialism: Ideological Boundaries and Visionary Frontiers.* London: Macmillan, 1983.

Reed, Ishmael. *Flight to Canada.* New York: Random House, 1976.

Robertson, P. J. M. "*Things Fall Apart* and *Heart of Darkness*: A Creative Dialogue." *International Fiction Review* 7.2 (Summer 1980): 106–11.

Ruppel, Richard. "Heart of Darkness and the Popular Exotic Stories of the 1890s." *Conradiana* 21.1 (1989): 3–14.

Said, Edward. "Intellectuals in the Post-Colonial World." *Salmagundi* 70/71 (Spring/Summer 1986): 44–64.

———. *Orientalism.* New York: Vintage, 1979.

Salih, Tayeb. *Season of Migration to the North.* Trans. Denys Johnson-Davies. New York: M. Kesend, 1989.

Sarvan, C. P. "Racism and the *Heart of Darkness.*" Conrad, 280–85. Also in *The International Fiction Review* 7 (1980): 6–10.

Scholes, Robert. "Aiming a Canon at the Curriculum." *Salmagundi* 72 (Fall 1986): 101–17.

Singh, Frances B. "The Colonialist Bias of *Heart of Darkness.*" Conrad, 268–80. Also in *Conradiana* 10 (1978): 41–54.

Viswanathan, Gauri. *Masks of Conquest: Literary Study and British Rule in India.* New York: Columbia University Press, 1989.

Watt, Ian. "Conrad's *Heart of Darkness* and the Critics." *North Dakota Quarterly* 57.3 (Summer 1989): 5–15.

Watts, Cedric. *Yearbook of English Studies* 13 (1983): 196-209.

West, Cornel. "Minority Discourse and the Pitfalls of Canon Formation." *The Yale Journal of Criticism* (1987): 193-201.

Wexler, Philip. "Structure, Text, and Subject: A Critical Sociology of School Knowledge." *Cultural and Economic Reproduction in Education: Essays on Class, Ideology, and the State.* Ed. Michael Apple. Boston: Routledge, 1982, 275–303.

14

MARA L. DUKATS

The Hybrid Terrain of Literary Imagination: Maryse Condé's Black Witch of Salem, Nathaniel Hawthorne's Hester Prynne, and Aimé Césaire's Heroic Poetic Voice

> Literature is not only fragmented, it is henceforth shared. In it lie histories and the voice of peoples.
>
> —Édouard Glissant

"Women have no mouth," (Schipper, 20) claims a Cameroon proverb. The corollary to such "common knowledge" is, of course, that women, by their very nature, cannot speak. Against this image of woman's essential silence, feminist writing has historicized and contextualized woman's absence and her enforced voicelessness. Charting the arduous journey from silence into speech, feminist writing has literally written women into existence and given a forum to words that have gone unheard.

"The concept of voicelessness necessarily informs any discussion of Caribbean women and literature," argue Carole Boyce Davies and Elaine Savory Fido (1). Voicelessness, as these authors claim, means not only the "historical absence of the woman writer's text," but also the "inability to express" and the "silence" of "articulation that goes unheard" (1). This same voicelessness surrounds the absent and silenced text of Tituba Indian, a Barbadian slave woman whom Marye Condé "resurrects" in the novel *I, Tituba, Black Witch of Salem.*[1]

The novel reconstructs the life of Tituba, sold in Barbados to the Reverend Samuel Parris, and brought to the American colonies to serve his family. Alleged to have bewitched the minister's daughter and his niece, causing the children severe fits of hysteria, and initiating the accusations, interrogations, and executions of the Salem witches, Tituba has become inseparably linked with the beginning of this notoriously odious chapter of American history.

Presented as Tituba's first person narrative that Condé, as "author," has transcribed, *I, Tituba* responds to the historical absence of Tituba's own narration of her life. As narrator in Condé's novel, Tituba emphasizes the fact that there is no written record of her existence: "I can look for my story among those of the witches of Salem, but it isn't there" (149). Indeed, Tituba experiences this deliberate omission and silencing as "a violent feeling of pain and terror" (110).

Halfway into the narrative, Condé has inserted extracts from Tituba's official deposition—the one safely deposited for posterity in the Essex County Archives in Salem, Massachusetts. Ironically, this recontextualization of Tituba's interrogation and of the words that she is recorded as having spoken, serves to underscore her voicelessness—her lack of access to a voice at the very moment when she is called upon to speak.

Tituba's confession, inserted into the narrative in the form of four pages of transcribed excerpts from the documents of her deposition, functions as the official text against which Condé's Tituba speaks and defines herself anew. *I, Tituba* is a retelling of history with Tituba as the first-person narrator and Condé as the scribe. This collaborative response to the "racism of the historians" (183) is thus a literal writing-into-being of an historically effaced woman.

Although historical reality is the basis for *I, Tituba*, Condé's narrative claims neither to be "history" nor constitute "historical truth." As Condé has said:

> A historian is somebody who studies the facts, the historical facts—somebody who is tied to reality, somebody who is tied to what actually happens. I am just a dreamer—my dreams rest upon a historical basis. Being a black person, having a certain past, having a certain history behind me, I want to explore that realm and of course I do it with my imagination and with my intuition. But I am not involved in any kind of scholarly research. ("An Interview," 201)

Involved in an imaginative exploration of the past, Condé counters the designation of *I, Tituba* as historical novel:

> For me Tituba is not a historical novel. Tituba is just the opposite of a historical novel. I was not interested at all in what her real life could have been. I had few precise documents: her deposition testimony. It forms the only historical part of the novel, and I was not interested in getting anything more than that. I really invented Tituba. ("An Interview," 200–201)

Filling in the blank spaces of lost history is thus not the primary focus of Condé's novel. Rather, it marks out a space for Caribbean woman's presence on the literary landscape by exposing her historical marginalization. Condé's explicit affirmation of the collaborative nature of *I, Tituba* is not so much a technique of postmodernist fiction or magical realism, as it is the assertion of the extent and duration of confinement and the surreal efforts necessary to move out of voicelessness. By incorporating and re-visiting the canonized texts of Aimé Césaire and Nathaniel Hawthorne, Condé reclaims Tituba's presence as a shaping force, as a background against which both the Caribbean hero and the American heroine took form.

Giving voice to a silenced Tituba, Condé recontextualizes her trial and the text of her deposition. Resituating this official text to the core of her novel, Condé allows Tituba a new hearing. Although these literary techniques clearly give Tituba a new visibility and force us to rethink the ways in which the past has been discursively constructed, the focus of my discussion is the way in which Condé's text rethinks literature itself.

Arguing for the hybridity of cultural processes, traditions, and formations, several contemporary theorists have advanced a view of culture as "a multivalent weave of dominant, residual, and emergent strands that are often in tension with one another" (Fraser, 18).[2] This view of culture necessarily implies a reconceptualization of agency and a rethinking of the ways in which the "dominant" is itself defined and conditioned by the residual and emergent. In this view "dominant" culture is no longer a closed and exclusive totality, but rather, a complex web of both hegemonic and counter-hegemonic forces. What I would like to suggest in the following discussion is that dominant culture shares with literary imagination its hybridity.

Condé's *mélange* of historical and literary texts makes of Tituba a symbolic presence that enables a revision of literary imagination. By literary imagination I mean the set of perceptual constructs within which a writer thinks, works, and creates at any given time. As the following discussion argues, literary imagination is a hybrid terrain, meaning not only that it is made up of a weave of diverse strands, but, more importantly, that within this hybrid terrain there are elements that are invisible, overshadowed, and suppressed. Moreover, these effaced elements often provide the enabling conditions for "dominant" cultural constructs, and thereby manifest themselves as shaping forces, albeit unacknowledged ones. Condé's *I, Tituba* brilliantly illustrates ways in which literary texts reclaim unacknowledged and effaced agency, thus reconceptualizing the processes of cultural formations and revealing the interrelational terrain, or hybridity, of literary imagination.

Similar to the concept of hybridity is that of *métissage*, defined by Françoise Lionnet as a concept that "allow[s] us to think *otherwise*," and "bypass the ancient symmetries and dichotomies that have governed the ground and the very condition of possibility of thought...in...Western philosophy" (*Autobiographical*, 6). In her theoretical work, Lionnet has used the concept of *métissage* to suggest a radical revision of the ways in which identity, culture, and counter-hegemonic practices have been conceptualized.

In "'*Logiques métisses*': Cultural Appropriation and Postcolonial Representations" (see chapter 5 above), for example, Lionnet sets forth the argument that the "ground upon which contemporary global culture can begin to be understood" is the ground made up of the "processes of adaptation, appropriation, and contestation that govern the construction of identity in colonial and postcolonial contexts" (111). Lionnet's quarrel with the way that the relationship between the colonized culture and the hegemonic system has generally been conceptualized is that it has emphasized only the subjugation, assimilation, and passivity of the colonized and has failed to assess the "transformative" processes and the "appropriative techniques" with which the colonized culture has actively "delegitimated" cultural hegemony and refuted the "paradigm of exoticism and/or victimization" (121–26). The "patterns of influence" between the colonized culture and the hegemonic system are "never unidirectional," but rather, "mutual and reciprocal" (115), argues Lionnet, quoting Toni Morrison: "Afro-American culture exists and though it is clear (and becoming clearer) how it has responded to Western culture, the instances where and means by which it has shaped Western culture are poorly recognized or understood" (114).

In *Playing in the Dark*, Toni Morrison takes up this very argument, claiming that black slavery created "a playground for the imagination" (38) of early American writers. Contrary to the conventionally accepted "knowledge" that "traditional, canonical American literature is free of, uninformed, and unshaped by the four-hundred-year-old presence of, first, Africans and then African-Americans in the U.S." (5), argues Morrison, the Africanist presence has provided the "arena for the elaboration of the quintessential American identity" (44) and furnished the major themes of American literature. This corresponds to what Lionnet, in the above-mentioned article, calls the "global mongrelization or *métissage* of cultural forms" (112). Lionnet's and Morrison's focus on the unacknowledged agency of historically marginalized voices in the shaping of dominant tradition, points to the Africanist other as the effaced enabling force behind such classics as *The Scarlet Letter*. In the discussion that follows, *I, Tituba* is read not primarily as a counter-text to historical lacuna, but rather, as a text that conceptualizes Tituba as the effaced and unacknowledged presence that conditions the construction of the canonized texts that it interrogates.

Set within the brutal, patriarchal, racist societies of New England and Barbados during the late seventeenth century, when collective hysteria was sweeping the villages of Massachusetts into a cruel witch-hunt and the slave trade was growing in intensity, *I, Tituba* presents itself as a corrective for historical oblivion—an explicit response to the "intentional or unintentional racism of the historians" (183) who have excluded Tituba from their accounts of the trials and executions of the alleged witches of Salem. As narrator, Tituba senses the cruelty of this effacement, this "injustice" (110), but knows that she will be immortalized in the hearts of her people, existing as the vital force that ignites revolt and sustains the dream of freedom.

This oppositional, or revolutionary, Tituba presents the other of the Tituba we have come to know via our history texts—the West Indian slave who, under torture, confessed that she had submitted to Satan's control and had tormented children. Condé's Tituba focuses on her enforced voicelessness. Forced to deny her self and to affirm her subjugation to a masculine power, she assumes the identity that her oppressors design. "Well spoken, Tituba. You understood what we expected of you" (106), Samuel Parris says after her interrogation. In response, Condé's Tituba can only acknowledge, to herself, the violent self-negation of her confession: "I hate myself as much as I hate him" (106).

Interestingly, this text of silenced history becomes a text that returns to other literary texts, and specifically to two texts that have been canonized as points of origin for their respective literary traditions. If Nathaniel Hawthorne's *The Scarlet Letter* has been regarded as the "true beginning of American prose fiction" (Bloom, 8), Aimé Césaire's "Notebook of a Return to the Native Land" has been canonized as a "fundamental" or "sacred" text (Condé, "Order," 126) that has given rise to all subsequent Caribbean francophone literature. Although Condé herself has acknowledged both the literary and political significance of Césaire's "Notebook,"[3] she takes issue with the way that it has been canonized, specifically, with the way that its reception has led to prescriptive "orders" for Antillean literature, stifling its creativity and perpetuating the oblivion and incomprehension of women writers of the West Indies ("Order," 122–34).

I, Tituba thus takes the events at Salem as a backdrop for the exploration of the ways in which Tituba's silenced narrative has been incorporated into canonized texts, and, more significantly, for an exploration of the ways in which this silenced text has functioned as an enabling or conditioning force for canonized texts. Condé's *I, Tituba* illustrates both what Lionnet calls the "*métissage* of cultural forms" and what Morrison identifies as the "compelling and inescapable" (46) ways in which unacknowledged presence shapes the texture of canonized literature.

If "Africanism is the vehicle by which the American self knows itself as not enslaved, but free; not repulsive, but desirable; not helpless, but licensed and powerful; not history-less, but historical; not damned, but innocent; not a blind accident of evolution, but a progressive fulfillment of destiny" (Morrison, 52), in short, if a negatively valued Africanism enables the construction of a positive American identity, then similarly, within the context of the witch trials of Salem, and within Condé's narrative, Tituba is the vehicle by which Puritan identity reestablishes itself as powerful, righteous, and innocent.

Tituba's "confession," the text of her deposition testimony, is the only historical document that Condé has at her disposal. The text of the novel is Tituba's second confession, and as Condé states in the epigraph, it contains her "endless conversations" with Tituba, conversations during which Tituba revealed things "she had confided to nobody else." This "second" and "private confession" (which is not really a confession at all, but rather, a co-authored life story resulting from a presumed and intimate woman-to-woman dialogue), in which Tituba claims her own identity with the words "I, Tituba," is countered by the first public confession, in which Tituba strives to follow Hester's recommendations and give the magistrates "their money's worth" (99), describing to them exactly what they believe, even if it has nothing to do with the truth. Hester thus advises Tituba to legitimate the beliefs of her persecuters, and not without good reason, because, by law, the life of a witch was spared if she confessed. By confessing then, Tituba escapes death, yet legitimates the authority of her oppressors.

If, after her public confession, Tituba hates herself because she has acquiesced and affirmed an identity that her oppressors have constructed for her, she nonetheless has also spoken a truth that Condé's novel unearths centuries later. *I, Tituba* is the text that allows Tituba to say to her oppressors, "you created me; you constructed and imposed a false identity upon me, but now that I have found a space in which I can speak openly, I am able to reveal not only my true self, but, as well, the ways in which I have shaped you and the ways in which I have informed your view of yourself." Tituba is thus able to illustrate that which might forever have remained unacknowledged.

Condé narrates the way that the American literary imagination has "played in the dark" and the way that the "dark and abiding presence" now reclaims its role as "mediating force" (Morrison, 46) through a rewriting of Hester Prynne, the heroine of the "quintessential American novel" (Baym, xxv), *The Scarlet Letter*. If for Morrison the "imaginative encounter with Africanism enable[d] white writers to think about themselves" (51), for Condé, the imaginative encounter between Tituba and Nathaniel Hawthorne's Hester Prynne enabled Condé to think about the way that her heroine, Tituba, had enabled Hawthorne to produce the "true beginning of American prose fiction." Condé thus returns to this canonized "absolute point of origin" (Bloom, 8) in order to reclaim Tituba's part in this origin, and to reaffirm Tituba's presence in what inevitably becomes a "wider landscape" (Morrison, 3), and a more hybrid lineage than heretofore imagined.

When asked about her incorporation of Hester Prynne in *I, Tituba*, Condé has replied:

> First of all I like the novel *The Scarlet Letter* and I read it often. Second, it is set in roughly the same period as *Tituba*. Third, when I went to Salem to visit the village, the place where Tituba used to live, I saw the house of Nathaniel Hawthorne, the House

> of the Seven Gables...meaning there was a link between Tituba and Nathaniel Hawthorne. ("An Interview," 202)

Condé's oblique answer refuses any comment on Hester and rather than drawing a link between herself and Hawthorne,[4] Condé forges a link between the voiceless Tituba and Nathaniel Hawthorne, the white male writer who, "with the publication of *The Scarlet Letter*...was instantly elevated to the position of the nation's foremost man of letters" (Baym, xxi).

This gesture is, on the one hand, ironic, since it implies that although Tituba was as much alive and real as Hawthorne, she was silenced for centuries and could not become a "writer" until the 1986 collaboration with Maryse Condé. The linking of Tituba and Hawthorne also comments on the way that popular imagination is formed and preserved. If Tituba's traces have been entirely erased from Salem, and Maryse Condé's trip to the village is a return to a place which might somehow stir her imagination or speak to her intuitively, The House of the Seven Gables physically imposes itself on the visitor, reinforcing what has already been immortalized in the popular imagination and canonized in the American literary tradition. Condé's connection between Tituba and Hawthorne thus has a trifold effect: first, it reveals an effacement; second, it reclaims the terrain of Salem as a shared terrain; and third, it reappropriates "the imaginative and historical terrain upon which early American writers journeyed" as a terrain "shaped by the presence of the racial other" (Morrison, 46).

It is no surprise then that Tituba is more present in the imaginative terrain, in literature,[5] than in "historical" documents. In her search for a "folk heroine of the West Indies" ("Je me suis réconciliée," 129), Condé revisits the American literary tradition, returning to the scarlet letter, the signifier of Hester Prynne's infamy.

The opening scene of *The Scarlet Letter* recounts the visual display of Hester's body in the marketplace. Rather than appearing disgraced, however, Hester emerges from the prison "marked with natural dignity and force of character" (Hawthorne, 54), proudly displaying her elaborately and artistically embroidered letter A. As one of the spectators remarks, Hester has made "pride" out of "punishment" (56). By embellishing the letter that is to mark her with ignominy, Hester transforms the sign into a complex and ambiguous symbol—one that signifies both Puritan control and domination, as well as the refusal and delegitimation of this control.

Likewise, *I, Tituba*, Tituba's autobiographical narrative, is the embellishment of a text (Tituba's deposition testimony) which signifies Tituba's guilt. Like Hester Prynne, Tituba refutes her subjugation by reappropriating, transforming, and signifying on a text which was intended as an unambiguous assertion of her fault. There is thus an alliance between Tituba and Hester, a connection which Condé imagines and narrates as the sisterhood and friendship between two victimized women.

Although it is unlikely that Hester Prynne is Hawthorne's intentional embodiment of an Africanist presence, I would like to suggest that the "invisible mediating force" (Morrison, 46) behind Hester is the Africanist presence, as formulated by Morrison. Indeed, Morrison has argued that it is "[e]ven, and especially, when American texts are not 'about' Africanist presences or characters or narrative or idiom, the shadow hovers in implication, in sign, in line of demarcation" (46–47). Hence Morrison contends that the Africanist presence acts "[a]s a metaphor for transacting the whole process of Americanization, while burying its particular racial ingredients" and "may be something the United States cannot do without" (47). By drawing a parallel between Tituba and Hester, Condé's text unburies this "racial ingredient," deciphering and making visible the complex workings of literary imagination. As Morrison says:

> For American writers...th[e] Africanist other became the means of thinking about body, mind, chaos, kindness, and love; provided the occasion for...the contemplation of freedom and of aggression; permitted opportunities for the exploration of ethics and morality, for meeting the obligations of the social contract, for bearing the cross of religion and following out the ramifications of power. (47–48)

Following this argument then, the Africanist other enabled, or made conceivable, the exploration of the issues central to *The Scarlet Letter*. Condé's novel thus not only fills a gap in the search for legendary Caribbean women, but it also reclaims the Africanist presence as a shaping force in canonical American literature.

In her rewriting of Hawthorne's Hester Prynne, Condé retains some of Hester's defining characteristics—such as the blackness of her physical traits—but, on the whole, Condé creates an altogether different Hester. Whereas Hawthorne's Hester gives birth to Pearl and lives according to what she feels is her maternal duty—to "conform with the most perfect quietude to the external regulations of society" (163)—Condé's Hester hangs herself in prison, before the birth of her child. Although Hawthorne's Hester contemplates suicide and infanticide, and although she is deeply critical of her society, she contents herself with a life of meditation, without investing her thought in action. If it weren't for Pearl, however, Hester might have attempted "to undermine the foundations of the Puritan establishment" (163–64).

In a sense, Tituba's return to Barbados and her decision to carry her child to term, can be read as her attempt to be like Hawthorne's Hester Prynne. In Hawthorne's text, the scarlet letter becomes legendary, assumes different meanings as time goes on, and, in the end, is even looked upon "with reverence" (261). Society denies Tituba such luxury—in Barbados she is still "the black witch of Salem," and she is hanged, pregnant with child. *I, Tituba* thus emphasizes the issue of agency. Whereas Hawthorne's Hester chooses not to speak (in order to conceal the identity of Chillingworth and Dimmesdale), Tituba is silenced. Although Condé's Hester is not to be envied, she is the author of her own death, unlike Tituba and unlike Abena.

As Bloom has noted, "every reader of *The Scarlet Letter* comes to feel a great regret at Hester's unfulfilled potential....Certainly we sense an unwritten book in her, a story that Hawthorne did not choose to write" (8). On another level then, we might read Tituba's participation in the slave revolt as an attempt to fulfill Hester's revolutionary potential. Back in Barbados, Tituba dreams of raising her yet unborn daughter in a different world. Nonetheless, the revolt she helps plan and carry out is unsuccessful. What *I, Tituba* suggests then, is that Tituba, by reason of her race, is in a no-win situation. She can neither be redeemed nor live out her life in tranquility as Hawthorne's Hester. She can neither successfully undermine the system that oppresses her, nor author her own death. Curiously then, if the Africanist presence generates the imaginative terrain for Hawthorne's narrative, when we paint Hester black, then *The Scarlet Letter*, as we know it, becomes inconceivable. Condé's text thus unearths this necessary camouflaging of the Africanist presence.

In the explicit rewriting of its own ending, however, the narrative allows us to envision an empowered Tituba. *I, Tituba* is not only a rewriting of Tituba's life, but also a rewriting of her fictional death. Although the novel ends with Tituba at the gallows, the "Epilogue" allows Tituba to speak once again, and to claim that her story really "has no end" (175). In this purely imaginative terrain of the "Epilogue," Tituba becomes a revolutionary and a mother by choice. Whereas *The Scarlet Letter* allows us to sense in Hester the unwritten book that Hawthorne chose not to write, *I,*

Tituba allows us to sense in Tituba an unwritten book that was denied expression.

If Hawthorne's heroine is one point of reference for Tituba, the Caribbean hero is another. Kathleen Balutansky has argued that "for contemporary women writers, imagining and representing fully autonomous Caribbean women seems paradoxical, especially when the governing symbol for the Caribbean condition remains that of Caliban" (29). Condé's claim that the text before us is the product of conversations between two women separated by three centuries of time allows Tituba to transcend time and signify on Aimé Césaire's "Notebook of a Return to the Native Land," and in particular its Calibanesque parthenogenesis. In terms of emplotment and imagery, Tituba's narrative echoes the "Notebook," inviting comparison between a text which gives voice to a forgotten and silenced black heroine and a text which has become inseparably linked with the origins of Antillean negritude. If Césaire's negritude renewed awareness in black culture and black identity, Condé's novel implies that this was largely a "male" identity, but an identity that obtained its insurrectional force from its own conscious or unconscious inscription of woman's experience.

Whereas the hero of the "Notebook" is an anonymous male who comes to embody the universal voice of his people, Tituba's story is the personal account of the life of an outcast. Unlike the male hero, who is able to establish fraternity with his people, the heroine remains a solitary figure whose revolt remains circumscribed by the limits society imposes on her gender. After her mother is hanged for having defended herself against the sexual aggression of her master, Tituba voices her impotence, alluding to the fact that Césairian heroism is inaccessible to her:

> Oh yes, I should have liked to unleash the wind like a dog from his kennel so that the white Great Houses of the masters would be blown away over the horizon, to order a fire to kindle and fan its flames so that the whole island would be purified and devastated. But I didn't have such powers. I only knew how to offer consolation. (12)

As argued by Janice Lee Liddell, the archetypal Caribbean woman is the "good mumma," and women are so constrained by this image that they can only be "something else" if the "mother spirit" is present in that "something else" (321). When Tituba returns to her island with a sense of revolt against injustice and finds herself pregnant again, even Man Yaya and Abena equate Tituba's maternity with her *nature*: "Well, this time you can't do away with it!

Your real nature has spoken!" (158). Indeed, Tituba's revolt is articulated within the maternal context, indicating that it is only possible where the "mother spirit" is clearly evident. Thus, she is asked to "disarm" (163) Christopher, being the only one who can do so, as she is carrying his child.

The turning points of Tituba's life—her rebirth into the world when her shackles and chains are smashed to pieces, the return to her island, her sacrificial offering and unsuccessful revolt—ironically echo the emplotment of Césaire's "Notebook." Upon their return, both Tituba and Césaire's hero are struck by the stench and ugliness of their native land. Tituba laments:

> my island did not exactly deck itself out to greet me....The streets were churned with muddy water in which men and beasts were splashing....How ugly my town was! Small. Petty. A colonial outpost of no distinction, reeking with the stench of lucre and suffering. (141)

Echoes of Césaire's "mute," "inert," and "sprawled-flat" town, the "hungry Antilles,...pitted with smallpox" and..."stranded in the mud" like a "bedsore on the wound of the waters" (35) immediately come to mind.

Although the poetic voice in the "Notebook" bemoans the "restrained conflagration of the morne" and the "sob gagged on the verge of a bloodthirsty burst" (37), his "male thirst" allows the hero to overcome voicelessness and become "the mouth of those calamities that have no mouth" (45). Tituba's narrative, on the other hand, is punctuated with the screams of women, yet these are screams that go unheard, and ultimately, communicate to no one.

Tituba's voicelessness becomes all the more evident with the incessantly muted screams that cannot but echo back to Césaire's text and its development of an ever-more resounding and self-affirmative voice. As she witnesses the hanging death of Goody Glover, for example, Tituba recalls: "I *screamed*, and the more I *screamed* the more I felt the desire to *scream*. To *scream* out my suffering, my revolt, and my powerless rage" (49, my emphasis). This "powerless rage" later becomes the scream of her aborted child. When she learns of Hester's suicide, Tituba identifies herself with a screaming fetus who fights not for life, but for death:

> I *screamed* down the door of my mother's womb. My fist broke her bag of waters in rage and despair. I choked and suffocated in this black liquid. I wanted to drown myself....Mother, will our torture never end? If this is how things are, I shall never emerge into the light of day. I shall remain crouched in your waters,

> deaf, dumb, and blind, clinging like kelp to your womb. I shall cling so tightly you'll never expel me and I shall return to dust without you, without ever having known the curse of day. Mother, help me! (111, my emphasis)

Whereas the male hero is able to "forc[e] the vitelline membrane that separates [him] from [him]self" (57), to give birth to himself, to imagine a "yet undared form" issuing from "man's unfathomable sperm" (67), and to claim an identity, Tituba's text is marked with impotence.

It is particularly with the metaphors of blood and birth that the heroine's text returns to the hero's poem as a native to an alien land. The blood of revolt, so prominent in the "Notebook," becomes, in Tituba's text, the blood of the violated woman. This blood precariously unites Tituba and her mistress, Elizabeth Parris, when Samuel Parris strikes the two women. It is the blood of aborted birth, the black stinking blood of the sacrificial rabbit, which unites with Tituba's own blood as she wounds herself with the knife she uses to slit the rabbit's belly. The puddle of blood at her feet reminds Tituba of Yao's words, words which echo, not surprisingly, the words of the "Notebook": "Our memory will have to be covered in blood....Our memories will have to float to the surface like water lilies" (165).

The irony of the use of Césaire's "Notebook" as subtext is compounded when Tituba is called upon to command to the elements. Compared to the male sorcerer, Tituba, the tortured and misunderstood sorcière, has no alchemic or metamorphic powers. Unlike the male hero-narrator, she is "nothing but a common Negress" (155). "Do I have to go on to the end?" (166) she asks as her narrative draws to a close, emphasizing the difference between her muffled dissent and the powerful, rising, and climactic poetic voice that closes Césaire's "Notebook."

Voicelessness—so crucial an issue for an understanding of Caribbean women's creativity (Davies and Fido, 1)—is deeply tied to historicity and to the reconstitution of black women's history. As Angela Davis has said in her Foreword to the translation of *I, Tituba*:

> [a]s Condé offers to Tituba the possibility of filling the silence and voids with voice and presence, we who are Tituba's cultural kin experience the possibilities of our own history....And when Tituba takes her place in the history of the Salem witch trials, the recorded history of that era—and indeed the entire history of the colonization process—is revealed to be seriously flawed. (xii)

Because voicelessness, as suppressed history and unacknowledged agency, is so central an issue in Tituba's life story, the very fact of presenting the possibility of her narrative is empowering. Not only does Tituba's voice participate in the reconstruction of the suppressed history of black women and challenge the ways that the past has been encoded, but it also reveals the presence of subdued voice in canonized literary texts.

As Ann Armstrong Scarboro points out, "Condé does not merely retell Tituba's story; she recreates it to new purposes" (213). Condé's recreation of Tituba's life allows the silenced heroine to intervene in the canon by proposing a revision of the way that we read texts. Tituba subverts the canon not by replacing some texts with others, but by articulating the need for alternative reading practices. By encoding the hybrid terrain of literary imagination, the narrative offers an alternative perspective on the enabling and formative conditions of canonized texts. *I, Tituba* also suggests a renewed awareness of the complexity of cultural formations and the way that the discursive features of a text actively revise, transform, and establish interrelations which in turn lead to the revaluation of power and the renegotiation of social relations.

NOTES

1. Condé's *Moi, Tituba, sorcière...Noire de Salem* (Paris: Mercure de France, 1986) has been translated by Richard Philcox (Charlottesville: University Press of Virginia, 1992). All textual references are from this translation.

2. I borrow this formulation from Nancy Fraser who uses it in her Introduction to *Revaluing French Feminism* to define "two antithetical conceptions of culture," the other being the view that culture is "monolithically phallocentric, everywhere instantiating the same hierarchical binary oppositions and eternally repressing feminine difference" (17–18).

3. See her *Cahier d'un retour au pays natal: Césaire: analyse critique* (Paris: Hatier, 1978) and *La poésie antillaise* (Paris: Nathan, 1978).

4. A link for which there are clear grounds: both authors claim to have found "evidence"—in Condé's case, the deposition, in Hawthorne's, the scarlet letter—which marks their respective heroines and inspires the narratives created about them, narratives both dealing thematically with guilt, confession, silence, and retribution.

5. Jeanne Snitgen in "History, Identity and the Constitution of the Female Subject: Maryse Condé's Tituba," *Black Women's Writing: Crossing the Boundaries*, ed. Carole Boyce Davies (Frankfurt: Holger Ehling, 1989), gives the following list: Henry Wadsworth Longfellow's

Giles Corey of the Salem Farms, William Carlos Williams' *Tituba's Children*, Arthur Miller's *The Crucible*, and Ann Petry's *Tituba of Salem Village*.

WORKS CITED

Balutansky, Kathleen M. "Creating Her Own Image: Female Genesis in *Mémoire d'une amnésique* and *Moi, Tituba sorcière....*" *L'Héritage de Caliban*. Ed. Maryse Condé. Guadeloupe: Jasor, 1992, 29–48.

Baym, Nina. *The Scarlet Letter: A Reading*. Boston: Twayne, 1986.

Bloom, Harold. "Introduction." *Nathaniel Hawthorne's The Scarlet Letter*. Ed. Harold Bloom. New York: Chelsea, 1986, 1–8.

Césaire, Aimé. "Notebook of a Return to the Native Land." *The Collected Poetry*. Trans. Clayton Eshleman and Annette Smith. Berkeley: University of California Press, 1983, 32–85.

Condé, Maryse. "An Interview with Maryse Condé." By Ann Armstrong Scarboro. "Afterword." *I, Tituba, Black Witch of Salem*. Trans. Richard Philcox. Charlottesville: University Press of Virginia, 1992, 198–213.

———. *I, Tituba, Black Witch of Salem*. Trans. Richard Philcox. Charlottesville: University Press of Virginia, 1992.

———. "'Je me suis réconciliée avec mon île'/'I Have Made Peace with My Island': Une interview de Maryse Condé/ An Interview with Maryse Condé." By VèVè A. Clark. *Callaloo* 12 (Winter 1989) : 85–133.

———. "Order, Disorder, Freedom, and the West Indian Writer." *Yale French Studies* 83 (1993) : 121–35.

Davies, Carole Boyce and Elaine Savory Fido. "Introduction: Women and Literature in the Caribbean: An Overview." *Out of the Kumbla: Caribbean Women and Literature*. Ed. Carole Boyce Davies and Elaine Savory Fido. Trenton, NJ: African World, 1990, 1–24.

Davis, Angela Y. Foreword. *I, Tituba, Black Witch of Salem*. By Maryse Condé. Trans. Richard Philcox. Charlottesville: University Press of Virginia, 1992, xi–xiii.

Fraser, Nancy. "Introduction." *Revaluing French Feminism: Critical Essays on Difference, Agency, and Culture*. Ed. Nancy Fraser and Sandra Lee Bartky. Bloomington: Indiana University Press, 1992, 1–24.

Hawthorne, Nathaniel. *The Scarlet Letter*. Ed. Harry Levin. Boston: Houghton, 1960 [1850].

Liddell, Janice Lee. "The Narrow Enclosure of Motherdom/Martyrdom: A Study of Gatha Randall Barton in Sylvia Wynter's *The Hills of Hebron.*" *Out of the Kumbla: Caribbean Women and Literature.* Ed. Carole Boyce Davies and Elaine Savory Fido. Trenton, NJ: Africa World, 1990, 321–30.

Lionnet, Françoise. *Autobiographical Voices: Race, Gender, Self-Portraiture.* Ithaca: Cornell University Press, 1989.

———. "'*Logiques métisses*': Cultural Appropriation and Postcolonial Representations." *College Literature* 19.3 (October 1992): 100–20; also, present volume, 111–36.

Morrison, Toni. *Playing in the Dark: Whiteness and the Literary Imagination.* Cambridge, MA: Harvard University Press, 1990.

Scarboro, Ann Armstrong. "Afterword." *I, Tituba, Black Witch of Salem.* Trans. Richard Philcox. Charlottesville: University Press of Virginia, 1992, 187–225.

Schipper, Mineke. "Women and Literature in Africa." *Unheard Words: Women and Literature in Africa, the Arab World, Asia, the Caribbean and Latin America.* Trans. Barbara Potter Fasting. London: Allison & Busby, 1985, 19–58.

15

ARUN P. MUKHERJEE

Other Worlds, Other Texts: Teaching Anita Desai's *Clear Light of Day* to Canadian Students

My teaching of Commonwealth/Third World/Postcolonial/South Asian/Indian literature is deeply influenced by my consciousness of my cultural and linguistic differences from the host society, Canada.[1] These differences structure my consciousness and make me aware of the culture-specific meanings that often escape cultural outsiders.[2] As a South Asian Canadian who received her first graduate degree in English literature from an Indian university, I became acutely conscious of the contribution of commonplace allusions to the texture of meanings in a literary text since I had to learn these meanings by going to encyclopedias and other "extra-literary" sources. I will never forget being stymied by the word "barbecue" that I encountered for the very first time in *Gone With the Wind*, read during my undergraduate days in India. The short, and several, explanations in my *Shorter Oxford Dictionary* didn't help since it was such an alien concept for me, a teenager growing up in a vegetarian family in a small central Indian town where vegetarians formed such an overwhelming majority that the one and only market lacked a meat store.[3] My father, who had earned a master's degree in English in the mid-1930s, was also unaware of the word as well as the ritualistic nature of the activity it denotes for those familiar with North American culture.

He told me not to bother to decode such cruxes when I read English language texts but to move on with the text. His theoretical advice was that everything in the text was not understandable, or worth understanding. He also advised me to skip the narratorial comments and long descriptions of any kind, things that, according to him, slowed down the unfolding of the plot. I suppose that must have been the pedagogical ideology that he was subjected to at Forman Christian College in Lahore in the mid-1930s.

My encounter with such enigmas in the text made me aware very early on in my study of literature how important culturally coded meanings are. This awareness has made me wary of theories that speak of "universality" and "autonomy" of literature. For, as several Third World writers and critics have suggested, "universality" in such theoretical exercises has really come down to a demand that the literary work not contain any references to the local or regional, since the New York- or London-based critic cannot be bothered to waste time acquainting him/herself with Yoruba myths or Indian scriptures (Mukherjee, "Vocabulary").

One result of this lack of desire on the part of the majority of Euro-American critics writing on non-Western texts has been a paucity of readings that bring out the culture-specific meanings of these texts. What we have, instead, are readings and theorizations that focus on a homogenized "postcolonial" text whose postcoloniality remains constant across cultural and geographic distances. In the name of "postcolonial" texts and "postcolonial" theories, current critical work brings out the "resisting," "parodic," and "allegorical" aspects of the "postcolonial" text, but only in relation to the imperial "center." Fredric Jameson's "Third World Literature in the Era of Multinational Capitalism" and Ashcroft's, Griffiths' and Tiffin's *The Empire Writes Back* provide quintessential examples of such an approach.

Such universalizing frameworks are beginning to be questioned after almost a decade of academic hegemony enjoyed by them. Recent critiques have focused on postcolonial theory's "ahistorical and universalizing deployments, and [its] potentially depoliticizing implications" (Shohat, 99). If there is a common thread in these writings, it is their assertion that a single theory, whatever its pedigree, is incapable of coming to terms with the multiplicity and heterogeneity of the world's cultural and social formations (Ahmad; Mukherjee, "Exclusions"; McClintock; Shohat). As McClintock suggests, what we need is not yet another single term to substitute for "postcolonialism" and its variants but "rethinking the global situation as a *multiplicity* of powers and histories which cannot be marshaled obediently under the flag of a single theoretical term, be that feminism, Marxism, or postcolonialism" (97).

Moving from singularity towards multiplicity would mean dismantling the current canon of "postcolonial literature" and the rubric under which it is taught. It seems to me that monolithic theories proposed by Jameson or Ashcroft, Griffiths, and Tiffin are determining what texts will be selected for teaching and how they will be taught. One does not have to go too far except to check a few departmental calendars and recent issues of journals in the field to discover that a canon of "postcolonial literature" has evolved that is heavily androcentric and biased in the favor of texts that can give back the analysis based on proving "parody" and "nationalist allegory." The critical work being published on this canon is predictably concerned with demonstrating intertexuality or the search of the "colonized" for authentic identity and lost history.

My problem with this canon and its interpretation is that in its desire to establish the parodic intertexuality of non-European texts with European ones, it overlooks the parodic and non-parodic functions that the text may be performing in the place of its origin. On the other hand, in their focus on the colonizer/colonized binary, such interpretations fail to notice that the "colonized" may also be an internal colonizer. Thus, Raja Rao's valorization of Brahminical culture in *The Serpent and the Rope* has remained unproblematic for critics who have seen the work as an assertion of "Indian" culture and "Indian" identity. Similarly, the androcentrism of Achebe's or Soyinka's texts is a topic one seldom hears about (a graduate student of mine recently encountered much harsh criticism when she read a feminist paper on the absence of the mother in Achebe's novels).

My subject position as an Indo-Canadian makes me very sensitive to the homogenizing tendencies of literary and critical discourses. India, as I have known it, is a multicultural, multiracial and unequal society and Indian texts are marked by the tensions that are produced when multiple discourses compete for domination. My consciousness of India's plurality also means that I am generally suspicious of all *a priori* homogenizations.

I have felt that postcolonial theory, the dominant critical theory in the field at the moment, overlooks the diversities within any society on the one hand, and, on the other, the diversities across postcolonial societies when it tries to speak of them all in terms of the colonizer/colonized binaries. In terms of pedagogy, postcolonial theory allows teachers and critics to speak about postcolonial literature(s) in the singular and design and teach omnibus courses called "postcolonial literature" that incorporate works of authors from far-flung regions of the world. Bringing together these works is justified in terms of their use of a common language, English, and a "common" experience of colonialism. Such a stance, in its privileging of commonalities, de-emphasizes differences or erases them outright. The commonalities, which have been identified as loss of identity in the form of lost history, lost languages and lost traditions, internalization of the colonizer's values, search for authenticity, forging of new identity, and cursing the colonizer, to name the more prominent ones, are highlighted at the expense of differences as well as other possible commonalities such as ethnic and religious tensions, gender oppression, poverty, and economic exploitation. The choice of commonalities, I am suggesting, is arbitrary as well as unconvincing.

This omnibus Commonwealth/postcolonial course militates against my desire to teach in ways that bring out the text's affiliation with the literary tradition it is a part of on the one hand, and, on the other, its engagements with the discourses and ideologies of the society it emerged from. For, the moment one tries to teach individual texts in terms of cultural and literary traditions and specific social realities, the rationale of a unitary postcolonial/Commonwealth course that brings together what are called "five regions" by Canadian departments of English is called into question. The rationale, whether stated or unstated, is based on the premise that the literatures of all these five "regions" harbor commonalities and that these commonalities will be brought out as we study their texts in contiguity. The moment one wants to explore a text in terms of its engagement with and representation of "a" social reality, one begins to swim against the predefined directions that *a priori* constitute "the postcolonial" as undifferentiated.

In my pedagogical practice, I have tried to move away from the omnibus Commonwealth/postcolonial course that packs the "five regions" into one and design courses that focus on a single region, or, at most, two. I feel that the rationale that supports the omnibus course is based on two *a priori* assumptions that haven't been analyzed rigorously. The first is that postcolonial societies are similar because of their "shared" experience of colonialism (Mukherjee, "Exclusions"). The second piggybacks on the first, and implies that because the societies are similar their literatures are as well. Since I believe that the social formation of each postcolonial society is unique and has to be studied on its own terms, I am opposed in principle to the omnibus course that preempts an inquiry into individual social formations and individual literary traditions. Unfortunately, it is the omnibus course that is entrenched in the majority of Western universities and it is very difficult to argue for space for five or more separate courses under the postcolonial/Commonwealth rubric when even the one or two omnibus courses are resented by the protectors of the canon.

While it may not be possible for teachers of postcolonial/ Commonwealth/Third World literatures to demand more space, given our marginalized position in English departments focused heavily on the study of British literature, it is necessary that the hidden assumptions of the omnibus course be brought out in the open. Its single-minded focus on commonalities among post-colonial societies and literatures and its strategies of reading, which privilege parodic intertextuality of some postcolonial texts with Western texts, necessarily prevent an engagement with the cultural apparatus—the totality of the symbolic resources of a culture—that informs a literary text. And its silent exclusion of texts that may not be about the anticolonial struggle or may not employ parody of Western texts reinforces the assumption that all postcolonial societies have similar concerns and similar mindsets.

I believe that the kind of attention I want to pay to a literary text is not possible in the format of the omnibus course that flits from region to region, leaving little time or room to explore intra-cultural intertextualities and linkages of other kinds than works from one social formation have. I have come to believe strongly that the cultural context is an integral aspect of the literary text and neither its form nor its content can be grasped without paying attention to the former. When postcolonial critics focus on comparisons and commonalities, they overlook the fact that the postcolonial texts do not speak only to the empire but that they are also in conversation with those on the home territory. That is, as "*strategic* [and] *stylized* answers" they participate in all the other discourses of their society and situate their own discourse by taking a position against or for these oppositional or friendly discourses (Burke, 1). I believe that the omnibus course, first through its selection and exclusion of texts and then through the kind of themes and formal strategies it chooses to highlight, forecloses the possibilities of inquiry into the engagement of the text with local realities.

For example, how are we to find commonalities for unique Indian institutions such as *sati* and untouchability? Conversely, how is our understanding of the temple-mosque dispute that is currently raging in India and threatens its dissolution enhanced by our comparative studies based on the premise of colonial domination? As Anne McClintock has suggested, postcolonial theory leads to "an entranced suspension of history, as if definitive historical events have preceded us, and are not now in the making" (86).

Since history is not a closed book, and since it neither began nor ended with the era of colonialism, I feel that there is no substitute for studying a literary text in its own sociohistorical context. When several literary texts from the same area and tradition are studied together, the recurrence of socially shared narratives and shared cultural assumptions links them for us in various interesting ways.

Such a pedagogical and interpretational ideology implies that a critic must bring to the text an extratextual knowledge about the multiple discourses circulating in a society rather than rely solely on the text. In pedagogical terms, this stance means that the text should be situated on an ideological spectrum—not universally, but in the context of the cultural ideologies operating in the place of its production.

I find that a good number of my Canadian students have very little knowledge about the geographic region known as the Indian subcontinent, except for some well-worn stereotypes learned from high school textbooks and Hollywood movies. Most of them do not know anything about ancient or modern Indian history, religions, or cultural traditions and customs. Such lack of basic knowledge on their part demands that I contextualize the text for them by talking in detail about things such as the epics *Mahabharata* and the *Ramayana*, independence and partition, contemporary social, political and cultural trends and films and other popular media. As Gerald Graff has noted:

> What a teacher is to *say* about a literary work [is] something that hinges on matters of purpose, context, and situation that are not pre-given either in literary works themselves or our experience of them. If works of literature "speak for themselves," they do so only up to a point, for their authors were not aware, and could not have been aware, of the kinds of situations in which their works would later be read and taught and the different problems of comprehension and appreciation these situations might occasion. (255)

I have already engaged with the "purpose...and situation" of my teaching in my earlier discussion of my problems with the purpose of the omnibus Commonwealth/postcolonial course and the premises that support it. The "context" of teaching, I think, has to do with taking into account the fact that an Indian text taught in India will need a different pedagogical and interpretive strategy than when it is taught in a different land and to a different body of students.

Since my Canadian students know very little about Indian history, literatures, religions, gender relations, and construction of the self in India, I become a narrator myself, recounting the shared narratives of India that are embedded in the literary text. This tale telling is educational both for me and my students. It makes me conscious of the unconscious interpretive activity that I bring to bear on texts from India whereas my students learn about the culture-specific nature of literary language. The point is brought home to them when we discuss that what to them is the crystal-clear textuality of a Canadian work becomes opaque to readers uninitiated in Canadian history, literature, and culture when they come across expressions such as "two solitudes," "the maple leaf," "the great white north," "survival," "the garrison mentality," and many others like these.

My aim as a teacher, then, is to acquaint my students with the allusive nature of the text. These allusions are not just to literary texts but, as I have said elsewhere, also to "collectively shared knowledge and experiences of a society: experience of colonialism, legends of heroes and villains, deeply-held belief systems, rhetorical pronouncements of local elite such as politicians, businessmen and movie stars" ("Vocabulary," 13). I try to steer my students away from their deeply entrenched habit of focusing solely on the character(s) in isolation by bringing to their attention the fact that such an isolationist move is ethnocentric insofar as they impose their own cultural values on the behavior and motivation of the character(s). Instead, I focus on acquainting them with the total web of significations that structure the narrative.

I would now like to focus on one particular fictional text, Anita Desai's *Clear Light of Day*, and elaborate on my pedagogical strategies as well as my students' responses. I have chosen this particular text since it is widely taught and has also received considerable critical attention. However, few of the research articles in journals and books—focusing on aspects such as intertextuality of the text with British literature and American pop music, "universal" themes such as quest, search for identity, loss of innocence, and, more recently, postcolonial "resistance" to the colonizer's impositions—provide much help to my students in coming to grips with the cultural premises that are embedded in the text and account for its "Indianness."

It is these cultural premises that I am interested in exploring and explaining to my students so that they may become aware of the dependence of the literary text on the totality of the symbolic resources of the culture the text emanates from. Often, it is the questions or the interpretations of my students that alert me to the culture-specific aspect of these symbolic codes as I had passed over them in my own reading, unaware of my own special knowledge as a "cultural insider" in my encounter with the text. For instance, if the text were being taught in India to Indian students, the teacher would not have to inform the students that the white sari of Mira Masi signifies her widowhood. However, the Canadian students need to be informed of this symbolism. Such realizations on our part make me and my students aware how culture-specific literary texts are and how important it is to know the social text if we really want to understand the literary text.

The growth of such an awareness, I believe, ought to be the end result of my teaching. As a teacher, my aim is to move students away from the fake "universality" that denies differences only because it projects its own ethnocentrism on the "other." Polly Young-Eisendrath has defined this imperialist universalism very well:

> Our ethnocentrism, as North Americans, frequently enters into our discussions about self-constructs of other cultures. We tend to believe that individuality, individual freedom, and self-reflectiveness are the truest, most valuable and least contestable aspects of self. In other words, we universalize the aspects of selfhood that suggest personal uniqueness and separateness. (158)

It is the "self-constructs of other cultures"—what is worth telling, how it is to be told, what is considered a good life—that I focus on in my classroom, in the hope that my students will become critically conscious of their own ethnocentrism. Much of the learning, and laughter, in my classroom, in fact, is born out of cross-cultural encounters since my classes at York University are increasingly multicultural and multiracial, which was not the case even five years ago. One of the recent encounters, for instance, was on the institution of arranged marriage. Whereas a white student admitted to considering the institution "weird" and "funny," a South Asian student accused her of applying a "Judaeo-Christian framework." The point I wish to make is that the multicultural Canadian classroom of the nineties is a deeply contested space and the pedagogical strategies I adopt are tailored to the realities of my classroom and may not be relevant to a monocultural, monoracial classroom, such as the classrooms that I encountered in Canada in the seventies and eighties, both as a graduate student and as a teacher, where I would often be the only nonwhite.

Having said that, perhaps one insight that I can share with other teachers of cross-cultural texts is the need to tell stories that are only partially referred to in the text because they are the common property of a culture. There are many such stories in *The Clear Light of Day*, and they require explaining to readers who are not acquainted with Indian culture and literature. One cluster of such stories, perhaps the most important since it resonates throughout the text, is woven around the Jumna river and its importance as a holy river as well as the playground of Krishna. It begins very early on in the text. In response to Tara's disappointment at seeing the summer-shrunk Jumna, Bim says:

> "Nothing?" she repeated Tara's judgment. "The holy river Jumna? On whose banks Krishna played his flute and Radha danced?"
>
> "Oh Bim, it is nothing of the sort," Tara dared to say, sure she was being teased. "It's a little trickle of mud with banks of dust on either side."
>
> "'It's where my ashes will be thrown after I'm dead and burnt," Bim said unexpectedly and abruptly. "It is where Mira-masi's ashes were thrown." (24)

There are two major cultural narratives here, and they convey deeply charged messages to a reader familiar with Hinduism and Hindu Indian culture. One refers to the rituals of a Hindu death, the other to Krishna's dancing and flute-playing by the banks of the Jumna and his flirtations with the cowgirls of Vrindavan. The reference to Krishna's and Radha's dancing and adulterous love-making by the banks of Jumna recalls a ubiquitous theme in Hindu Indian culture, which encompasses medieval lyrics by Surdas and Mira, idols of Radha and Krishna in Hindu temples, Indian sculpture and painting, Indian classical and folk music, and, finally, Indian films and film music. The theme, when presented straight, suggests religious ecstasy, sexual freedom, equality of women, pastoral harmony, and an overall feeling of plenitude. As Sudhir Kakar puts it, "In psychological terms, he [Krishna] encourages the individual to identify with an ideal primal self, released from all social and superego constraints. Krishna's promise, like that of Dionysus in ancient Greece, is one of utter freedom and instinctual exhilaration" (142).

Although my students have some idea of Krishna's association with ecstatic dancing and singing, thanks to the popularity of the Hare Krishna cult, in order for them to grasp the novel's utilization of the theme, I have to tell them stories about Krishna's days as a cowherd in Mathura and Vrindavan, particularly the stories about Krishna's dancing and flute-playing and how Radha and the other cowgirls were so mesmerized by them that the moment they heard the flute beckoning them, they left whatever they were doing to join him in his dancing, even at midnight. I cannot, of course, tell them all the stories, given the constraints of class time, but the point I wish to impress on them is the text's utilization of, and its dependence on, the socially shared narratives.

The text, however, inverts these narratives of joyous adulterous love by pointing out their patriarchal underpinnings. While these narratives idealize the explicit sexuality of the Krishna-Radha legend as the allegorical rendering of the pining of a devotee for the incarnate God, Desai's use of the legends brings out their total irrelevance to the lived experience of Indian women. She suggests that dancing and teaching these stylized dances celebrating the love of Radha and Krishna is no exhilarating experience for Jaya and Sarla, the Misra sisters:

> Walking up the Misras' driveway, they [Bim and Tara] could hear instead the sounds of the music and dance lessons that the Misra sisters gave in the evenings after their little nursery school had closed for the day, for it seemed that they never ceased to toil and the pursuit of a living was unending....Bim stood apart, feeling a half-malicious desire to go into the house and watch the two grey-haired, spectacled, middle-aged women—once married but both rejected by their husbands soon after their marriage—giving themselves up to demonstrations of ecstatic song and dance, the songs always Radha's in praise of Krishna, the dance always of Radha pining for Krishna. She hadn't the heart after all....After a while, the teachers, too, emerged on the veranda. They too drooped and perspired and were grey with fatigue. There was nothing remotely amusing about them. (30)

The emphasis on "always" in "the songs always Radha's in praise of Krishna, the dance always of Radha pining for Krishna," brings out the selectiveness and repetitiveness of the thematizations utilized by the classical schools of Indian dancing, which are all heavily focused on the theme of Radha's and Krishna's lovemaking, carried out "always" in terms of Krishna's flirtations and ultimate abandonment of Radha. Desai's questioning of this art form pokes holes in the vocabulary of high seriousness that Indian dance critics employ. Her vocabulary seems to parody the mystical-formalistic mode of dance critics like Ananda Coomaraswamy, Sunil Kothari, and Kapila Vatsyayan whose studies of Indian classical dance have been published in expensive, lavishly illustrated books: "The poor Misra girls, so grey and bony and needle-faced, still prancing through their Radha-Krishna dances and impersonating lovelorn maidens in order to earn their living....Bim shook her head."

As the term "always" had emphasized the frozen-in-time quality of the form, the term "prancing" mocks those who speak of it only in terms like "fluidity," "ecstasy," and "gracefulness." It asks us whether watching and enacting the same theme over and over again does not risk boredom. And it asks us to question the disjunction between the "lovelorn maidens" and the aging Misra sisters who must "impersonate" them in order to make their living. The novel, by giving voice to the plight of these aging and abandoned sisters, sets itself up in antithesis to the art form they must practice despite the fact that it obliterates their own sad realities. Unlike the novel, the dance has no room for women other than "lovelorn maidens."

One can only understand the boldness of this attack if one knows about the discursive idealizations of this dance form in the official cultural discourses of India that occurred under the nationalist project of manufacturing a new cultural identity. Beginning in the 1940s, nationalist cultural critics sanitized the history of India's classical dance forms by renaming the dance as well as writing out of its history the prostitutes and temple dancers (*devdasis*) who made their living by performing these dances for the entertainment of their rich clients. In fact, temple dancing by *devdasis* was outlawed by the passage of a bill in the Madras legislative assembly in 1947 in the name of morality and national honor. The dance was then "revived" under the aegis of "nationalization of Indian art and life and its almost 'religious' idealization...was in no small measure itself an effect of westernization" (Srinivasan, 196).

Supported by huge subsidies from the government and business patrons, India's classical dances were given a new cultural script. Nowadays, India's classical dancers present the eternal love play of Krishna and Radha in opulent concert halls, both at home and abroad. Indian dance critics comment on the "spirituality" of these dances in expensively produced and subsidized hard-cover volumes. Their exalted language hides the inability of the exponents of the dance form to connect and expand their art to encompass the lives of flesh and blood women. Desai's narrative, by bringing out the repetitiveness and frozen-in-time aspect of these dance forms creates a dissonance in the discursive consensus around India's high culture, which speaks of such things as "the attainment of the Infinite," and "absolute bliss in the *Brahman*" (Vatsyayan, 5) but not about day-to-day life and its iniquities.

This idealized view of classical Indian art is further critiqued in the novel in an exchange between Bakul and Bim that occurs only a few paragraphs after the passages quoted earlier:

> Elegantly holding his cigarette in its holder at arm's length, Bakul told them in his ripest, roundest tones, "What I feel is my duty, my vocation, when I am abroad, is to be my country's ambassador....I refuse to talk about famine or drought or caste wars or—or political disputes....I choose to show them and inform them only of the best, the finest."
>
> "The Taj Mahal?" asked Bim.
>
> "Yes, exactly," said Bakul promptly. "The Taj Mahal—the Bhagvad Gita—Indian philosophy—music—art—the great, immortal values of ancient India." (35)

I tell my students that Bakul's view presents the officially sanctioned view of Indian culture—the culture Indian government exhibits at great cost at Indian fairs held in New York and Moscow. It is a view of culture frozen in the past and unable to encompass "famine or drought or caste wars." And it is highly selective. In Susie Tharu's words, this nationalist construction has produced "an almost unbearably tasteful past and an exquisite tradition." In it, "Women are no longer people, but goddess spirits. And as such, not alive or growing, but sculpted by the requirement of the emerging power" (262–63).

Desai's ironic uncovering of this "exquisite tradition" is, for me, the achievement of her text. Against the conflictless high culture's promotion by Bakul, who is appropriately a high-ranking civil servant, the novel uncovers the anguished history of fratricide, of partition, of religious bigotry, of treatment and representation of women, and finally, of the destruction of Islamic Indian culture. Raja's inability to go to Jamia Milia to pursue a degree in Islamic studies and the inability of his sisters to read his verses written in Urdu thematize the deliberate erasure of Islamic culture and Urdu literature in modern India. The Hindu bias in post-independence Indian historiography and Indian literary history are themes that are now being written about in oppositional terms by Muslim writers like Rahi Masoom Raza and Manzoor Ehtesham. Anita Desai's contribution to this oppositional discourse is indeed a gesture of tremendous integrity.

However, this oppositional aspect of the novel will remain inaccessible to my students unless I acquaint them with the politics of language and culture in modern India. Part of my work is done by Attia Hosain's powerful novel *Sunlight on a Broken Column*, which I teach before teaching *Clear Light of Day*. It describes vividly to them the partition of the country on the basis of religion and prepares them for the events and politics narrated in *Clear Light of Day*. Some stories still need to be told by me, however. I tell them about my father's education in English, Persian, and Urdu whereas my mother was educated, like Bim and Tara, in English, Hindi, and Punjabi. I tell them that this was so because of the combined impact of gender and religion. And, finally, I tell them of my own lack of education in Urdu and of the gap it leaves in my knowledge of my past. I tell them of major Indian writers like Prem Chand who wrote in both Hindi and Urdu, and how their Urdu writings have been forgotten.

The text's radical questioning of this forgetting and its intertextualizing of such famous Urdu poets as Zauq, Ghalib, Daag, Hali, and Iqbal can only be appreciated if we know the politics of language in contemporary India. For Canadian students, these aspects of the text, once explained, become illuminative of their own country's struggles around language and culture.

The text, in my classroom, thus, is read as a contested site, as a "dialogic" gesture that supports or opposes the discourses that share the social-cultural space with it. Its language, I insist, is contextualized and its narrative weaves in several other narratives. To read the text, then, is to read the culture, and there is no short cut around it.

Perhaps the best description, for me, of the pedagogical process has been given by Alice Walker in her novel *Meridian*.

Meridian, the protagonist, says, "I imagine good teaching as a circle of earnest people sitting down to ask each other meaningful questions. I don't see it as a handing down of answers" (188). Walker's and Paulo Freire's "Pedagogy of the Question" gave me the idea of asking my students to prepare their seminar presentations around questions that they would ask the class. I tell them that they must take it for granted that many things in the text will not make sense to them and they must question me and the class about those aspects of the text. These questions evoke multiple answers in the form of "perhaps" or "may be" from the class and often end up with my recounting a story, which is really my life history as part of the history of my people.

I will end with one more passage from the novel that appears quite transparent on the surface but is really a deconstructive intertextualization with one of the grand themes of Bengali literature and culture. Dr. Biswas, the Bengali doctor who has been trying to court Bim, unsuccessfully, thinks that her reluctance to marry him is caused by her responsibility for looking after Mira-masi, Raja and Baba:

> "Now I understand why you do not wish to marry. You have dedicated your life to others—to your sick brother and your aged aunt and your little brother who will be dependent on you all his life. You have sacrificed your own life for them." (97)

Desai's heroine, Bim, is shocked "at being so misunderstood, so totally misread" (97). Desai's use of the term, "misread" once again reminds us of the power of social texts. For Dr. Biswas' "misreading" of Bim is informed by scores of Bengali novels and films. The rejection of marriage and love on the part of a young woman for the sake of providing for her family is a perennial theme in Bengali literature and has also been rendered on screen by such talented filmmakers as Ritvik Ghatak in his classic film *Meghe Dhaka Tara*.

On the surface, Bim's predicament appears quite similar to these sacrificing heroines of Indian fiction and Indian cinema who abjure marriage because of family responsibilities, and it is because of the cultural ubiquity of this theme that Dr. Biswas so confidently "misreads" Bim. By making Bim "reject" Dr. Biswas because she considers him a wimp and not because she is burdened by dependent family members, Desai parodies the sacrificial, sentimental heroine popularized by the stalwarts of Bengali fiction and cinema. By creating a heroine who wants autonomy rather than domestic bliss, and having her turn down the Bengali doctor, Desai creates a new script for Indian women at the same time that she mocks the earlier ones. There is perhaps no other heroine in Indian literature(s) who utters words such as Bim's with such emotional force:

> She was looking down, across the lighted, bustling garden to her own house, dark and smouldering with a few dim lights behind the trees, and raised her hands to her hair, lifting it up and letting it fall with a luxuriant, abundant motion. "I shall work—I shall *do* things," she went on, "I shall earn my own living—and look after Mira-masi and Baba and—and be independent. There'll be so many things to do—when we are grown up—when all this is over—" and she swept an arm out over the garden party, dismissing it. "When we are grown up at last—then—then—" but she couldn't finish for emotion, and her eyes shone in the dusk. (141)

While the emotional charge of these words is not hard for my students to understand, surrounded and influenced as they are by feminist theories and feminist activism, they appreciate the text's radical stance even better when they learn about its oppositional intertextuality with the Bengali and Hindi texts about the sacrificing spinster who remains unappreciated by her ungrateful family members and ends up in a sanatorium. By creating a spinster heroine who refuses to be "read" in the framework of these discourses and by refusing to render her, as they do, as the object of pity and guilt, Desai's text engages in a discursive battle with the texts about sentimentalized femininity that continue to be churned out in great numbers in India. The terms of its battle are specific, not universal, just as the constructions of gender and femininity are culture-specific.

My classroom, then, is a place to explore the kind of meanings that a text generates in its place of production. Such an exploration presupposes that human beings, both the author and her/his characters, are social and historical beings, and their subjectivity is formed by their response to their concrete historical situation. To the extent that I focus on the text's relationship with the other discourses and material realities of a society, I steer my students away from the notions of universality as they operate in literary criticism, both in terms of technique and themes. I see my goal as a teacher to be to wean my students away from the ethnocentric universality that unproblematically applies the thought and behavior patterns of a critic's own culture to the rest of humanity, refusing to acknowledge and/or value difference. If I succeed in making my students aware of the universalizing tendencies of Western literary theory, I consider my teaching to have attained its desired goal.

NOTES

1. "Commonwealth/Postcolonial literature" until 1992–93. The 1993–94 calendar has quietly dropped the dual label and adopted the term "Postcolonial literature."

2. "Cultural outsider" and "Cultural insider" are not biological or ascriptive categories for me. To paraphrase Simone de Beauvoir's famous sentence about the process of becoming a woman, one can say that "One is not born a cultural insider but becomes one." Thus, Basil Davidson's work on Africa amply demonstrates his cultural insider status. Having worked for more than twenty years on U. S. and Canadian cultures, I consider myself a cultural insider although I have been denied teaching positions in American Studies because I am not American. From my perspective, anyone, born in whatever cultural or racial group, has the capacity to become a cultural insider. The tragedy, however, is that there are few scholars working on "Postcolonial literatures" who can claim that status. As Aijaz Ahmad says, "[R]are would be...a major literary theorist in Europe or the United States who has ever bothered with an Asian or African language" (5). Michael Sprinker also comments on "our general and shameful ignorance of the native languages themselves—not to mention the cultural, social, and political histories attendant upon specific texts" (59).

3. Rohinton Mistry's *Such a Long Journey* (Toronto: McClelland and Stewart, 1991) has thematized the subterfuges a meateater in India has to resort to because of the vegetarians' intolerance toward meateaters.

WORKS CITED

Ahmad, Aijaz. "Jameson's Rhetoric of Otherness and the 'National Allegory.'" *Social Text* 17 (Fall 1987): 3–25.

Ashcroft, Bill, Gareth Griffiths, and Helen Tiffin. *The Empire Writes Back: Theory and Practice in Post-Colonial Literatures*. London: Routledge, 1989.

Burke, Kenneth. *The Philosophy of Literary Form: Studies in Symbolic Action*. Baton Rouge: Louisiana State University Press, 1967.

Coomaraswamy, Ananda. *The Dance of Shiva: Fourteen Indian Essays*. Bombay: Asia Publishing House, 1948.

Desai, Anita. *Clear Light of Day*. London: Penguin, 1980.

Freire, Paulo. *The Pedagogy of the Oppressed*. New York: Herder and Herder, 1970.

Graff, Gerald. *Professing Literature: An Institutional History*. Chicago: University of Chicago Press, 1987.

Jameson, Fredric. "Third-World Literature in the Era of Multinational Capitalism." *Social Text* 15 (1986): 65–88.

Kakar, Sudhir. *The Inner World: A Psycho-analytic Study of Childhood and Society in India*. 2nd ed. Delhi: Oxford University Press, 1981.

Kothari, Sunil. ed. *Bharatnatyam: Indian Classical Dance Art*. Bombay: Marg Publications, 1982.

McClintock, Anne. "The Angel of Progress: Pitfalls of the Term 'Post-Colonialism.'" *Social Text* 31/32 (1992): 84–98.

Mukherjee, Arun. "The Exclusions of Postcolonial Theory and Mulk Raj Anand's *Untouchable*: A Case Study." *Ariel* 22.3 (July 1991): 27–48.

———. "The Vocabulary of the 'Universal': The Cultural Imperialism of the Universalist Criteria of Western Literary Criticism." *Towards an Aesthetic of Opposition: Essays on Literature, Criticism and Cultural Imperialism*. Stratford, Ontario: Williams-Wallace, 1988, 10–20.

Shohat, Ella. "Notes on the 'Post-Colonial.'" *Social Text* 31/32 (1992): 99–113.

Sprinker, Michael. "Marxism and Nationalism: Ideology and Class Struggle in Premchand's *Godan*." *Social Text* 23 (Fall/Winter 1989): 59–82.

Srinivasan, Amrit. "Reform or Conformity? Temple 'Prostitution' and the Community in Madras Presidency." *Structures of Patriarchy: State, Community and Household in Modernising Asia*. Ed. Bina Agarwal. New Delhi: Kali for Women, 1988, 175–98.

Tharu, Susie. "Tracing Savitri's Pedigree: Victorian Racism and the Image of Women in Indo-Anglian Literature." *Recasting Women: Essays in Colonial History*. Eds. Kumkum Sangari and Sudesh Vaid. New Delhi: Kali for Women, 1989, 254–68.

Vatsyayan, Kapila. *Classical Indian Dance in Literature and the Arts*. New Delhi: Sangeet Natak Akademi, 1977.

Walker, Alice. *Meridian*. New York: Pocket Books, 1976.

Young-Eisendrath, Polly. "The Female Person and How We Talk about Her." *Feminist Thought and the Structure of Knowledge*. Ed. Mary McCanney Gergen. New York: New York University Press, 1988, 152–72.

16

SUSAN GARDNER

"And Here I Am, Telling in Winnebago How I Lived My Life": Teaching Mountain Wolf Woman

> I learned that Indians had a bad rap and that they can write. Big deal!
>
> This course has completely transformed my life, and should be an absolute requirement for graduation.
>
> This literature is my Shakespeare. Neither I nor my writing will ever be the same.

These comments (the third from a Lumbee Indian student), evaluations of my third-year "topics" course—Native North American Indian Literatures: An Introduction—represent the extremes of student response concerning this offering (since 1991) at a mainstream, largely white, southern state university.[1]

At least the course is not, as a department chair at another university pronounced when I proposed teaching it, "eccentric and irrelevant, of no interest to undergraduate teaching." It fulfills three of the six hours of American literature required for English majors, and three of the six hours of the cross-cultural/international requirement for graduation. I may regret instigating the latter, as the course was already fully subscribed when I taught it two semesters back-to-back. (I no longer do so, observing the taboo on storytelling once the ice on the lakes breaks up. An advantage of offering it in fall semester, of course, is that students come to regard Columbus Day and Thanksgiving differently—whether critically or defensively—and have the opportunity to visit local pow-wows.) My heart sank the first two times around, as I entered a classroom crammed to its capacity of forty and more, with some students on the floor and others perched in windowsills, and with waiting lists making worse-than-usual havoc of any order until drop-add. Nothing could be less characteristic of traditional Native pedagogy: learning through observation, mimesis, repetition, and participation. Some students, I was soon to learn, anticipated an easy, exotic semester: Crystals, Drums, and Beads 101.

Using *Mountain Wolf Woman, Sister of Crashing Thunder* as my example, I wish to discuss some difficulties—not to say perils—when non-Indians attempt "teaching" American Indian materials. For those of us formed by the traditional Western canon (or, for that matter, coming to Native studies as I did, after some years of immersion in feminist and postcolonial theories), a major retooling is imperative if we are not to misread and, therefore, misrepresent Native texts.

Yet within the context of this particular volume it must seem at most absurd, and at least inappropriate, to discuss a text which I regard as neither postcolonial nor (as far as the narrator's intentions were concerned) "literary." But when I was hired to teach at the University of North Carolina at Charlotte (UNCC), my brief was to introduce "Third World" literatures, *including* American Indian. "Third World" impressed me as condescending—can any so-called "Third World" country eventually achieve "First World" status?—not to mention irrelevant, as the "Second World" was then tumbling down. Besides, I wondered, if any worlds are "first," surely they are those of indigenous peoples? Do "Third World" people think of themselves as "marginal," "ex-centric," "peripheral," "Other"?[2] What was I really being asked to teach?

I thus changed my job description to "Postcolonial and American Indian Literatures," reflecting a not yet wholly articulated sense that American Indian literatures are *not, cannot* be, "postcolonial," an issue I discuss below. What I didn't expect was that I would eventually question whether some literatures conventionally accepted as such are "postcolonial," either.

Several American Indian scholars reject "postcolonial" as an adequate description of Native American literary output. Jack Forbes (Renape, Lenape, and Sapori), for instance, regards most contemporary Native writing, even by such recognized figures as Leslie Marmon Silko (Laguna Pueblo), N. Scott Momaday (Kiowa), James Welch (Blackfeet), and Paula Gunn Allen (Laguna/Sioux), "as a colonized and submerged literature. *Even the oral segments of the literature are impacted by colonialism*" (22; my emphasis). To be authentically Native American requires that a piece of literature have not only a Native writer, but a predominantly Native *audience.* Instead, Forbes asserts, the audience for contemporary American Indian literature consists of readers and citizens of a "mature colonialism," which is to say a mainstream/Euramerican one. Such readers prefer:

> nostalgic, romantic works which falsify or distort the colonial situation and which depict the Native people as simple victims of alcoholism, poverty, or personal alienation. The dominant elites in the Americas can tolerate novels about Indian poverty and personal drama so long as it appears that the oppression depicted is not a concrete result of an entire system of relationships. (20)[3]

One of the most vehement Native critics of the term "post-colonial," Thomas King, ringingly refuses to use it:

> While post-colonialism purports to be a method by which we can begin to look at those literatures...formed out of the struggle of the oppressed against the oppressor, the colonized and the colonizer, the term itself assumes that the starting point for that discussion is the advent of Europeans in North America. At the same time, the term organizes the literature progressively suggesting that there is both progress and improvement. No less distressing, it also assumes that the struggle between guardian and ward is the catalyst for contemporary Native literature, providing those of us who write with method and topic. And, worst of all, the idea of post-colonial writing effectively cuts us off from our traditions...traditions which have come down to us through our cultures in spite of colonization, and it supposes that contemporary Native writing is largely a construct of oppression. Ironically enough, while the term itself—post-colonial—strives to escape to find new centres, it remains, in the end, a hostage to nationalism. (11–12)

He concludes: "[I] cannot let post-colonial stand—particularly as a term—for, at its heart, it is an act of imagination and an act of imperialism that demands that I imagine myself as something I did not choose to be, as something I would not choose to become" (16).

Intellectuals from regions more commonly regarded as "post-colonial" also do not endorse the term, for varied reasons. For Ghanaian Kwame Anthony Appiah, "All aspects of contemporary African cultural life...have been influenced, often powerfully, by the transition of African societies through colonialism, but they are not in the relevant sense *post*colonial." *Post*coloniality is "the condition of what we might ungenerously call a *comprador* intelligentsia: a relatively small, Western-style, Western-trained group of writers and thinkers, who mediate the trade in cultural commodities of world capitalism at the periphery. In the West they are known through the Africa they offer" (348). For Arun P. Mukherjee:

> [Postcolonial] theory insists that the subjectivity of post-colonial cultures is inextricably tied to their erstwhile occupiers. It claims that we do nothing but search for or mourn the loss of our authentic pre-colonial identities or continuously resist the encroachment of the colonizers to our cultural space....[But] our cultural productions are created in response to our own needs. (5–6)

To my mind, if American Indian literatures are to be associated with others, a more relevant comparison is with indigenous verbal art (oral or textual) in other former colonies of (in this instance) anglophone settlement: Australia, New Zealand, South Africa, Canada. As a brief illustration, consider some similarities between American Indian and black South African literatures.

My impetus for this comparison may seem fortuitous; coincidence (which may not be accidental at all) sometimes does. Having lived in South Africa for some years, on my first day back in the United States I was walking down Wisconsin Avenue in Milwaukee. A plaque on a hotel wall caught my attention: the site, it was blandly stated, had originally been occupied by a Potowatami village, but in 1838 the inhabitants had been "removed" west of the Mississippi by the federal government.

"Removed," of course, is one of the most sinister words in the apartheid lexicon, and denotes much the same process of enforced dispossession and internal diaspora, including the brutal displacement of peoples into areas of the Western nation-state not native to them. Structurally, I realized, American Indians and black South Africans are equivalent groups. Historically, their identity has not been that which they ascribed to themselves, but defined by the European state in terms of blood quantum and paperwork.[4] How very different, I wondered, are 1620 and 1652, Plymouth Rock and the Castle? South African "homelands" and reservations? Colonial warfare/resistance waged to regain the land? "Kaffir" wars as opposed to "King Philip's War" or Pontiac's "rebellion"?

The beginnings of both literatures in English were near-strangulated by the censorship of missionary presses. Repressive schooling in both cases inadvertently created a pan-tribal and, indeed, pan-continental awareness, as well as a shared (colonial) language, although both retain a concept of the author as communal storyteller. And Forbes' description of the dependency of American Indian literatures applies also to black South African literature. Neither is "the literature of a people who have been able to evolve slowly, gradually absorbing alien elements." Neither is "the literature of a people who have possessed ownership of printing presses, magazines, newspapers, bookstores, radio stations...(until very recently and only partially even now)." Neither is "the literature of a people who have been able to control a national territory with statutory laws to protect an indigenous communications system." Neither is "the literature of a people secure in their racial pride and comfortable with their self-identity." Neither is "the literature of a people whose creative persons can make a living by selling their products to people of their own culture and nationality" (19).

There are, of course, differences. The most obvious is demographic: black South Africans are the majority of South Africans, American Indians are the smallest—although fast-growing—"minority" of Americans, about 1½ percent of the population. Due to the racialized character of South African capitalism, moreover, black South African literature is more urban and class-conscious, as well as more militant: the American Indian Movement in its present state can hardly be compared to the African National Congress or Inkhata. To borrow Abdul JanMohamed's distinction, South African colonialism has been "dominant" (overt), the U.S. variant "hegemonic" (covert): colonialism, in other words, is not homogeneous, and is differently experienced, but historical study reveals the United States only too clearly as also internally imperialist. The bland term "multicultural," subsuming Native American cultures, mystifies and occludes the colonial origin of their contemporary voices in English. Although universities in the United States, South Africa, Canada, and Australasia are among the significant generators of postcolonial theories, scholars often inadequately conceptualize and contextualize the literatures within their own national frontiers, failing to address the imperialist origins and continuing implications of our own institutional and personal positions.

Salman Rushdie, arguing for the dismissal of the term "Commonwealth literature" (the precursor of "postcolonial"), envisages a different comparative world literature in English: "It is possible,

I think, to begin to theorize common factors between writers from these societies—poor countries, or deprived minorities in powerful countries—and to say that much of what is new in world literature comes from this group. This seems to me...a 'real' theory, bounded by frontiers which are neither political nor linguistic but imaginative" (69). "Postcolonial," using political sovereignty as its benchmark, cannot apply to U.S. ethnic "minority" literatures, whether native or immigrant. I've also suggested that it may be challenged as an accurate, meaningful term for societies with formal ("flag") independence insofar as they remain intellectually and economically bound to their former colonizers. Once I run out of the thousands of business cards that the university demands (but does not pay for!) as a minimum order, I'll probably change my title yet again, this time to "indigenous world literatures," saving caveats, qualifications, and distinctions for whatever "native" cultural group is under study, and challenging the so-called "major" world literatures to define, rather than to assume, their standing for a change.

As both a Euramerican and a member of the academy, I have various qualms about what I teach (while, paradoxically, my institution urges me to teach more such, so that in 1994 I offered the first graduate course throughout the sixteen-campus North Carolina system on American Indian literature—a theory-intensive study of Native North American Indian "autobiography," with a fieldwork component, interviewing local Indian people over 80 for the American Indian Heritage Council of Charlotte and the North Carolina Indian Cultural Center in Pembroke). Or, perhaps more precisely, *how* I teach what I teach. Paula Gunn Allen calls for instructors "to present [American Indian] literatures as they were intended to appear to the primary audience" (xii)—meaning, I assume, the traditional oral literatures, and, therefore, an impossible brief. But even when teaching bicultural texts (narrated by a Native and transcribed, translated, edited, and contorted to form a European narrative), or the most contemporary literature, it is easy to run afoul.

Although I focus here on a single text, *Mountain Wolf Woman, Sister of Crashing Thunder*, many of the teaching strategies I have adopted in the undergraduate course apply to other American Indian texts, particularly when taught by non-Indians to non-Indians. I am not advocating academic apartheid, by which *only* members of the culture being studied are able to teach about it: an outsider's view, *self-recognized as such*, can provide perspectives beyond the purview of some insiders. I agree with Edward Said that "On its own, ethnic particularity does not provide for intellectual process—quite the contrary" (183), and with JanMohamed and David Lloyd that "a rigorously critical minority discourse...should not merely fall back on the oppositional affirmation of an essential ethnic or gender identity" (16). But I do urge that we non-Natives examine our motivations, acknowledge our shortcomings and biases, and *never* presume to "teach the Other" without respect and a great deal of cultural and historical information, as well as seeking guidance from the People. Otherwise our teaching is patronizing and exploitative.[5]

Mountain Wolf Woman enjoys an unusual popularity for academic texts. It has been continuously in print since 1961, no doubt due to the upsurge of interest in American Indian studies and women's studies. Originally its editor, anthropologist Nancy Lurie, thought that an autobiography by her adoptive aunt Stella would be interesting in itself and, as the subtitle indicates, as a gender-specific comparison with the autobiography of Mountain Wolf Woman's (MWW) brother Crashing Thunder produced by Paul Radin. By classifying them as "autobiography," a familiar genre with which young people identify readily, we make these texts seem more easily accessible than they are.

For neither of these is an autobiography in such a conventional Western sense as "confessional in form, exploring the inner labyrinth of the psyche, recording the emotional vibrations of the writer as well as the cultural milieu, documenting historic events and the autobiographer's relationships with members of society, encompassing both the inner and public lives of the subject over a lengthy period of time" (Bataille and Sands, 4). David Brumble does claim in *American Indian Autobiography* that Sam Blowsnake ("Crashing Thunder") produced a parallel to the conversion narrative of St. Augustine. It most certainly is an account of salvation, but with Radin's heavy editorial control, Blowsnake's contribution is difficult to assess. Radin described it as a "rake's progress" and compared Blowsnake to Candide. Such an imposition of Western categories on a non-Western text is understandable, but also misleading. Thanks to Arnold Krupat's detailed study in *For Those Who Come After* of many nineteenth- and early twentieth-century American Indian autobiographies as "original, bi-cultural composite composition," the complexities of rendering an "authentic" Indian voice can be understood as another process whereby Western culture appropriates "the other" on its own terms, domesticating it.

Bataille and Sands, in *American Indian Women Telling Their Lives*, do accept Mountain Wolf Woman's narrative as "literary," by which they mean techniques usually associated with Western textual aesthetics: "dialogue, expression of inner emotions and responses to events, a first-person omniscient viewpoint, latitude in handling time and sequence of events, and an awareness of audience" (11). But such techniques are not limited to self-consciously "literary" artifacts, and *MWW* most certainly is not one. When MWW narrated in Winnebago what she thought was her complete story, which Lurie then asked a grandniece of MWW's to translate into English, Lurie was very disappointed. MWW used no more than a half reel of tape, and this version is included as appendix A in Lurie's edited version. I suggest having students read this appendix first, to appreciate, once reading the preceding edited narrative (expanded both chronologically and thematically), how Lurie transformed her aunt's seemingly random and schematic recollections (which to MWW, of course, were not) into a form familiar to Western readers.

Unlike many previous bicultural composers, Lurie makes no claims of having little influence on her subject's story. Unlike Radin, who borrowed from other narratives by Crashing Thunder (CT), including some which may not even be by him but reflect Radin's understanding of Winnebago (male) culture over many years, Lurie scrupulously sets out her own methodology and motivation. CT's narrative (one of them, at least) was *written* in a Winnebago syllabary by CT for pay, whereas MWW *told* her story as a favor to her niece. Lurie meticulously outlines every step, and employs extensive notes to add information for us that MWW assumed, correctly, any Winnebago relative—such as her adoptive niece—would understand. The narrator's intended audience, then, is Winnebago, not us. In a sense, we eavesdrop on a private conversation.

One result of Lurie's and MWW's collaboration is, as David Murray has commented in *Forked Tongues*:

> [a] typical multi-layered sandwich, where we are given a foreword, a preface, the text with extensive footnotes, then the first brief version of her life given by MWW, which she extended when she saw Lurie's disappointment—indicating the role of white expectations in the creation of such texts....At several points Lurie refers to "literary" and "scholarly" criteria which decided the style of the English version. Unfortunately [and rather like Bataille and Sands] she never develops what she means by these terms, and when we look at all of the layers of

> the "sandwich," questions of authenticity [and, I would amplify, "authorship"] become even more confusing. What role...does a letter from MWW, written in non-standard English...play in the combination of voices?...We are offered either her poor written English—which leaves us at a distance from her "real" voice, though it is her own actual product—or a translation of her speaking Winnebago which uses all the (white) literary and scholarly resources available to recreate a sense of her real presence and speech. (74–75)

However, rather than a static sandwich (in which MWW's contribution in English would represent a dab of mustard), what we have is a plurivocal, indeed intervocal text that does not pretend to answer, only to raise, issues of cultural translation. This is hardly a feature of American Indian texts alone, but exploring Krupat's principle of original, bicultural composition encourages students to ponder Western notions of "authorship"/ ownership:

> The author-ity of the author, in the [European] view, derives not from his predecessors and their productions, nor from his contemporaries and theirs, but, instead, from his personality, his imagination, or, arriving at the ultimate mystification, from his individual genius which transcends the society that would seek to contain it. This particular mythology never developed in Native America, where the individual who spoke for himself spoke, therefore, for no one else. (*For Those Who Come After*, 12)

Comparing MWW's two narratives reveals several constant themes in her life (and other Winnebagoes'): her frequent travel is to visit a wide network of kin separated by various federal policies, and to search for work. She also develops a syncretically satisfying spirituality during a time of drastic change. (As with *Black Elk Speaks*, students, especially with backgrounds of Southern evangelical fundamentalism, find it initially difficult to understand this: MWW's calm acceptance of traditional Winnebago, Christian, and peyote beliefs baffles some of them). Both versions start with "Mother" (not with "I") and both show her own satisfaction as mother, wife, and provider. She is no proto-feminist, and women's studies courses will properly teach her narrative as an illustration of non-Western gender arrangements.[6]

In the following, I give some of the techniques I have worked out to alleviate tokenistic, ghettoizing teaching, but without any illusion that I have achieved much change except in interstices of an institutional structure that remains, basically, hierarchical and hegemonic.[7] In both American Indian courses, interaction with members of the cultures being "taught" is built in, as are forms of community service such as internships (for academic credit) with the Coordinator of Indian Education Programs at the Charlotte-Mecklenburg Public Schools (helping her with administrative work or mentoring at-risk Indian schoolchildren) and the Indian Parents' Committee (helping to produce their newsletter and to host community events) or presentations at schools K–12, sharing some of what my students have learned. Panels of locally available Indian people (teachers, scientists, social workers, an assistant chief, a tribal attorney; Lumbees, Catawbas, Cherokees, Lakotas, and Gros Ventre, a group of teen-aged Lakota drummers) join us for discussion followed by an American Indian cook-in; students attend pow-wows and conferences. Thus they have no opportunity to divorce the classroom content from contemporary social realities for, at least, Indian professional people. Yet I realize that both the Indian participation and my students' "giving back" in the form of community service are symbolic at best, although both are aspects of the course that students really enjoy: "I liked the combination of literature and film lab to get a closer insight into Indian life. Our evening spent with Indian guests and our dinner made the course not only a college class but a chance to get to know the human beings behind it."

Students involved in certain internships, such as the "Read Aloud" program, which involves finding, evaluating, and reading culturally relevant/sensitive materials to Indian elementary- and middle-school children, have also had to fight some battles. In one case, the principal of an elementary school allowed a student to visit her reading partner twice a week for 20 minutes, on a sofa in an open corridor. Another principal resented a student arranging free breakfast for those in her Read Aloud group, even though none of the funding came from his budget. He equally opposed, but eventually without success, a free excursion for Indian parents and children to a local hands-on science museum. But greater numbers of my students show interest in such activities than actually perform them: such commitments are time-consuming, requiring considerable dedication.

As I involved Indian people in the course planning and implementation, hoping to mitigate (though I cannot eliminate) my role as "authority," my guest-speakers were once dismissed by a colleague as "Uncle Toms and cigarstore Indians." This was profoundly insulting, less to myself than to my Indian colleagues, who are, after all, fully capable of making their own decisions. They understand the elitist university framework for what it is (several of them have completed higher degrees at UNCC), yet utilize the chance to address its audiences/fora. The days of "native informants" and collaborators are over. My guest-friends simply feel, as I do, that complete separation from the mainstream/malestream is not possible, and try to influence institutions through their politic participation within them.

Not for a moment, though, do any of us think curricular change equals social change, or will guarantee it. As Jonathan Jansen argues from a South African context: "Curricular change is more a reflector than a generator of social change or development" (330). Instead, and as he argues, we are more likely providing for the "maintenance of the status quo through incremental changes in existing curricula" (327), as long as other teaching remains largely unaffected.

bell hooks has similarly noted the dangers facing feminist pedagogy: "the mechanisms of appropriation within white-supremacist, capitalist patriarchy are able to co-opt with tremendous ease that which appears merely radical or subversive.... Within [the corporate university's] walls, I have tried to teach literature and Women's Studies courses in a way that does not reinforce structures of domination: imperialism, racism, sexism, and class exploitation" (51, 101). As she warns readers in a number of essays, this may lead to harsh student and peer evaluations. Those who do try to redefine our pedagogy as well as our course content often find ourselves regarded as more activist than scholarly (an opposition only monocentric, "masculinear" thinking could devise) although my South African experiences had taught me the impossibility of separating the two. For, "Committed research and scholarship...must eschew neutrality and detachment where the human condition demands drastic amelioration—a scholarship that is catalytic and cathartic is imperative" (Nkomo, 303).

For pedagogy as well—to borrow from Spivak—"The real task here is to displace and undo that killing opposition between the text narrowly conceived as the verbal text and activism narrowly conceived as some kind of mindless engagement" (120–21). Clearly, what is at issue here is "objectivity" itself; I would argue that a course *about* contemporary peoples not one's own cannot *be* "objective" unless accompanied by involvement *with* them.

In this process of redefining collegiality, and the more I explored the paradox of a non-Indian "teaching" Native materials to a mostly non-Indian audience, I also began to conceive of my audience (more properly, audiences) differently. Students, of course; the tenure and promotion audience, necessarily; but the extra-university audience must include members of the communities whose cultures are being "taught." I am, above all, accountable to them. They are not specimens, and cannot be dissected. They must know who I am, where I'm coming from, and what I'm doing. I do not want to be the literary counterpart of an archaeologist colleague who offered credit for a dig in Cherokee country without consulting with the local Cherokees. In short, I want neither my scholarship nor my career to be at others' expense.

(A few) Euramerican colleagues assumed that my close association with the local and state Indian communities meant that I was in their pay (only people knowing nothing about Indians could make that assumption!). My (invited) participation in Indian activities (conferences, workshops, celebrations) meant a loss of professional neutrality: surely I was being censored? It took some time, at least two years, before I could convince those who mattered—the review committee, in other words—that my involvement was not "community service" but a dialogic relationship with my peers (many of whom I began to consider as my elders). With the hindsight of several years, I now realize that my *alliances* with Indian people were perceived as *identification*, which therefore made me seem untrustworthy, a dissident daughter of the white patriarchy. Which I am! But dissent is not the same as rejecting one's home culture, or annexing the struggles of others.

Similarly, it took a while to redefine other relationships "within the profession," such as funding projects carried out on a reservation as research or course development, and convincing peers that such activity is as "scholarly" and significant as that of a colleague studying, say, Beckett manuscripts at Trinity College in Dublin. Multicultural teaching of indigenous materials may well lead the scholar along centripetal, not centrifugal by-ways. For just as I felt my courses must have links to the local and statewide Indian communities, it seemed that there must also be a relationship with a reservation; in which case, I had to establish one. During the summers of 1992 and 1993, the university awarded me a curriculum and instruction development grant to attend the Lakota Cultural Studies Summer Institute at Oglala Lakota College, Pine Ridge reservation—and that changed everything, irrevocably. My course was given a focus it had lacked—how is one to teach, in fifteen weeks, hundreds of centuries of oral traditions, and contemporary American Indian literature, without grossly simplifying and homogenizing? This is as impossible as it is marginalizing, ghettoizing.[8]

From now on, then, I am going to "teach" whatever group(s) I have learned about the most, from the People themselves. The courses at Oglala Lakota College in oral traditions, music, games, rituals, gender roles, and ethnobotany, and the visits to sacred and historical sites in four surrounding states, made the Lakota materials I had already read leap from the page. I returned, not really capable of "assuming the subject position of the Other" (121), which Spivak exhorts of those possessing hegemonic discourse, but capable of apprehending what it is like. I yearned for my students to have a similar opportunity, and am now working on various arrangements by which they could attend the summer institute for academic credit at UNCC (independent study, as a continuing education course, attending the Summer Institute as an elective, a co-op or summer internship with the Office of Experiential Learning, national student exchange).

One of the most important goals of the courses is for students to gain some, however limited, experience in non-Western reading. It is hard to relinquish such concepts as the tragic (usually male) hero, protagonist and antagonist, or linear plot with a clear conclusion. But students learn how encoded (rather than "obvious," "natural") Western literary criteria are. Thus, through learning to read American Indian narratives, students can realize that many of the world's indigenous tales have no clear-cut ending or beginning, are not arranged around conflict, climax, and individual achievement, and are told by narrators for whom quality of performance matters more than originality of conception.

Most interesting has been the disruption of the process I call "I-dentification," by which students find themselves reflected in characters. One gets weary of the predictable, subjectivist comment, "For me personally...." Here, solipsism masquerading as critical response is not possible: students are obligated to focus on how a story works to achieve meaning—a meaning not necessarily evident or transparent. This, of course, should be true of any literary criticism, but more difficult to impart when the texts are from the students' own cultural heritage.

Sooner or later the twin issues of white shamanism and white guilt surface, along with such comments as: "Of course they should get their land back, but not my front yard!" and the inevitable "I'm not responsible for what my ancestors did." (The first few class sessions demystify the predictable Cherokee "princess" in the background: one in five black Southerners, and one in ten whites, has a Native ancestor, so there is nothing particularly extraordinary about it. Romanticism isn't difficult to deal with, but exploitation is: several feel entitled to state or federal scholarships because they "are Indian," which of course is not the case.) I explain Adrienne Rich's distinction between guilt and accountability—the former paralyzing, the latter enabling—and use myself as an example: No, I'm not responsible for my great-great-great grandfather the Indian fighter, nor for the fact that the deeds to my parents' yard clearly demonstrate its extortion from Indians during Polk's presidency. But I have benefited every day of my life—indeed, in the womb and before—from "what my ancestors did" (or failed to do, or ignored): I owe my health, education, global travels, profession—my very presence in our classroom—to privilege wrested from others' oppression.

This doesn't necessarily work—a white professor, particularly a female one, can again be seen as a traitor rather than a mediator. But a number of my students become ponderous bores to their friends and families, and the Director of Under-Graduate Studies assures me that the community service component, far from alienating students, has touched a vein of idealism neither he nor I expected.[9] This is nice, I guess (so long as students don't regard themselves as "helping" Indians to surmount their "plight"), but it isn't the primary aim of my teaching, which is informed consciousness-raising, not missionary work. Similarly, my conception of multiculturalism is that it is a life-work, a process of recovery, a progress towards humanistic sanity.

As I've observed the early stages of multicultural teaching at my university, I understand that it has offered me unparalleled opportunities within a network of painful contradictions. Not that UNCC stands out in this regard: rather, mainstream universities have historically been *mono*versities where cultural differences have been tolerated on condition that they were elective (i.e., don't "count for anything," are a luxury), rather than transforming the entire curriculum, so that we might finally be teaching in "pluriversities."

So far, the structures have resisted struggle, fearing their demolition rather than the liberation for *everyone* that multicultural teaching intends. There are bad (often unintentionally comic) days, when I read in a journal entry that "General Custard was defeated by the LaQuotas at Little Knee" (in the same vein, "Toni Morrison won the Nobel Prize for *Uncle Tom's Cabin*").

Pondering some Euramerican students' downright refusal (coupled with repelled fascination) to admit any Indian viewpoint, I used to agree entirely with (Cherokee) Louis Owens' insight: "[A]t the heart of America's history of Indian hating is an unmistakable yearning to *be* Indian" (3). In many cases this is probably true, but at this stage, having taught the undergraduate course four times, I conclude rather less elegantly: For Euramericans to remain comfortable with themselves, Indian people must be viewed in certain ways only. If that is the case, then my teaching is not really about Native America: it is about our fragile, conflict-ridden, haunted selves.

NOTES

1. For stylistic reasons, I'll use "American Indian," "Indian," "Native American," and "Native" interchangeably, although the correct usage is to refer to Indian peoples by the affiliations they use to name themselves.

2. Trinh T. Minh-ha asserts in *Woman Native Other*: "To survive, 'Third World' must necessarily have negative *and* positive connotations: negative when viewed in a vertical ranking system—'under-developed' as compared to over-industrialized...and positive when understood sociopolitically as a subversive, 'non-aligned' force. Whether 'Third World' sounds negative or positive also depends on *who* uses it. Coming from you Westerners, that word can hardly mean the same as when it comes from Us members of the Third World" (97–99).

3. Blackfeet novelist James Welch describes the U.S. audience for American Indian writing as "quite small...and quite ineffectual; a few university professors, a few people...interested in Indians...not a large audience [and] a very nonpowerful audience" (196). Forbes further reminds us: "Few Indians, aside from university students, have probably ever seen most of the novels produced by these writers, let alone read them. Of necessity, Native writers producing novels have to write them in such a way that they will be attracted to an English-language audience which is predominantly non-Indian" (22).

Others may share my dispiriting experiences: a Euramerican lay public usually asks, "Are there any Indians left? I didn't know they wrote!" whereas Native colleagues and students usually ask me to recommend an imaginative work. What educational experiences would have exposed either group to the traditional or contemporary literatures? Since many of my Native acquaintances are urban, professionals, and community activists, they have little time to read for pleasure. My familiarity with the literature, and the literary research, results from race and class privilege; a Wisconsin Chippewa woman, raised in an orphanage cum boarding school, once asked me to recommend books by or about Chippewas, "so that I can learn who I am."

4. In emphasizing structural dependency, I do not mean to imply that black South Africans or American Indians have no sense of identity other than those legislated by their colonizers. Many American Indian groups are sovereign nations in international law, and the political rhetoric of Inkhata, for example, is based—however dubiously—upon a legitimating identification with precolonial Zulu "nationalism."

5. Student opinion on this matter of cross-cultural teaching is contradictory. Almost all, African-American or Euramerican, can give instances of teachers who, for them, crossed borders without transgressing: an African-American teacher of French, or of Shakespeare, for example. Matters become trickier when I ask if they would be comfortable with an American Indian professor. Most are too polite to intimate their present instructor is anything but fine: "Our instructor made us aware of her shortcomings at every step, but I did not feel uncomfortable with her." But some indicate anxieties: perhaps, "like" Asian teaching assistants, the Native professor would not speak English very well (!); or, more ominously, perhaps such a class would resemble African-American studies classes, where Euramericans feel "discriminated against." A Native American literature course in such circumstances—where I've never had more than one Indian student per semester, if any (though I have plenty of wannabes)—owes its popularity in no small part to its apparently nonthreatening character.

6. A video is available from a freelance producer (Jocelyn Riley, Her Own Words, P.O. Box 5264, Madison, WI 53705) in which MWW's granddaughter ("who sounds much like her," Lurie writes) narrates sections of the text; a teaching guide is also available. The seventeen-minute video, ISBN 1-877933, © 1990, costs $95, and the teaching guide, $20.

7. These include a mandatory film lab, faithfully attended, much to my astonishment, on Friday afternoons! The idea was my students', who came to realize how much of their previous "knowledge" of Indians was pure Hollywood. Whenever available I include Native responses to contemporary films. Some appear on electronic mail networks such as NativeNet. I also supply film assessment guidelines. The changes in representation when Indians portray themselves and produce their own films is of course enormous, and thus teaches students how to analyze the rhetoric of social "texts," not just printed artifacts.

Another feature is a topic recurrent throughout the semester in their journals: their observations of brand/marketing names (such as the odiously named Crazy Horse malt liquor, "Sundance" flavored waters, Red Man tobacco, Land O' Lakes butter, collector plates of the "Little Princess" and "Vanishing Indian" stereotypes, postage stamps of conquered heroes, and cars and helicopters too numerous to mention here). This intends to show them how a culture can be commodified, reified, and fetishized by its conquerors. A useful counter-stereotypical exercise has been to ask—in journals and in the classroom—what words immediately come to mind (positive or negative, it doesn't matter) when they hear the words, "American Indian"? We repeat this exercise at semester's end, and I am pleased when some students reject the term "American Indian" altogether, using instead "Lakota people," or "Cherokee people."

8. Cf. Arun P. Mukherjee: "I think those of us who teach 'post-colonial' literatures...should point out the absurdity of our being saddled with the responsibility of teaching about two-thirds of the world that our institutional position forces us into" (7).

9. One year nearly a quarter of the students were African-Americans, far better equipped to understand militant rage and protest. One of the most satisfying achievements, in the racially polarized South, is to create a classroom where neither group, for once, is at odds with the other. I often start the course with a reading from *Black Issues in Higher Education* comparing Indians and African-Americans as "minorities." Evaluations from black students have been very positive: "The course helped me break down my own personal stereotypes of Indians. In all actuality, it helped me to realize that I had them."

WORKS CITED

Allen, Paula Gunn. *Studies in American Indian Literatures.* New York: MLA, 1983.

Appiah, Kwame Anthony. "Is the Post- in Postmodernism the Post- in Postcolonial?" *Critical Inquiry* 17 (Winter 1991): 336–57.

Bataille, Gretchen, and Kathleen Mullen Sands. *American Indian Women: Telling Their Lives.* Lincoln: University of Nebraska Press, 1984.

Brumble, H. David III. *American Indian Autobiography.* Berkeley: University of California Press, 1990 [1988].

Forbes, Jack. "Colonialism and Native American Literature: An Analysis." *Wicazo Sa Review* 3.2 (1987): 17–23.

Hooks, Bell. *Talking Back: Thinking Feminist, Thinking Black.* Boston: South End Press, 1989.

JanMohamed, Abdul R., and David Lloyd, eds. *The Nature and Context of Minority Discourse.* New York: Oxford University Press, 1990.

Jansen, Jonathan. "Curriculum in a Post-Apartheid Dispensation." Nkomo, *Pedagogy of Domination,* 325–39.

King, Thomas. "Godzilla vs. Post-Colonial." *World Literature Written in English* 30.2 (1990): 10–16.

Krupat, Arnold. *For Those Who Come After: A Study of Native American Autobiography*. Berkeley: University of California Press, 1985.

———. *The Voice in the Margin: Native American Literature and the Canon.* Berkeley: University of California Press, 1989.

Lurie, Nancy Oestreich, ed. *Mountain Wolf Woman, Sister of Crashing Thunder: The Autobiography of a Winnebago Indian*. Ann Arbor: University of Michigan Press, 1990 [1961].

Mukherjee, Arun P. "Whose Post-Colonialism and Whose Post-Modernism?" *World Literature Written in English* 30.2 (1990): 1–9.

Murray, David. *Forked Tongues: Speech, Writing and Representation in North American Indian Texts*. Bloomington: Indiana University Press, 1991.

Nkomo, Mokubung. "Post-Apartheid Education: Preliminary Reflections." Nkomo, *Pedagogy of Domination*, 291–323.

———, ed. *Pedagogy of Domination: Toward a Democratic Education in South Africa.* Trenton: Africa World Press, 1990.

O'Brien, Eileen M. "Isolation Leads to Little Conflict Between Indians, Other Minorities." *Black Issues in Higher Education* 7.20 (6 December 1990): 1, 20–25.

Owens, Louis. *Other Destinies: Understanding the American Indian Novel.* Norman: University of Oklahoma Press, 1992.

Radin, Paul, ed. *Crashing Thunder: The Autobiography of an American Indian.* Foreword and appendix by Arnold Krupat. Native American Autobiography. Ed. H. David Brumble III and Arnold Krupat. Lincoln: UNE Bison Books, 1983 [1926].

Rushdie, Salman. "'Commonwealth Literature' Does Not Exist." *Imaginary Homelands: Essays and Criticism 1981–1991*. London: Granta/ Viking, 1991.

Said, Edward W. "The Politics of Knowledge." *Raritan* 11.1 (Summer 1991): 17–31.

Spivak, Gayatri Chakravorty. *The Post-Colonial Critic.* Ed. Sarah Harasym. New York: Routledge, 1990.

Trinh T. Minh-ha. *Woman, Native, Other: Writing Postcoloniality and Feminism.* Bloomington: Indiana University Press, 1989.

Wong, Hertha Dawn. *Sending My Heart Back Across the Years: Tradition and Innovation in Native American Autobiography*. New York: Oxford University Press, 1992.

17

DEREK WRIGHT

Parenting the Nation: Some Observations on Nuruddin Farah's *Maps*

Perhaps the most startling and unforeseen consequences of the recent breakup of Central and Eastern Europe have been the release of resurgent micronationalisms and a reversion to absolutist ideas of the "ethnic nation": ideas that have habitually taken uncharitable views of "migrant" or "minority" cultures. No doubt, as the whole concept of "Soviet literature" is gradually displaced, questions of national identity—Ukrainian, Kazakhstani, Azerbaijani—will be drawn up along exclusive ethnic, cultural, and religious lines as alternatives to those framed by political ideology and legated by Soviet imperialism. In fact, something much like this has already happened in another part of the world—on the African continent, where tribal nationalisms have long overridden the constructs of political geography, and African literature has recorded the process in some spectacular examples. The fiction of the Somali writer Nuruddin Farah is a nomadic fiction, drawing upon many cultural and religious sources and upon readings in many of the world's literatures. It is a living testament to the cultural mongrelization which has become a standard feature of the colonial and postcolonial world, and his strange novel of the 1976 war in the Ogaden, *Maps*, dramatizes the resistance to this phenomenon by resurrected ethnocentrisms. In this short article I propose to review Farah's treatment of the latter resistive process and the implications of cultural exclusiveness for his handling of personal, national, and sexual identity.

Maps is the story of Askar, an orphaned Somali child of the disputed Ogaden, and his shifting relationship with his adoptive mother Misra, an Oromo woman from the Ethiopian Highlands who is doubtfully accused of betraying the Somali army to the forces of her homeland during Ethiopia's reconquest of the Ogaden and is murdered by the Western Somali Liberation Front, of which Askar is a member. Indeed, on the last page of the novel Askar is arrested by the Mogadiscio police, presumably on suspicion of having had a hand in her murder. Askar's retrospective narrative, which is told by turns in the first, third, and speculative second person ("You are a question to yourself...You doubt, at times, if you exist outside your own thoughts"), recounts the traumas and triumphs of his Ogadenese childhood spent with Misra and, more briefly, his adolescence in Mogadiscio with an adoptive uncle and aunt. The narrative is haunted throughout by memories and intuitions of his foster mother's physical presence and of a sometimes excruciating intimacy with her, dating from the crucial early years. This bodily closeness, which allows the motherless male child and the childless surrogate mother to live, complementarily, inside each other, later resists the abstract intellectual hatreds of creed and country that are awakened by the Somali-Ethiopian War in the Ogaden.

In this novel—not surprisingly in Farah's fiction, where domestic and political patriarchies are mutually reinforcing—the relations between a nation and its members are expressed through the roles of parents, or guardians, and children. The postcolonial nation is parented or, more precisely, foster-parented. Nationality categories are most accurately read through the positions assumed by the novel's various surrogate parents towards their charges. Conversely, the destabilization of these categories is perceived through a series of pseudo-incestuous role-reversals that subvert these positions. The postcolonial territory of Askar's birth is, like Askar himself, without natural parentage. Neither is it self-creating, as Askar fancies himself to be—"I had made myself, as though I was my own creation" (23)—though it may have the opportunity to take charge of its own destiny. Such territories are, in reality, the imaginative constructs of colonial and postcolonial cartographers (British, Italian, Ethiopian, Somali), conceived not biologically but intellectually: Askar, who is the human analogue of the Somali Ogaden, describes himself as "a creature given birth to by notions formulated in heads, a creature brought into being by ideas" (3). Such creatures are adopted beings with adopted identities defined by adoptive parents, and Farah sustains the analogues between the child's ties with the family and the individual's more artificial ties with the nation only by replacing Askar's real parents with a range of surrogates and guardians. These are his foster-mother Misra who, albeit in a purely nominal way, represents the Ethiopian occupier; the childless Mogadiscio intellectuals Hilaal and Salaado, who represent the modern Somali Republic, seeking to complete itself by the addition of the motherless child of the Ogaden; the Koranic teacher Aw-Adan, who represents the unifying power of Islam; and the brutal Ogadenese Somali Uncle Qorrax. At the end of the book each of Askar/Ogaden's five guardians has had parts of him/herself chopped away. Misra undergoes a mastectomy (and is then murdered and mutilated, her heart torn out); Hilaal has had a vasectomy, his wife Salaado a hysterectomy; Aw-Adan has had a leg amputated; and Qorrax has had blood exacted. These truncations seem to signify, allegorically, the further dismemberment and fragmentation of the Ogaden.

In the book's allegoric scheme Askar, representing the Ogaden, is born to two patriotic martyrs who give their lives for the cause of its liberation from Ethiopian occupation: his father dies on the day of his birth and his mother soon afterwards. He is thus the posthumous mythic offspring of Somali nationalist aspiration and the mother-republic, and he signifies what is salvaged by his country from the colonial carve-up of the Horn of Africa (his mother's unread journal, predating Somali orthography, is written in Italian). Askar-Ogaden is then, strangely, entrusted by her to the "enemy" in the form of the Oromo-Amhara woman Misra, who cannot be said to be of the same blood as the child, either in the matrilineal or ethnic sense. The child's budding nationalist aspirations are subsequently grounded in the special stifling, suffocating intimacy generated by the one-parent-one-child family, in which the gender-confused male child first identifies with and then seeks to exorcize the oppressively close maternal presence. As he grows up Askar feels a natural need to live a life independent of Misra and expresses the desire of each man to kill the "mother" in him: "To live, I will have to kill you" (57). But these emotions get mixed up with a felt imperative to shoulder the burden of his biological inheritance, left him by his natural mother, by defending his country from the people of his nurturing mother, even though he has only the most theoretical sense of the former, compared with the intensely felt proximity of the latter. Askar has a strange obsession with the idea that there is "a woman living inside him," but this has curiously little to do with Misra, the woman who is most physically present in his life. It seems rather to be tied up with an abstract guilt complex over the spectral figure of his biological mother, "she who claimed she 'lived' in him who had survived her" (105), and whom he accuses himself of killing at his own birth: "I feel as if my mother's death was my birth, or, if you prefer, her death gave birth to me" (151). The feeling is thus more filial than sexual: it is specifically the mother, rather than the woman in him, whom Askar desires to preserve.

At his circumcision, which is his first lesson in frontiers, Askar is ritually separated from Misra and begins to define his "specific" Somali adult maleness against his "generic" Ethiopian mother-figure (the terms are those of his uncle Hilaal, who argues that Somalis have their own unique and exclusive language, culture, and destiny, while "Ethiopia" is a "generic notion, expansive, inclusive," being merely "the generic name of an unclassified mass of different peoples" [148]). After his painful separation from his adoptive mother, he is given his first maps and calendars and these become the "mental charts" on which he measures, in time and space, both "the uncoverable distance between Misra and himself" (97) and the Somali advances and retreats in the Ogaden. Significantly, as the war in the Ogaden escalates, the seven-year-old Askar is physically removed to Mogadiscio and his childhood dependence on Misra comes to an end. Askar's first steps towards psychological independence have thus initiated, quite fortuitously, an involvement with his homeland's political independence, and from the moment of his arrival in the Somali capital, national military progress in the Ogaden is measured, symbolically, by the distance that has grown between the Somali child and the adoptive "Ethiopian" mother whose foreign presence within him he feels he must rid himself of. This physical distance between "your anatomy and mine" (18) becomes, increasingly, a perceptual distance between her physical reality and his mental image of her. When he meets her again in the capital years later, he feels "totally detached" and "weaned" from his "mother-figure," for "in the process of looking for a substitute, he had found another—Somalia, his mother country" (96). He now feels that he can espouse one of his rival adoptive mothers only by denying the other, and the earlier ominous words of his childhood, "To live, I will have to kill you," now take on, in the quite different context of her suspected betrayal of the Somali army, the tone of patriotic duty. Yet his sense of his separate identity is continually undermined by his long and deep intimacy with Misra and, when placed beside this, his claims for the primacy within himself of his unknown biological mother are less than persuasive. Indeed, Askar is culturally formed and molded by Misra in his upbringing. For example, his fantasy that he is one of the race of epic miracle children who kill their mothers at birth is implanted in his mind by Misra's Oromo oral tales and folklore: thus, even the idea of his natural mother's special moral claim upon him derives, ironically, from the culture of his adoptive mother.

In the historical period covered by the novel Askar, like his beloved Ogaden, is separated from both his mothers—from his Somali motherland at his birth and from his Ethiopian stepmother at her death—and the latter separation, in the lives of both individual and nation, is the costlier affair. During the "tragic weekend" in which Russian-backed Ethiopian forces retake the Ogaden, six hundred Somali patriots are betrayed to the enemy and massacred, and among the refugees flooding into Mogadiscio is Misra, the one accused of the betrayal. Embarrassed by her arrival in the capital and by reports of her reputed treachery, Askar is then further traumatized by her final abduction and death at the hands of the Liberation Front (her mutilated corpse is fished out of the bay) and he falls mysteriously and evasively ill at each of these crisis points. It later transpires that one of the things he has been evading may be his own ill-defined complicity with Misra's murder, for which he is, apparently, detained and interrogated by the police at the end of the novel. In this respect *Maps* might be compared with Graham Swift's novel *Waterland*, in which the protagonist also tries to hide from himself (and from the reader) his involvement in a murder. The difference is that whereas Swift, a late modernist-realist, is concerned with the ultimate meaning of the deed performed by the guilty party and with the gradual revelation of his hidden traumas, Farah, in more postmodernist fashion, poses the ontological question of *what* it is that the narrator has done and is now concealing from himself or, indeed, *whether* he has done anything (which things are clear neither to the reader nor to the character himself). There are, for example, two passages in *Maps*—where Askar pictures a soldier standing over a wounded woman with a blood-stained knife and then imagines himself a fish feeding from Misra's blood (211, 214)—which could be construed to mean that Askar, if not the initiator, was at least an accomplice in Misra's murder and dismemberment. But as both of these passages are presented in the form of dream sequences, it is difficult to say exactly what is happening or when, or at what level the images are meant to be read.

To return to the fable of national identity: the association of Misra with the foreign occupation of the Ogaden is ultimately a spurious one. She is, after all, an Amharic-speaking Oromo, not a full-blooded Ethiopian, and she has more natural affinity with the occupied zone than with the occupier. She is herself an occupied possession on Somali as on Ethiopian territory, a slave-girl sexually colonized by a host of "uncles": the Ogaden's symbolic guardian is herself the guarded property, violated by various occupying patriarchal wardens. Also Misra, like Askar, is an uprooted orphan and her Oromo culture, like the Somali one, has been historically marginalized by its orality and oppressed by a literate Ethiopia. She is, in fact, doubly displaced: first as an Oromo living in Ethiopia and forced to speak the language of the dominant Amharic culture, and then as an "Ethiopian" reviled by Somali ethnocentrism. Ironically, Misra is, much more precisely than Askar, a fitting image of the Ogaden that she is accused of betraying. Like the Ogaden, she is brutally abused by Somali patriarchy, is raped by her supposed defenders (by a vengeful pack of Liberation Front patriots), and is finally mutilated and dismembered, her heart torn out by war. For the bigoted members of the Liberation Front, who are convinced they need no proof of Misra's guilt, she is the diseased part of the Somali heritage, to be surgically removed (such is their perverse reading of her mastectomy). But those who live fragmentarily, through a number of cultures as Misra does, always have missing parts of themselves elsewhere, on the other side of some border, whether in Mogadiscio or in Ethiopia. Misra is not a unitary being who can be comprehensively enclosed and defined by maps but represents the various parts of cultures and countries—Oromo, Ethiopian, Somali—which are to be found in mongrelized, migration-prone areas like the Ogaden. Farah has said that the Kallafo of his Ogaden childhood "boasted a Somali-speaking civilian population, a large Arab community engaged in business, as well as Amharic-speaking soldiers...recruited from all the ethnic groups of the Ethiopian empire" ("Childhood," 1264). Askar likes to think of Ethiopia as a "patchwork country," but it is really the Ogaden—crossed, as a veteran soldier remarks, by different waves of migrants twenty, fifty, or a hundred years apart over a period of centuries—which best expresses the hybridization of cultural reality. This irretrievable hybridization is most keenly represented in the novel by Misra.

Misra is the daughter of an Amhara nobleman and an Oromo servant. She lives with a Somali family, and has Qotto and

Ethiopian lovers. Accordingly, she has access to and concourse with all of the fertile neighboring microcultures and tribal nationalisms by which the Ogaden is hedged around and diversified, in spite of its narrowly ethnocentric efforts to resist them. Creative energy, it seems, lives, liminally, along these borders: Askar notes that two-thirds of Somalia's major poets come from its marginal territories and that one such peripheral people, the Boran, provide the Mogadiscio *mingis* with its ceremonial language. Appropriately, the Ogaden, which is a collection of border territories, is symbolically entrusted by Askar's natural mother to a border person, to one of mixed descent and therefore with a choice of identities. This entrustment by a Somali woman to an Oromo servant-girl, reaching across artificial boundaries erected by male nationalistic obsessions, is done, it seems, in recognition of their common Cushitic heritage and interpenetrating cultures. The reputedly "specific" Somali culture which uncle Hilaal theorizes at length about is seen, in reality, to participate in a broader generic group and it is surely no accident that, for all his talk of Somali specificity, there are actually few "pure" Somalis in the novel and those who exist are surrounded by people of Oromo, Qotto, Boran, Adenese, Arab, and Ethiopian extraction. Misra's name exists in three of these languages and in its Somali form is an incomplete version of the Ethiopian "Misrat," meaning "foundation of the earth." Referring as it does to the elemental and nonpartisan, unmapped and unfrontiered earth, it is an appropriately loose signifier for an area as diverse as the Ogaden.

Two key motifs in the novel contest this linguistic and cultural hybridization and play contrapuntally against them in the text: the first is incest, the second maps. Askar says quite early in the novel that Misra regards the fabric of Somali society as "basically incestuous." In the course of his narrative incest becomes an expressive image of the narrow, inward-looking ethnocentrism of Somali culture, its failure to diversify itself by recognizing its kinship with neighboring peoples in a broader generic family. It is also used to demonstrate the way in which the patriarchal abuse of power in the Ogaden shores up micronational divisions among its chequered subjects. The region's paternal guardians seem to make a habit of abusing the foreign wards entrusted to their care and protection, thus committing a figurative incest and identifying the national or ethnic "other" as a mere object of degradation. The Somali boys are abused by the Adenese; the Ogadenese foster-child by the Islamic schoolteacher and lover of his adoptive mother; and the abducted Oromo girl Misra by the Somali patriarchs and the wealthy Muslim Abdullah who forces her to switch roles from adopted daughter to wife. In each case the child looks to its false foster-parent, as the Ogaden to its latest political guardian, for self-definition, moral example, and leadership. Instead he or she finds paternal and avuncular responsibilities betrayed and traditional relationships inverted: "uncles" become rapists, fathers husbands, daughters wives. Askar is himself complicit with this incestuous abuse of power. When Misra's nocturnal male visitors force themselves upon her in the Ogadenese household, the child's rage is clearly colored by an incestuous Oedipal envy of her violators. And it is significant that Misra allows herself to be blackmailed into sleeping with uncle Qorrax because only by so doing is she able to sleep with Askar, thus implicating the child in her own quasi-incestuous humiliation. Askar specifically likens himself to a "third leg" lying "somewhere between her [Misra's] opened legs" (24); the image identifies him explicitly with the wooden leg that the crippled Aw-Adan removes before intercourse with Misra and thence, vicariously, with Aw-Adan's penis; and during her sexual climax Misra sighs the same endearments to her lover as the ones she uses to the child Askar ("my man!"). Not surprisingly, the adolescent Askar is plagued by subconscious guilt over his physical attachment to his stepmother, and his elected psychological ruse for escaping this guilt is to externalize his incestuous desires and alienate them to Misra herself, thus turning the victim into the aggressor. To this end, he falsifies Misra's past, accusing her of murdering her adoptive father/husband "during an excessive orgy of copulation," whereas the truth is that her guardian forced himself upon her and a likelier cause of death was the old man's sexual overenthusiasm. The role of incestuous murderer is clearly more convenient for Askar's newly adopted image of Misra as "enemy-barbarian." More incredibly, he recasts an Ethiopian army captain with whom she enters into a sexual liaison during the invasion of the Ogaden as a half-brother, thus transferring his own incestuous desires to the lover and substituting for him in his own fantasies.

On the narrative level, Misra's relations with Askar are not entirely normal, being full of incestuous echoes like the ones mentioned above. But the Ogaden is symbolically entrusted to her because, in the Brechtian phrase, she is good for it, and its paternal guardians—be they Somali, Qotto, or Amhara—clearly are not. "We're in each other's life now. No more wars. We're a family," says uncle Hilaal as he hugs Askar to him, and in this he speaks, unconsciously, for the multicultural, mongrel spirit of the Ogaden, which desires only that its various guardians live at peace with its occupants and they with one another. Misra is the good guardian because, unlike her shifting political counterparts, she is sufficiently conversant with and tolerant of all her people's cultures to make allowance for their different partisan relevancies and myopias. She is the true mother who sees all the blind spots on her child's body and "soaps them all and, in the end, washes them clean" (110–11). When she admits to buying milk for the Ethiopian soldiers, she protests that "she was doing something for 'her people,'" and then adds the comment, "the problem is, who are 'my people'?" (184). The phrase is, of course, deliberately ambiguous. Both sides are "her people" and she provides both with what they most need: milk for the Ethiopians, money for the Somalis. Misra serves all members of her larger, generic Ogaden "family," giving to each what is good for them and overriding the incestuous inwardness of Somali ethnicity.

The second and stronger bastion of resistance to cultural and linguistic diversification is Askar's maps. Farah has said of the colonial maps of Africa that "we should redraw [them] according to our economic and psychological and social needs, and not accept the nonsensical frontiers carved out of our regions" ("Wretched" 54). And yet it is no accident that Askar has a nostalgic hankering for the time, during World War Two, when all of the Somali territories except for Djibouti were united under a single, colonial administration: his own politico-linguistic map of Greater Somalia is, in reality, as much a fiction of cultural geography as the colonial maps were figments of political geography. History, Hilaal reminds us, is made by those who have access to sign-systems (168) and is imposed upon those who have not, and the coercive cartographic enclosures enforced by the newly-literate Somalis override sociopolitical (and, increasingly, cultural) divisions as the old Western imperial ones overrode ethnic and linguistic barriers. Their ethnocentric organization of political space is, arguably, as distortive of reality as the Mercator projection's Eurocentric organization of geographical space. The Somalis of the WSLF regard their people as united by language, divided by maps, and the independent nation-state of the Somali Republic imagines that its cultural-linguistic "specificity" gives it a unique claim on those territories where Somali, in one fashion or another, is still spoken. The chief objection to this new cartographic hegemony, after noting the shakiness of its political propositions, is that it claims to unite people who, both linguistically and in other respects, are becoming more and more diverse—who have in fact become irredeemably mongrelized—while it artificially sets apart other groups of people who, in reality, are much more closely bonded. In the former category are the Somalis scattered through Kenya and Tanzania, like the tutor of Cusmaan, Askar's intellectual mentor in Mogadiscio. These, when they are not speaking Swahili, use a bastardized, ungrammatical form of Somali similar to that spoken by the Ogadenese Somalis, and their subscription to Somali cultural values is as adulterated and compromised by the dominant host-cultures as is that of the Ogadenese marginal groups, the Oromo and Qotto, by the Somali one. Much closer to home, the Westernized urbanites of Mogadiscio, at the hub of the nation-state, do not identify closely with their Ogadenese brethren but snobbishly regard them not only as linguistically incompetent but also as lacking in self-sufficiency and wholeness. No sooner has Hilaal declared categorically that "you are either a Somali or you aren't" (148) than he proceeds to postulate a halfway classification of extra-territorial "unpersons" who cannot be admitted to a full Somali identity. All the indicators suggest that the linguistic homogeneity and cultural exclusiveness of Greater Somalia, if they ever existed, are rapidly disintegrating. Conversely, in the second category there is Misra, a non-ethnic Somali speaker who, though fully acculturated, is automatically mistrusted and is denied a place on her ward's identity papers that she has done more than enough to earn. Misra fosters a Somali child and teaches it its national language and folklore, slaves in a Somali-Ogaden household where she is sexually abused by Somali men, and is, at last, doubtfully accused of treachery by them and murdered. Meanwhile, in the same Greater Somalia where children are made to learn their genealogies by heart as proof of ethnicity (Lewis, 10–11), honorary citizenship is granted to another non-ethnic Somali, the sullen Qotto schoolteacher Aw-Adan, for no other reason than that his Arabic input into Somali culture is, politically, more acceptable than Misra's Amharic one (significantly it is Aw-Adan, whose loyalty is never questioned, who accuses Misra of treachery, thus, perhaps, making his own insecure position a little safer by denouncing another foreigner).

What is a Somali and what does it mean to be one? The question opens up a Pandora's box of political, ethnic, and moral quandaries. Is it to speak or to read the language, or to be born in the homeland or in one of its territories? (In fact, few of the novel's Somali speakers are Somalis by birth.) Is it to be a patriot in the cause of the Ogaden? In which case what right has Qorrax, who openly collaborates with the Ethiopian conquerors, to his Somali identity? Who, if anyone, is fit to be political guardian of the disputed Ogaden territory to which Somalia lays claim? Who can claim to have "authored" it parentally? Certainly, the criteria for nationhood postulated by Askar, Hilaal, and the Western Somalia Liberation Front patriots are as erratic and capricious as the Somali map of the Ogaden, which ignores its multilingual character and fifty percent Amharic-speaking population. Little ground is left for belief in anything that could be described as a "pure," "authentic," or "natural" Somali identity. In one way or another, each of the novel's characters stands, like a girl-apparition in one of Askar's many dreams, "in a borrowed skin," and the Somali map, in its peculiarly monolithic contours and fine disregard of multiculturalism, provides an inexact, inadequate model of reality. Maps, like the wars fought over them to redraw national terrains, distort and destroy, and they are, appropriately, attended by funereal images throughout the book. The "notional truths" expressed by the Somali maps correspond to the political actuality of the Horn of Africa as little as Askar's moral conception of Misra coincides with the real woman (Misra, significantly, has no understanding of maps). Misra, like the political map of the territory of which she is the figurative custodian, is in his consciousness a suitably floating signifier, zoned into many stereotyped figures and rival fantasy embodiments: on one side, mother-martyr and victimized nation; on the other, wicked stepmother, betrayer, and national enemy. A nominal sense of reality so prevails over the actual, and the signifier over its referent, that at one point Askar even thinks of her as "a creature of his own invention" (107), and it is difficult to say exactly what does constitute her reality, since she seems (like the Ogaden) to have her being solely through the guardians and wards who control her existence in one way or another.

Askar, the girl in his dream tells him, is "almost always satisfied with the surface of things...a mirror in which your features...may be reflected" (130). For him Misra is an image of the Ogaden insofar as both are mirrors in which the beholder sees his own desires reflected, and maps, like mirrors, reflect the dispositions of their makers. "There is truth in maps," Hilaal concedes but, aware of the dangers of ethnocentric myths, adds the rider: "The question is, does truth change?...The Ogaden, as

Somali, is truth. To the Ethiopian map-maker, the Ogaden, as Somali, is untruth" (217–18). In the novel's allegoric scheme Askar comes to represent a chauvinistic Somali concept of the Ogaden, as his real mother represents the dead dream of an ethnic nation, of "Mother Somalia" as the Ogaden's natural parent, "getting together" with "the Ogaden/child separated from her" (97). Misra signifies a broader, hybrid, generic concept of the Ogaden as a place of mixed ethnicity, and her hybridization signifies everything that Askar must resist and destroy to realize his sectarian Somali dreams. "One day, you will identify yourself with your people and identify me out of your community," she prophesies, "you might even kill me to make your people's dreams become a tangible reality" (95). What Askar does is tantamount to these things. Together with his uncles, he "others" Misra, misogynistically and xenophobically, as woman and foreigner, as a sexual and political territory to be invaded and colonized; and this separative process, even as it destabilizes roles in the parent-child relationship, reaffirms divisive gender and nationality categories. Meanwhile, like Misra, the neutral ground of the disputed strip of land ("the foundation of the earth") does not discriminate between its diverse occupying nationalities and the rival maps that overlay it like the layers of a palimpsest. The "truth" of maps is, finally, a highly subjective, ethnocentric kind of truth, and the stable identity presupposed by the idealistic vision of the map-maker nonexistent.

Some recent writing from the postcolonial world, particularly that from the white Commonwealth of Australia and Canada (Malouf, Atwood, Kroetsch) has challenged the homogeneity of ethnocentric colonial discourses by projecting spaces other than those inscribed on the prevailing hegemonic map. These resistive readings celebrate the diversity and mixed ethnicity of formerly colonized cultures, previously ignored or stigmatized by the dominant colonial one, and indicate a shift away from cultural homogeneity. In the contemporary Africa of *Maps*, however, the new dominant discourse is itself insularly and oppressively ethnic. Ethnicity is here the hegemonic and reterritorializing power, not the revisioning agent or counterdiscourse: the regional map is the instrument of new, postcolonial ethnocentrisms and false cultural homogeneities forced upon a hybrid, mongrelized reality. Africa's internal imperialisms have taken over from where the alien, external ones left off. Farah's novel offers us new maps for old.

WORKS CITED

Farah, Nuruddin. "Childhood of My Schizophrenia." *The Times Literary Supplement*, 23–29 November 1990: 1264.

———. *Maps*. London: Picador, 1986.

———. "Wretched Life." Interview with Patricia Morris. *Africa Events*, September 1986: 54.

Lewis, I. M. *A Modern History of Somalia: A Nation and State in the Horn of Africa*. London: Longman, 1980.

18

F. TIMOTHY RUPPEL

"Re-inventing Ourselves a Million Times": Narrative, Desire, and Identity in Bharati Mukherjee's *Jasmine*

> We are the outcasts and deportees, strange pilgrims visiting outlandish shrines, landing at the end of tarmacs, ferried in old army trucks where we are roughly handled and taken to roped-off corners of waiting rooms where surly, barely wakened customs guards await their bribes. We are dressed in shreds of national costumes, out of season, the wilted plumage of inter-continental vagabondage. We only ask one thing: to be allowed to land; to pass through; to continue.
>
> —Bharati Mukherjee, *Jasmine*, 90–91

Who are these "strange pilgrims"? Certainly, we see them infrequently on the evening news when their "vagabondage" becomes intolerable, when their passage can no longer be ignored, when they put spectacular pressure on our borders. Then, these "outcasts and deportees" emerge into a brief visibility beneath Western eyes. Watching television the other night, I saw Haitian "boat people" crammed on their small, overcrowded crafts off the Florida shore. Through its spokesman, the U.S. administration reasonably explained its policy of denying these refugees entry, citing a benevolent and humanitarian concern with the possible loss of life. In other words, their "vagabondage" was being treated as an issue of water safety, of laudable nautical rigor, rather than as an issue of political and material conditions. In addition, and due to the interests of electronic brevity, the Haitians had been resolutely fixed into the already known, and therefore available, category of "boat people," a distinction that defined them as a collective identity. As

Chandra Mohanty writes, "the idea of abstracting particular places, peoples, and events into generalized categories, laws, and politics is fundamental to any form of ruling" (16).

We are thus insulated from the historical trajectories that set this population in motion, the contradictions and ruptures that have propelled them out of their native culture. This insulation involves a substitution, a metalepsis, where a sociopolitical effect is identified as a cause. As a result, these "strange pilgrims" become the originary cause of scrutiny, interest, or benevolence, of a discourse that seeks to situate them in teleological narratives of Western civilization and progress, rather than as the effects of these same narrative gestures. In this paper, I want to suggest that texts such as Bharati Mukherjee's *Jasmine* attempt to disrupt this even flow of narrative historiography with a counter-discourse that thematizes prior narratives of enforced identity—narratives that through accumulation and repetition seek to define and circumscribe identity as a fixed and available resource, constituted wholly by another's desire.

Although *Jasmine* is a narrative of emergence, I do not wish to assert, in any sense, that this novel relates an immigrant's success story, charting a steady and inevitable progress that culminates in the achievement of an autonomous, unified self. Nor is it a completely realized postcolonial text, since Mukherjee's portrayal of India relies on the trope of the Manichean allegory. Rather, *Jasmine* is a novel that resists closure and suggests a strategy of continual transformation as a necessary and historically contingent ethic of survival. This continual remaking of the self invokes "two temporalities: that of oppression, memory, and enforced identity, and that of emergence after the 'break,' the counter memory, and heterogeneous difference" (Radhakrishnan, "Ethnic Identity" 211). On the one hand, *Jasmine* thematizes narration and identity by bringing into focus how differences are social products of interested desire. At the same time, it offers the symbolic possibility of the emergence of a reinvented, paralogical, heterogeneous "family," based on affinity and multiplicity rather than fixed identity. Thus, I will be reading *Jasmine* as a counter-narrative where "re-inventing ourselves a million times" becomes a reflexive, historically situated strategy for negotiating power.

Discussing narrative history, Frantz Fanon writes that when the colonizer comes to write the history of the colonial encounter "the history which he writes is not the history of the country which he plunders but the history of his own nation" (41). Such interested productions become, for Lila Abu-Lughod, "the great self-congratulatory literature of the rise of the West, which for so long has shaped our view of the past" (111). Suggesting that this literature should be "revaluated" and "remade," Abu-Lughod recommends an analysis based on triangulation, or multiple, contradictory points of view (112).[1] It is just this voice of the excluded and marginalized respondent that feminist, Afro-American, and multicultural studies tries to recover. But, at the same time, this voice is seen as a threat to the accomplishments and values of Western culture simply because it has been historically marginalized and may have a different story to tell. In other words, the silent, demarcated subject who is the product of Western and patriarchal historiography built upon theories of synchronous development is again resituated just at the very moment of emergence, at the very moment s/he speaks.

Moreover, as Edward Said suggests, when the postcolonial subjects speak, they are considered by many Western intellectuals to be merely "wailers and whiners," denouncing the evils of colonialism. They are thus implicated in the politics of blame. As Said explains, such a politics proceeds from a willingness to assert that colonialism has ended. Therefore, "any claims about or reparations for its damages and consequences into the present are dismissed as both irrelevant and preposterously arrogant" ("Intellectuals" 54). The phrase "into the present" is crucial. As I mentioned earlier, the former colonial subject becomes an originary cause, a source of discourse. Instead of being grateful for what "we" have historically done for them, "they" are constituted in the present as a pack of unappreciative whiners. They have declined the invitation, refused the call to step up into a world that is not of their own making. They are then implicated in a failure of recognition that only confirms their essential and underdeveloped nature.[2]

This rhetorical and strategic resituating of the resisting respondent tends to maintain boundaries of exclusion. What is at risk here is the erasure of those traces of resistance that might disrupt the inevitability of the Western narrative of progress and benevolence. These exclusions occlude the complete record of colonialism, even as they resolutely try to define the excesses of colonialism as the product of aberrant individuals, a succession of Kurtzes, rather than as effects of the system that produced them. Such an experience of colonialism does continue into the present, producing an endless ripple of effects. For specific reasons, different in each case, the historical discourse produced by the colonizer created a system of representations (mostly centered around, and justified by, supposed traits of the native) that totally effaced the possibility of resistance. Resistance to domination was portrayed as an essential misrecognition on the part of the native. In other words, the native had failed to answer the call of Western ideology.

This is the complex of concerns articulated by *Jasmine*: resistance, hierarchical distinctions, and boundaries that exclude and include. In what follows I will be examining these in light of what Chandra Mohanty calls (following Dorothy Smith) "relations of ruling"—a model for cultural analysis that "posits multiple intersections of structures of power and emphasizes the *process* or *form* of ruling, not the frozen embodiment of it" (14). In *Jasmine* these concerns, embedded in relations of ruling, reveal themselves through the actions of the religious fundamentalist, Sukhwinder, the rapist, Half-Face, and the seemingly benevolent banker, Bud Ripplemeyer, individuals who continually attempt to place Jasmine into prior narratives of desire that would define her as a known, visible, and essential self conforming to one or another of the myths that their narrativized knowledge of her authorizes and legitimizes.

Confronted by the repeated pleas from Bud Ripplemeyer, the father of her unborn child, the narrator of *Jasmine* reflects upon how much he doesn't know about her. In fact, he has studiously avoided such knowledge, since her "genuine foreignness frightens him" (22). Instead, his desire and interest are spurred by his image of "Eastern" women. For her prospective husband, she is "darkness, mystery, inscrutability. The East plunges me into visibility and wisdom" (178). This visibility then involves an identity as an already known subject. But she knows differently: she has been "many selves" and has "survived hideous times" (190). In contrast to her, Bud lives innocently within "the straight lines and smooth planes of his history" (190).

Two versions of history and narration emerge in the narrator's comments. For Jasmine, history is the discontinuity and rupture produced by material and political events and, as a result, the self becomes plural and contradictory. Her survival depends upon a flexible strategy of appropriation and transformation. For Bud, history is a straight line, a teleological and progressive ordering of existence where the phenomenological world is transparent and the self is unified and autonomous. It is "a history whose perspective on all that precedes it implies an end of time, a completed development" (Foucault, 152). The narrator's displacement of fixed identity and these two views of history provide a point of entry into Mukherjee's *Jasmine*. In the course of the novel, the narrator is Jyoti, Jasmine, Jane, and Jase. Each of her names represents a transitional self as she travels from Hasnapur, India to Baden, Iowa. Rather than a recapitulation of the stereotype of the deceitful, mendacious Asian, these name changes can be seen as a response to the still ongoing effects of colonialism. She must change to survive and to continue her journey. In fact, the narrative structure is that of a journey and passage, a liminal state, which places the Third World inside the First World. In the process, the narrator must continually remake herself to avoid the threat posed by enforced identity. She must avoid the limiting boundaries that seek to confine her in traditional and specific gendered roles, both in India and America.

As a village girl from Hasnapur, she is "born to that kind of submission, that expectation of ignorance" (204). Her transformation from Jyoti to Jasmine represents her ability to escape from "a social order that had gone on untouched for thousands of years" (204). This social order can be seen as symptomatic of the relations of ruling I discussed earlier. For Jyoti and the other women of Hasnapur, these relations of ruling involve a submission to the patriarchal order, which demands arranged marriages, constant reproduction, ritual suicide upon the death of the husband, and the prohibition against their remarriage as a widow. These gendered restrictions are also configured along the lines of class and religion in *Jasmine*. Jyoti's expectations as a bride are limited by the fact that she is undowered. Her husband dies in sectarian religious violence. As the fifth daughter of nine children, Jyoti is born into a culture where daughters are a curse, since they must have dowries—which her family is unable to provide. Jyoti's mother, in an effort to spare Jyoti from a history similar to hers, a history of incessant childbearing and beatings, tries to kill her at birth. This is a culture that brings up daughters "to be caring and have no minds of our own" (39). Nevertheless, her mother fights to keep Jyoti in school for six years and to prevent her from being married at the age of eleven to a widowed landlord.

When Jyoti does marry, it is to Prakash Vijh, a city man whose values are those of Gandhi and Nehru. In contrast to the other men of the traditional culture, Prakash does not see marriage as the cultural sanctioning of patriarchal control and enforced obedience. He renames Jyoti as Jasmine, a symbolic break with her feudal past. Yet this break causes Jyoti/Jasmine deep conflict. As a traditional woman she wants to get pregnant immediately to prove her worth and to validate her identity. Indeed, in this society, pregnancy is the *only* available identity. Jyoti still feels "eclipsed by the Mazbi maid's daughter, who had been married off at eleven, just after me, and already had had a miscarriage" (70).

The point to note here, as Jasmine later realizes, is that Prakash does exert a Pygmalion effect on her, since he wanted "to make me a new kind of city woman" (70)—a new woman for his new India. Thus, Prakash is entirely determining Jyoti's new identity. He tells her that it "was up to women to resist" (70). Despite his modern views, Prakash is first defining Jyoti's role in the new political landscape of India, and then he is telling Jyoti how to be this new woman. As such, Prakash exerts a more subtle form of patriarchal control, disguised as benevolence and demanding her active complicity. Jyoti fully recognizes her husband's limitations. She instinctively hides her detergent sales' commissions from Prakash. "For all his talk of us being equal, was he possessive about my working?" she wonders (74). Indeed, his talk of equality contradicts his belief that a "husband must protect the wife whenever he can" (82). At the same time, Jyoti begins to read, even reading Prakash's repair manuals. Her ability to read and understand technical manuals leads to the turning point in their marriage: the night when they work together, repairing a VCR with an equal division of labor. They dream of opening their own business, Vijh & Vijh. This vision is important in the narrative economy of *Jasmine*, since it provides the first model of the reconstituted family in the novel.

However, this possibility is decisively put to an end by the religious fundamentalist, Sukhwinder, who has "unforgiving eyes" and a "flat, authoritative voice" (57). Conveniently forgetting the history of violence that followed Partition, Sukhwinder wants to create the new, separatist state of "Khalistan, the Land of the Pure" for believers who renounce "filth and idolatry" (57). Within this codified economy of sameness, "whorish women" would be kept off the streets. Indeed, "all women are whores," and "'the sari is the sign of the prostitute'" (58). Sukhwinder thus wishes to uphold the traditional rigid segregation of the sexes and the exclusion of women as a corollary of his religious beliefs. For Sukhwinder, the nation-state is an exclusionary border, an enclave that celebrates the will to sameness in its univocal narrative of historical and human destiny.

But Jasmine and Prakash cannot escape the sectarian violence that has spread from the provinces to the city. Prakash is killed by a bomb wired into a radio as his assassin yells "'Prostitutes! Whores!'" (85). The bomb is meant for Jasmine, who becomes a political target because her aspirations pose a threat to the social order built on women's subjection. Like Jasmine's father, and later Professor Devinder Vadhera, Sukhwinder and his cohorts desire to return to an imagined, timeless, and seamless moment that, to them, reflects the natural order.[3] For Jasmine, this political killing means an abrupt end to the dreams of Vijh & Vijh. Instead, she must join her mother in enforced widowhood. As she laments, "I am a widow in the war of feudalisms" (88). In spite of this temporary recognition, however, she is still balanced precariously between Jyoti and Jasmine. Her place, her "mission," is to travel to the United States and commit ritual suicide, *suttee*, where Prakash intended to go to school. As such, she is still ensnared in the same imaginary relations as her contemporary from the village of Hasnapur, Vimla. When Vimla's husband dies of typhoid, Vimla, although just twenty-two, douses herself with kerosene and flings herself on the stove. "In Hasnapur, Vimla's isn't a sad story" (12). A similar destiny propels Jasmine into the "shadow world" of "outcasts and deportees" (90).

At this point in the novel, India merely serves as a regressive and repressive background to further Mukherjee's thematic aims. It is a timeless India that is forever feudal, undeveloped, and barbaric, and, hence, still in need of Western guidance. On strictly literary grounds, Mukherjee argues that "I had to give her [Jasmine] a society that was so regressive, traditional, so caste-bound, genderist, that she could discard it" much easier than "a fluid American society" could be discarded ("Interview," 19). Here, India's stalled backwardness is unfavorably contrasted to the more attractive fluidity of Western society. Following Abdul JanMohamed, we can see that Mukherjee deploys the trope of the Manichean allegory in her representation of India, since "the putative superiority of the European" depends upon "the supposed inferiority of the native" (82). As JanMohamed explains, the Manichean allegory exerts such a powerful influence, consciously or subconsciously, that "even a writer who is reluctant to acknowledge it and who may indeed be highly critical of imperialist exploitation is drawn into its vortex" (82). Mukherjee's interests in *Jasmine* do not include such a critical attitude towards "imperialist exploitation" or the practice of *suttee*.[4] Instead, her focus remains on the gendered subject in transit from the Third World to the First World. For Mukherjee, then, a critique of stereotypes based on gender and exoticism supersedes a critique of imperialist influence in India.[5] In many ways, this omission points to the inherent difficulties involved in avoiding the powerful attraction of the Manichean allegory and, again, indicates the pervasive effects of colonialism continuing into the present.

These effects become more apparent in Mukherjee's novel when Jasmine leaves Hasnapur. She joins the dangerous, unstable category of "refugees and mercenaries and guest workers," slipping into "a shadow world" of interchangeable bodies (90). This floating population only asks to be allowed "to continue" (91), while it journeys, simultaneously and side-by-side, with the tourists and businessmen who travel through legal channels of access and availability. These pilgrims are thus seen and unseen. They are ignored because of their obscene message that colonialism is not over yet. Colonialism has merely shifted into a different register. As Donna Haraway writes, the international economy of electronics and capital has redefined the notion of work. This new worker is "female and feminized," conforming to the twin imperatives of constant vulnerability and availability, as she is thoroughly "exploited as a reserve labor force" (190).

For the refugees, the goal is simply to survive. However, this survival is threatened at the moment of their emergence into visibility. They then become the locus of suspicion and discourse. As a "'visible minority,'" these refugees are enveloped in an "atmosphere of hostility" based upon a whole series of "'crippling assumptions'" ("Interview," 12) that are the product of prior colonialisms, textualities, and cultural myths. These myths then represent and influence behavior towards the native. For Jasmine, these myths of the available and passive Eastern woman create the climate that legitimizes her rape.

Jasmine's journey has taken her from Hasnapur to the United States aboard unregistered aircraft and ships. As an illegal immigrant traveling on a forged passport, she must complete her pilgrimage to Tampa aboard *The Gulf Shuttle*, a shrimper engaged in "the nigger-shipping bizness" (99). She ends up in a motel room at the run-down Florida Court with the captain of the trawler, Half-Face, whose name derives from the loss of an eye, an ear, and half his face in Vietnam, where he served as a demolitions expert. Half-Face, a character "from the underworld of evil" (103), is thus marked by his neocolonialist experience in Southeast Asia, and in this sense is like the young man at the bar later in the novel who reacts to Jasmine's entrance with the remark that "'I know whore power when I see it'" (179). Recognition and association are immediate: "His next words were in something foreign, but probably Japanese or Thai or Filipino, something bar girls responded to in places where he'd spent his rifle-toting youth" (179). The young man and Half-Face, both veterans of the East, respond similarly because Jasmine represents an already known and undifferentiated gendered subject.

With banal conviction, Half-Face tells Jasmine, "You know what's coming, and there ain't nobody here to help you, so my advice is to lie back and enjoy it. Hell, you'll probably like it. I don't get many complaints" (102). For Half-Face, Jyoti's vulnerability is a "sort of turn-on" (101), and his boast implies a prior knowledge/narrative of known Eastern women and an entire history of others who have not complained. In other words, for Half-Face and his cohorts, women have not complained because ultimately they accepted the inevitability of the hierarchical situation and their sexual nature, thus discovering that they "really" liked it after all. In this interested configuration of desire, cause and effect are conflated, and the threat of violence occluded. The myth of the available and passive Eastern woman eliminates any possibility of resistance, any possibility that these women did not "really" like it. For Half-Face, Jyoti is merely "one prime piece," an identity that "cancels out" any other considerations (103). With mechanical and perfunctory obliviousness, Half-Face drinks, rapes, and then falls asleep. As a consequence of her "personal dishonor," Jasmine considers killing herself as Half-Face snores in the next room.

Occurring at the exact center of the novel, Jasmine's rape signals a crucial moment in her successive transformations and in the formation of her ethics of survival. Instead of killing herself and passively conforming to an identity politics that would define her solely as a victim, she decides instead to kill her attacker. With ritualistic attentiveness, she first thoroughly cleanses her body, and then she purifies her soul through prayer. She has a small knife, given to her by Kingsland, a savvy fellow nomad traveling aboard *The Gulf Shuttle*. She first uses it on herself, cutting a strip across her tongue. As Mukherjee explains, Jasmine becomes "Kali, the goddess of destruction, since "Kali has her red tongue hanging out" ("Interview," 21). In addition, this gesture of marking and naming reclaims her body. It is an active intervention in the relations of ruling that provided the justification of her rape and her subsequent conception of herself as a victim.

One further observation here has implications for Jasmine's later desertion of her crippled husband. Mukherjee has remarked that Kali is "the goddess of destruction, but not in a haphazard, random way. She is the destroyer of evil so that that world can be renewed" ("Interview," 21). As such, this restructuring and renewing function of Jasmine as Kali provides a key to the possibility of a postcolonial politics where resistance to the myths, histories, and narratives of the metropolitan center involves an active thematizing of the structures of enforced identity, and an affirmative transformation that involves appropriating the weapons and technologies that have served to maintain the center. Jasmine's killing of Half-Face involves a reappropriation—a violent sundering and subsequent adapting of the controlling strategies of violence and desire—and the reinscription of active resistance into the patriarchal narrative of vulnerability and availability. She appropriates the knife/phallus, and she penetrates his body. Then, instead of committing *suttee*—burning the suit of her dead husband and then lying on the fire, the "mission" that controlled her journey to the United States—Jasmine burns Prakash's suit and her Indian clothes in a trash can next to the motel. She breaks the chain of causality, the metalepsis that continually tries to substitute cause for effect in the relations of ruling, the terrible causality that led to her being "raped and raped and raped in boats and cars and motel rooms" on her journey to America (114). With the killing of Half-Face, Jasmine passes from innocence and enacts a radical break, suggesting a form of resistance that is contingent, disruptive, and strategic. Rather than reifying a past that is continuous and identical with itself, *Jasmine* suggests a history dislodged from origins and a self fractured from organic wholeness.

As R. Radhakrishnan writes, "[t]he task for radical ethnicity is to thematize and subsequently problematize its entrapment within these binary elaborations with the intent of stepping beyond to find its own adequate language" ("Ethnic Identity," 216). For Jasmine, this "adequate language" involves the ability "to adjust, to participate," without succumbing to the desire to hold on to the past and certainty (128). To do so would be to become like Professor Vadhera and his family who recreate an "artificially maintained Indianness" (145). In contrast, Jasmine must seek to negotiate and resituate, continually, the horizon of her fears and desires. Her articulation of a desire denied her in the patriarchal relations of ruling propels her to New York, where she acquires an illegal green card and comes to work as a domestic in the Hayes household. In the process, she is again renamed. Like Prakash, Taylor Hayes acknowledges her liminal state: "Taylor didn't want to change me. He didn't want to scour and sanitize the foreignness. My being different...didn't scare him" (165). In contrast to her earlier transformations, she asserts that "I changed because I wanted to" (165). She thus becomes "Jase, the prowling adventurer" (157).

But Sukhwinder reappears in New York. To protect her new family, Jase escapes to Baden, Iowa. Here again, she changes, exchanging Jase for Jane. The point to note here is that she is actively changing her name, rather than passively accepting a name as she had with Prakash. But this new role requires a "regression, like going back to village life, a life of duty and devotion" ("Interview," 31). Settling in Baden as the wife of Bud Ripplemeyer, the head of the local bank, would be the same as remaining in Hasnapur, since becoming Bud's wife would be merely another form of enforced identity. As Jane, she only feels affection for Bud. Crippled by a distraught farmer whom his bank has foreclosed on, Bud appeals to her feelings of responsibility to be a caregiver as she had been in the Hayes' family. To become Mrs. Jane Ripplemeyer, therefore, would require renouncing her desire to gain control of her body and destiny.

I began my reading of *Jasmine* with Jane and Bud by noting their two different conceptions of narrative and history, and I want to return to the connection between these conceptions and the production of enforced identity through another's desire. These two contrasting views become apparent when Bud and Jane are driving through Baden and pass "half-built, half-deserted cinder-block structures at the edge of town" (97). The "empty swimming pools and plywood panels in the window frames" remind her of the Florida Coast motel where she was raped because as constructed by prior narratives of female identity she could be imagined as provocatively vulnerable and available.

Bud reacts differently to the cinder-block structures. Contemplating these undeveloped resources, Bud "frowns because unproductive projects give him a pain" (97). In fact, Bud sees these unproductive resources and can only wonder "who handled their financing" (97). For Bud then, individuals, resources, and land are only understandable within an economy of productivity and efficiency. Thus, "Asia he'd thought of only as a soy-bean market," presumably tended by productive and silent natives. And, indeed,

Bud imagines the natives of his own region in terms of similar evaluative categories. A "good man" is one who displays "discipline, strength, patience, character. Husbandry" (20). To Bud, individuals like Darryl who do not want to be tied down by the family farm, who want to make "something more of his life than fate intended" (71), are irreducibly "flawed" (21).

Bud Ripplemeyer is like a series of characters in this novel—Sukhwinder, Professor Vadhera, and Jyoti's father—who want to preserve a vision of the past as a pure, uncontested, and originary terrain. This nostalgia precludes change while it authorizes relations of ruling that seek to deny the interested subordination of oppositional voices and knowledges. Thus, the narrator can easily "wonder if Bud ever sees the America I do" (97). The answer is no. Bud's desire manifests itself in the will to possess and to define. Jasmine has learned a different lesson from history.

Rather than preservation, stasis, and attachments, Mukherjee's novel proposes a counter-narrative that suggests that "transformation" must be embraced (214). Such a strategy questions the drive to essentialize that characterizes Sukhwinder, Half-Face, and Bud Ripplemeyer. It also suggests a different relationship between former colonial partners, a resituating of history that involves a thematizing of prior myths of enforced identity and a breaking into a new space, provisional and based on affinity, not identity. This postcolonial space is portrayed symbolically as the reconstituted family that emerges at the end of the novel: Jase is carrying Bud's child, Duff is an adopted child, and Taylor is emerging from a failed marriage. In addition they are going to California to be reunited with Du and his sister, victims of Vietnam's colonial past.

In the reconstituted family, they do not have the certainty of Bud's straight line of history, but neither do they have those benevolent assumptions that authorize exclusions based on fear of immigrants. Here, individuals survive through a flexible strategy of "scavenging, adaption, and appropriat[ing] technology" (138), not exactly because they want to, but because they must in order to survive. It is not coincidental that the skills of Prakash and Du involve the rewiring of the circuitry of electronic machinery. Yet this skill can also be turned to destructive ends, since Sukhwinder and his cohorts, the Khalsa Lions, wire bombs into radios. In this sense, an affinity that recognizes difference and contradiction, rather than an affiliation solely based on identity politics, becomes a necessity.

But survival also depends on a recognition of the historical and material forces that set this floating population in motion. As

I indicated earlier, such a recognition might have informed Mukherjee's portrayal of India and her understanding of the ideological complexity of *suttee*. With its title character scarred by history, Mukherjee's *Jasmine* concludes with an image of affiliation through affinity—a hopeful imaging of a postcolonial world where difference is acknowledged and history is reconfigured. Yet, at the same time, this achieved state or topos of the reconstituted family cannot be seen as fixed and realized. Instead, Jasmine wonders how many "more selves" are in her (190). There are no answers to these questions in *Jasmine*, since any answer would involve a refutation of the novel's ethic of survival, adaptation, and transformation.

"Re-inventing ourselves" may be seen as an active strategy that implies the possibility of resistance and reappropriation through a reconfiguring of the received knowledges that constitute colonial history. As JanMohamed and Lloyd note, such a critical reinterpretation "assert[s] that even the very differences which have always been read as symptoms of inadequacy are capable of being re-read transformatively as indications and figurations of values opposed to the dominant discourse" (10). Thus, this archival work involves a strategy of rereading the received history of the past, with particular attention to its silences, ruptures, and contradictions.[6] It strives to avoid mistaking effects for causes, and to maintain a critical activity that sees differences as a product of competing discursive fields. Identity is never reducible to one stable and essential position, but is an effect of these discourses and contestations. To think only in terms of the implacable opposition of center to margin is to revalidate the essentializing binary grid of identity.[7] To think in terms of shifting the center, decentering, is to imagine an ascendancy of the margins, a simple reversal, where "interested" versions of heterogeneity vie for prominence. A third option is to illuminate the borders where centers and margins rub against each other in often contradictory ways. It is to bring the border into visibility, while resisting the urge to speak for it.

Jasmine examines this play of borders. As such, the novel avoids becoming a simple attack upon identity-based discursive formulas. Instead, it addresses the multiplicity of material forces and discursive regimes that seek to position the gendered subject. Put another way, *Jasmine* examines the doubleness involved in being "always moving and always still" (37), a shifting and multiple identity that is in a state of perpetual transition.[8] This novel presents the possibility of the acceptance of a plural self, one that resists the impulse towards certainty and totalization. In addition, resistance and transgression become viable alternatives, since, as the narrator remarks, "[t]here are no harmless, compassionate ways to remake oneself" (25). Remaking oneself becomes the only possible response to enforced identity and subjugated knowledge.

It is a mistake, I think, to seek agency at the conscious level of enactment. Even when there is a face on the machine—for instance, Half-Face or Bud Ripplemeyer—it is only one of many replaceable faces. The task for the intellectual is to delineate the workings of the machine, the relations of ruling, at its tentacle extension, at the extended point where it is most vulnerable, disputed, and diffused. Such a strategy involves a reappropriation, *but also a negotiation*, since negotiation recognizes difference as a site of both affinity and contestation. Negotiation is a desire to open up larger spaces in a common field of dialogical interaction. Yet, at the same time, there is the persistent danger noted by R. Radhakrishnan, related to the "profound contradictions that underlie the attempt to theorize change," that "our attempts to change the subject" may be "potentially wrong and repressive, even barbaric" ("Changing Subject," 127, 147). In other words, there is the real danger of reproducing the very same relations of ruling that we have identified. To some extent, these processes occur in *Jasmine*.

Rather than locating agency in a unified subject position capable of correctly reading the real, a subject who has somehow "successfully" resisted its interpellation, Mukherjee's *Jasmine* struggles to articulate an other form of knowledge. This negotiated knowledge is a modality of action predicated on a series of shifting subject positions. These temporary roles then become vectors of intersection and intervention, and, because they are temporary and mobile, possibly prevent succumbing to the desire for certainty and completeness. A "role" is not originary, unique, or substantial. In fact, it points to the fictiveness of the gesture towards complete, realized development and continuity; it reveals discontinuity beneath the "role," the mask. Rather than a frozen category, identity, then, becomes an historically specific strategy: not a "free" subject acting, but an available site for negotiation. Mukherjee has argued that an ability to adapt and appropriate is transformative, establishing the "sense of two-way traffic" ("Interview," 20). This "two-way traffic" captures the sense of Said's call for "a tremendously energetic attempt to engage with the metropolitan world in a common effort at re-inscribing, re-interpreting and expanding the sites of intensity and the terrain contested with Europe" ("Intellectuals," 54).

No doubt, this "common effort" does not in any way help the Haitian "boat people" that I began this paper with. Nor will it probably help the next floating population of refugees and deportees. The failure lies in the too-easy conflation of cause and effect and the ready availability of abstract categories, so that these people are not seen as the effects of colonialisms "into the present." We can, however, continue to create the conditions where these silent people might speak of a different history. I think Mukherjee's strategy of "re-inventing ourselves" does open up the transformative possibility of not only interrogating these structures of power and knowledge, but also suggesting a historically situated strategy where borders serve as multiple sites of contestation, transformative rereadings, and affinity. As such, the visible border becomes the site for critical interruption and discontinuity, for rewiring the circuitry.

NOTES

1. Abu-Lughod goes on to note that "only a more fine-grained contextual analysis of historic change that pays attention to both extrinsic world-system transformations and developments of a more internal origin can satisfy the minimum requirements of credulity" (121).

2. Fanon writes that the colonial world is a "Manichean world" where the native is not only represented as the "quintessence of evil," but also as the very "negation of values" (33, 54). In other words, the native subject serves as an active and persistent threat to Western values.

3. *Jasmine* can be read as a text that demonizes the Sikhs, since they are solely portrayed as violence-crazed fundamentalists. This essentializing precludes diversity in their community and the possibility of legitimate political demands. As such, complex historical forces are reduced to simple binary oppositions. Here, as in her portrayal of the asymmetrical relationship between India and the West, Mukherjee succumbs to those relations of ruling that, at other points, she struggles to dismantle.

4. Such a critical perspective continually informs Gayatri Spivak's discussion of *suttee* as an "ideological battleground" ("Subaltern," 300). See especially 294–308.

5. Mukherjee's comment about "being taken for a smelly, dark, alien other" in Canada suggests her personal investment in a critique of stereotypes based on gender and exoticism ("Interview," 12).

6. Michel Foucault writes that the "traditional devices for constructing a comprehensive view of history and for retracing the past as a patient and continuous development must be systematically dismantled" (153). Thus the "historical sense" that he recommends has three uses: opposition to history as either recognition, tradition, or knowledge (160). In all these instances, identity is then revealed as plural, a site where "numerous systems intersect and compete" (161). In terms of my discussion, Foucault presents a strategy for reading identity and the body.

7. Spivak has noted how the margin must be seen in terms of the center, "as an accomplice of the center," rather than in opposition to it, since an oppositional notion of marginality "implicitly valorizes the center." Thus, she can speak of the "concept-metaphor of margins" as "the place for argument, the place for the critical moment, the place of interests, for assertions rather than a shifting of the center" as she previously suggested (*Post-Colonial*, 156). Such a position places Spivak in opposition to Mohanty, who writes of the "necessary process of pivoting the center (in Bettina Apieker's terms) for the assumed center (Europe and the United States) will no longer hold" (2). I would assert that the center/margin binarism reproduces those relations of ruling explicit in the opposition between power and resistance.

8. Naomi Schor writes that doubling "may well be the feminine mode of subverting the unitary subject," since doubling "holds open *for now* a space that has only begun to be explored" (58).

WORKS CITED

Abu-Lughod, Lila. "On The Remaking Of History: How To Reinvent The Past." *Remaking History*. Ed. Barbara Kruger and Phil Marlani. Seattle: Bay Press, 1989, 111–29.

Fanon, Frantz. *The Wretched of the Earth*. New York: Grove, 1966.

Foucault, Michel. "Nietzsche, Genealogy, History." *Language, Counter-Memory, and Practice*. Trans. Donald F. Bouchard and Sherry Simon. Ithaca: Cornell University Press, 1977, 139–64.

Haraway, Donna. "A Manifesto for Cyborgs: Science, Technology, and Socialist Feminism in the 1990s." *Coming To Terms: Feminism, Theory, Politics*. Ed. Elizabeth Weed. New York: Routledge, 1991, 173–204.

JanMohamed, Abdul R. "The Economy of the Manichean Allegory: The Function of Racial Difference in Colonialist Literature." *"Race,"*

Writing, and Difference. Ed. Henry Louis Gates, Jr. Chicago: University of Chicago Press, 1985, 78–106.

JanMohamed, Abdul R., and David Lloyd. "Introduction: Toward a Theory of Minority Discourse." *Cultural Critique* 6 (1987): 5–12.

Mohanty, Chandra Talpade. "Introduction: Cartographies of Struggle: Third World Women and the Politics of Feminism." *Third World Women and the Politics of Feminism*. Bloomington: Indiana University Press, 1991, 1–47.

Mukherjee, Bharati. "An Interview with Bharati Mukherjee." *The Iowa Review* 20.3 (1990): 7–32.

———. *Jasmine*. New York: Fawcett Crest, 1989.

Radhakrishnan, R. "The Changing Subject and the Politics of Theory." *Differences: A Journal of Feminist Cultural Studies* 2.2 (1990): 126–52.

———. "Ethnic Identity and Post-Structuralist Differance." *Cultural Critique* 6 (1987): 199–220.

Said, Edward. "Intellectuals in the Post-Colonial World." *Salmagundi* 70/71 (1986): 44–64.

———. "Third World Intellectuals and Metropolitan Culture." *Raritan* 9.3 (1990): 27–50.

Schor, Naomi. "Dreaming Dissymmetry: Barthes, Foucault, and Sexual Difference." *Coming to Terms: Feminism, Theory, Politics*. Ed. Elizabeth Weed. New York: Routledge, 1991, 47–58.

Spivak, Gayatri Chakravorty. "Can the Subaltern Speak?" *Marxism and the Interpretation of Culture*. Ed. Cary Nelson and Lawrence Grossberg. Urbana: University of Illinois Press, 1988, 270–313.

———. *The Post-Colonial Critic: Interviews, Strategies, Dialogues*. New York: Routledge, 1990.

INDEX